Audit: Workbook

Azhar ul Haque Sario

Published by Azhar ul Haque Sario, 2023.

AUDIT: WORKBOOK

First edition. August 2, 2023.

ISBN: 979-8223155478

Written by Azhar ul Haque Sario.

Table of Contents

Audit: Workbook

Published by Azhar ul Haque Sario
azhar.sario@hotmail.co.uk

Foreword

This comprehensive workbook is an invaluable tool for those seeking to delve into the world of auditing. With an exploration of 65 key auditing concepts, followed by an extensive set of questions and answers, the reader is guided towards a thorough comprehension and understanding of the field. It is not just a theoretical guide, but also a practical one, filled with real-life examples demonstrating the application of these concepts.

The book begins by laying the groundwork with fundamental concepts such as the definition of an audit, its cost, and its objectives. It then takes the reader on a journey through the intricacies of audit planning, the role of the audit committee, and the importance of auditor independence. The workbook also facilitates a deep understanding of concepts like audit thresholds and the auditor-client relationship.

As the reader progresses through the workbook, they will gain insights into international auditing standards, including Generally Accepted Auditing Standards (GAAS) and International Standards on Auditing (ISA). Complex concepts such as audit scope, control procedures, tests of controls, materiality, and different types of risks are simplified and made accessible.

The workbook further covers a whole spectrum of audits including the Sarbanes-Oxley Act, risk-based audit, compliance audit, forensic audit, financial audit, and more. It provides a detailed explanation of audit sampling and delves into the balance sheet and income statement audits.

The workbook also touches upon the internal control system, due diligence, audit evidence, compliance testing, scope limitation, substantive procedures, and more. It elucidates on audit software and assertions, and critical components of audit engagement, peer review, audit findings, management letter, audit opinion, and auditor's report.

As a resource for students, professionals, or anyone interested in auditing, this workbook merges theory, practicality, and application. Readers will not only acquire a profound understanding of auditing concepts but also be able to apply this knowledge in real-world scenarios. This is an essential and comprehensive learning tool for anyone seeking to become proficient in the world of auditing.

Audit Cycle

Theoretical

Q: What is the Audit cycle?

A: The audit cycle is the process of auditing from the beginning to the end. It includes planning, fieldwork, reporting, and follow-up.

Q: How does the audit cycle begin?

A: The audit cycle begins with planning. This involves identifying the scope of the audit, creating an audit plan, and preparing for the audit.

Q: What is involved in the planning stage of the audit cycle?

A: The planning stage involves identifying the objectives and scope of the audit, assessing risks, and developing an audit plan.

Q: What happens during the fieldwork stage of the audit cycle?

A: During the fieldwork stage, auditors gather evidence through various methods such as observation, inquiry, inspection, and confirmation.

Q: What is the purpose of the reporting stage in the audit cycle?

A: The purpose of the reporting stage is to communicate the findings of the audit to the relevant parties.

Q: How does the follow-up stage of the audit cycle contribute to the process?

A: The follow-up stage ensures that any issues identified during the audit are addressed and corrected.

Q: What is the role of risk assessment in the audit cycle?

A: Risk assessment helps auditors identify areas of high risk that need more attention during the audit.

Q: How long does an audit cycle typically last?
A: An audit cycle can last anywhere from a few weeks to several months, depending on the size and complexity of the organization.
Q: Why is documentation important in the audit cycle?
A: Documentation provides evidence of the audit process and supports the auditor's findings and recommendations.
Q: What is the aim of creating an audit plan?
A: An audit plan outlines the procedures to be followed during the audit, the areas to be audited, and the timeline for the audit.
Q: How are audit findings communicated?
A: Audit findings are usually communicated through an audit report, which details the findings and recommendations.
Q: What happens if an organization fails to address issues identified in an audit?
A: If an organization fails to address audit findings, it can lead to further audits, penalties, or even legal action.
Q: What is the role of an internal auditor in the audit cycle?
A: An internal auditor plans and conducts the audit, gathers evidence, documents findings, and communicates results.
Q: Can the audit cycle be skipped or shortened?
A: No, the audit cycle is a crucial process that ensures the accuracy and integrity of an organization's financial statements.
Q: Who are the key stakeholders in an audit cycle?
A: Key stakeholders in an audit cycle include management, the audit committee, and external auditors.
Q: How is the scope of an audit determined?
A: The scope of an audit is determined based on the objectives of the audit, the size and complexity of the organization, and the areas of risk.
Q: What is the role of an audit committee in the audit cycle?

A: An audit committee oversees the audit process, ensures the audit is carried out objectively, and reviews the audit findings.

Q: How does an auditor gather evidence during the fieldwork stage?

A: An auditor gathers evidence through various methods such as observation, inquiry, inspection, and confirmation.

Q: What is an audit report?

A: An audit report is a document that communicates the findings of the audit, including any issues or discrepancies identified, and recommendations for improvement.

Q: What are some common risks identified during the planning stage of the audit cycle?

A: Common risks include errors or fraud in financial reporting, non-compliance with laws and regulations, and operational inefficiencies.

Q: How can an organization prepare for an audit?

A: An organization can prepare for an audit by maintaining accurate and complete financial records, understanding the audit process, and cooperating with the auditors.

Q: What is the relationship between the audit cycle and financial reporting?

A: The audit cycle checks the accuracy and integrity of financial reporting, ensuring that the financial statements present a true and fair view of the organization's financial position.

Q: How often should an audit cycle be carried out?

A: Typically, an audit cycle is carried out annually, but it can vary depending on the organization's needs and regulatory requirements.

Q: What is the role of external auditors in the audit cycle?

A: External auditors independently assess the accuracy and integrity of the organization's financial statements and internal controls.

Q: Why is independence important in the audit cycle?
A: Independence ensures that the auditor can objectively assess the organization's financial statements without any bias or conflict of interest.
Q: What is the purpose of the follow-up stage in the audit cycle?
A: The follow-up stage ensures that any issues identified during the audit are addressed and corrected, and that the organization is implementing the auditor's recommendations.
Q: How is the effectiveness of an audit cycle evaluated?
A: The effectiveness of an audit cycle can be evaluated through the quality of the audit report, the improvements made as a result of the audit, and the organization's satisfaction with the audit process.
Q: What are some challenges in the audit cycle?
A: Challenges can include a lack of cooperation from the organization, incomplete or inaccurate financial records, and complex or changing regulations.
Q: What are some ways to improve the audit cycle?
A: Improvements can include better planning, more effective risk assessment, improved communication between auditors and the organization, and regular follow-ups.
Q: What is the relationship between the audit cycle and corporate governance?
A: The audit cycle is a key part of corporate governance, ensuring that the organization is operating effectively, efficiently, and in compliance with laws and regulations.
Q: Can technology be used in the audit cycle?
A: Yes, technology can be used to automate parts of the audit process, analyze large amounts of data, and improve the accuracy and efficiency of the audit.
Q: How can an organization benefit from an audit cycle?

A: An organization can benefit from an audit cycle by identifying areas for improvement, ensuring compliance with laws and regulations, and enhancing its reputation for transparency and integrity.

Q: What is the impact of regulatory changes on the audit cycle?

A: Regulatory changes can affect the scope and objectives of the audit, the methods used to gather evidence, and the way the audit findings are reported.

Q: What is the role of management in the audit cycle?

A: Management is responsible for maintaining accurate and complete financial records, providing necessary information to the auditors, and implementing the auditor's recommendations.

Q: How can the audit cycle contribute to an organization's strategic planning?

A: The audit cycle can provide valuable insights into the organization's operations and performance, helping to inform strategic planning and decision-making.

Q: What is the relationship between the audit cycle and internal controls?

A: The audit cycle evaluates the effectiveness of internal controls, ensuring that they are operating as intended and identifying any weaknesses.

Q: Can an audit cycle detect fraud?

A: While not its primary purpose, an audit cycle can detect signs of fraud, such as discrepancies in financial records, unusual transactions, or inadequate internal controls.

Q: How is materiality considered in the audit cycle?

A: Materiality refers to the significance of an item or error that could influence the decisions of users of financial statements. Auditors consider materiality when planning the audit and evaluating the audit findings.

Q: What skills are important for an auditor in the audit cycle?

A: Important skills for an auditor include analytical thinking, attention to detail, understanding of accounting principles and regulations, and good communication skills.

Q: How can an audit cycle support an organization's risk management?

A: The audit cycle can identify risks in the organization's operations and financial reporting, helping to inform risk management strategies.

Q: What is a quality control review in the context of the audit cycle?

A: A quality control review is a process to ensure that the audit has been conducted according to the standards and that the audit report is accurate and complete.

Q: Can an audit cycle be outsourced?

A: Yes, an organization can hire external auditors to conduct the audit cycle. This can bring a fresh perspective and expertise, but it also requires careful management to ensure a successful audit.

Q: What is the role of ethics in the audit cycle?

A: Ethics are crucial to ensure the integrity of the audit process. Auditors should conduct their work with honesty, objectivity, and professionalism, and respect confidentiality.

Q: How is an audit cycle different from a financial review?

A: An audit cycle provides a more detailed and comprehensive assessment of the organization's financial statements and internal controls, while a financial review is a less intensive examination of the financial statements.

Q: How does the audit cycle relate to an organization's stakeholders?

A: The audit cycle provides assurance to stakeholders about the accuracy of the organization's financial statements, enhancing their confidence and trust in the organization.

Q: Can the results of an audit cycle be disputed?

A: Yes, the organization has the right to dispute the audit findings if it believes they are inaccurate or unfair. This usually involves a discussion and review with the auditors.

Q: How does the audit cycle contribute to transparency in an organization?

A: The audit cycle checks the accuracy of the organization's financial statements, ensuring that they present a true and fair view of its financial position, which contributes to transparency.

Q: What is the role of professional judgment in the audit cycle?

A: Professional judgment is crucial in many aspects of the audit cycle, such as assessing risks, choosing audit procedures, interpreting findings, and formulating recommendations.

Q: How is confidentiality maintained in the audit cycle?

A: Confidentiality is maintained through professional ethics and legal requirements, which prohibit auditors from disclosing sensitive information without the organization's consent.

Q: What is the role of communication in the audit cycle?

A: Effective communication is crucial throughout the audit cycle, such as between the auditors and the organization, within the audit team, and in reporting the audit findings.

Applications

Scenario 1: A company named XYZ Corp is planning an audit for the financial year ending in 2020. However, due to the COVID-19 pandemic, their regular auditors are unable to travel to their offices to conduct the audit. How should XYZ Corp handle this situation?

Solution: In this unprecedented situation, XYZ Corp should leverage technology and shift towards a remote auditing approach. They can use secure digital platforms to share necessary financial documents and records with the auditors. While this is a shift from traditional auditing practices, it allows the audit to continue while maintaining the safety and health of all parties involved.

Scenario 2: ABC Enterprises has discovered discrepancies in their financial records during an internal audit. It's suspected that an employee within the accounting department has been manipulating the books. How should ABC Enterprises handle this situation?

Solution: ABC Enterprises should engage an external audit firm to conduct a forensic audit. The aim is to identify the extent of the discrepancies, trace the irregularities back to their source, and suggest measures to prevent such occurrences in the future. The company may also need to involve law enforcement, depending on the severity of the fraud. Scenario 3: A newly established company, DEF Industries, is preparing for its first audit. However, the company's management is unsure about the kind of documents and records they need to provide to the auditors. How should DEF Industries prepare for the audit?

Solution: DEF Industries should consult with their auditors before the audit begins. Generally, they need to provide documents related to assets, liabilities, income and expenses, such as bank statements, invoices, receipts, payroll records, and tax returns. By having these documents organized and ready, DEF Industries can facilitate a smoother and more efficient audit process.

Scenario 4: GHI Tech, a tech startup, has never conducted an audit before. With the company growing fast, the management realizes the importance of having their financial statements audited. However, they have limited knowledge of the audit process. How should GHI Tech approach this situation?

Solution: GHI Tech should hire a reputable audit firm to conduct their first audit. Before the audit, the auditors will explain the process, what information they need, and how long the audit will take. The auditors will also provide recommendations for improving their financial management based on the audit findings.

Scenario 5: JKL Retail has recently undergone an audit. The audit report highlighted several areas where the company is not complying with the Generally Accepted Accounting Principles (GAAP). How should JKL Retail address these issues? Solution: JKL Retail should take the audit findings seriously and take immediate action to rectify the issues. They should revisit their accounting policies and practices, provide additional training to their accounting staff, and possibly hire a consultant to ensure compliance with GAAP. This will not only improve their financial management but also increase the credibility of their financial statements.

Cost of Audit

Theoretical

What is the cost of audit?

The cost of audit refers to the total fee that an organization pays to an accounting firm for the auditing services they provide.

How is the cost of audit determined?

The cost of audit is usually determined by a variety of factors, including the size and complexity of the organization, the scope of the audit, the risk involved, and the time required to complete the audit.

Is the cost of an audit fixed?

No, the cost of an audit can vary greatly depending on the factors mentioned above. It's important for organizations to negotiate the cost with the auditing firm before the audit begins.

Why is it important for companies to audit their financial statements?

Audits provide an independent verification of a company's financial statements, which increases their credibility and reliability. This can be beneficial for stakeholders, such as investors and creditors, who rely on these statements to make informed decisions. Can the cost of audit be a barrier to small businesses?

Yes, the cost of audit can be a significant barrier for small businesses, as they may not have the resources to afford a full-scale audit.

What are the benefits of auditing that justify its cost? Auditing can help identify errors or fraud, improve financial reporting processes, and provide assurance to stakeholders. These benefits can outweigh the costs for many organizations.

Why do some companies choose to have an internal audit function?

Some companies choose to have an internal audit function to provide continuous oversight of their financial and operational processes. This can help identify issues early and reduce the risk of significant errors or fraud.

What is the role of an audit committee in managing audit costs?

An audit committee is responsible for overseeing the audit process, including the selection of the auditor and negotiation of the audit fee. They can help manage audit costs by ensuring that the scope of the audit is appropriate for the organization's needs.

How can a company reduce its audit costs?

A company can reduce its audit costs by improving its internal controls and financial reporting processes, which can reduce the time and effort required for the audit. What is the impact of audit risk on audit cost? The audit risk refers to the potential for the auditor to give an inaccurate assessment of the financial statements.

Higher audit risk can increase the audit cost, as the auditor may need to perform more procedures to reduce this risk.

How does the complexity of a company's operations affect audit cost?

More complex operations usually require more time and expertise to audit, which can increase the audit cost.

How does the size of a company affect audit cost?

Larger companies typically have more complex operations and financial transactions, which can increase the audit cost. However, they may also have more sophisticated internal controls, which can reduce the audit cost. What is the relationship between audit fees and audit quality?

There is not a direct relationship between audit fees and audit quality. High audit fees do not necessarily indicate high-quality audits, and low audit fees do not necessarily indicate low-quality audits.

Is there a regulatory body that oversees audit costs?

Yes, in many countries, audit fees are regulated by professional bodies or government agencies to ensure that they are fair and reasonable.

How does the auditor's expertise affect the cost of audit?

The more expertise an auditor has, the higher their fees may be. This is because their expertise can add value to the audit by identifying complex issues and providing high-quality recommendations.

How does the audit process impact the cost of audit?

The audit process impacts the cost of audit through the time and resources required. The more detailed and thorough the audit process, the higher the cost. What is the role of technology in reducing audit costs?

Technology can automate many audit tasks, reducing the time and effort required and thereby reducing audit costs.

How does the auditor's reputation impact the audit cost?

Auditors with a strong reputation can command higher fees, as their reputation can provide assurance of high-quality work.

How do external factors like economic conditions impact audit costs?

Economic conditions can impact audit costs by affecting the risk of the audit. For example, in a weak economy, the risk of business failure and fraud may be higher, which can increase audit costs.

Can a company negotiate the cost of audit?

Yes, a company can negotiate the cost of audit with the auditor. However, the auditor must ensure that the fee is not so low that it

compromises the quality of the audit. How does industry specialization of the auditor impact audit cost?
Auditors with industry specialization may charge higher fees due to their specific knowledge and expertise, but they may also be able to conduct the audit more efficiently. How does the geographical location of a company affect audit cost?
The geographical location can impact the audit cost due to variations in travel expenses, local regulations, and market rates for audit services.
Does the cost of an audit include only the auditor's fees?
No, the cost of an audit can also include other expenses, such as travel expenses, out-of-pocket expenses, and other direct costs related to the audit. How does the timing of the audit affect its cost?
The timing of the audit can affect its cost. For example, if the audit is conducted during the company's busy season, it may require more resources and thus be more costly.
What is the impact of legislative changes on audit cost?
Legislative changes can impact audit cost by introducing new requirements that require additional work from the auditor.
How do changes in accounting standards impact audit costs?
Changes in accounting standards can impact audit costs by requiring additional work to ensure compliance with the new standards. How does the cost of audit impact a company's financial performance?
The cost of audit is an expense that can impact a company's profitability. However, the benefits of an audit, such as improved financial reporting and risk management, can outweigh this cost.
How does the auditor's independence impact audit cost?
An auditor's independence is crucial to a quality audit, and any threats to this independence can increase the audit cost due to the additional procedures required to mitigate these threats.

How does the scope of the audit impact its cost? The scope of the audit refers to the areas and transactions that will be audited. A broader scope can increase the audit cost due to the additional work required.

What are some common misconceptions about audit costs? Some common misconceptions about audit costs include the belief that higher audit fees always mean higher quality, and that small businesses cannot afford to have their financial statements audited.

How does the materiality level set by the auditor affect audit cost? The materiality level is the threshold above which errors or misstatements are considered significant.

A lower materiality level can increase the audit cost, as it requires more detailed testing to ensure that no material misstatements exist.

How does the company's internal control system impact audit cost?

A strong internal control system can reduce the audit cost by reducing the risk of errors and fraud, and thus reducing the amount of work required by the auditor.

How does the company's financial condition impact audit cost? If a company is in poor financial condition, the risk of errors or fraud may be higher, which can increase the audit cost.

How does the use of an audit team impact audit cost? The use of an audit team can increase the audit cost due to the additional personnel involved. However, it can also improve the quality and efficiency of the audit.

How does the company's business model affect audit cost? A complex business model may require more time and expertise to audit, which can increase the audit cost.

How does the company's transaction volume impact audit cost?

A high transaction volume can increase the audit cost due to the additional testing required. How does the company's risk profile impact audit cost? A high-risk profile can increase the audit cost due to the additional procedures required to manage the risk.
How can a company budget for audit costs?
A company can budget for audit costs by estimating the scope of the audit and the time and resources required, and by negotiating the audit fee with the auditor. How does the company's regulatory environment impact audit cost?
A complex regulatory environment can increase the audit cost due to the additional work required to ensure compliance.
How does the company's industry impact audit cost? Certain industries may have specific risks or complexities that can increase the audit cost.
What is the difference between the cost of an internal audit and an external audit?
The cost of an internal audit is often lower than that of an external audit, as it is conducted by the company's own staff. However, an external audit provides a higher level of assurance due to the auditor's independence. How does the auditor's liability impact audit cost?
The auditor's liability for an incorrect audit opinion can increase the audit cost, as the auditor may need to perform more procedures to reduce this risk.
How does a company's growth rate impact audit cost?
A high growth rate can increase the audit cost due to the additional work required to audit the expanding operations. How does a company's capital structure impact audit cost?
A complex capital structure can increase the audit cost due to the additional work required to audit the various sources of capital.
How does a company's ownership structure impact audit cost?

A complex ownership structure can increase the audit cost due to the additional work required to audit the relationships between the owners.

How does the number of a company's locations impact audit cost?

A large number of locations can increase the audit cost due to the additional travel and coordination required.

How does a company's level of debt impact audit cost?

A high level of debt can increase the audit cost due to the additional work required to audit the debt agreements and related transactions.

How does a company's level of inventory impact audit cost?

A high level of inventory can increase the audit cost due to the additional work required to audit the inventory counts and valuation.

How does a company's level of technology usage impact audit cost?

A high level of technology usage can increase the audit cost due to the additional work required to audit the IT controls and data integrity.

How does a company's level of outsourcing impact audit cost?

A high level of outsourcing can increase the audit cost due to the additional work required to audit the relationships with the outsourced service providers.

Applications

Scenario 1: A manufacturing company, XYZ Ltd., has recently completed its annual audit. The company spent $100,000 on the audit, which is a significant increase from the $70,000 spent the previous year. The management is concerned about the escalating audit cost and wants to know if this cost is justified. Solution: The effectiveness of the audit can be evaluated based on the value it has added to the organization. If the audit has identified significant financial discrepancies, inefficiencies, or risks that the company was not aware of, and if addressing these issues could lead to cost savings or increased revenue in the future, then the audit cost could be justified. However, if the audit has simply confirmed the information that the company already knew and has not provided any new insights, then the increased audit cost may not be justified.

Scenario 2: A retail company ABC Corp. employs an external audit firm that charges a fixed fee for its services. The company's management is considering switching to an audit firm that charges based on the number of hours worked. They believe this could potentially reduce the audit cost.

Solution: Switching to an audit firm that charges based on the number of hours worked may or may not reduce the audit cost. It would depend on the efficiency and effectiveness of the audit firm. If the new firm is able to complete the audit in less time due to better efficiency, then the audit cost could potentially be reduced. However, if the new firm takes longer to complete the audit, the cost could increase. Scenario 3: A tech start-up, DEF Inc., is considering conducting an internal audit for the first time. The company's management is unsure about the cost implications and wants to know how to manage the cost of the audit effectively.

Solution: The cost of an internal audit can be managed effectively by planning the audit properly. This includes setting clear objectives for the audit, ensuring that the audit team has the necessary skills and resources, and establishing a realistic timeline for the audit. The company could also consider hiring an external audit firm on a contractual basis, which could potentially be more cost-effective than hiring a full-time internal audit team.

Scenario 4: A non-profit organization, GHI NGO, has received a grant from a government agency. The grant agreement requires the organization to conduct an annual audit. The organization is concerned about the cost of the audit and wants to know how to minimize it.

Solution: The organization can minimize the cost of the audit by ensuring that its financial records are well-organized and up-to-date. This would reduce the amount of time that the auditors need to spend on the audit, therefore reducing the audit cost. The organization could also negotiate the audit fee with the audit firm or consider getting quotes from different audit firms to find the most cost-effective option.

General Audit

Theoretical

Q: What is an audit's main goal?

A: The main objective of an audit is to conduct a neutral third-party review of a company's financial statements, which enhances the trustworthiness and credibility of the financial data prepared by the company's management.

Q: How does internal auditing differ from external auditing? A: An internal audit is performed by the company's internal staff, whereas an external audit is conducted by independent auditors.

Q: Could you explain what a statutory audit is?

A: A statutory audit is a legally mandated check of a company's financial records' accuracy.

Q: What is an auditor's function in the auditing process?

A: An auditor's role is to scrutinize a company's financial statements and give an opinion on whether they are free of significant errors.

Q: Can you define auditing evidence?

A: Auditing evidence comprises the data gathered for a company's financial transactions review, internal control practices, and other factors essential for an auditor's financial statements certification.

Q: Could you explain what audit risk is?

A: Audit risk refers to the possibility of an auditor incorrectly giving a clean audit opinion when the financial statements contain significant errors.

Q: What part does internal control play in the auditing process?

A: Internal control procedures aid in ensuring the reliability of the financial statements and in preventing fraud and errors.

Q: Can you explain what auditing materiality is?

A: Materiality in auditing pertains to the importance of an amount, transaction, or discrepancy.

Q: Could you differentiate between a qualified and an unqualified audit report?

A: A qualified audit report signifies that the auditor has concerns about the financial statements, while an unqualified report indicates that the auditor believes the statements are free from significant misstatements.

Q: What is the function of a management letter in the auditing process?

A: A management letter is a formal note from the auditor to the management, highlighting areas where management can enhance its controls and procedures.

Q: What is the aim of an audit engagement letter?

A: An audit engagement letter defines the audit's scope, the responsibilities of the auditor, and the engagement's terms.

Q: Can you define a compliance audit?

A: A compliance audit is a review carried out to ensure a company is adhering to the regulations and rules set by regulatory bodies.

Q: What does professional skepticism mean in auditing?

A: Professional skepticism in auditing involves maintaining a mindset that includes questioning and critically assessing audit evidence.

Q: Could you explain what audit scope is?

A: An audit scope delineates the specific areas or components of the financial statements that the auditor will examine.

Q: How does a review differ from an audit?

A: A review offers limited assurance about the financial statements, whereas an audit provides reasonable assurance.

Q: Could you explain what an operational audit is?
A: An operational audit assesses a company's operating procedures and methods for effectiveness and efficiency.
Q: How does a financial audit differ from a performance audit?
A: A financial audit assesses whether financial statements are presented according to applicable accounting standards, while a performance audit assesses whether resources are being used efficiently and effectively.
Q: What is the function of an audit committee?
A: The audit committee supervises the financial reporting process, chooses and oversees the independent auditors, and monitors the company's internal controls and compliance with laws and regulations.
Q: How does auditing differ from accounting?
A: Accounting involves recording, reporting, and analyzing financial transactions, while auditing evaluates the accuracy of the financial statements prepared by the accountants.
Q: Could you explain what substantive testing in auditing is?
A: Substantive testing in auditing is the detailed testing of transactions and account balances to detect significant errors in the financial statements.
Q: What is an integrated audit?
A: An integrated audit is a process that combines a review of the financial statement alongside an evaluation of the internal control over financial reporting.
Q: Could you explain what an audit trail is?
A: An audit trail is a record that documents who has accessed a computer system, what actions they performed during a specific period, and what data was affected.
Q: Could you explain what a financial statement audit is?

A: An independent auditor's review of an organization's financial statements and related disclosures is known as a financial statement audit.

Q: What is a forensic audit?

A: A forensic audit is a review of an entity's financial records to produce evidence that can be used in a court of law or legal proceeding.

Q: Could you explain what an audit plan is?

A: An audit plan is a comprehensive plan of the specific auditing procedures the auditor needs to carry out to complete the audit.

Q: Could you define a performance audit?

A: A performance audit is an impartial examination of a program, function, operation, or the management systems and procedures of a governmental or non-profit organization. The aim is to evaluate if the organization is using its resources economically, efficiently, and effectively.

Q: What is the purpose of conducting an internal audit?

A: The aim of an internal audit is to evaluate an organization's risk and management systems and to suggest improvements.

Q: Can you explain what a risk-based audit approach is?

A: A risk-based audit approach is a methodology that focuses on the inherent risk involved in an organization's activities or systems.

Q: What role does an auditor play during a tax audit?

A: During a tax audit, an auditor checks the accuracy of the tax returns filed by a taxpayer and ensures compliance with tax laws.

Q: What is an information systems audit?

A: An audit of information systems involves assessing the management controls within an IT infrastructure.

Q: How does an audit contribute to corporate governance?

A: An audit plays a crucial role in corporate governance by improving the reliability of financial information used by investors and other stakeholders.

Q: How does an audit report differ from an audit certificate? A: An audit report is a formal document that communicates the audit's results, while an audit certificate is a written confirmation that an audit has occurred.

Q: What is a surprise audit?

A: A surprise audit is an unannounced audit carried out to prevent fraudulent activities within an organization.

Q: What is an environmental audit?

A: An environmental audit evaluates an organization's compliance with environmental laws and regulations.

Q: Could you explain what an audit universe is?

A: An audit universe is a list of all areas within an organization that could potentially be audited.

Q: How does a balance sheet audit differ from a profit and loss audit?

A: A balance sheet audit assesses an organization's financial position at a specific point in time, while a profit and loss audit concentrates on the income and expenses during a particular period.

Q: What is the role of a lead auditor?

A: A lead auditor is in charge of managing the audit team during an audit, coordinating the audit process, and communicating the audit findings.

Q: What is a peer review in auditing?

A: A peer review in auditing is a review of an auditor's work by another auditor to ensure compliance with professional standards.

Q: What is a process audit?

A: A process audit examines a process's effectiveness and efficiency in achieving its objectives.

Q: What is an audit finding?

A: An audit finding is a conclusion that an auditor arrives at based on the audit evidence gathered.

Q: What is an audit questionnaire?
A: An audit questionnaire is a list of questions that auditors use to collect information from the auditee.
Q: What is audit assurance?
A: Audit assurance refers to the level of confidence that the auditor provides regarding the accuracy and fairness of the financial statements.
Q: What is an audit adjustment?
A: An audit adjustment is a change made to the financial statements during the audit process to correct a misstatement.
Q: What is the function of an audit program?
A: An audit program is a detailed plan of the audit procedures to be carried out, the audit objectives to be met, and the specific audit steps to achieve the audit objectives.
Q: How do first-party, second-party, and third-party audits differ?
A: A first-party audit is an internal audit, a second-party audit is performed by a party having an interest in the audited organization, and a third-party audit is carried out by an independent auditing firm.
Q: What is a desktop audit?
A: A desktop audit is an audit conducted remotely, often by reviewing electronic records and conducting interviews via video conference.
Q: What is a tax audit?
A: A tax audit is a review of an individual's or organization's tax return to verify that financial information is being reported correctly.
Q: How does a special audit differ from a regular audit?
A: A special audit is conducted to investigate a specific issue or area, whereas a regular audit is a routine examination of financial statements.
Q: What is an exit meeting in an audit?

A: An exit meeting in an audit is a meeting between the auditors and the auditee at the end of the audit to discuss the audit findings and recommendations.

Q: What is a follow-up audit?

A: A follow-up audit is an audit carried out after a certain period to check whether the auditee has implemented corrective action based on the audit findings.

Applications

Scenario 1: Internal Control System Consider a manufacturing company that has an internal control system in place. However, there have been several incidents of financial discrepancies that have raised questions about the effectiveness of this system. As an auditor, how would you assess the internal control system's efficiency?

Solution: In this scenario, an auditor would first evaluate the design and operation of the internal control system. They would identify areas of weakness and potential fraud risks, such as lack of segregation of duties or weak oversight over financial reporting. They would then test the operational effectiveness of the controls by sampling transactions and observing procedures. The auditor would also conduct interviews with employees to understand their knowledge and compliance with control procedures.

Effectiveness: This approach is effective as it provides a comprehensive evaluation of the internal control system. It identifies both design and operational weaknesses, enabling the company to take corrective action.

Scenario 2: Fraud Detection Consider a retail business where there has been suspected fraudulent activity in the form of inventory theft. As an auditor, how would you go about detecting and verifying this fraud?

Solution: An auditor would start by comparing the company's inventory records with the physical count of inventory. They would also analyze sales records and any unusual inventory shrinkage. Additionally, they may use data analytics to identify patterns or anomalies that could indicate fraud, such as unusual inventory movements or inconsistencies between recorded inventory and sales. Effectiveness: This approach is effective as it combines multiple methods of fraud detection, increasing the likelihood of identifying fraudulent activity. It also provides evidence to support any findings of fraud.

Scenario 3: Compliance with Laws and Regulations Suppose you are auditing a pharmaceutical company that must comply with numerous laws and regulations. How would you evaluate the company's compliance?

Solution: As the auditor, you would review the company's policies and procedures to ensure they align with the relevant laws and regulations. You would also evaluate the company's training programs to ensure staff understand and comply with these requirements. Further, you would review any incidents or violations reported and how the company responded.

Effectiveness: This approach is effective as it provides a detailed evaluation of the company's compliance efforts. It identifies areas where the company may be falling short, allowing them to take corrective action and mitigate the risk of non-compliance.

Audit Objective

Theoretical

Q: What is the primary objective of auditing?

A: The main goal of auditing is to provide an opinion on whether the financial statements have been created in complete accordance with the relevant financial reporting framework.

Q: What is the significance of materiality in auditing?

A: Materiality in auditing relates to the importance of an item, transaction, or discrepancy that could influence the decisions of the users of financial statements.

Q: What is the role of evidence in audit objectives?

A: Evidence plays a critical role in audit objectives. It is used to support the auditor's opinion and ensure that the financial statements are free from material misstatement.

Q: What is the importance of independence in auditing?

A: Independence is crucial in auditing to ensure that the auditor's opinion is unbiased and objective.

Q: How does an auditor ensure reliability in an audit?

A: An auditor ensures reliability in an audit through thorough verification of data and transactions, using sampling techniques and other audit procedures.

Q: What is the objective of a compliance audit?

A: The objective of a compliance audit is to ensure that an organization is adhering to regulatory guidelines.

Q: What is the aim of an operational audit?

A: The aim of an operational audit is to evaluate the efficiency and effectiveness of an organization's operations and processes.

Q: How is the objective of a financial audit different from a compliance audit?

A: The objective of a financial audit is to ensure that the financial statements are free from material misstatement, while a compliance audit ensures that the organization is adhering to regulatory guidelines.

Q: What is the purpose of risk assessment in an audit?

A: The purpose of risk assessment in an audit is to identify and assess risks that could lead to material misstatement in the financial statements.

Q: What is the role of internal controls in an audit?

A: The role of internal controls in an audit is to ensure the reliability of financial reporting, compliance with laws and regulations, and effective and efficient operations.

Q: What is the objective of an information systems audit?

A: The objective of an information systems audit is to evaluate the system's internal controls to ensure the integrity, confidentiality, and availability of data.

Q: What is the objective of an environmental audit?

A: The objective of an environmental audit is to ensure that an organization is complying with environmental laws and regulations.

Q: What is the objective of a fraud audit?

A: The objective of a fraud audit is to detect and prevent fraudulent activities.

Q: What is the role of professional skepticism in an audit?

A: The role of professional skepticism in an audit is to ensure that the auditor does not accept evidence at face value and continuously challenges the evidence obtained.

Q: What is the objective of a quality audit?

A: The objective of a quality audit is to assess whether a company's quality management system is effective and meets specified requirements.

Q: What is the objective of a tax audit?

A: The objective of a tax audit is to verify the accuracy of a taxpayer's returns and ensure compliance with tax laws.

Q: What is the significance of audit planning?

A: Audit planning is significant as it helps auditors to identify high-risk areas, decide the nature, timing, and extent of audit procedures, and organize the audit work.

Q: What is the objective of a performance audit?

A: The objective of a performance audit is to evaluate the performance of an organization in terms of its efficiency, effectiveness, and economy.

Q: What is the objective of a forensic audit?

A: The objective of a forensic audit is to investigate fraud or financial irregularities for legal proceedings.

Q: How does an auditor assess the going concern of an entity?

A: An auditor assesses the going concern of an entity by evaluating the entity's ability to continue its operations in the foreseeable future.

Q: How does an auditor ensure the completeness of financial statements?

A: An auditor ensures the completeness of financial statements by verifying that all transactions and events have been recorded.

Q: What responsibilities does the audit committee have?

A: The audit committee provides oversight of the financial reporting process, the audit process, the company's system of internal controls, and compliance with laws and regulations.

Q: What is the objective of an internal audit?

A: The objective of an internal audit is to improve an organization's operations by evaluating its internal controls, risk management, and governance processes.

Q: What is the objective of a management audit?

A: The objective of a management audit is to evaluate the effectiveness of management in achieving the organization's objectives.

Q: What is the role of materiality in determining the scope of an audit?

A: Materiality plays a key role in determining the scope of an audit as it helps auditors to identify areas that may have a significant effect on the financial statements.

Q: What is the objective of an integrated audit?

A: The objective of an integrated audit is to evaluate both the financial statements and the effectiveness of an entity's internal control over financial reporting.

Q: What is the objective of a statutory audit?

A: The objective of a statutory audit is to ensure that an organization is providing a true and fair view of its financial position and performance in its financial statements.

Q: What is the role of professional judgment in an audit?

A: The role of professional judgment in an audit is to apply knowledge, experience, and understanding in making informed decisions about the appropriate actions in the audit process.

Q: What is the objective of a cost audit?

A: The objective of a cost audit is to ascertain whether the cost of production is being maintained in accordance with cost accounting principles.

Q: What is the objective of a social audit?

A: The objective of a social audit is to assess an organization's social responsibility performance.

Q: What is the objective of a value-for-money audit?

A: The objective of a value-for-money audit is to evaluate an organization's use of resources in terms of economy, efficiency, and effectiveness.

Q: What is the role of the internal auditor in achieving audit objectives?

A: The role of the internal auditor in achieving audit objectives is to evaluate and improve the effectiveness of risk management, control, and governance processes.

Q: What is the objective of a due diligence audit?

A: The objective of a due diligence audit is to investigate a business before a significant financial decision, such as a merger or acquisition.

Q: What is the significance of an unqualified audit opinion?

A: An unqualified audit opinion signifies that the financial statements present a true and fair view in all material respects.

Q: What is the objective of a follow-up audit?

A: The objective of a follow-up audit is to verify that management has taken corrective action on the issues identified in the previous audit.

Q: What is the objective of a safety audit?

A: The objective of a safety audit is to assess the safety procedures and policies of an organization.

Q: What is the significance of confidentiality in an audit?

A: Confidentiality in an audit is significant as it ensures that sensitive information obtained during the audit is not disclosed to unauthorized individuals.

Q: What is the objective of a human resources audit?

A: The objective of a human resources audit is to evaluate the HR policies, practices, and systems of an organization.

Q: How does an auditor ensure the accuracy of financial statements?

A: An auditor ensures the accuracy of financial statements by verifying the correctness of the amounts and disclosures in the financial statements through substantive procedures.

Q: What is the objective of a data audit?

A: The objective of a data audit is to ensure the accuracy, completeness, and reliability of data.

Q: What is the role of an external auditor in achieving audit objectives?

A: The role of an external auditor in achieving audit objectives is to provide an independent opinion on the truth and fairness of the financial statements.

Q: What is the objective of a process audit?

A: The objective of a process audit is to evaluate the effectiveness and efficiency of a process or operation.

Q: How does an auditor ensure the timeliness of financial reporting?

A: An auditor ensures the timeliness of financial reporting by verifying that the financial statements are prepared and presented within the specified time frame.

Q: What is the objective of a systems audit?

A: The objective of a systems audit is to ensure that the systems are operating efficiently and effectively, and are free from material misstatement.

Q: What is the objective of an energy audit?

A: The objective of an energy audit is to identify energy-saving opportunities by assessing the energy use and efficiency of a facility.

Q: What is the significance of an adverse audit opinion?

A: An adverse audit opinion signifies that the financial statements do not present a true and fair view due to material misstatements.

Q: What is the objective of a security audit?

A: The objective of a security audit is to assess the effectiveness of an organization's information security measures.

Q: What is the role of an audit program?

A: The role of an audit program is to provide a step-by-step guide for the audit procedures to be performed to achieve the audit objectives.

Q: What is the objective of a quality control review in an audit?

A: The objective of a quality control review in an audit is to ensure that the audit work complies with professional standards and regulatory requirements.

Q: What is the objective of a sustainability audit?

A: The objective of a sustainability audit is to evaluate an organization's environmental, social, and economic performance.

Applications

Scenario 1: In an IT firm, the internal audit team discovered that some employees were bypassing the control measures put in place to regulate access to certain sensitive information.

The team suspects this could potentially lead to data breach or unauthorized use of data. How should the audit team address this issue?

Evaluation: The audit team should immediately report these findings to the management. They should also recommend strengthening the control systems, possibly through the use of advanced security measures or by enhancing employee training on data security. This scenario highlights the importance of monitoring controls during an audit. (Source: ISACA)

Scenario 2: A manufacturing company has been consistently reporting high profits. However, the auditors have noticed a large number of obsolete inventories in the warehouse not reflected in the financial statements. How should the auditors respond?

Evaluation: The auditors should consider this as an indication of potential overstatement of inventory and subsequently the profits.

They should recommend the management to write off or adjust the value of obsolete inventory. This highlights the role of auditors in ensuring the accuracy of financial records. (Source: AICPA)

Scenario 3: A retail store has been experiencing inconsistencies in their cash register. The daily records from the cash register do not match with the sales recorded. What should be the auditor's course of action?

Evaluation: Auditors should first check if this discrepancy is due to clerical errors. If the problem persists, they should recommend the implementation of a more robust system for cash handling and recording. This scenario underlines the role of auditors in identifying and addressing operational inefficiencies. (Source: IIA)

Scenario 4: An insurance company has received customer complaints about incorrect billing. The internal audit reveals that the billing software has some glitches. What should be the audit conclusion?

Evaluation: The audit conclusion should be that there is a need to fix the software glitches to prevent incorrect billing. The auditor should recommend a review of the software and necessary corrections. This scenario shows the importance of IT systems in operational efficiency and the auditor's role in ensuring these systems are working correctly. (Source: NAIC)

Scenario 5: A pharmaceutical company has failed to comply with the industry environmental standards, which was discovered during an internal audit. What should be the auditor's recommendation?

Evaluation: The auditor should recommend that the company immediately take steps to comply with the environmental standards to avoid legal implications. They also should recommend ongoing audits to ensure compliance. This scenario highlights the importance of compliance audits in protecting the company from legal and reputational risks. (Source: EPA)

Audit Plan

Theoretical

Q: What is an audit plan?

A: An audit plan is a detailed strategy devised for conducting an audit of an organization's financial records.

Q: What are the key components of an audit plan?

A: The main components include the scope of the audit, audit procedures, audit objectives, and timelines.

Q: Why is an audit plan important?

A: An audit plan is vital as it ensures an organized and systematic approach towards the audit, which enhances its efficiency and effectiveness.

Q: How is the scope of the audit determined in an audit plan?

A: The scope of the audit is determined by identifying the areas of the organization's financial records that will be inspected.

Q: What is the role of audit objectives in an audit plan?

A: The audit objectives define the purpose of the audit and guide the development of the audit procedures.

Q: How are audit procedures developed in an audit plan?

A: Audit procedures are developed based on the audit objectives and scope, and they outline the steps to be taken during the audit.

Q: What is the significance of timelines in an audit plan?

A: Timelines ensure that the audit is completed within a specific period, thereby facilitating efficient resource management.

Q: How does an audit plan enhance the effectiveness of an audit?

A: The plan provides a clear roadmap for the audit, enabling the auditors to conduct a thorough and comprehensive review of the financial records.

Q: Can an audit plan be changed once it's made?

A: Yes, an audit plan can be modified if necessary, especially when new information or changes in the organization's operations emerge.

Q: What factors are considered while forming an audit plan?

A: Factors such as the organization's size, industry, operations, and previous audit findings are considered.

Q: How does an audit plan help in risk assessment?

A: It helps in identifying and assessing potential risk areas in the organization's financial records.

Q: What is the role of an audit plan in communication?

A: An audit plan facilitates communication between the auditors and the organization, ensuring everyone is on the same page regarding the audit process.

Q: How does an audit plan contribute to the audit's efficiency?

A: By providing a clear plan of action, it helps to avoid unnecessary steps and ensures all necessary areas are covered.

Q: What is the relationship between an audit plan and audit evidence?

A: The audit plan guides the collection of audit evidence by identifying the areas to be audited and the procedures to be followed.

Q: How is an audit plan used in the evaluation of audit findings?

A: The plan provides a benchmark against which the audit findings can be evaluated.

Q: Can an audit plan help in detecting fraud?

A: Yes, by focusing on high-risk areas, an audit plan can help in detecting potentially fraudulent activities.

Q: How is an audit plan documented?

A: The plan is typically documented in a formal written format, outlining all its components.

Q: Who is responsible for creating an audit plan?

A: The audit team, with the audit manager or lead auditor, typically develops the audit plan.

Q: How often should an audit plan be reviewed?

A: Ideally, the audit plan should be reviewed at the start of each audit to ensure its relevance and effectiveness.

Q: Can an audit be conducted without an audit plan?

A: Technically, yes, but without a plan, the audit is likely to be disorganized and inefficient.

Q: How does an audit plan aid in resource allocation?

A: By outlining the tasks and timelines, an audit plan helps in determining the resources required for each phase of the audit.

Q: What is the role of an audit plan in resolving audit disputes?

A: An audit plan can provide a reference point for resolving disputes by clarifying the scope, objectives, and procedures of the audit.

Q: How is technology used in the development of an audit plan?

A: Technology can be used for risk assessment, data analysis, and the development of audit procedures, among other things.

Q: How does an audit plan address the issue of auditor independence?

A: An audit plan ensures that the audit procedures are unbiased and objective, thereby upholding the principle of auditor independence.

Q: How does an audit plan help in managing audit risks?

A: The plan helps in identifying and assessing audit risks, which aids in their management and mitigation.

Q: How does an audit plan facilitate compliance with audit standards?

A: By outlining the audit procedures and objectives, an audit plan ensures that the audit is conducted in line with established audit standards.

Q: How does an audit plan assist in the interpretation of audit findings?

A: The plan provides a context for understanding the audit findings, making it easier to interpret them.

Q: How does an audit plan ensure audit quality?

A: It ensures that the audit is conducted systematically and thoroughly, thereby enhancing the quality of the audit.

Q: How are stakeholders involved in the audit planning process?

A: Stakeholders can provide valuable input during the planning process, particularly regarding risk assessment and the determination of audit objectives.

Q: What is the role of an audit plan in audit reporting?

A: The plan can serve as a guide for structuring the audit report, ensuring that all important areas are covered.

Q: How does an audit plan promote transparency in the audit process?

A: By outlining the audit procedures and objectives, an audit plan ensures that the audit process is transparent and open to scrutiny.

Q: Can an audit plan help in preventing audit failures?

A: Yes, a well-structured audit plan can help in identifying potential issues early and taking appropriate corrective action.

Q: How does an audit plan support the auditor's professional judgment?

A: It provides a framework within which the auditor can apply their professional judgment effectively.

Q: How does an audit plan handle the issue of materiality in an audit?

A: The plan helps in determining the levels of materiality for the audit, which guides the collection and evaluation of audit evidence.

Q: How does an audit plan help in managing audit costs?

A: By ensuring an efficient and systematic audit process, an audit plan can help in controlling audit costs.

Q: What is the role of an audit plan in the audit follow-up process?

A: The plan can guide the follow-up process by identifying areas that require further investigation or action.

Q: How does an audit plan deal with the issue of audit sampling?

A: The plan outlines the approach to audit sampling, including the selection of samples and the evaluation of sample results.

Q: How does an audit plan aid in the assessment of internal controls?

A: The plan guides the evaluation of the organization's internal controls as part of the audit process.

Q: How does an audit plan ensure consistency in the audit process?

A: By providing a standard approach for conducting the audit, the plan ensures consistency in the audit process.

Q: How does an audit plan address the issue of audit documentation?

A: The plan outlines the requirements for audit documentation, ensuring that all necessary records are kept.

Applications

Scenario 1: Inconsistencies in the Financial Statements XYZ Ltd. has just completed its fiscal year and its financial statements show a significant increase in profit compared to the previous year. However, the auditors have noticed some inconsistencies in the accounts. They suspect that the management has overstated the revenues and understated the expenses to inflate the profits. How should the auditors approach this situation?

Solution: The auditors should gather sufficient appropriate evidence to substantiate the figures presented in the financial statements. They can do this by performing substantive testing on transactions and balances, such as checking sales invoices and expense receipts. If the suspicions are confirmed, they should communicate these findings to the audit committee and recommend a restatement of the financial statements.

Effectiveness: This solution is effective as it ensures that the financial statements present a true and fair view of the company's financial position. It also complies with auditing standards, which require auditors to obtain reasonable assurance that the financial statements are free from material misstatement.

Scenario 2: Insufficient Audit Evidence ABC Corp. is an e-commerce company that operates in multiple countries. Due to the vastness of its operations, the auditors are having a hard time obtaining sufficient audit evidence. What should the auditors do in such a situation?

Solution: The auditors can use Computer Assisted Audit Techniques (CAATs) to gather audit evidence. CAATs allow auditors to test large volumes of data quickly and accurately. They can also take a risk-based approach, focusing on areas that are likely to give rise to material misstatements.

Effectiveness: This solution is effective as it enables the auditors to gather sufficient audit evidence despite the complexity of the company's operations. It also ensures that the audit is conducted efficiently and effectively.

Scenario 3: Lack of Independence The auditors of PQR Ltd. have been providing non-audit services to the company, which has raised concerns about their independence. How should this issue be addressed?

Solution: To maintain their independence, the auditors should stop providing non-audit services to the company. Alternatively, a different team within the audit firm can provide these services. The auditors should also disclose the provision of non-audit services to the audit committee and assess whether it impairs their independence.

Effectiveness: This solution is effective as it ensures that the auditors remain independent and objective in their audit work. It also complies with the ethical standards for auditors, which require them to avoid any situations that could compromise their independence.

Audit Program

Theoretical

Question: What is an audit program?
Answer: An audit program is a detailed plan of action for an audit process. It outlines the specific procedures and methods auditors will use to gather and evaluate evidence.
Question: Why is an audit program necessary?
Answer: An audit program is necessary to ensure that the audit process is systematic, efficient, and covers all areas of an organization's operations. It also provides a roadmap for the audit team.
Question: What is the role of an auditor in an audit program?
Answer: The auditor's role in an audit program is to plan and execute the audit procedures outlined in the program, gather evidence, evaluate the evidence, and draw conclusions based on their findings.
Question: What are the key components of an audit program?
Answer: The key components of an audit program include the audit objectives, scope, methodology, and procedures. It also includes timelines and resources required for the audit. Question: What is the purpose of an audit objective in an audit program?
Answer: The audit objective defines what the audit aims to achieve. It provides direction and focus for the audit process.
Question: What does the scope of an audit program entail?

Answer: The scope of an audit program outlines the boundaries of the audit. It specifies the areas to be audited, the time period, and the extent of the audit procedures.

Question: What is the importance of audit methodology in an audit program?

Answer: The audit methodology provides a systematic approach for conducting the audit. It includes techniques and procedures to be used in gathering and analyzing evidence.

Question: How does an audit program enhance efficiency in the audit process?

Answer: An audit program enhances efficiency by providing a systematic approach to the audit process. It outlines clear steps and procedures to be followed, reducing the risk of overlooking important areas.

Question: How does an audit program support risk assessment in the audit process?

Answer: An audit program supports risk assessment by outlining procedures to identify and evaluate risks in the organization's operations. It also provides steps to assess the effectiveness of internal controls.

Question: What is the role of documentation in an audit program?

Answer: Documentation in an audit program provides evidence of the audit process. It records the audit procedures performed, the evidence gathered, and the conclusions reached.

Question: How is an audit program different from an audit plan?

Answer: An audit program is a detailed set of instructions for the audit process, while an audit plan is a broader document outlining the overall strategy and direction of the audit.

Question: Can an audit program be modified during the audit process?

Answer: Yes, an audit program can be modified during the audit process if new information or conditions warrant a change in the audit procedures.
Question: What factors influence the design of an audit program?
Answer: Factors that influence the design of an audit program include the nature of the organization, its size, the complexity of its operations, and the risks identified in the audit process.
Question: How does an audit program contribute to the reliability of audit findings?
Answer: An audit program contributes to the reliability of audit findings by providing a systematic approach to the audit process. It ensures that all relevant areas are covered and that evidence is gathered and evaluated in a consistent manner. Question: What is the relationship between an audit program and audit evidence?
Answer: An audit program guides the process of gathering audit evidence. The procedures outlined in the program are designed to gather sufficient, reliable evidence to support the auditor's conclusions.
Question: How does an audit program support communication in the audit process?
Answer: An audit program supports communication by providing a clear roadmap for the audit process.
It outlines the procedures to be performed, the expected outcomes, and the roles and responsibilities of the audit team.
Question: What is the importance of timing in an audit program?
Answer: Timing in an audit program ensures that the audit procedures are performed within a reasonable time frame. It also ensures that the audit findings are reported in a timely manner.
Question: How does an audit program assist in resource allocation in the audit process?

Answer: An audit program assists in resource allocation by outlining the resources needed for each audit procedure. This helps in planning and managing the audit resources effectively.
Question: How does an audit program contribute to accountability in the audit process?
Answer: An audit program contributes to accountability by outlining the roles and responsibilities of the audit team. It provides a clear roadmap for the audit process, ensuring that everyone involved understands their duties.
Question: What is the role of technology in an audit program?
Answer: Technology in an audit program supports the execution of audit procedures, data analysis, and reporting.
This improves the effectiveness and precision in the auditing process.
Question: How does an audit program support compliance with audit standards?
Answer: An audit program supports compliance with audit standards by outlining procedures that align with the standards. It ensures that the audit process is conducted in a manner that meets the required professional and ethical standards.
Question: How does an audit program impact the quality of an audit?
Answer: An audit program impacts the quality of an audit by providing a systematic approach to the audit process. It ensures that all relevant areas are covered, and that evidence is gathered and evaluated in a consistent and thorough manner.
Question: How does an audit program assist in the identification and management of audit risks?
Answer: An audit program assists in the identification and management of audit risks by outlining procedures to identify and evaluate risks. It also provides steps to assess the effectiveness of the organization's internal controls in managing these risks.

Question: How does an audit program support the independence of the auditor?

Answer: An audit program supports the independence of the auditor by providing a clear and systematic approach to the audit process. It ensures that the auditor's judgments and conclusions are based on objective evidence, not influenced by external pressures or biases.

Question: Can an audit program be used for different types of audits?

Answer: Yes, an audit program can be tailored to different types of audits, such as financial audits, operational audits, or compliance audits. The specific procedures and methods may vary, but the general approach remains the same.

Question: How does an audit program contribute to the transparency of the audit process?

Answer: An audit program contributes to the transparency of the audit process by outlining the steps and procedures to be followed. It provides a clear roadmap for the audit process, making it easier for stakeholders to understand how the audit was conducted and how conclusions were reached.

Question: How does an audit program assist in the evaluation of internal controls?

Answer: An audit program assists in the evaluation of internal controls by outlining procedures to assess the effectiveness of the controls. It provides steps to test the controls and identify any weaknesses or deficiencies.

Question: How does an audit program support the objectivity of the auditor?

Answer: An audit program supports the objectivity of the auditor by providing a systematic approach to the audit process. It ensures that the auditor's judgments and conclusions are based on objective evidence, not influenced by personal biases or preferences.

Question: How does an audit program facilitate the audit reporting process?

Answer: An audit program facilitates the audit reporting process by providing a clear record of the audit procedures performed, the evidence gathered, and the conclusions reached. This information forms the basis for the audit report. Question: How does an audit program assist in the training and development of audit staff?

Answer: An audit program assists in the training and development of audit staff by providing a clear outline of the audit process. It serves as a learning tool, helping audit staff understand the procedures and techniques used in an audit.

Question: How does an audit program support decision-making in the audit process?

Answer: An audit program supports decision-making in the audit process by providing a systematic approach to gathering and evaluating evidence. The conclusions drawn from this evidence inform the auditor's decisions.

Question: How does an audit program ensure consistency in the audit process?

Answer: An audit program ensures consistency in the audit process by providing a standard set of procedures to be followed. This ensures that the audit is conducted in a consistent manner, regardless of who is performing the audit.

Question: How does an audit program assist in the management of audit resources?

Answer: An audit program assists in the management of audit resources by outlining the resources needed for each audit procedure. This helps in planning and managing the audit resources effectively.

Question: How does an audit program support the credibility of the audit process?

Answer: An audit program supports the credibility of the audit process by providing a systematic and transparent approach to the audit. It ensures that the audit is conducted in a manner that is consistent, thorough, and based on objective evidence.

Question: How does an audit program contribute to the effectiveness of the audit process?

Answer: An audit program contributes to the effectiveness of the audit process by providing a clear and systematic approach to the audit. It ensures that all relevant areas are covered, and that evidence is gathered and evaluated in a thorough and consistent manner.

Question: How does an audit program assist in the management of audit time?

Answer: An audit program assists in the management of audit time by outlining the timelines for each audit procedure. This helps in planning and managing the audit process effectively.

Question: How does an audit program support the accountability of the audit team?

Answer: An audit program supports the accountability of the audit team by outlining the roles and responsibilities of each team member. It ensures that everyone involved in the audit process understands their duties and is accountable for their performance.

Question: How does an audit program assist in the identification of audit issues?

Answer: An audit program assists in the identification of audit issues by outlining procedures to gather and evaluate evidence. It provides steps to identify potential issues and evaluate their impact on the audit findings.

Question: How does an audit program support the resolution of audit issues?

Answer: An audit program supports the resolution of audit issues by providing a systematic approach to the audit process. It outlines steps to identify and address issues, ensuring that they are resolved in a timely and effective manner.

Question: How does an audit program assist in the evaluation of audit performance?

Answer: An audit program assists in the evaluation of audit performance by providing a clear record of the audit procedures performed, the evidence gathered, and the conclusions reached. This information can be used to assess the efficiency and effectiveness of the audit process.

Question: How does an audit program support continuous improvement in the audit process?

Answer: An audit program supports continuous improvement in the audit process by providing a systematic approach to the audit. It outlines steps to identify and address issues, and to evaluate the effectiveness of the audit process, enabling continuous learning and improvement.

Question: How does an audit program contribute to the integrity of the audit process?

Answer: An audit program contributes to the integrity of the audit process by providing a systematic and transparent approach to the audit.

It ensures that the audit is conducted in a manner that is consistent, thorough, and based on objective evidence.

Question: How does an audit program support stakeholder confidence in the audit process?

Answer: An audit program supports stakeholder confidence in the audit process by providing a systematic and transparent approach to the audit.

It ensures that the audit is conducted in a manner that is consistent, thorough, and based on objective evidence, enhancing stakeholder trust and confidence.

Question: How does an audit program support the professionalism of the audit team?

Answer: An audit program supports the professionalism of the audit team by providing a systematic approach to the audit process. It outlines clear procedures and standards to be followed, promoting professionalism in the conduct of the audit.

Question: How does an audit program assist in the management of audit risks?

Answer: An audit program assists in the management of audit risks by outlining procedures to identify and evaluate risks. It also provides steps to assess the effectiveness of the organization's internal controls in managing these risks.

Question: How does an audit program support the thoroughness of the audit process?

Answer: An audit program supports the thoroughness of the audit process by providing a systematic approach to the audit. It ensures that all relevant areas are covered, and that evidence is gathered and evaluated in a thorough and consistent manner.

Question: How does an audit program assist in the monitoring of the audit process?

Answer: An audit program assists in the monitoring of the audit process by providing a clear record of the audit procedures performed, the evidence gathered, and the conclusions reached. This information can be used to monitor the progress and effectiveness of the audit process.

Question: How does an audit program support the fairness of the audit process?

Answer: An audit program supports the fairness of the audit process by providing a systematic approach to the audit. It ensures that the auditor's judgments and conclusions are based on objective evidence, not influenced by personal biases or preferences.

Question: How does an audit program contribute to the accountability of the organization being audited?

Answer: An audit program contributes to the accountability of the organization being audited by providing a systematic approach to the audit. It outlines steps to evaluate the organization's operations and internal controls, promoting accountability and transparency.

Question: How does an audit program support the audit conclusion?

Answer: An audit program supports the audit conclusion by providing a systematic approach to gathering and evaluating evidence. The conclusions drawn from this evidence form the basis for the audit conclusion.

Applications

Scenario 1: Company A recently underwent an internal audit and the auditor, Mr. Smith, found that there were some discrepancies in the company's financial statements. He found that the company had been overstating its assets and understating its liabilities.

Question: How should Mr. Smith, as an auditor, handle this situation?

Answer: As an auditor, Mr. Smith's primary responsibility is to report his findings to the company's management and suggest corrective actions. He must also verify the accuracy of the financial statements by cross-checking them with other records. If corrections are not made, he should report these discrepancies to the appropriate regulatory bodies. Effectiveness: This answer effectively demonstrates the auditor's role in ensuring the integrity of financial statements and the procedure he should follow if discrepancies are found.

Scenario 2: Company B is a small business that has never had an audit before. The owner, Mrs. Jones, is unsure of what to expect during an audit and what her responsibilities are. Question: What should Mrs. Jones expect during an audit and what are her responsibilities?

Answer: During an audit, Mrs. Jones can expect the auditor to thoroughly examine her company's financial records, assets, and liabilities. She will need to provide all necessary documentation and answer any questions the auditor may have. Her responsibilities include ensuring all records are accurate and up-to-date, and any discrepancies are corrected. Effectiveness: This answer effectively outlines what a small business owner can expect during an audit and their responsibilities during the process.

Scenario 3: Company C is a large corporation that has been audited many times. However, the recent audit revealed significant financial misstatements. The CEO, Mr. Brown, is worried about the potential legal repercussions.

Question: What potential legal repercussions could Company C face as a result of these financial misstatements?

Answer: Depending on the severity of the misstatements and whether they were intentional, Company C could face fines, penalties, or even criminal charges. Additionally, the company's reputation could be severely damaged, leading to a loss of business. Effectiveness: This answer effectively highlights the potential legal repercussions a company could face as a result of financial misstatements.

Audit Charter

Theoretical

Q: What is the primary purpose of an audit charter?

A: The primary purpose of an audit charter is to establish the authority, scope, and responsibilities of the audit function within an organization.

Q: How does an audit charter provide independence to the internal audit function?

A: An audit charter provides independence by clearly stating that the internal audit function has unrestricted access to all functions, records, property, and personnel of the organization.

Q: What elements should be included in an effective audit charter?

A: An effective audit charter should include the purpose, authority, and responsibility of the internal audit function, the nature of audit services provided, the reporting structure of the internal audit function, and the standards to which the internal audit function adheres.

Q: Who usually approves the audit charter?

A: The board of directors or the audit committee typically approves the audit charter.

Q: How often should the audit charter be reviewed and updated?

A: Ideally, the audit charter should be reviewed and updated annually to ensure that it is still relevant and effective.

Q: What role does the audit charter play in risk management?

A: The audit charter sets the tone for how internal audit will address risk management within the organization, including the scope of its risk assessment activities and its role in the organization's overall risk management framework.

Q: What are the consequences of not having an audit charter in place?

A: Without an audit charter, there may be confusion about the role and responsibilities of the internal audit function, which can lead to inefficiencies, misunderstandings, and potential conflicts.

Q: How does an audit charter promote transparency?

A: An audit charter promotes transparency by clearly defining the roles, responsibilities, and reporting relationships of the internal audit function.

Q: Who should be involved in the development of the audit charter?

A: The development of the audit charter should involve key stakeholders including the board of directors, audit committee, management, and the chief audit executive.

Q: Can the scope of the internal audit function as defined in the audit charter be changed?

A: Yes, the scope can be changed, but any changes should be approved by the board or the audit committee and documented in a revised audit charter.

Q: What is the relationship between the audit charter and the internal audit plan?

A: The audit charter establishes the framework within which the internal audit plan is developed and executed.

Q: How does an audit charter support accountability?

A: An audit charter supports accountability by clearly defining the roles and responsibilities of the internal audit function and the expectations of the board and management.

Q: What is the role of the audit charter in establishing the internal audit function's reporting relationship with the board or audit committee?
A: The audit charter should clearly state that the chief audit executive reports functionally to the board or audit committee, which promotes the independence and objectivity of the internal audit function.
Q: How does the audit charter help in defining the scope of the internal audit function?
A: The audit charter clearly outlines the areas and functions within the organization that the internal audit function is authorized to review and assess.
Q: What role does the audit charter play in conflict resolution within the organization?
A: The audit charter can help resolve conflicts by providing a clear reference point for the roles and responsibilities of the internal audit function.
Q: Can an audit charter be used in external audits?
A: While primarily designed for internal audits, the audit charter can provide useful information for external auditors about the scope and function of the internal audit department.
Q: Why is it important for the audit charter to be in written form?
A: A written audit charter provides a formal and tangible document that can be referred to and reviewed by all stakeholders.
Q: How does the audit charter contribute to the professional practice of internal auditing?
A: The audit charter provides a foundation for the professional practice of internal auditing by establishing the purpose, authority, and responsibility of the internal audit function.
Q: Can the audit charter limit the scope of the internal audit function?

A: While the audit charter defines the scope of the internal audit function, it should not unduly limit the areas and functions that internal audit can review and assess.

Q: How does the audit charter promote adherence to the International Standards for the Professional Practice of Internal Auditing?

A: The audit charter can explicitly state that the internal audit function will adhere to these standards, thereby promoting their consistent application.

Q: What role does the audit charter play in defining the relationship between the internal audit function and management?

A: The audit charter should clearly define the reporting relationship between the internal audit function and management, including the process for handling audit findings and recommendations.

Q: Why is it important for the audit charter to be communicated to all employees?

A: Communicating the audit charter to all employees helps to promote understanding and acceptance of the internal audit function.

Q: How does the audit charter facilitate the planning of audit activities?

A: The audit charter defines the scope and responsibilities of the internal audit function, which provides a basis for planning audit activities.

Q: How does the audit charter contribute to the credibility of the internal audit function?

A: The audit charter contributes to the credibility of the internal audit function by clearly establishing its authority and independence.

Q: What role does the audit charter play in the recruitment and selection of internal audit staff?

A: The audit charter can serve as a reference for the skills and competencies required for the internal audit function, thereby guiding the recruitment and selection process.

Q: How does the audit charter support the continuous improvement of the internal audit function?

A: The audit charter provides a framework for evaluating the performance of the internal audit function and identifying areas for improvement.

Q: Can the audit charter help in resolving disputes between the internal audit function and management?

A: Yes, the audit charter can provide a basis for resolving disputes by clearly defining the roles and responsibilities of the internal audit function and management.

Q: How does the audit charter promote the objectivity of the internal audit function?

A: The audit charter promotes objectivity by stating that the internal audit function should have no operational responsibilities and should be free from any influences that could impair its ability to make impartial judgments.

Q: What is the role of the audit charter in the overall governance of an organization?

A: The audit charter contributes to the overall governance of an organization by establishing the role and responsibilities of the internal audit function in relation to the board, audit committee, and management.

Q: How does the audit charter support the alignment of the internal audit function with the organization's strategic objectives?

A: The audit charter can state that the internal audit function should assist the organization in achieving its strategic objectives by providing assurance and consulting services related to governance, risk management, and internal control processes.

Q: What is the relationship between the audit charter and the organization's code of ethics?

A: The audit charter can reinforce the organization's code of ethics by requiring the internal audit function to adhere to high standards of honesty, integrity, and professional conduct.

Q: How does the audit charter support the quality assurance and improvement program of the internal audit function?

A: The audit charter provides a basis for assessing the quality of the internal audit function by establishing its purpose, authority, and responsibility.

Q: How can the audit charter help to manage the expectations of stakeholders about the internal audit function?

A: The audit charter provides a clear and comprehensive description of the internal audit function, which can help manage the expectations of stakeholders.

Q: How does the audit charter contribute to the ethical climate of the organization?

A: The audit charter can contribute to the ethical climate of the organization by stating that the internal audit function should adhere to high standards of professional conduct.

Q: Can the audit charter be used to justify the resources allocated to the internal audit function?

A: Yes, the audit charter can be used to justify the resources allocated to the internal audit function by outlining its scope and responsibilities.

Q: How does the audit charter support the integration of the internal audit function into the organization's culture?

A: The audit charter can articulate the value and contributions of the internal audit function, thereby promoting its acceptance and integration into the organization's culture.

Q: What is the role of the audit charter in the evaluation of the performance of the internal audit function?
A: The audit charter provides a basis for evaluating the performance of the internal audit function by defining its purpose, authority, and responsibility.
Q: How does the audit charter promote the professionalism of the internal audit function?
A: The audit charter can promote professionalism by requiring the internal audit function to adhere to recognized standards of internal auditing.
Q: How does the audit charter contribute to the trust and confidence of stakeholders in the internal audit function?
A: The audit charter contributes to the trust and confidence of stakeholders by clearly establishing the authority, independence, and professionalism of the internal audit function.
Q: Can the audit charter be used as a tool for marketing the internal audit function within the organization?
A: Yes, the audit charter can be used as a tool for marketing the internal audit function by articulating its value and contributions to the organization.
Q: How does the audit charter support the development of a risk-based internal audit plan?
A: The audit charter provides a foundation for developing a risk-based internal audit plan by defining the scope and responsibilities of the internal audit function in relation to risk management.
Q: How does the audit charter contribute to the consistency and continuity of the internal audit function?
A: The audit charter contributes to the consistency and continuity of the internal audit function by providing a stable reference point for its role and responsibilities.

Q: How does the audit charter support the communication of audit findings and recommendations?
A: The audit charter can outline the process for communicating audit findings and recommendations, thereby promoting clarity and understanding.
Q: How does the audit charter contribute to the accountability of management for addressing audit findings and recommendations?
A: The audit charter can state that management is responsible for addressing audit findings and recommendations, thereby promoting accountability.
Q: How does the audit charter support the training and development of internal audit staff?
A: The audit charter can serve as a reference for the skills and competencies required for the internal audit function, thereby guiding the training and development of internal audit staff.
Q: How does the audit charter contribute to the resilience of the internal audit function in times of change or crisis?
A: The audit charter provides a stable reference point for the role and responsibilities of the internal audit function, thereby contributing to its resilience in times of change or crisis.
Q: How does the audit charter support the management of relationships with external auditors and regulators?
A: The audit charter can outline the role and responsibilities of the internal audit function in relation to external auditors and regulators, thereby promoting effective relationship management.
Q: How does the audit charter contribute to the integrity of the internal audit function?
A: The audit charter contributes to the integrity of the internal audit function by clearly establishing its authority, independence, and adherence to high standards of professional conduct.
Q: How does the audit charter support the management of conflicts of interest within the internal audit function?

A: The audit charter can require the internal audit function to adhere to a code of ethics, which can provide guidance for managing conflicts of interest.

Q: How does the audit charter contribute to the value and impact of the internal audit function?

A: The audit charter contributes to the value and impact of the internal audit function by clearly defining its purpose, authority, and responsibility, and by promoting its independence, objectivity, and professionalism.

Applications

Scenario 1: Business Name: MaxTech Inc.

MaxTech Inc., a tech firm, is in its initial phase of development and has not established an audit charter. As the internal auditor, you discover irregularities in the company's financial reporting. What measures would you implement to handle this situation? To evaluate the effectiveness of the solution, one would first create an audit charter that outlines the responsibilities, authority, and accountability of the internal audit function. This will provide a clear framework for conducting audits and addressing irregularities. The charter will also help in establishing a direct communication line with the audit committee, making it easier to report any issues. The next step would be to investigate the irregularities and report them to the audit committee. The effectiveness of the solution can be measured by how quickly and efficiently the irregularities are addressed.

Scenario 2: Business Name: GreenLife Organics GreenLife Organics, an organic food company, has an audit charter in place. However, the internal audit function seems to be ineffective as there are recurring financial irregularities. As the chief audit executive, how would you address this issue? The effectiveness of this solution can be evaluated by assessing the effectiveness of the audit charter. This can be done by reviewing the charter, identifying any gaps or weaknesses, and making necessary amendments. Also, regular training and development sessions should be conducted to ensure that the internal audit team is equipped with the knowledge and skills required to carry out their duties effectively. The effectiveness of the solution can be measured by the decrease in financial irregularities and improved performance of the internal audit function.

Scenario 3: Business Name: Fashionista Boutique Fashionista Boutique, a fashion retail store, has an audit charter but is facing issues with its implementation due to lack of understanding among employees. As an internal auditor, how would you ensure effective implementation of the audit charter? The effectiveness of the solution would be evaluated by conducting awareness sessions to educate the employees about the importance and benefits of the audit charter. As part of these sessions, real-life examples can be given to demonstrate the consequences of not adhering to the charter. The effectiveness of the solution can be measured by the increased understanding and adherence to the audit charter among the employees.

Scenario 4: Business Name: QuickTravel Agency QuickTravel Agency, a travel agency, has an audit charter, but the senior management often interferes in the auditing process, undermining the authority of the internal audit function. As the head of the audit committee, how would you handle this situation? The effectiveness of the solution would be evaluated by reinforcing the authority and independence of the internal audit function as outlined in the audit charter. This can be done by holding discussions with the senior management to address the issue and ensuring that the audit charter is respected and adhered to. The effectiveness can be measured by observing a decrease in interference from the senior management in the audit process.

Audit Committee

Theoretical

Q: What is the principal role of an audit committee?

A: The principal role of an audit committee is to oversee the integrity of the company's financial reporting process, the system of internal controls and management of financial risks, and the audit process.

Q: What are the primary duties of an audit committee?

A: The key responsibilities of an audit committee include overseeing financial reporting, reviewing the company's internal controls, managing relations with the external auditor, and assessing risk management policies.

Q: Who typically makes up an audit committee?

A: An audit committee is typically made up of at least three members of the board of directors, with a majority being independent non-executive directors.

Q: How often should an audit committee meet?

A: An audit committee should meet at least four times a year, and as many times as necessary to perform its duties effectively.

Q: Why is independence important for an audit committee?

A: Independence is important for an audit committee to ensure that it can objectively assess the company's financial statements and internal controls without being influenced by management.

Q: What is the relationship between an audit committee and the external auditor?

A: The audit committee is responsible for the appointment, remuneration, and oversight of the external auditor, and for reviewing and discussing the auditor's reports.

Q: What skills and knowledge should members of an audit committee possess?

A: Members of an audit committee should have a good understanding of finance and accounting, as well as knowledge of the company's industry and business model.

Q: Can the CEO be a member of the audit committee?

A: No, the CEO cannot be a member of the audit committee as this would compromise the committee's independence.

Q: What are the potential consequences for a company if its audit committee does not perform its duties effectively?

A: If an audit committee does not perform its duties effectively, it could lead to inaccurate financial reporting, regulatory sanctions, damage to the company's reputation, and loss of investor confidence.

Q: What is the role of the audit committee in risk management?

A: The audit committee is responsible for overseeing the company's risk management policies and procedures, and for ensuring that significant risks are properly identified, assessed, and managed.

Q: Why is it important for an audit committee to have a charter?

A: A charter is important for an audit committee as it outlines the committee's purpose, responsibilities, and authority, and provides a framework for its activities.

Q: What is the difference between an audit committee and a finance committee?

A: An audit committee is primarily concerned with oversight of financial reporting and audit processes, while a finance committee is typically responsible for strategic financial planning and budgeting.

Q: What is the role of the audit committee in corporate governance?

A: The audit committee plays a crucial role in corporate governance by ensuring the integrity of financial reporting, which contributes to the transparency and accountability of the company's management.

Q: How does the audit committee contribute to the credibility of financial reporting?

A: The audit committee contributes to the credibility of financial reporting by overseeing the audit process, reviewing the financial statements for accuracy and completeness, and ensuring that the company complies with accounting standards and regulations.

Q: What are the key qualities of an effective audit committee?

A: The key qualities of an effective audit committee include independence, financial literacy, industry knowledge, integrity, objectivity, and good judgment.

Q: Can a member of the audit committee be a member of the management team?

A: No, a member of the management team cannot be a member of the audit committee as this would compromise the committee's independence.

Q: What is the role of the audit committee in relation to internal audit?

A: The audit committee is responsible for overseeing the activities of the internal audit function, including its scope, budget, and staffing.

Q: How should an audit committee handle disagreements between management and the external auditor?

A: An audit committee should objectively assess the arguments of both sides, seek additional information if necessary, and make a decision that is in the best interest of the company and its shareholders.

Q: How does an audit committee ensure the independence of the external auditor?

A: The audit committee ensures the independence of the external auditor by taking responsibility for the auditor's appointment and remuneration, reviewing the auditor's work, and limiting the non-audit services provided by the auditor.

Q: What is the role of the audit committee in fraud prevention and detection?

A: The audit committee plays a role in fraud prevention and detection by overseeing the company's internal controls and risk management systems, and by ensuring that there is a mechanism for employees to report suspicious activities.

Q: Why is financial literacy important for members of the audit committee?

A: Financial literacy is important for members of the audit committee so that they can understand and evaluate the company's financial statements, assess the appropriateness of accounting policies, and challenge the management's assumptions and judgments.

Q: What is the relationship between an audit committee and the board of directors?

A: The audit committee is a subcommittee of the board of directors, and it reports its findings and recommendations to the full board for approval.

Q: Can an audit committee make decisions on behalf of the board of directors?

A: No, an audit committee can only make recommendations to the board of directors, who are ultimately responsible for making decisions.

Q: What is the impact of an ineffective audit committee on a company?

A: An ineffective audit committee can lead to inaccurate financial reporting, regulatory sanctions, damage to the company's reputation, and loss of investor confidence.

Q: How does an audit committee add value to a company?

A: An audit committee adds value to a company by enhancing the credibility of financial reporting, improving the effectiveness of internal controls, and contributing to good corporate governance.

Q: What is the role of the audit committee in the audit process?

A: The audit committee oversees the audit process by selecting the external auditor, defining the scope of the audit, reviewing the audit findings, and ensuring that the management takes corrective action if necessary.

Q: How should an audit committee handle conflicts of interest?

A: An audit committee should handle conflicts of interest by establishing a conflict of interest policy, requiring members to disclose potential conflicts, and ensuring that conflicted members do not participate in related decisions.

Q: What is the role of the audit committee in relation to the company's internal controls?

A: The audit committee is responsible for reviewing the effectiveness of the company's internal controls and ensuring that weaknesses are addressed.

Q: Why is it important for the audit committee to have a good relationship with the external auditor?

A: A good relationship with the external auditor is important for the audit committee to ensure open communication, mutual understanding, and effective oversight of the audit process.

Q: What are the steps an audit committee should take if it identifies a significant weakness in the company's internal controls?

A: If the audit committee identifies a significant weakness in the company's internal controls, it should report the weakness to the board of directors, recommend corrective action, and monitor the management's progress in addressing the weakness.

Q: What is the role of the audit committee in ensuring compliance with laws and regulations?

A: The audit committee is responsible for overseeing the company's compliance with laws and regulations, and for ensuring that any violations are identified, reported, and addressed.

Q: Can the audit committee override the decisions of the management?

A: No, the audit committee cannot override the decisions of the management, but it can challenge the management's judgments and recommendations, and report its concerns to the board of directors.

Q: How should an audit committee handle allegations of fraud or misconduct?

A: An audit committee should handle allegations of fraud or misconduct by conducting or overseeing an investigation, ensuring that the allegations are thoroughly and impartially examined, and recommending appropriate action.

Q: Why is it important for an audit committee to be transparent in its activities?

A: Transparency in the activities of the audit committee is important to demonstrate its accountability, maintain the trust of shareholders, and enhance the credibility of the company's financial reporting.

Q: What should an audit committee consider when selecting an external auditor?

A: When selecting an external auditor, an audit committee should consider the auditor's independence, qualifications, experience, reputation, and understanding of the company's industry and business.

Q: How does an audit committee ensure the objectivity of the internal audit function?

A: The audit committee ensures the objectivity of the internal audit function by overseeing its activities, ensuring its independence from the management, and reviewing its findings and recommendations.

Q: What is the role of the audit committee in relation to the company's ethics and compliance program?

A: The audit committee is responsible for overseeing the company's ethics and compliance program, and for ensuring that the company operates in a legal, ethical, and socially responsible manner.

Q: How should an audit committee handle sensitive issues such as executive compensation and related party transactions?

A: Sensitive issues such as executive compensation and related party transactions should be handled by the audit committee with objectivity, transparency, and in accordance with the company's policies and applicable laws and regulations.

Q: What is the impact of a strong audit committee on a company's performance?

A: A strong audit committee can enhance a company's performance by improving the quality of financial reporting, strengthening internal controls, reducing risk, and contributing to good corporate governance.

Q: Can the audit committee fire the external auditor?

A: Yes, the audit committee has the authority to recommend the dismissal of the external auditor to the board of directors, if it believes that the auditor is not performing its duties effectively or independently.

Q: How should an audit committee communicate its activities and decisions to stakeholders?

A: An audit committee should communicate its activities and decisions to stakeholders through the audit committee report in the company's annual report, and through other appropriate disclosure mechanisms.

Q: What is the role of the audit committee in relation to the company's financial policies and procedures?

A: The audit committee is responsible for reviewing the company's financial policies and procedures, and for ensuring that they are consistent with accounting standards, laws and regulations, and best practices.

Q: What is the role of the audit committee in relation to the company's disclosure controls and procedures?

A: The audit committee is responsible for reviewing the company's disclosure controls and procedures, and for ensuring that material information is accurately and timely disclosed.

Q: Can the audit committee initiate an investigation into the company's operations?

A: Yes, the audit committee has the authority to initiate an investigation into the company's operations, if it has concerns about potential fraud, misconduct, or violation of laws and regulations.

Q: How should an audit committee handle a whistleblower complaint?

A: A whistleblower complaint should be handled by the audit committee with confidentiality, thoroughness, and impartiality, and the committee should ensure that the whistleblower is not retaliated against.

Q: What is the role of the audit committee in relation to the company's strategic planning?

A: While strategic planning is not a primary responsibility of the audit committee, the committee can contribute to strategic planning by ensuring that financial risks and implications are considered, and that the company's strategy is aligned with its risk appetite.

Q: What is the role of the audit committee in relation to the company's capital structure and financing decisions?

A: The audit committee can contribute to the company's capital structure and financing decisions by ensuring that financial risks are properly assessed, and that the decisions are consistent with the company's financial policies and risk appetite.

Q: How should an audit committee keep itself updated on changes in accounting standards and regulations?

A: An audit committee can keep itself updated on changes in accounting standards and regulations through continuing education, consultation with experts, and engagement with professional and regulatory bodies.

Q: Can the audit committee engage external advisors?

A: Yes, the audit committee has the authority to engage external advisors, such as lawyers and consultants, to assist it in its duties, at the expense of the company.

Q: What is the role of the audit committee in relation to the company's sustainability and social responsibility?

A: The audit committee can contribute to the company's sustainability and social responsibility by ensuring that related risks and opportunities are considered in the company's strategy, and that the company's performance in these areas is accurately reported.

Applications

Scenario 1: ABC Company has been experiencing declining profits for the last few years, despite an increase in sales. As a member of the audit committee, you are tasked with investigating the cause of this decline.

Answer: By conducting a financial audit, we can identify areas of inefficiency and wastage. Our investigation reveals that the company is spending excessively on raw materials due to poor inventory management. By implementing a robust inventory control system, we can significantly reduce costs and increase profitability. Evaluation: This answer effectively addresses the problem by identifying and rectifying the root cause of the declining profits.

Scenario 2: XYZ Company has recently undergone a merger. There are concerns about inconsistencies and discrepancies in the financial statements of the two entities. As an auditor, how would you address these issues? Answer: By conducting a comprehensive audit, we can identify and reconcile any inconsistencies or discrepancies in the financial statements. This may involve reviewing and comparing the financial records of the two entities, and verifying the accuracy of the information provided. Evaluation: This answer is effective as it outlines a thorough and systematic approach to resolving the issues related to the merger.

Scenario 3: DEF Company has been accused of tax evasion. As a member of the audit committee, how would you investigate these allegations? Answer: Through a forensic audit, we can investigate the allegations of tax evasion. This involves examining the company's financial records, transactions, and tax returns to detect any fraudulent or illegal activities. If any irregularities are found, we can recommend corrective measures to ensure compliance with tax laws. Evaluation: This answer is effective as it outlines a robust and comprehensive approach to investigating allegations of tax evasion.

Scenario 4: GHI Company is planning to expand its business operations overseas. As an auditor, what would you do to ensure the company's financial readiness for this expansion? Answer: By conducting a financial audit, we can assess the company's financial health and readiness for expansion. This involves reviewing the company's financial statements, cash flow, and liquidity to determine if it has the financial resources to support the expansion. Evaluation: This answer is effective as it provides a clear strategy for assessing the company's financial readiness for expansion.

Scenario 5: JKL Company has been experiencing a high turnover of staff in the finance department. As a member of the audit committee, how would you address this issue? Answer: By conducting an operational audit, we can identify the factors contributing to the high staff turnover. This may involve reviewing the company's HR policies, work environment, and employee satisfaction levels. Based on our findings, we can recommend measures to improve staff retention. Evaluation: This answer is effective as it addresses the issue in a comprehensive and systematic manner.

Auditor Independence

Theoretical

Q: What is the concept of auditor independence?

A: Auditor independence refers to the state of an auditor being free from any influence, bias or conflict of interest that could affect their professional judgment or objectivity during the audit process.

Q: Why is auditor independence crucial in auditing?

A: Auditor independence is essential to uphold the credibility and reliability of the audit report. It ensures that the auditor's opinion is objective and free from any influence, thus providing accurate and trustworthy information to stakeholders.

Q: What are the two main types of auditor independence?

A: The two main types of auditor independence are independence in fact and independence in appearance.

Q: What is meant by 'independence in fact'?

A: Independence in fact refers to the actual state of the auditor being impartial and unbiased in their work, regardless of any external influences or pressures.

Q: What does 'independence in appearance' refer to?

A: Independence in appearance refers to the perception that others, such as stakeholders or the public, have of the auditor's independence.

Q: How can an auditor maintain independence in fact and appearance?

A: An auditor can maintain independence by avoiding situations that may lead to conflicts of interest, ensuring a proper rotation of audit assignments, and adhering to professional ethics and standards.

Q: What are some threats to auditor independence?

A: Some threats to auditor independence include self-interest threat, self-review threat, advocacy threat, familiarity threat, and intimidation threat.

Q: What is self-interest threat?

A: A self-interest threat occurs when an auditor could benefit, financially or otherwise, from the outcome of the audit.

Q: What is self-review threat?

A: A self-review threat occurs when an auditor has to review and assess work that they or their colleagues have performed.

Q: What is advocacy threat?

A: Advocacy threat arises when an auditor becomes an advocate for their client, compromising their ability to remain impartial.

Q: What is familiarity threat?

A: Familiarity threat occurs when an auditor becomes too familiar with the client, impacting their ability to remain objective.

Q: What is intimidation threat?

A: An intimidation threat arises when an auditor feels threatened or pressured by the client into providing a favorable audit opinion.

Q: What measures can be taken to mitigate threats to auditor independence?

A: Measures include implementing safeguards, adhering to professional ethics, maintaining professional skepticism, and ensuring a proper rotation of audit assignments.

Q: How do safeguards help maintain auditor independence?

A: Safeguards help manage potential threats and conflicts of interest that could compromise independence by providing a framework for ethical decision-making and behavior.

Q: What is the role of professional ethics in maintaining auditor independence?

A: Professional ethics guide auditors in upholding their integrity, objectivity, and professional competence and due care, all of which are vital for maintaining independence.

Q: What is the importance of professional skepticism in auditor independence?

A: Professional skepticism ensures that auditors don't accept information at face value and question everything, thereby enhancing their independence.

Q: How does rotation of audit assignments help maintain auditor independence?

A: Rotation of audit assignments prevents auditors from becoming too familiar with the client, mitigating the familiarity threat to independence.

Q: What is the impact of auditor independence on the reliability of financial statements?

A: Auditor independence enhances the reliability of financial statements by ensuring the auditor's opinion is impartial and unbiased.

Q: How does auditor independence affect stakeholders' confidence?

A: Auditor independence boosts stakeholders' confidence in the audit report as they can trust that the auditor's opinion is objective and free from any influence.

Q: How can potential conflicts of interest be managed to maintain auditor independence?

A: Potential conflicts of interest can be managed by implementing safeguards, maintaining professional ethics, and ensuring a proper rotation of audit assignments.

Q: What is the role of audit committees in maintaining auditor independence?

A: Audit committees help maintain auditor independence by overseeing the audit process, ensuring the auditor's objectivity, and managing potential conflicts of interest.

Q: How can regulatory bodies ensure auditor independence?

A: Regulatory bodies can ensure auditor independence by setting and enforcing stringent ethical standards and conducting regular inspections of audit firms.

Q: How does auditor independence contribute to the quality of an audit?

A: Auditor independence enhances the quality of an audit by ensuring the auditor's judgment is impartial, unbiased, and based solely on the audit evidence.

Q: What are the consequences of a lack of auditor independence?

A: A lack of auditor independence can lead to a compromised audit quality, misleading financial statements, and loss of stakeholder trust.

Q: Can an auditor provide non-audit services to an audit client without compromising independence?

A: While it's possible for an auditor to provide non-audit services, it can pose a threat to independence if the auditor ends up auditing their own work or advising the client in decision-making.

Q: What is the link between auditor remuneration and independence?

A: Auditor remuneration, if contingent upon certain outcomes or overly generous, can threaten independence by creating a self-interest threat.

Q: How can an auditor's independence be compromised by their relationship with the client's management?

A: If an auditor develops a close personal relationship with the client's management, it can create a familiarity threat, compromising their independence.

Q: What is the danger of long-term auditor-client relationships?

A: Long-term auditor-client relationships can lead to a familiarity threat, whereby the auditor becomes too comfortable or complacent, compromising their independence.

Q: Can auditors accept gifts from clients without compromising their independence?

A: Accepting gifts from clients, particularly if significant, can create a self-interest threat and compromise the auditor's independence.

Q: How does the size of an audit firm impact auditor independence?

A: The size of an audit firm can impact auditor independence, as larger firms may have more robust safeguards and rotation policies in place to maintain independence.

Q: How can an auditor ensure independence when they have a financial interest in the client?

A: An auditor should avoid having any financial interest in the client, as it creates a self-interest threat to their independence.

Q: How can a firm-wide culture of ethics and integrity help maintain auditor independence?

A: A firm-wide culture of ethics and integrity can help maintain auditor independence by setting the right tone at the top and promoting ethical behavior at all levels.

Q: How does client pressure impact auditor independence?

A: Client pressure can create an intimidation threat, potentially influencing the auditor's judgment and compromising their independence.

Q: How does auditor rotation impact auditor independence?

A: Auditor rotation helps maintain auditor independence by preventing the auditor from becoming too familiar with the client and their operations.

Q: What is the importance of transparency in maintaining auditor independence?

A: Transparency is crucial in maintaining auditor independence, as it ensures that any potential threats to independence are disclosed and appropriately addressed.

Q: How can personal relationships with the client impact auditor independence?

A: Personal relationships with the client can create a familiarity threat, potentially compromising the auditor's independence.

Q: How can an auditor's past employment with the client impact their independence?

A: An auditor's past employment with the client can create a familiarity or self-review threat, potentially compromising their independence.

Q: How can an auditor's future employment prospects with the client impact their independence?

A: The prospect of future employment with the client can create a self-interest threat, potentially compromising the auditor's independence.

Q: What is the role of external peer reviews in maintaining auditor independence?

A: External peer reviews can help maintain auditor independence by providing an independent assessment of the audit work and the auditor's compliance with ethical standards.

Q: How can the provision of non-audit services impact auditor independence?

A: The provision of non-audit services can pose a threat to auditor independence if the auditor ends up auditing their own work or becomes too involved in the client's decision-making.

Q: How does the client's governance structure impact auditor independence?

A: The client's governance structure can impact auditor independence, as a strong governance structure can mitigate potential threats to independence by overseeing the auditor's work and managing conflicts of interest.

Q: How does the auditor's reporting line impact their independence?

A: The auditor's reporting line can impact their independence, as reporting directly to an audit committee rather than management can help maintain independence.

Q: How can the auditor's compensation structure impact their independence?

A: The auditor's compensation structure, if linked to the audit outcome, can create a self-interest threat and compromise their independence.

Q: How does an auditor's professional competence impact their independence?

A: An auditor's professional competence impacts their independence, as a competent auditor is more likely to resist pressures that could compromise their independence.

Q: What is the role of continuous professional development in maintaining auditor independence?

A: Continuous professional development helps maintain auditor independence by enhancing the auditor's competence and ability to exercise professional judgment.

Q: How can an auditor's reputation impact their independence?

A: An auditor's reputation can impact their independence, as an auditor with a strong reputation has more incentive to uphold their independence to maintain their credibility.

Q: How does the client's financial condition impact auditor independence?

A: The client's financial condition can impact auditor independence, as a financially distressed client may exert more pressure on the auditor to provide a favorable audit opinion.

Q: How can an auditor's moral courage help maintain their independence?
A: An auditor's moral courage can help maintain their independence, as it equips the auditor to resist pressures and uphold their professional ethics.
Q: How can an auditor's personal values and beliefs impact their independence?
A: An auditor's personal values and beliefs can impact their independence, as these can influence their judgment and ability to remain impartial.
Q: How can an auditor's use of professional skepticism help maintain their independence?
A: The use of professional skepticism helps maintain auditor independence by ensuring the auditor does not accept information at face value and questions everything.

Applications

Scenario 1: An auditor, who is also a significant shareholder of the company he is auditing, has decided to continue with the audit. The effectiveness of this situation is highly questionable. Auditor independence, both in mind and appearance, is crucial for the credibility of the audit report. The auditor's financial interest in the company can impair his professional judgement and objectivity, leading to potential bias in the audit process and conclusions. In this scenario, it would be best if another auditor who does not have any financial ties with the company conducts the audit.

Scenario 2: An auditing firm has been providing consulting services to a company for several years and is now asked to perform an audit. The effectiveness of the audit is compromised in this situation. The auditing firm may not be able to objectively assess the company's financial statements due to their long-standing relationship. This can lead to biased results and potential conflicts of interest. To resolve this, the company should engage a different firm for the audit process. Scenario 3: An auditor has a close personal relationship with the CFO of the company being audited. This could significantly affect the effectiveness of the audit as the auditor may be influenced by the CFO and may not critically assess the company's financial statements. To maintain independence and ensure the validity of the audit, another auditor without any personal connections with the company's officers should be appointed.

Scenario 4: The same auditing firm has been auditing a company for the past twenty years. This could lead to familiarity threat where the auditor could become too comfortable and potentially overlook discrepancies. To deal with this, the company should consider rotating auditors every few years to ensure fresh perspectives and unbiased assessments.

Scenario 5: An audit firm is auditing a company that contributes a significant proportion of the firm's total revenue. This situation can create a self-interest threat where the auditing firm may not want to risk losing a major client by reporting a negative audit opinion. The solution would be to limit the proportion of revenue an auditing firm can receive from a single client to maintain auditor independence.

Audit Technique

Theoretical

Q: What is the primary purpose of an audit technique?

A: The primary purpose of an audit technique is to examine the financial statements, transactions, and operations of an organization to ensure accuracy, reliability, and adherence to regulations and standards.

Q: What are the main types of audit techniques?

A: The main types of audit techniques include inspection, observation, inquiry, confirmation, and analytical procedures.

Q: What is the role of inspection in audit techniques?

A: Inspection involves examining records, documents, or physical assets to obtain audit evidence.

Q: How does observation function as an audit technique?

A: Observation involves watching a process or procedure being performed by others to gain understanding and insights.

Q: What is inquiry as an audit technique?

A: The process of inquiry entails obtaining information from individuals within the company who are knowledgeable in both financial and non-financial roles.

Q: Why is confirmation an important audit technique?

A: Confirmation provides a direct response from a third party verifying an aspect of a transaction or account balance.

Q: How are analytical procedures used in audit techniques?

A: Analytical procedures refer to the assessment of financial information by examining the logical connections between financial and non-financial data.

Q: Can audit techniques vary depending on the nature of the business?

A: Yes, audit techniques can vary depending on the nature, size, complexity, and risk profile of the business.

Q: What is the importance of risk assessment in selecting audit techniques?

A: Risk assessment helps in determining the nature, timing, and extent of audit procedures that need to be applied to reduce audit risk to an acceptable level.

Q: How does an auditor use professional judgement in applying audit techniques?

A: An auditor uses professional judgement to decide which audit techniques to use, the extent of their application, and interpretation of the results.

Q: What is the role of sampling in audit techniques?

A: Sampling allows the auditor to draw conclusions about an entire data set by examining a subset of it.

Q: What is the importance of documentation in audit techniques?

A: Documentation provides evidence of the auditor's basis for a conclusion and also shows that the audit was performed in accordance with standards.

Q: How does understanding internal controls help in selecting audit techniques?

A: Understanding internal controls helps the auditor to assess the risk of material misstatement and to design the nature, timing, and extent of further audit procedures.

Q: How does the use of technology impact audit techniques?

A: Technology can enhance the efficiency and effectiveness of audit techniques through data analysis, automation of routine tasks, and enhanced reporting capabilities.

Q: Why is continuous auditing an important audit technique? A: Continuous auditing allows for real-time, or near real-time, assurance and timely identification of issues.

Q: How do inquiry and observation complement each other as audit techniques?

A: Inquiry provides verbal evidence while observation provides visual evidence. Together, they provide a more complete understanding of the audited area.

Q: How does the auditor maintain objectivity when applying audit techniques?

A: The auditor maintains objectivity by not allowing personal views or biases to influence professional judgement.

Q: What is the role of professional skepticism in applying audit techniques?

A: Professional skepticism involves maintaining an attitude of questioning mind and critical assessment of audit evidence.

Q: How does understanding the company's business environment impact the selection of audit techniques?

A: Understanding the business environment helps the auditor to identify areas of higher risk and tailor the audit techniques accordingly.

Q: How does the concept of materiality influence the application of audit techniques?

A: The concept of materiality helps the auditor to focus on the areas that are significant to the fair presentation of financial statements.

Q: What is the main objective of using analytical procedures as an audit technique?

A: The main objective is to detect unusual transactions or events, and amounts, ratios, and trends that might indicate matters that have financial statement and audit planning implications.

Q: What is the purpose of a walk-through in audit techniques?

A: A walk-through helps the auditor to understand the client's processes and controls and to identify potential areas of risk.

Q: How does the auditor ensure reliability of information obtained through audit techniques?

A: The auditor ensures reliability by assessing the source of information, the accuracy of the data, and the methods used to produce the information.

Q: How does the auditor assess the sufficiency and appropriateness of audit evidence?

A: The auditor assesses sufficiency by considering the quantity of evidence and appropriateness by considering the quality or relevance and reliability of the evidence.

Q: How does the auditor deal with discrepancies identified through audit techniques?

A: The auditor investigates discrepancies to determine their cause and impact, may revise risk assessments, and modify audit procedures as necessary.

Q: What is the role of vouching in audit techniques?

A: Vouching involves checking the authenticity and validity of the transactions recorded in the books of accounts.

Q: How does the auditor use assertions in applying audit techniques?

A: Assertions are used by the auditor to consider the different aspects of information in the financial statements, which helps in determining the types and extent of audit procedures.

Q: What is the purpose of a management representation letter in audit techniques?

A: A management representation letter is used to obtain written representations from management to confirm certain matters or support other audit evidence.
Q: How does the auditor handle uncertainties identified during the audit?
A: The auditor discusses uncertainties with management, considers their impact on the financial statements, and may adjust the audit approach or report as necessary.
Q: What is the role of professional ethics in applying audit techniques?
A: Professional ethics guide the auditor's behavior and decisions, ensuring independence, integrity, objectivity, confidentiality, and professional competence.
Q: How does the auditor evaluate the reasonableness of estimates in the financial statements?
A: The auditor evaluates the reasonableness of estimates by considering the method, assumptions, and data used by management and comparing them with independent expectations.
Q: How does the auditor verify the existence and rights of assets?
A: The auditor verifies the existence and rights of assets through physical inspection, confirmation, examination of documents, and inquiry of management.
Q: How does the auditor verify the occurrence and completeness of transactions?
A: The auditor verifies the occurrence and completeness of transactions through inspection of documents, observation, inquiry, and analytical procedures.
Q: How does the auditor assess the valuation and allocation of assets and liabilities?
A: The auditor assesses the valuation and allocation of assets and liabilities through inspection of documents, analytical procedures, and inquiry of management.

Q: What is the role of substantive procedures in audit techniques?
A: Substantive procedures are performed to detect material misstatements at the assertion level and provide direct evidence about the completeness, accuracy, and existence of account balances, transactions, and disclosures.
Q: How does the auditor test the operating effectiveness of controls?
A: The auditor tests the operating effectiveness of controls through inquiry, observation, inspection of documents, and re-performance of controls.
Q: What is the purpose of a management letter in audit techniques?
A: A management letter is used to communicate significant deficiencies in internal control and other issues identified during the audit to those charged with governance.
Q: How does the auditor evaluate the appropriateness of the accounting policies applied by the company?
A: The auditor evaluates the appropriateness of the accounting policies by considering their consistency with the applicable financial reporting framework and their relevance and reliability in presenting the financial position and performance of the company.
Q: How does the auditor assess the presentation and disclosure of financial statements?
A: The auditor assesses the presentation and disclosure of financial statements by considering their completeness, classification, understandability, and comparability.
Q: How does the auditor communicate with those charged with governance?
A: The auditor communicates with those charged with governance through meetings, written reports, and letters,

discussing the scope and timing of the audit, significant findings, and other matters.

Q: How does the auditor deal with fraud and non-compliance with laws and regulations?

A: The auditor maintains professional skepticism, identifies and assesses the risks of fraud and non-compliance, designs and implements responsive procedures, and communicates with management and those charged with governance.

Q: How does the auditor evaluate the going concern assumption?

A: The auditor evaluates the going concern assumption by considering the company's ability to continue its operations for the foreseeable future, based on evidence obtained during the audit.

Q: What is the role of related parties in the audit?

A: The auditor identifies and assesses the risks of material misstatement associated with related party transactions and balances, and applies appropriate procedures to address those risks.

Q: How does the auditor conclude on the audit?

A: The auditor concludes on the audit by considering all the audit evidence obtained, evaluating the overall financial statement presentation, and forming an opinion.

Q: How does the auditor report on the audit?

A: The auditor provides a report on the audit, giving their opinion about whether the financial statements have been prepared according to the relevant financial reporting structure in all significant aspects.

Q: What is the role of quality control in the audit?

A: Quality control ensures that the audit is performed in accordance with professional standards and regulatory and legal requirements, and that the auditor's report is appropriate in the circumstances.

Q: How does the auditor consider subsequent events?
A: The auditor considers subsequent events by performing procedures to obtain sufficient appropriate audit evidence about whether any events occurring between the date of the financial statements and the auditor's report require adjustment or disclosure.
Q: How does the auditor consider the company's use of the work of a specialist?
A: The auditor evaluates the competence, capabilities, and objectivity of the specialist, the appropriateness of the specialist's work as audit evidence, and the appropriateness of the specialist's findings in the context of the audit.
Q: How does the auditor use the work of internal auditors? A: The auditor evaluates the objectivity and competence of the internal auditors, the scope and results of their work, and coordinates with them to ensure efficient and effective audit coverage.
Q: How does the auditor handle disagreements with management?
A: The auditor discusses disagreements with management to resolve them, and if not resolved, considers the impact on the auditor's report and communicates with those charged with governance.

Audit Threshold

Applications

Q: What is an audit threshold?

A: An audit threshold refers to the minimum level or limit at which a financial transaction or a series of transactions becomes subject to auditing.

Q: Why is the audit threshold significant?

A: The audit threshold is significant because it determines which businesses require an audit, helping to ensure that transactions are correctly recorded, and preventing financial mismanagement or fraud.

Q: How is the audit threshold determined?

A: The audit threshold is usually determined by regulatory bodies and can depend on factors like the size of the company, the industry it operates in, and its annual turnover.

Q: Can the audit threshold vary between different countries?

A: Yes, the audit threshold can vary between different countries based on their respective financial laws and regulations.

Q: Can a company choose to have an audit even if it falls below the threshold?

A: Yes, a company can choose to have an audit even if its financial activities fall below the threshold for a variety of reasons such as improving financial controls or satisfying investor requirements.

Q: What is the impact of a high audit threshold?

A: A high audit threshold can reduce the financial and administrative burden on smaller companies, but it may also increase the risk of financial mismanagement going undetected.

Q: What happens if a company exceeds the audit threshold?

A: If a company exceeds the audit threshold, it becomes mandatory for it to undergo an audit to ensure the accuracy of its financial statements.

Q: Can the audit threshold change over time?

A: Yes, the audit threshold can change over time due to changes in regulations or changes in the company's size or turnover.

Q: Does exceeding the audit threshold imply financial mismanagement?

A: No, exceeding the audit threshold does not imply financial mismanagement. It simply means that the company's financial activities have reached a level where an audit is required.

Q: What is the relationship between the audit threshold and audit risk?

A: The audit threshold and audit risk are inversely related. As the audit threshold increases, the audit risk decreases because fewer transactions are subject to audit.

Q: Does a lower audit threshold always mean more accuracy in financial reporting?

A: Not necessarily. While a lower audit threshold means more transactions are audited, it doesn't guarantee more accuracy as errors can still occur.

Q: Who sets the audit threshold?

A: The audit threshold is typically set by regulatory bodies or financial authorities.

Q: What factors might lead to a change in a company's audit threshold?

A: Changes in a company's financial status, size, or regulatory changes can lead to a change in a company's audit threshold.

Q: Is the audit threshold the same for all types of businesses?
A: No, the audit threshold can vary depending on the type of business and the industry it operates in.
Q: What impact can the audit threshold have on small businesses?
A: The audit threshold can impact small businesses by determining whether they need to undergo an audit. This can have implications for their financial management and administrative burden.
Q: Is the audit threshold applicable to non-profit organizations?
A: Yes, the audit threshold can also apply to non-profit organizations, though the specific threshold may differ.
Q: Can a company's audit threshold change during a financial year?
A: Typically, the audit threshold is set for a financial year. However, significant changes in a company's circumstances might necessitate a mid-year change.
Q: What role does the audit threshold play in fraud detection? A: The audit threshold can play a critical role in fraud detection as it determines which transactions are audited and scrutinized.
Q: How does the audit threshold contribute to a company's financial transparency?
A: By determining which transactions are audited, the audit threshold contributes to a company's financial transparency by ensuring the accuracy of its financial reporting.
Q: Do all companies need to adhere to the audit threshold?
A: Yes, all companies need to adhere to the audit threshold as set by the relevant financial authorities.
Q: How does a company determine if it has exceeded the audit threshold?
A: A company can determine if it has exceeded the audit threshold by analyzing its financial transactions and comparing it to the set threshold.

Q: What is the penalty for not complying with the audit threshold requirements?

A: The penalty can vary, but it generally involves fines or legal action, and can also damage the company's reputation.

Q: Can a company's audit threshold be lower than the set regulatory threshold?

A: Yes, a company can choose to set its audit threshold lower than the regulatory threshold for its own internal controls.

Q: Does the audit threshold affect the scope of an audit?

A: Yes, the audit threshold can affect the scope of an audit as it determines which transactions are audited.

Q: How does the audit threshold impact the cost of an audit?

A: The audit threshold can impact the cost of an audit. A lower threshold can increase the cost as more transactions need to be audited.

Q: Does the audit threshold apply to both internal and external audits?

A: The audit threshold typically applies to external audits. However, companies may choose to apply it to internal audits as part of their internal controls.

Q: Can the audit threshold be different for different departments within a company?

A: The audit threshold is usually set for the company as a whole, but different departments may have different internal audit thresholds based on their specific risks and activities.

Q: How does the audit threshold relate to the concept of materiality in auditing?

A: The audit threshold and the concept of materiality are closely related as both determine the level of transactions that are significant enough to influence the decisions of users of financial statements.

Q: Does a company's audit threshold need to be made public?

A: The regulatory audit threshold is usually public knowledge, but a company's internal audit threshold may not be publicly disclosed.

Q: What role does the audit threshold play in corporate governance?

A: The audit threshold plays a key role in corporate governance by ensuring that financial transactions are adequately monitored and reported, contributing to accountability and transparency.

Q: Can the audit threshold be used as a tool for risk management?

A: Yes, the audit threshold can be used as a tool for risk management by helping to identify areas of financial risk in a company's operations.

Q: How does the audit threshold affect stakeholders' confidence in a company?

A: The audit threshold can affect stakeholders' confidence in a company. A high threshold may lead to less confidence as fewer transactions are audited, while a low threshold may increase confidence.

Q: What is the impact of regulatory changes on the audit threshold?

A: Regulatory changes can impact the audit threshold. For example, changes in financial laws or regulations can lead to a change in the audit threshold.

Q: Can a company's audit threshold be affected by its growth?

A: Yes, a company's audit threshold can be affected by its growth. As a company grows and its financial transactions increase, it may exceed the set audit threshold.

Q: How does the audit threshold affect a company's financial strategy?

A: The audit threshold can affect a company's financial strategy by influencing its approach to financial management and reporting, and its efforts to manage financial risk.

Q: Can the audit threshold be used as a measure of a company's financial health?

A: While the audit threshold doesn't directly measure a company's financial health, consistently exceeding the threshold might indicate robust financial activities.

Q: Does the audit threshold affect the level of scrutiny a company's financial transactions receive?

A: Yes, the audit threshold affects the level of scrutiny a company's financial transactions receive, determining which transactions are audited.

Q: Can the audit threshold be adjusted to account for inflation?

A: In some cases, the audit threshold may be adjusted to account for inflation. However, this depends on the regulations of the specific jurisdiction.

Q: How does the audit threshold affect a company's audit timeline?

A: The audit threshold can affect a company's audit timeline. If a company exceeds the threshold, it may require more time for the audit to be completed due to the increased number of transactions to be audited.

Q: Can a company's audit threshold change if it enters a new market or industry?

A: Yes, entering a new market or industry could potentially change a company's audit threshold, especially if the new market or industry has different regulations or financial risks.

Q: Does the audit threshold affect a company's audit methodology?

A: The audit threshold can influence a company's audit methodology, as it determines the scope and depth of the audit.

Q: Can a company have multiple audit thresholds for different types of transactions?

A: Yes, a company can have multiple internal audit thresholds for different types of transactions based on their varying levels of risk.

Q: Can the audit threshold affect a company's credit rating?

A: While the audit threshold itself may not directly affect a company's credit rating, the results of an audit triggered by exceeding the threshold may impact it.

Q: Does the audit threshold need to be reviewed periodically?

A: Yes, it is good practice to review the audit threshold periodically to ensure it remains relevant and effective.

Q: Can the audit threshold be a tool for financial planning?

A: Yes, understanding the audit threshold can be a helpful tool in financial planning as it provides insight into when an audit will be required.

Q: How does the audit threshold affect a company's risk profile?

A: The audit threshold can affect a company's risk profile by influencing the level of financial oversight and scrutiny the company's transactions receive.

Q: How does the audit threshold relate to a company's internal controls?

A: The audit threshold can be an important part of a company's internal controls, helping to determine which transactions need to be audited and reviewed.

Q: Can the audit threshold be a factor in a company's audit budget?

A: Yes, the audit threshold can be a factor in a company's audit budget, as it influences the scope and potentially the cost of an audit.

Q: How does the audit threshold help in maintaining financial integrity?

A: The audit threshold helps maintain financial integrity by ensuring that transactions above a certain level are audited and accurately reported.

Q: Can the audit threshold affect a company's compliance with financial regulations?
A: Yes, the audit threshold can affect a company's compliance with financial regulations, as exceeding the threshold requires the company to undergo an audit which checks for compliance.

Applications

Scenario 1: A mid-sized organization XYZ Ltd has recently been taken over by a larger entity. The new management insists on an audit of the previous year's financial statements. How should the auditor approach this scenario? The auditor should begin the process by understanding the audit threshold. As XYZ Ltd is a mid-sized organization, the auditor must establish if it meets the criteria for mandatory auditing. The auditor must also ascertain the new management's objectives concerning the audit. This will allow the auditor to tailor the audit approach accordingly, ensuring that the audit is effective in meeting the set objectives.
Scenario 2: You are the auditor for a small start-up, Alpha Enterprises. They have never undergone an audit before and are not sure about the process. How should you, as the auditor, approach this scenario? The auditor should first explain the concept of Audit Threshold to the management of Alpha Enterprises. Since this is a small start-up, they may not meet the criteria for a mandatory audit. However, the auditor can still conduct an audit if it's beneficial for the organization. The auditor should try to understand the company's financial position and operations thoroughly. This will allow the auditor to provide a comprehensive and effective audit that not only complies with regulations but also adds value to the business.
Scenario 3: A multi-national corporation, Beta Corp, has undergone an audit. However, the senior management is not satisfied with the results.

They believe that the audit threshold was not properly considered and that the audit was not comprehensive enough. What steps should be taken in this scenario? The auditor needs to address the concerns of the senior management at Beta Corp. First, they should explain how the audit threshold was determined and why it was deemed appropriate for the organization. The auditor should also provide a detailed explanation of the audit procedures followed and how they were suitable for the organization's size and complexity. If the management still feels the audit was not thorough enough, the auditor may consider conducting a more in-depth review or a forensic audit to address their concerns. Scenario 4: Gamma Ltd, a large corporation, is about to undergo an audit. However, they have a very complex financial system with multiple subsidiaries and cross-border transactions. How should the audit threshold be determined in this case? In this case, the auditor needs to consider the complexity and size of Gamma Ltd. The audit threshold needs to be set at a level that considers all the subsidiaries and the international transactions. The auditor needs to have a deep understanding of the company's operations, financial systems, and internal controls. This will help them determine the appropriate audit threshold and conduct an effective and comprehensive audit.

Audit Client

Theoretical

Q: What is an audit client?

A: An audit client is an entity whose financial statements and internal controls are evaluated during an audit process.

Q: What is the significance of an audit client in an audit process?

A: The audit client is significant as it is their financial records and systems that are being audited to ensure transparency, accuracy and adherence to financial laws and regulations.

Q: What is the relationship between an audit client and an auditor?

A: The relationship between an audit client and an auditor is professional. The auditor is hired to provide an independent review of the client's financial statements and internal controls.

Q: What are the responsibilities of an audit client?

A: The responsibilities of an audit client include providing all necessary financial records, ensuring all transactions are recorded accurately, and implementing recommendations made by the auditors.

Q: What does the term 'client acceptance' mean in auditing? A: Client acceptance refers to the process where an auditor decides whether to accept a new client or continue with an existing client based on a risk assessment.

Q: What is 'audit independence'?

A: Audit independence refers to the auditor's ability to perform their work freely and without any influence from the audit client or other parties.

Q: What are some factors that could compromise the independence of an auditor?

A: Factors that could compromise audit independence include financial or personal relationships with the audit client, fear of losing the client or pressure from the client to alter audit findings.

Q: What is the impact of compromised auditor independence on the audit process?

A: Compromised auditor independence can undermine the integrity and credibility of the audit process, leading to inaccurate audit reports and potential legal issues.

Q: What is the role of an audit committee in relation to the audit client?

A: The audit committee acts as a mediator between the audit client and the auditor to ensure the audit process is carried out transparently and objectively.

Q: What is the purpose of an engagement letter in an audit process?

A: An engagement letter outlines the scope of the audit, the responsibilities of both the auditor and the audit client, and the terms of the engagement.

Q: Why is maintaining confidentiality crucial in an audit process?

A: Maintaining confidentiality is crucial to protect sensitive information of the audit client and to uphold the integrity and professionalism of the audit process.

Q: What is the importance of audit evidence?

A: Audit evidence is important as it forms the basis of the auditor's report. It helps to substantiate the auditor's opinion on the fairness and accuracy of the client's financial statements.

Q: What is the difference between internal and external auditors?

A: Internal auditors are employed by the audit client to review internal controls and processes, while external auditors are independent professionals hired to review the client's financial statements.

Q: What factors does an auditor consider when assessing audit risk?

A: An auditor considers factors such as the client's internal control system, the nature of the client's business, and the client's financial stability when assessing audit risk.

Q: How does an auditor maintain objectivity during an audit process?

A: An auditor maintains objectivity by avoiding any personal or financial relationships with the audit client, and by conducting their work in a fair and unbiased manner.

Q: What is the importance of communication between an auditor and an audit client?

A: Effective communication between an auditor and an audit client ensures that all relevant information is shared, misunderstandings are avoided, and the audit process runs smoothly.

Q: What is meant by 'audit scope'?

A: Audit scope refers to the breadth and depth of the audit, including the areas to be audited, the period of time covered, and the nature of the audit procedures to be used.

Q: How does an auditor evaluate the effectiveness of an audit client's internal control system?

A: An auditor evaluates the effectiveness of an audit client's internal control system by testing controls, observing operations, and reviewing documentation.

Q: What is materiality in an audit process?

A: Materiality in an audit process refers to the significance of an item or an error that could influence the decisions of users of the client's financial statements.

Q: What is the role of professional skepticism in an audit process?

A: Professional skepticism involves the auditor having a questioning mind and a critical assessment of audit evidence. This helps to identify irregularities and errors in the client's financial statements.

Q: Why is it important for an auditor to understand the audit client's business?

A: Understanding the client's business helps the auditor to identify potential risks, understand the client's financial transactions, and make informed decisions during the audit process.

Q: What is fraud risk in an audit process?

A: Fraud risk in an audit process refers to the risk that the client's financial statements may contain material misstatements due to fraud.

Q: How does an auditor assess fraud risk?

A: An auditor assesses fraud risk by understanding the client's business and industry, assessing the client's internal controls, and using professional skepticism.

Q: What is the role of audit sampling in an audit process?

A: Audit sampling involves the auditor selecting a subset of transactions or accounts from the client's records to test. This helps to obtain sufficient audit evidence without reviewing all transactions.

Q: What is the difference between a compliance audit and a financial audit?

A: A compliance audit evaluates whether the client is following laws, regulations, and company policies, while a financial audit evaluates the accuracy and fairness of the client's financial statements.

Q: How does an audit client prepare for an audit?

A: An audit client prepares for an audit by organizing and reviewing their financial records, understanding the scope of the audit, and communicating effectively with the auditor.

Q: What is the role of management representation in an audit process?

A: Management representation involves the client's management providing written assertions to the auditor about the accuracy and completeness of the financial statements.

Q: What is audit documentation?

A: Audit documentation refers to the records kept by the auditor of the procedures performed, the evidence obtained, and the conclusions reached during the audit.

Q: What is the importance of audit planning?

A: Audit planning is important to ensure that the audit is conducted efficiently and effectively. It involves understanding the client's business, assessing risks, and determining the audit procedures to be used.

Q: What is the relationship between audit risk and materiality?

A: Audit risk and materiality are inversely related. The lower the level of materiality (i.e., the smaller the size of an error or omission that could be considered significant), the higher the audit risk.

Q: What is a substantive test in an audit process?

A: A substantive test is an audit procedure designed to detect material misstatements at the assertion level. It involves detailed testing of transactions and balances.

Q: What is the difference between a clean audit report and a qualified audit report?

A: A clean audit report indicates that the auditor believes the client's financial statements are free of material misstatements. A qualified report indicates that the auditor has identified certain issues that limit their ability to give a clean opinion.

Q: How does an auditor test an audit client's inventory?

A: An auditor tests an audit client's inventory by observing the physical count of the inventory, reviewing procedures for recording inventory transactions, and inspecting inventory records.

Q: How does an auditor verify an audit client's cash balance?

A: An auditor verifies an audit client's cash balance by confirming the balance with the client's bank, reviewing bank statements, and testing the client's procedures for handling cash.

Q: What is going concern assumption in auditing?

A: The going concern assumption is the assumption that the audit client will continue its operations in the foreseeable future. The auditor assesses whether there are any factors that may cast doubt on the client's ability to continue as a going concern.

Q: What are related party transactions and why are they significant in an audit process?

A: Related party transactions are transactions between the audit client and entities or individuals that have a close relationship with the client. They are significant because they may not be conducted at arm's length and may pose a risk of material misstatement.

Q: How does an auditor test an audit client's revenue recognition?

A: An auditor tests an audit client's revenue recognition by reviewing sales contracts, verifying the timing and amount of revenue recorded, and assessing the client's revenue recognition policies.

Q: What is the difference between a statutory audit and a voluntary audit?

A: A statutory audit is legally required, usually for public companies or for companies of a certain size. A voluntary audit is not legally required but is conducted at the discretion of the company's management or shareholders.

Q: What is internal control over financial reporting and why is it crucial in an audit process?

A: Internal control over financial reporting refers to the procedures and systems implemented by the audit client to ensure the accuracy and integrity of financial reporting. It is crucial in an audit process as it can help prevent and detect material misstatements.

Q: What is an audit adjustment?

A: An audit adjustment is a correction of a misstatement identified by the auditor in the client's financial statements.

Q: How do changes in an audit client's industry affect the audit process?

A: Changes in the client's industry, such as new regulations or economic shifts, can affect the client's business and financial risks, which in turn can affect the focus and scope of the audit.

Q: What is the importance of an exit meeting in an audit process?

A: An exit meeting provides an opportunity for the auditor to discuss their findings and recommendations with the client's management, to clarify any issues, and to ensure that the management understands the content of the audit report.

Q: What is the difference between a single audit and a program-specific audit?

A: A single audit is an audit of an entity as a whole, while a program-specific audit focuses on one specific program or operation within the entity.

Q: How does an auditor assess the reasonableness of an audit client's accounting estimates?

A: An auditor assesses the reasonableness of the client's accounting estimates by understanding how the estimates are made, reviewing the data used, and comparing the estimates to actual results or to estimates made in prior periods.

Q: What is an audit finding?

A: An audit finding is a conclusion reached by the auditor based on the audit evidence obtained. It could relate to a material misstatement, a weakness in internal control, or a non-compliance with laws or regulations.

Q: What is the importance of professional ethics in an audit process?

A: Professional ethics guide the auditor's conduct during the audit process, ensuring that the auditor acts with integrity, maintains confidentiality, and performs their work objectively and competently.

Q: How does an auditor obtain an understanding of an audit client's system of internal control?

A: An auditor can obtain an understanding of the client's internal control system by interviewing personnel, observing operations, reviewing documentation, and performing walkthroughs of the controls.

Q: How does an audit differ from a review?

A: An audit provides a high level of assurance on the client's financial statements based on detailed testing and evaluation, while a review provides a moderate level of assurance based on limited procedures such as analytical review and inquiries.

Q: How does an auditor address the detection of fraud during an audit?

A: If an auditor detects fraud during an audit, they should communicate the issue to the client's management and consider the implications for the audit, including the need for revisions to the audit plan or the auditor's opinion.

Q: What is the relationship between an audit client's business risks and the audit risk?

A: The client's business risks can affect the risk of material misstatement in the financial statements, which in turn affects the audit risk – the risk that the auditor may express an inappropriate audit opinion.

Applications

Scenario 1 A tech startup company has recently hired an independent auditor to perform an audit for the first time. The auditor identifies a discrepancy in the company's reported financial statements and the actual financial transactions. The management is reluctant to correct the error, arguing that it will affect their upcoming funding round. How should the auditor handle this situation? Solution: The auditor should remain firm and insist that the discrepancies must be corrected. The auditor is responsible for providing an accurate and fair representation of the company's financial state in the audit report. Any compromise on the auditor's part will undermine the integrity of that report and the reliability of the audit. The auditor should also remind the management of the potential legal and financial repercussions of knowingly publishing incorrect financial statements.

Scenario 2 An auditor is auditing a manufacturing company and discovers that some of the company's inventory is obsolete and has not been written off. The company insists that the inventory still holds value and refuses to write it off. How should the auditor proceed? Solution: The auditor should advise the company on the need to write off the obsolete inventory from the books. It is a common practice in auditing to write off such inventory because it does not hold any resale value. If the company refuses, the auditor should express an opinion on the company's financial statements reflecting the overstatement of the inventory and its potential impact on the financial health of the company.

Scenario 3 During an audit of a retail business, the auditor discovers that the company has been using a faulty sale tracking system, leading to overstatements of sales. The management is unwilling to correct the error as it would mean a significant decrease in reported revenues. What actions should the auditor take? Solution: The auditor should insist on the correction of the errors. If the management refuses, the auditor should qualify the audit report to reflect the inaccuracies in the sales figures. It is crucial for the auditor to maintain integrity and objectivity in their role, despite any potential backlash from the company's management.

Scenario 4 An auditor is auditing a nonprofit organization and comes across a large donation that does not have adequate documentation. The organization argues that this is a common occurrence in the nonprofit sector, and it doesn't necessarily indicate fraud. How should the auditor handle this? Solution: The auditor should insist on proper documentation for all transactions, including donations. Without proper documentation, the auditor cannot verify the authenticity of the transaction. If the organization fails to provide the necessary documents, the auditor should express a qualified opinion on the organization's financial statements, highlighting the lack of documentation for the said donation.

Generally Accepted Auditing Standards (GAAS)

Theoretical

Q: What are the Generally Accepted Auditing Standards (GAAS)?

A: GAAS are a set of systematic guidelines used by auditors when conducting audits on companies' finances, ensuring the accuracy, consistency, and verifiability of auditors' actions and reports.

Q: How many sections does GAAS encompass?

A: GAAS encompasses three sections - General Standards, Standards of Field Work, and Standards of Reporting.

Q: What is the first general standard in GAAS?

A: The first general standard is that the audit must be performed by a person or persons having adequate technical training and proficiency as an auditor.

Q: What is the importance of independence in the GAAS?

A: Independence is vital in the GAAS because it ensures that the auditor is unbiased and does not have a conflict of interest in the results of the audit.

Q: What is meant by "Due Professional Care" in GAAS?

A: "Due Professional Care" implies that the auditor must exercise a high level of care and caution in the auditing process, ensuring accuracy and thoroughness in their work.

Q: What is the purpose of the Standards of Field Work?

A: The Standards of Field Work guide how the audit is conducted, including planning the audit, understanding the entity and its environment, and assessing the risks of material misstatement.

Q: What does the third standard of fieldwork require?

A: The third fieldwork standard mandates the auditor to gather adequate and suitable audit evidence through conducting audit processes. This provides a reasonable foundation for forming an opinion on the audited financial statements.

Q: What is meant by "reasonable assurance" in GAAS?

A: "Reasonable assurance" means that the auditor is not absolutely guaranteed that the financial statements are correct, but has obtained enough evidence to believe they are largely free from material misstatement.

Q: What does the first standard of reporting require?

A: The first standard of reporting requires the report to state whether the financial statements are presented in accordance with Generally Accepted Accounting Principles (GAAP).

Q: What is the significance of the phrase "in all material respects" in GAAS?

A: "In all material respects" suggests that the financial statements are free from material misstatement and give a true and fair view of the financial position of the company.

Q: What are the types of opinions an auditor can express according to GAAS?

A: According to GAAS, an auditor can express four types of opinions: unqualified opinion (clean), qualified opinion, adverse opinion, and disclaimer of opinion.

Q: What is an unqualified opinion?

A: An unqualified opinion is when the auditor concludes that the financial statements give a true and fair view in accordance with the financial reporting framework used for the creation and display of the financial statements.

Q: What does a qualified opinion imply?
A: A qualified opinion implies that except for certain issues, the financial statements give a true and fair view in accordance with the financial reporting framework used for the creation and display of the financial statements.
Q: What is an adverse opinion?
A: An adverse opinion is when the auditor concludes that the financial statements do not give a true and fair view in accordance with the financial reporting framework used for the preparation and presentation of the financial statements.
Q: What is a disclaimer of opinion?
A: An opinion disclaimer occurs when an auditor cannot gather enough suitable audit evidence to form an opinion, leading to the conclusion that the potential impact on the financial statements could be significant and widespread.
Q: What is the principle of consistency in GAAS?
A: The principle of consistency requires that the auditors should use the same accounting principles and methods from one period to another.
Q: What is meant by "disclosure" in GAAS?
A: "Disclosure" in GAAS refers to the requirement for financial statements to include all necessary information for a clear understanding of the company's financial position.
Q: How does the GAAS relate to the Generally Accepted Accounting Principles (GAAP)?
A: GAAS provides a framework for conducting audits, while GAAP provides a framework for preparing and presenting financial statements. GAAS requires auditors to determine whether the financial statements are prepared in accordance with GAAP.
Q: What is the role of the American Institute of Certified Public Accountants (AICPA) in GAAS?

A: The AICPA establishes the GAAS and provides guidance and interpretation on their application.

Q: How does GAAS enhance the credibility of financial statements?

A: By requiring auditors to follow a set of standards when conducting an audit, GAAS ensures that the audit is conducted in a consistent and thorough manner, which enhances the reliability and credibility of the financial statements.

Q: What is the Planning and Supervision component of GAAS?

A: The Planning and Supervision component of GAAS requires the auditor to adequately plan the work and properly supervise any assistants.

Q: What does the Understanding the Entity and Its Environment and Assessing the Risks of Material Misstatement component of GAAS involve?

A: This component involves understanding the entity's operations, the nature of its assets, and the transactions it has engaged in. It also involves assessing the risks of material misstatement in the financial statements.

Q: What does it mean to have sufficient appropriate audit evidence?

A: Having sufficient appropriate audit evidence means the auditor has enough reliable information to base their opinion on the financial statements.

Q: What is the importance of audit documentation in GAAS? A: Audit documentation is important as it provides evidence of the auditor's basis for a conclusion about the achievement of the overall objectives of the auditor.

Q: What does the term "materiality" refer to in GAAS?

A: Materiality refers to the significance of an amount, transaction, or discrepancy. If something is material, its omission or misstatement could influence the economic decisions of users taken on the basis of the financial statements.

Q: What is the role of professional judgment in GAAS?

A: Professional judgment is essential in the application of GAAS. It is required to determine the nature, timing, and extent of audit procedures, to evaluate the results of those procedures, and to draw conclusions.

Q: What is the purpose of an audit risk assessment?

A: The purpose of an audit risk assessment is to identify and assess the risks of material misstatement in the financial statements, in order to determine the nature, timing, and extent of further audit procedures.

Q: What are control activities in the context of GAAS?

A: Control activities consist of the guidelines and processes that assist in fulfilling managerial orders. They have a part in averting, or identifying and rectifying significant inaccuracies in financial reports.

Q: What is the purpose of substantive procedures in GAAS?

A: Substantive procedures are created to identify significant inaccuracies at the assertion stage. These involve detailed tests and substantive analytical methods.

Q: What is the importance of communication in the context of GAAS?

A: In GAAS, communication is pivotal as it facilitates the acquisition of audit-relevant information by the auditor. Additionally, it provides the auditor with the opportunity to clearly convey their responsibilities as well as the intended scope and timeline of the audit.

Q: How important is the consideration of laws and regulations in GAAS?

A: Auditors need to consider the applicable laws and regulations in planning and conducting the audit, as non-compliance by the entity with laws and regulations could have a material effect on the financial statements.

Q: What is the role of the audit committee in the context of GAAS?

A: The audit committee serves as a focal point for communication between other directors, the external auditors, and management as their mandates relate to financial and other reporting, internal controls, risk assessment and audit activities. Q: What is the concept of audit evidence in GAAS?

A: Audit evidence refers to the data that the auditor utilizes to draw conclusions which form the basis of their opinion. This evidence encompasses information found in the accounting records that support the financial statements, as well as additional information.

Q: What is the relationship between audit evidence and audit procedures?

A: Audit procedures are used to gather audit evidence. The appropriateness and sufficiency of audit evidence is a matter of professional judgment.

Q: What is the relevance of using analytical procedures in GAAS?

A: Analytical procedures help to comprehend the business of the entity and identify potential risk areas.

Q: What is the concept of risk assessment procedures in GAAS?

A: Risk assessment procedures are used to obtain an understanding of the entity and its environment, including its internal control. This helps the auditor identify and assess risks of material misstatement.

Q: What is the significance of understanding the entity and its environment in GAAS?

A: By comprehending the entity and its surroundings, the auditor can pinpoint the risks of significant inaccuracies in the financial statements and plan the character, schedule, and scope of additional audit procedures.

Q: How does GAAS treat the concept of fraud in financial statements?

A: The Generally Accepted Auditing Standards (GAAS) mandate that auditors consistently exercise professional skepticism during an audit. They must consider the possibility of management bypassing safeguards and acknowledge that auditing methods effective in identifying errors might not be as successful in discovering fraud.

Q: What is the role of internal controls in GAAS?

A: Understanding internal controls is crucial in GAAS as it helps the auditor to identify the types of potential misstatements, consider factors that affect the risks of material misstatement, and design tests of controls and substantive procedures.

Q: How important is the consideration of subsequent events in GAAS?

A: Subsequent events are significant in GAAS as they may significantly affect the financial statements and may, therefore, require adjustment or disclosure in the statements.

Q: How does GAAS approach the concept of going concern?

A: GAAS requires the auditor to evaluate during the audit whether there is substantial doubt about the entity's ability to continue as a going concern for a reasonable period of time. Q: What is the relevance of estimates in GAAS?

A: GAAS acknowledges that making estimates involves decision-making based on the available information at the time of estimation. It is the responsibility of auditors to evaluate the suitability of the estimates provided by the management within the overall context of the financial statements.

Q: How does GAAS view the concept of related parties?

A: The Generally Accepted Auditing Standards (GAAS) mandates auditors to evaluate the potential risk of significant inaccuracies linked with transactions involving related parties. It also necessitates that auditors gather enough suitable audit proof to confirm if these transactions have been correctly identified, recorded, and revealed in the financial reports.

Q: What is the concept of audit sampling in GAAS?

A: Audit sampling is the application of audit procedures to less than 100% of items within an account balance or class of transactions. It is used to enable auditors to obtain and evaluate audit evidence about some characteristic of the items selected in order to form a conclusion concerning the population.

Q: What is the importance of written representations in GAAS?

A: The auditor requires written representations as essential information related to the audit of an entity's financial statements. These representations constitute part of the audit evidence that the independent auditor gathers. However, they alone do not offer enough suitable audit evidence concerning any of the issues they address.

Q: What is the role of management in GAAS?

A: The responsibility of management entails preparing and presenting the financial statements accurately and fairly according to the relevant financial reporting framework. The auditor, on the other hand, is tasked with giving an opinion on the financial statements, which is founded on the audit.

Q: How does GAAS view the concept of professional skepticism?

A: Professional skepticism is an attitude that includes a questioning mind and a critical assessment of audit evidence. It is necessary for the auditor to challenge the management's assertions and to consider the possibility of fraud.

Q: What is the relationship between GAAS and quality control?

A: The firm's system of quality control includes policies and procedures that address, among other things, the conduct of individual audits. It is the foundation for the conduct of an audit in accordance with GAAS.

Q: What is the concept of audit strategy in GAAS?

A: An audit strategy sets the scope, timing, and direction of the audit and guides the development of the audit plan.

Q: What is the concept of audit planning in GAAS?

A: Planning an audit entails formulating a broad strategy and a comprehensive plan for the anticipated scope, schedule, and extent of the audit. This process includes factors such as acceptance and continuation of the client, gaining an understanding of the client's business and industry, evaluating client risk, and setting materiality levels.

Applications

Scenario 1: Company A has recently been acquired by Company B. The new management has requested an audit to assess the financial health of their new subsidiary. As the auditor, you are tasked with performing the audit as per GAAS. How would you approach this scenario? Evaluation: The effectiveness of the audit would rely heavily on understanding and applying the GAAS principles. Firstly, the auditor must have adequate technical training and proficiency to perform the audit. Secondly, it is imperative for the auditor to uphold an independent mindset in all audit-related matters. Lastly, due care should be exercised during the performance of the audit and the preparation of the report.

Scenario 2: You've been hired as an independent auditor by Company C, a medium-sized manufacturing firm. During your audit, you discover several inconsistencies in their inventory records. What would your next steps be, according to GAAS? Evaluation: As per GAAS, the auditor must obtain sufficient appropriate audit evidence by performing audit procedures to afford a reasonable basis for an opinion regarding the financial statements under audit. In this case, the auditor should further scrutinize these inconsistencies, possibly involving a third-party inventory count or other confirmatory procedures.

Scenario 3: Company D has contracted you to perform an audit for them. During your audit, you discover some transactions that the company failed to disclose in their financial statements. How would you handle this situation following GAAS? Evaluation: According to GAAS, the auditor should identify and assess the risks of material misstatement, whether due to fraud or error, at the financial statement and assertion levels. In this scenario, the auditor should bring these undisclosed transactions to the attention of the management. If they continue to withhold this information, the auditor should express a qualified opinion or a disclaimer of opinion in their audit report.

Scenario 4: You're auditing Company E, a start-up tech company. The company has been growing rapidly, but you notice their internal controls are weak. According to GAAS, how should you approach this issue? Evaluation: As per GAAS, the auditor must understand the entity and its environment, including its internal control, to assess the risk of material misstatement of the financial statements whether due to fraud or error, and to design the nature, timing, and extent of further audit procedures. In this scenario, the auditor should recommend that the company strengthen its internal controls to prevent any potential financial misstatements.

Scenario 5: You're conducting an audit for Company F. During your audit, you find that one of the company's significant revenue streams is based on an illegal activity. How should you handle this situation according to GAAS? Evaluation: As per GAAS, the auditor must plan the audit in such a way as to detect material misstatements due to fraud or error. In this scenario, the auditor should report the illegal activity to the appropriate legal authorities, discontinue the audit, and notify the company's management and board of directors.

International Standards on Auditing (ISA)

Theoretical

Q: What is the purpose of International Standards on Auditing (ISA)?

A: The purpose of ISA is to set uniform guidelines and procedures for auditors to follow when conducting an audit of financial statements.

Q: Who issues the ISA?

A: The International Auditing and Assurance Standards Board (IAASB) issues the ISA.

Q: How many standards does the ISA currently consist of? A: There are currently 36 ISAs.

Q: What is the significance of ISA 200?

A: ISA 200 sets the overall objectives of the independent auditor when conducting an audit of financial statements.

Q: What is ISA 315?

A: ISA 315 relates to the auditor's responsibility to identify and assess the risks of material misstatement in the financial statements.

Q: What does ISA 520 entail?

A: ISA 520 provides guidance on the use of analytical procedures as a substantive test to obtain audit evidence.

Q: What is the focus of ISA 700?

A: ISA 700 focuses on forming an opinion and reporting on financial statements.

Q: How does ISA 610 relate to the use of internal auditors?

A: ISA 610 provides guidelines for the external auditor's use of the work of internal auditors.

Q: What is the aim of ISA 505?

A: ISA 505 aims to guide auditors on the process of obtaining external confirmations as audit evidence.

Q: What does ISA 320 cover?

A: ISA 320 outlines the auditor's duty to apply the principle of materiality when planning and executing an audit.

Q: How does ISA 500 relate to audit evidence?

A: ISA 500 outlines the auditor's responsibility to design and implement responses to assess the risks of material misstatement.

Q: Explain ISA 530.

A: ISA 530 deals with the auditor's use of statistical and non-statistical sampling as an audit procedure.

Q: What is the consideration in ISA 540?

A: ISA 540 addresses the auditing of accounting estimates, including fair value accounting estimates, and their related disclosures.

Q: What does ISA 220 pertain to?

A: ISA 220 pertains to the quality control for an audit of financial statements.

Q: What is the importance of ISA 240?

A: ISA 240 emphasizes the duties of the auditor in relation to fraud during a financial statement audit.

Q: What is the objective of ISA 560?

A: ISA 560 deals with the auditor's responsibilities relating to subsequent events.

Q: What does ISA 570 cover?

A: ISA 570 outlines the duties of an auditor regarding the audit of financial statements, particularly in relation to a company's capacity to remain operational.

Q: What is ISA 230?

A: ISA 230 outlines the auditor's obligation to create and maintain documentation pertaining to a financial statement audit.

Q: What does ISA 250 refer to?

A: ISA 250 refers to the auditor's responsibilities relating to laws and regulations in an audit of financial statements.

Q: How does ISA 300 relate to planning an audit?

A: ISA 300 sets out the considerations relevant to planning an audit of financial statements.

Q: What is the role of ISA 402?

A: ISA 402 provides guidance when an entity uses a service organization for its operational activities.

Q: What does ISA 210 cover?

A: ISA 210 covers the terms of audit engagements.

Q: How does ISA 620 relate to the work of an expert?

A: ISA 620 provides guidance on using the work of an expert to obtain audit evidence.

Q: What is the purpose of ISA 450?

A: ISA 450 deals with the evaluation of misstatements identified during the audit.

Q: What does ISA 580 entail?

A: ISA 580 requires the auditor to obtain written representations from management and, where appropriate, those charged with governance.

Q: What is the objective of ISA 260?

A: ISA 260 outlines the auditor's responsibility to communicate with those charged with governance in an audit of financial statements.

Q: How does ISA 265 relate to communicating deficiencies?

A: ISA 265 addresses the auditor's responsibility to communicate appropriate matters related to internal control deficiencies to those charged with governance and management.

Q: What does ISA 550 cover?

A: ISA 550 deals with related party transactions in the audit of financial statements.

Q: What is the role of ISA 520 in analytical procedures?

A: ISA 520 guides the auditors on the use of analytical procedures as a substantive test to obtain audit evidence.

Q: What is the focus of ISA 501?

A: ISA 501 focuses on specific considerations for selected items in the audit of financial statements.

Q: What is ISA 800 about?

A: ISA 800 relates to special considerations in the audit of financial statements prepared in accordance with a special purpose framework.

Q: How does ISA 805 relate to single financial statements?

A: ISA 805 provides guidance on audits of single financial statements and specific elements, accounts, or items of a financial statement.

Q: What is the objective of ISA 810?

A: ISA 810 pertains to the duties of an auditor in relation to engagements that involve reporting on condensed financial statements.

Q: What does ISA 600 cover?

A: ISA 600 encompasses the specific considerations in auditing group financial statements, including the tasks performed by component auditors.

Q: What is the importance of ISA 700?

A: ISA 700 outlines the form and content of the auditor's report issued as a result of an audit of financial statements.

Q: What is ISA 701?

A: ISA 701 communicates key audit matters in the independent auditor's report.

Q: What is the focus of ISA 705?

A: ISA 705 focuses on modifications to the opinion in the independent auditor's report.

Q: How does ISA 706 relate to paragraph emphasis?

A: ISA 706 pertains to extra communication in the auditor's report, encompassing paragraphs that emphasize particular points and other related matters.

Q: What does ISA 710 cover?

A: ISA 710 outlines comparative information corresponding figures and comparative financial statements.

Q: What is the objective of ISA 720?

A: ISA 720 deals with the auditor's responsibilities relating to other information in documents containing audited financial statements.

Q: Why is ISA 330 important?

A: ISA 330 provides guidance on the auditor's responses to the risks of material misstatement.

Q: How does ISA 340 relate to segment reporting?

A: ISA 340 does not relate to segment reporting. ISA 340 is not yet issued.

Q: What is the focus of ISA 220?

A: ISA 220 is focused on the quality control for audits of financial statements.

Q: What is the importance of ISA 315?

A: ISA 315 is important because it deals with the auditor's responsibility to identify and assess the risks of material misstatement in the financial statements.

Q: How does ISA 240 relate to fraud in financial statements?

A: ISA 240 outlines the auditor's responsibilities relating to fraud in an audit of financial statements.

Q: What does ISA 320 cover?
A: ISA 320 covers the concept of materiality in the audit of financial statements.
Q: What is the role of ISA 402?
A: ISA 402 provides guidance when an entity uses a service organization for its operational activities.
Q: What is the purpose of ISA 450?
A: ISA 450 is concerned with the evaluation of misstatements identified during the audit.
Q: What does ISA 580 entail?
A: ISA 580 requires the auditor to obtain written representations from management and, where appropriate, those charged with governance.
Q: What is the focus of ISA 501?
A: ISA 501 is focused on audit evidence and specific considerations for selected items.

Applications

Scenario: The ABC Company has recently undergone an audit as per the International Standards on Auditing (ISA). The auditors detected that the company had not adequately assessed the risks of material misstatements in their financial reports. As an auditor, how would you address this situation? Solution: As an auditor, I would first communicate this issue to the management and those charged with governance. I would then recommend a thorough risk assessment procedure to identify and evaluate the risks of material misstatements.

This could include understanding the entity's environment, internal control, and the applicability of other ISAs.

This process would enhance the reliability of the financial reports and ensure compliance with the ISA.

Effectiveness: This solution is effective as it directly addresses the identified issue and ensures the company's compliance with the

ISA. It also enhances the reliability of the financial reports, thus increasing stakeholder confidence.

Scenario: The XYZ Corporation has been audited according to ISA. The auditors discovered that the company had not maintained proper documentation of its audit procedures, which is a requirement under ISA 230 (Audit Documentation). How would you, as an auditor, address this problem?

Solution: I would advise the corporation's management to implement a comprehensive system for documenting their audit procedures, including the nature, timing, and extent of the audit procedures performed. This would provide a clear record of the work performed and the basis for the audit conclusions.

Effectiveness: This solution ensures that the corporation maintains proper audit documentation, thus complying with ISA 230. It also provides a clear basis for the audit conclusions and enhances the transparency of the audit process.

Scenario: A newly established firm, DEF Ltd., has been audited as per ISA. However, the auditors discovered that the firm did not have a sufficient understanding of the entity and its environment, including its internal control, which is a requirement under ISA 315 (Identifying and Assessing the Risks of Material Misstatement). How would you address this issue?

Solution: I would recommend DEF Ltd. to conduct a comprehensive review of its business environment and its internal control. This could include an analysis of the industry, regulatory factors, the entity's operations, and its financial performance. I would also advise the firm to establish a robust system of internal control to manage and mitigate risks. Effectiveness: This solution ensures that DEF Ltd. has a deeper understanding of its business and its environment, which is vital for identifying and assessing the risks of material misstatements. It also ensures the firm's compliance with ISA 315 and enhances the effectiveness of its internal control. Scenario: GHI Inc., audited according to ISA, found that the company had not adequately dealt with the identified misstatements that could be material, which is a requirement under ISA 450 (Evaluation of Misstatements Identified during the Audit). How would you handle this situation?

Solution: I would advise GHI Inc. to reassess the identified misstatements and determine their significance to the financial statements.

If these misstatements are found to be material, the company should correct them promptly. I would then reevaluate the audit evidence to ensure that the corrected financial statements are free from material misstatement. Effectiveness: This solution ensures that GHI Inc. adequately deals with the identified misstatements, thus complying with ISA 450. It also enhances the reliability of the company's financial statements and increases stakeholder confidence.

Audit Scope

Theoretical

Q: What is the meaning of audit scope?

A: Audit scope refers to the extent and boundaries of an audit, encompassing the depth and duration of audit procedures, the departments or locations that will be included, and the audit period.

Q: What is the purpose of defining the audit scope?

A: The purpose is to provide a clear framework for the audit, outlining what will be examined, thereby ensuring that the audit is focused, efficient, and effective.

Q: How does the scope of an audit affect the audit process?

A: The scope determines the extent of the audit procedures to be carried out, directly influencing the resources required, the duration of the audit, and the level of detailed analysis.

Q: What factors influence the determination of an audit scope?

A: Factors include the organization's structure, industry regulations, the complexity of the organization's operations, and the objectives of the audit.

Q: Can the scope of an audit change during the audit process?

A: Yes, if during the audit process, issues arise that were not originally considered, the scope can be adjusted to accommodate the necessary investigations.

Q: What would be an example of a broad audit scope?

A: A broad scope might include all departments of a company, multiple fiscal years, and comprehensive examination of all financial statements.

Q: What would be an example of a narrow audit scope?

A: A narrow scope might focus on a single department, specific transactions, or a single fiscal year.

Q: Who typically defines the scope of an audit?

A: The scope is usually defined by the audit team in collaboration with the client, considering the objectives of the audit.

Q: What is the relationship between audit scope and audit risk?

A: The broader the scope, the greater the potential for uncovering issues, reducing audit risk. However, a broader scope also requires more resources.

Q: What is an audit scope limitation?

A: This refers to a situation where the auditor is unable to obtain sufficient appropriate audit evidence, which could lead to a limitation in the scope of the audit.

Q: How can an audit scope limitation impact the audit opinion?

A: If significant enough, the limitation can lead to a qualified or disclaimer of opinion, indicating that the auditor was not able to obtain a complete understanding of the company's financial situation.

Q: What is the difference between audit scope and audit objective?

A: The audit scope refers to the boundaries of the audit, while the audit objective refers to what the audit aims to achieve.

Q: Can audit scope be too broad or too narrow?

A: Yes, if too broad, it may become unmanageable and inefficient. If too narrow, it may not cover all relevant areas, leading to insufficient evidence and higher audit risk.

Q: How does audit scope relate to materiality in auditing? A: The scope determines the level of detail in the audit, which influences the identification of material misstatements.

Q: What is the role of audit scope in internal auditing?

A: The audit scope in internal auditing determines the areas to be audited within the organization, including operational activities, risk management, and control processes.

Q: What happens when there is disagreement on the audit scope?

A: Disagreements on the audit scope can be resolved through discussions between the auditor and the client, or by involving a third party such as an audit committee.

Q: How does the audit scope affect the audit report?

A: The scope determines the extent of the audit procedures and hence the level of assurance provided in the audit report.

Q: What is the role of audit scope in planning an audit?

A: The audit scope guides the planning process by defining what will be audited, helping the auditor allocate resources appropriately.

Q: How is audit scope communicated to the audit team?

A: The scope is usually communicated through the audit planning document or audit engagement letter.

Q: What is the role of the audit scope in external auditing?

A: In external auditing, the audit scope provides a framework for the audit, outlining the areas to be audited and the level of detail required.

Q: How does audit scope contribute to audit quality?

A: A well-defined audit scope ensures that all relevant areas are covered, contributing to the completeness and accuracy of the audit, thereby enhancing audit quality.

Q: What happens if the audit scope is not clearly defined?

A: If not clearly defined, the audit may lack focus, become inefficient, and may not provide a sufficient level of assurance.

Q: Can the audit scope be different for different audits?
A: Yes, the scope can vary depending on the objectives of the audit, the auditee, and the specific circumstances of the audit.
Q: How does the size of the organization affect the audit scope?
A: Larger organizations typically require a broader audit scope due to their complexity and the greater number of transactions.
Q: How does the audit scope relate to audit evidence?
A: The scope determines the extent of the audit procedures, which in turn determines the amount and type of audit evidence to be collected.
Q: Why is it important to document the audit scope?
A: Documenting the scope provides a reference for the audit team and ensures that everyone understands the extent of the audit.
Q: How does the audit scope relate to the audit strategy?
A: The audit scope informs the audit strategy by defining what will be audited, which the auditor then uses to determine how the audit will be conducted.
Q: What is the role of audit scope in compliance audits?
A: In compliance audits, the audit scope determines the regulations and standards to be checked for compliance.
Q: How does the audit scope contribute to stakeholder confidence?
A: A comprehensive audit scope can enhance stakeholder confidence by demonstrating that the audit is thorough and covers all relevant areas.
Q: How does the audit scope relate to the audit approach?
A: The scope influences the approach by defining what will be audited, which affects the audit procedures to be used.
Q: How does the audit scope affect the time frame of the audit?
A: A broader scope generally requires a longer time frame due to the greater number of areas to be audited and the level of detail required.

Q: Does the audit scope affect the cost of the audit?
A: Yes, a broader scope usually requires more resources and hence is more costly.
Q: How does the audit scope relate to the concept of professional skepticism in auditing?
A: The scope guides the auditor on what to examine, but professional skepticism is necessary to critically assess the evidence obtained.
Q: Can the auditor expand the audit scope based on findings during the audit?
A: Yes, if the auditor identifies issues that require further investigation, they can expand the scope accordingly.
Q: How does the audit scope relate to the audit objective? A: The audit scope should be sufficiently broad to meet the audit objective, providing adequate assurance on the subject matter.
Q: What is the relationship between audit scope and audit planning?
A: The audit scope is a key input in audit planning, guiding the auditor in determining the resources required, the timing, and the audit procedures to be used.
Q: How does the nature of the auditee's operations affect the audit scope?
A: The more complex the operations, the broader the scope is likely to be in order to address the various aspects of the operations.
Q: How does the audit scope relate to the audit risk model?
A: The audit scope, by determining the extent of the audit procedures, influences the detection risk component of the audit risk model.
Q: What is the role of the audit scope in performance audits?
A: In performance audits, the audit scope determines the operations to be audited for efficiency and effectiveness.

Q: How does the audit scope relate to the concept of materiality in auditing?

A: The audit scope guides the identification of material areas or transactions that require more detailed examination.

Q: Can the audit scope be different for different types of audits (e.g., financial, operational, compliance)?

A: Yes, the scope varies depending on the type of audit, with each focusing on different aspects of the auditee's operations.

Q: What is the role of the audit committee in determining the audit scope?

A: The audit committee can provide input on the areas of concern that should be included in the scope, and also approve the final audit scope.

Q: How does the audit scope relate to the auditor's responsibility?

A: The auditor is responsible for conducting the audit within the defined scope and ensuring that the scope is sufficient to meet the audit objectives.

Q: How does the audit scope relate to the concept of audit assurance?

A: The audit scope, by determining the extent of the audit procedures, influences the level of assurance that the auditor can provide.

Q: How does the audit scope relate to the auditor's independence?

A: The scope does not directly affect the auditor's independence, but if the scope is unduly restricted by the auditee, this could raise questions about the auditor's independence.

Q: What is the relationship between audit scope and audit report?

A: The audit scope determines the areas covered in the audit, which are then reported on in the audit report.

Q: How does the audit scope relate to the audit methodology?

A: The audit scope informs the choice of audit methodology by defining what will be audited.

Q: Can the audit scope have a bearing on the level of audit risk?

A: Yes, a broader scope can reduce audit risk by increasing the likelihood of detecting material misstatements.

Q: How does the audit scope relate to the concept of sampling in auditing?

A: The audit scope guides the selection of items for sampling, with broader scopes typically requiring larger sample sizes.

Q: How does the audit scope relate to the concept of audit assertions?

A: The audit scope determines the assertions to be tested, such as existence, completeness, accuracy, and valuation.

Applications

Scenario 1: A company, ABC Ltd, has recently expanded its operations across multiple states. The audit team is tasked with auditing all the branches but the time allowed for the audit is tight.

How can the audit scope be defined to ensure an effective audit?

Answer: In this scenario, the audit scope should be defined by focusing on the areas of highest risk. The audit team should prioritize branches with the largest operations or those that have had issues in the past. They should also focus on the key areas of operations like procurement, sales, and finance. This approach ensures a focused and effective audit.

Effectiveness: This answer is effective as it highlights the importance of risk-based auditing. It emphasizes that instead of trying to audit everything within a limited time, the audit team should focus on the areas that present the highest risk.

Scenario 2: XYZ Corporation recently experienced a major theft in one of its warehouses. The management has requested an audit to identify any loopholes in the security system.

How should the audit scope be defined in this case?
Answer: The audit scope should specifically focus on the warehouse's security systems. This includes physical security measures, access controls, surveillance systems, and employee training on security measures. It should also look into the procedures for reporting and investigating any security breaches.
Effectiveness: The answer adequately defines a specific audit scope that focuses on the issue at hand, which in this case, is the security of the warehouse. This ensures that the audit will provide valuable insights on how to improve the security systems and prevent future thefts.
Scenario 3: A small business, PQR Enterprises, has never conducted an audit before. The owner wants to conduct an audit to understand the financial health of his business.
How should the audit scope be defined?
Answer: For a small business that has never undergone an audit, the scope should be comprehensive. The auditor should look into all aspects of the business, including revenues, expenses, assets, and liabilities. The auditor should also evaluate the company's internal control systems and accounting practices.
Effectiveness: This answer is effective as it provides a thorough approach to auditing for a small business that has never undergone an audit before. It ensures that all important aspects of the business are covered, providing a complete picture of the business's financial health.

Control Procedures

Theoretical

Q: What is the primary role of control procedures in auditing? A: The primary role of control procedures in auditing is to ensure the accuracy and reliability of financial reports and to prevent and detect fraud and errors.

Q: What are the two main types of control procedures in auditing?

A: The two main types of control procedures in auditing are preventive controls and detective controls.

Q: How do preventive controls differ from detective controls?

A: Preventive controls are proactive measures aimed at preventing errors or fraud, while detective controls are designed to identify and correct errors or irregularities that have already occurred.

Q: What is an example of a preventive control procedure in auditing?

A: An example of a preventive control procedure in auditing is the segregation of duties, which prevents a single individual from controlling all key aspects of a transaction.

Q: What is an example of a detective control procedure in auditing?

A: An example of a detective control procedure in auditing is regular financial statement reviews to identify any inconsistencies or irregularities.

Q: Why are control procedures important in the auditing process?

A: Control procedures are important in the auditing process because they help ensure the integrity and accuracy of financial information, thereby enhancing the reliability of financial reporting and preventing fraud.

Q: What are the steps involved in establishing control procedures in auditing?

A: The steps involved in establishing control procedures in auditing include identifying risks, designing and implementing control procedures, and monitoring and adjusting the controls as necessary.

Q: How do control procedures help in risk management during an audit?

A: Control procedures help in risk management during an audit by preventing, detecting, and correcting errors and irregularities, thus reducing the risk of material misstatement in financial reports.

Q: Can control procedures completely eliminate the risk of fraud or error in an audit?

A: No, control procedures cannot completely eliminate the risk of fraud or error in an audit, but they can significantly reduce the risk.

Q: What is the role of internal control procedures in an audit?

A: The role of internal control procedures in an audit is to help ensure the accuracy and integrity of financial information, and to facilitate efficient and effective operations.

Q: How do auditors assess the effectiveness of control procedures?

A: Auditors assess the effectiveness of control procedures by performing tests of controls, which involve evaluating the design of the controls and testing their operating effectiveness.

Q: What happens if control procedures are found to be ineffective during an audit?

A: If control procedures are found to be ineffective during an audit, the auditor must assess the impact on the audit and consider modifying the audit approach or increasing the extent of substantive testing.

Q: How do control procedures contribute to the quality of an audit?

A: Control procedures contribute to the quality of an audit by helping to ensure the reliability and accuracy of financial information, thus facilitating the auditor's ability to express an opinion on the financial statements.

Q: What is the relationship between control procedures and audit risk?

A: There is an inverse relationship between control procedures and audit risk. Effective control procedures reduce audit risk by minimizing the likelihood of material misstatement in the financial statements.

Q: What is a compensating control in auditing?

A: A compensating control in auditing is a control implemented to mitigate the risk when the primary control procedure is not effective or cannot be implemented.

Q: Can an auditor rely solely on control procedures to form an audit opinion?

A: No, an auditor cannot rely solely on control procedures to form an audit opinion. They must also perform substantive testing to gather sufficient appropriate audit evidence.

Q: What is the role of control procedures in the audit of financial statements?

A: The role of control procedures in the audit of financial statements is to ensure the accuracy and completeness of the data used to prepare the financial statements.

Q: What is the role of the management in establishing control procedures?

A: The management is responsible for establishing and maintaining an effective system of internal control, including designing and implementing control procedures.

Q: How do control procedures help in the detection of fraud during an audit?

A: Control procedures help in the detection of fraud during an audit by identifying discrepancies, irregularities, and deviations from normal patterns.

Q: What is a control deficiency in an audit?

A: A control deficiency in an audit is a weakness in the design or operation of control procedures that could adversely affect the organization's ability to record, process, summarize, and report financial data accurately.

Q: How does the auditor address control deficiencies identified during an audit?

A: The auditor addresses control deficiencies identified during an audit by communicating these deficiencies to the management and those charged with governance, and by modifying the audit plan as necessary.

Q: What is the difference between a control deficiency and a material weakness in an audit?

A: A control deficiency is a weakness that could adversely affect the organization's ability to process and report financial data accurately. A material weakness is a more severe control deficiency, or combination of deficiencies, that significantly increases the risk of a material misstatement in the financial statements.

Q: What is the role of IT controls in an audit?

A: IT controls play a crucial role in an audit by ensuring the integrity and security of financial data, particularly in organizations that rely heavily on IT systems for financial reporting.

Q: What is the difference between general IT controls and application controls in an audit?

A: General IT controls relate to the overall IT environment and affect multiple applications, while application controls are specific to individual applications and ensure the completeness and accuracy of the transactions processed by those applications.

Q: How do control procedures support the auditor's assessment of control risk?

A: Control procedures support the auditor's assessment of control risk by providing evidence about the effectiveness of the controls in preventing or detecting and correcting material misstatements.

Q: What is the difference between manual controls and automated controls in an audit?

A: Manual controls are performed by individuals, while automated controls are performed by IT systems. Manual controls may involve more human error, while automated controls may be more efficient and consistent.

Q: Can control procedures detect all instances of fraud or error in an audit?

A: No, control procedures cannot detect all instances of fraud or error in an audit. Some fraud or errors may be concealed or involve collusion, and some control procedures may not be 100% effective.

Q: What is the role of control procedures in the audit of cash transactions?

A: Control procedures in the audit of cash transactions help ensure the completeness and accuracy of cash receipts and payments, prevent theft or misappropriation of cash, and verify the existence and valuation of cash balances.

Q: What is a substantive test in an audit?

A: A substantive test in an audit is a procedure designed to obtain evidence about the completeness, accuracy, and validity of the data in the financial statements.

Q: How do control procedures relate to substantive testing in an audit?

A: Control procedures and substantive testing are complementary components of the audit process. If control procedures are effective, the auditor may rely on them and perform less substantive testing. Conversely, if control procedures are weak, the auditor may need to perform more substantive testing.

Q: What is the role of control procedures in the audit of inventory?

A: Control procedures in the audit of inventory help ensure the accurate recording of inventory transactions, the physical safeguarding of inventory, and the correct valuation of inventory in the financial statements.

Q: What is the difference between entity-level controls and transaction-level controls in an audit?

A: Entity-level controls are controls that apply to the entire organization, such as the control environment and management's risk assessment process. Transaction-level controls are specific to individual transactions or processes, such as approval of invoices or reconciliation of bank statements.

Q: How do control procedures help in the audit of sales transactions?

A: Control procedures in the audit of sales transactions help ensure the accurate recording of sales, the correct recognition of revenue, and the prevention of fictitious sales or revenue.

Q: What is the role of control procedures in the audit of payroll?

A: Control procedures in the audit of payroll help ensure the accurate calculation and recording of payroll expenses, the correct deduction and remittance of payroll taxes, and the prevention of fraudulent payroll transactions.

Q: How do control procedures help in the audit of purchases and payables?

A: Control procedures in the audit of purchases and payables help ensure the accurate recording of purchase transactions, the correct recognition of expenses and liabilities, and the prevention of duplicate payments or fictitious vendors.

Q: What is the role of control procedures in the audit of fixed assets?

A: Control procedures in the audit of fixed assets help ensure the accurate recording of asset acquisitions and disposals, the correct calculation and recording of depreciation, and the physical safeguarding of assets.

Q: How do control procedures help in the audit of investments?

A: Control procedures in the audit of investments help ensure the accurate recording of investment transactions, the correct valuation of investments, and the proper disclosure of investment information in the financial statements.

Q: What is the role of control procedures in the audit of loans and receivables?

A: Control procedures in the audit of loans and receivables help ensure the accurate recording of loan and receivable transactions, the correct calculation and recognition of interest income, and the proper evaluation and disclosure of credit risk.

Q: How do control procedures help in the audit of equity transactions?

A: Control procedures in the audit of equity transactions help ensure the accurate recording of equity transactions, the correct calculation and recognition of dividends, and the proper disclosure of equity information in the financial statements.

Q: What is the role of control procedures in the audit of tax transactions?

A: Control procedures in the audit of tax transactions help ensure the accurate calculation and recording of tax expenses and liabilities, the correct remittance of taxes to tax authorities, and the proper disclosure of tax information in the financial statements.

Q: How do control procedures help in the audit of related party transactions?

A: Control procedures in the audit of related party transactions help ensure the accurate identification and recording of related party transactions, the correct valuation and disclosure of these transactions, and the prevention of fraudulent related party transactions.

Q: What is the role of control procedures in the audit of contingent liabilities?

A: Control procedures in the audit of contingent liabilities help ensure the accurate identification and recording of contingent liabilities, the correct estimation and disclosure of these liabilities, and the prevention of fraudulent contingent liabilities.

Q: How do control procedures help in the audit of subsequent events?

A: Control procedures in the audit of subsequent events help ensure the accurate identification and recording of events occurring after the balance sheet date but before the issuance of the financial statements, and the proper disclosure of these events in the financial statements.

Q: What is the role of control procedures in the audit of earnings per share (EPS)?

A: Control procedures in the audit of EPS help ensure the accurate calculation and recording of basic and diluted EPS, and the proper disclosure of EPS information in the financial statements.

Q: How do control procedures help in the audit of segment information?

A: Control procedures in the audit of segment information help ensure the accurate identification and recording of segment revenues, expenses, assets, and liabilities, and the proper disclosure of segment information in the financial statements.

Q: What is the role of control procedures in the audit of financial statement disclosures?

A: Control procedures in the audit of financial statement disclosures help ensure the accurate and complete presentation of all required disclosures in accordance with the applicable financial reporting framework.

Q: How do control procedures help in the audit of fair value measurements?

A: Control procedures in the audit of fair value measurements help ensure the accurate identification and recording of fair value measurements, the correct application of fair value measurement techniques, and the proper disclosure of fair value information in the financial statements.

Q: What is the role of control procedures in the audit of accounting estimates?

A: Control procedures in the audit of accounting estimates help ensure the accurate identification and recording of accounting estimates, the correct application of estimation techniques, and the proper disclosure of estimate information in the financial statements.

Q: How do control procedures help in the audit of complex financial instruments?

A: Control procedures in the audit of complex financial instruments help ensure the accurate identification and recording of these instruments, the correct application of complex valuation techniques, and the proper disclosure of financial instrument information in the financial statements.

Q: What is the role of control procedures in the audit of non-financial information?

A: Control procedures in the audit of non-financial information help ensure the accurate collection, processing, and reporting of non-financial data, and the appropriate integration of this data with the financial information in the financial statements.

Applications

Scenario 1: A small business named GreenTech has had a recent change in management. The new manager is not satisfied with the current internal control procedures.

She has observed an increase in errors in financial reports and inventory discrepancies.

How can an auditor help GreenTech improve its control procedures?

Solution: An auditor evaluates the existing control procedures by examining the financial reports, conducting interviews with employees, and observing the operations. The auditor identifies the weak areas and recommends improvements.

For instance, if the inventory discrepancies arise from a lack of segregation of duties, the auditor advises the company to separate the responsibilities of recording and maintaining inventory. The effectiveness of this solution can be evaluated by the reduction in inventory discrepancies and errors in financial reports.

Scenario 2: A manufacturing company, BuildIt, has been experiencing frequent machine breakdowns leading to production delays. The management suspects that the maintenance department is not following the established control procedures.

How can an auditor address this issue?

Solution: The auditor can perform a compliance audit to check if the maintenance department is adhering to the control procedures. The auditor reviews the maintenance records, inspects the machines, and interviews the maintenance staff. If the auditor finds any lapses, he proposes corrective measures like training for the staff or revising the control procedures. The effectiveness of the solution can be assessed by the decrease in machine breakdowns and production delays.

Scenario 3: A retail store, ShopEase, has been receiving customer complaints about billing errors. The store manager believes that the cashiers are not following the control procedures.

How can an auditor assist ShopEase in resolving this problem?

Solution: The auditor can carry out a transaction audit to examine the billing process. The auditor checks the cash register logs, matches the bills with the inventory records, and observes the cashiers. If the auditor detects non-compliance with control procedures, he suggests improvements like cashier training or upgrading the billing system. The effectiveness can be determined by the decrease in customer complaints about billing errors.

Scenario 4: A restaurant, FoodHaven, is struggling with food wastage. The manager suspects that the kitchen staff is not adhering to the portion control procedures.

How can an auditor help FoodHaven manage its food wastage?

Solution: An auditor can conduct an operational audit to review the portion control procedures. The auditor assesses the food preparation process, measures the portion sizes, and talks to the kitchen staff. If the auditor uncovers non-compliance, he recommends corrective actions such as retraining the staff or adjusting the portion sizes. The effectiveness can be gauged by the reduction in food wastage.

Scenario 5: A software company, CodeCraft, has been losing clients due to delayed project deliveries. The CEO suspects that the project managers are not following the project management control procedures.

How can an auditor assist CodeCraft in delivering projects on time?

Solution: The auditor can undertake a performance audit to scrutinize the project management control procedures.

The auditor reviews the project plans, timelines, and progress reports, and interviews the project managers. If the auditor identifies any deviations, he advises reforms like project management training or revising the control procedures.

The effectiveness can be assessed by the improvement in project delivery times.

Test of Controls

Theoretical

Q: What is the purpose of the test of controls in an auditing process?

A: The primary purpose of the test of controls in an auditing process is to evaluate the effectiveness of an organization's internal controls system.

Q: What does the test of controls aim to achieve?

A: The test of controls aims to determine whether the internal controls are working as intended and effectively preventing errors or fraud.

Q: What are the steps involved in the test of controls?

A: The steps involved in the test of controls include identifying controls to be tested, designing tests, executing the tests, and evaluating the results.

Q: What are the types of test controls?

A: The types of test controls are inquiries, inspections, observations, and re-performance.

Q: How does an auditor determine which controls to test?

A: An auditor determines which controls to test based on their risk assessment. The controls that mitigate high-risk areas are likely to be tested.

Q: What is the significance of control risk assessment in the auditing process?

A: Control risk assessment helps the auditor to identify areas with high risk of material misstatement and thus, focus their testing efforts on these areas.

Q: What happens if a control fails a test of controls?

A: If a control fails a test of controls, the auditor may need to perform additional substantive testing or recommend improvements to the control.

Q: What is the role of evidence in a test of controls?

A: Evidence plays a crucial role in a test of controls as it supports the auditor's conclusion about the effectiveness of the control.

Q: What kind of evidence is considered in a test of controls? A: Evidence considered in a test of controls includes documents, records, and information that support the operation of the control.

Q: What is a control deficiency and how does it impact a test of controls?

A: A control deficiency is a flaw in the design or operation of a control. It impacts a test of controls by indicating that the control is not effective and may not prevent or detect errors or fraud.

Q: What is a material weakness in the context of a test of controls?

A: A material weakness is a type of control deficiency where the design or operation of a control does not prevent or detect errors or fraud on a timely basis.

Q: How is the severity of control deficiencies determined?

A: The severity of control deficiencies is determined based on the likelihood and magnitude of potential misstatements that could result from the deficiency.

Q: What is an integrated audit?

A: An integrated audit is an audit that includes both a test of controls and a substantive audit of the financial statements.

Q: How does an integrated audit benefit an organization?

A: An integrated audit benefits an organization by providing assurance on the effectiveness of internal controls and the accuracy of financial statements.

Q: How does an auditor document the results of a test of controls?

A: An auditor documents the results of a test of controls in the form of a report, including the procedures performed, the conclusions reached, and any identified control deficiencies.

Q: What is the difference between a test of controls and a substantive test?

A: A test of controls is focused on evaluating the effectiveness of internal controls, while a substantive test is focused on verifying the accuracy of account balances and transactions.

Q: What is the impact of effective internal controls on the audit process?

A: Effective internal controls can reduce the extent of substantive testing required, making the audit process more efficient.

Q: What is the role of management in the test of controls?

A: Management is responsible for the design and operation of internal controls, so their cooperation and support are crucial to the test of controls.

Q: What factors influence the scope of a test of controls?

A: Factors that influence the scope of a test of controls include the size and complexity of the organization, the nature of its operations, and the auditor's risk assessment.

Q: How does information technology impact the test of controls?

A: Information technology can significantly impact the test of controls by introducing new risks and controls to be tested, as well as by providing tools for conducting and documenting the tests.

Q: What are the potential outcomes of a test of controls?

A: The potential outcomes of a test of controls include the identification of control deficiencies or material weaknesses, recommendations for control improvements, and a reduction in control risk assessment.

Q: How does the test of controls relate to the overall audit opinion?

A: The results of the test of controls contribute to the auditor's overall opinion on the financial statements by providing assurance on the effectiveness of internal controls.

Q: What is the relationship between the test of controls and the audit risk model?

A: The test of controls is used to assess control risk, which is a component of the audit risk model.

Q: How does the auditor's understanding of the client's business affect the test of controls?

A: The auditor's understanding of the client's business helps to identify relevant controls to test and to interpret the results of the tests.

Q: What are some common challenges in performing a test of controls?

A: Some common challenges in performing a test of controls include obtaining sufficient appropriate evidence, dealing with complex information systems, and managing client relationships.

Q: How can the test of controls be used to identify fraud risk factors?

A: The test of controls can identify fraud risk factors by revealing control deficiencies that could allow fraud to occur undetected.

Q: What is the role of professional skepticism in the test of controls?

A: Professional skepticism is crucial in the test of controls, as the auditor must critically evaluate the evidence and not simply accept the client's assertions.

Q: What is the role of internal audit in the test of controls?

A: Internal audit plays a supportive role in the test of controls by providing independent assurance on the effectiveness of internal controls.

Q: How does a test of controls differ in a smaller vs. a larger organization?

A: In a smaller organization, the test of controls may be less formal and rely more on direct observation, while in a larger organization, it may involve more complex procedures and documentation.

Q: What is the importance of timing in a test of controls?

A: Timing is important in a test of controls because controls must be tested during the period under audit to provide evidence of their effectiveness during that time.

Q: What is a compensating control and how does it impact a test of controls?

A: A compensating control is a control that mitigates the risk of a control deficiency. It impacts a test of controls by providing additional assurance where a primary control is not effective.

Q: How does a test of controls contribute to the planning phase of an audit? A: A test of controls contributes to the planning phase of an audit by identifying areas of high risk that need more intensive substantive testing.

Q: How does the auditor communicate the results of a test of controls to the client?

A: The auditor communicates the results of a test of controls to the client through a written report, including identified control deficiencies and recommendations for improvement.

Q: How does a test of controls contribute to the auditor's assessment of going concern?

A: A test of controls can contribute to the auditor's assessment of going concern by identifying control deficiencies that could impact the organization's ability to continue as a going concern.

Q: What is the role of the audit committee in the test of controls?
A: The audit committee plays an oversight role in the test of controls, ensuring that the audit process is thorough and that identified control deficiencies are addressed.
Q: How does a test of controls contribute to the assessment of materiality in an audit?
A: A test of controls can contribute to the assessment of materiality by identifying control deficiencies that could lead to material misstatements.
Q: What is the impact of regulatory requirements on the test of controls?
A: Regulatory requirements can impact the test of controls by dictating certain mandatory testing procedures or by influencing the assessment of control risk.
Q: How does the concept of reasonable assurance relate to the test of controls?
A: The concept of reasonable assurance relates to the test of controls by acknowledging that no control is perfect and that the goal of testing is to provide a reasonable level of assurance about the effectiveness of controls.
Q: What is the impact of an organization's control environment on the test of controls?
A: The organization's control environment impacts the test of controls by influencing the design and operation of controls and thus, the effectiveness of those controls.
Q: How does the auditor's understanding of the client's industry affect the test of controls?
A: The auditor's understanding of the client's industry helps in identifying industry-specific risks and controls to be tested.
Q: What is the difference between a test of design and a test of operating effectiveness in a test of controls?

A: A test of design assesses whether a control is properly designed to prevent or detect errors or fraud, while a test of operating effectiveness assesses whether the control is operating as designed.

Q: What role does sampling play in a test of controls?

A: Sampling plays a crucial role in a test of controls, as it allows the auditor to draw conclusions about the entire population of transactions based on a sample.

Q: What factors influence the sample size in a test of controls?

A: Factors that influence the sample size in a test of controls include the level of control risk, the frequency of the control, and the tolerable error rate.

Q: What is the role of statistical vs. non-statistical sampling in a test of controls?

A: Statistical sampling employs mathematical methods to assess sample size and results, whereas non-statistical sampling depends on the auditor's discretion.

Q: How do deviations from controls identified in a test of controls affect the audit process?

A: Deviations from controls identified in a test of controls can increase the perceived level of control risk and thus, increase the extent of substantive testing required.

Q: What are the limitations of a test of controls?

A: The limitations of a test of controls include the possibility of sampling error, the inherent limitations of internal controls, and the potential for controls to be overridden.

Q: How does an auditor determine the sufficiency and appropriateness of evidence in a test of controls?

A: The auditor determines the sufficiency and appropriateness of evidence in a test of controls based on the risk of material misstatement, the quality of the evidence, and the results of other audit procedures.

Q: What is the difference between inherent risk and control risk in the context of a test of controls?

A: Inherent risk is the risk of a material misstatement occurring in the absence of controls, while control risk is the risk that a material misstatement will not be prevented or detected by the controls.

Q: How does the concept of segregation of duties relate to the test of controls?

A: The concept of segregation of duties relates to the test of controls by establishing that no single individual should have complete control over a process, reducing the risk of error or fraud.

Q: How does the auditor's professional judgment influence the test of controls?

A: The auditor's professional judgment influences the test of controls in various ways, including the selection of controls to test, the design of testing procedures, and the evaluation of test results.

Applications

Scenario 1: A small manufacturing company has been experiencing some discrepancies in their inventory levels.

The auditor was called in to conduct a test of controls.

The management states that they have a control in place where the warehouse manager checks the inventory at the end of each day and matches it with the sales record.

How effective is this control?

Evaluation: This control might be partially effective as it does allow for daily checks. However, it has its limitations.

The warehouse manager might not be completely objective and there is potential for errors or even fraud. A more effective control would be to include another level of check - perhaps someone from the finance department could also verify the records. This would provide a second layer of validation and ensure that any discrepancies are caught.

Scenario 2: A retail business has been facing frequent cash shortages. The management has implemented a control that requires two cashiers to be present at the time of cash counting. The auditor has been asked to test this control.

How effective is this control?

Evaluation: This control is effective in preventing internal fraud as it would require collusion between the two cashiers to manipulate cash. However, it does not prevent errors. A more effective control might be to have surprise cash counts by the finance department or the manager.

Scenario 3: A large corporation has been facing issues with its procurement process. The management put a control in place where all orders above a certain amount need to be approved by the CFO. The auditors have been asked to test this control. How effective is this control?

Evaluation: This control is effective in preventing unauthorized purchases or purchases over budget. However, it could create bottlenecks if the CFO is not available or does not have enough time to review all orders. A more effective control might be to have a procurement committee that can share the approval responsibility.

Scenario 4: A bank has implemented a control where all loan applications over a certain amount need to be reviewed by a loan committee. The auditor has been asked to test this control. How effective is this control?

Evaluation: This control is effective in preventing fraudulent or risky loans. However, it might slow down the loan approval process and could lead to loss of business. A more effective control might be to have a risk assessment team that can review the loan applications and make recommendations to the loan committee.

Scenario 5: A company has implemented a control where all expense reports need to be approved by the department head. The auditor has been asked to test this control.

How effective is this control?

Evaluation: This control is effective in preventing fraudulent or unnecessary expenses. However, it might create bottlenecks if the department head is not available or does not have enough time to review all expense reports. A more effective control might be to have a finance team that can review the expense reports and make recommendations to the department head.

Materiality

Theoretical

Q: What is materiality in auditing?

A: Materiality in auditing refers to the significance of an amount, transaction, or discrepancy that could influence the decisions of users relying on the financial statements.

Q: Why is materiality important in auditing?

A: Materiality is important in auditing as it helps auditors determine the nature, timing, and extent of audit procedures. It also guides the evaluation of audit findings and the overall impact on the financial statements.

Q: How is materiality determined in an audit?

A: Materiality is usually determined by the auditor based on their professional judgment, considering quantitative factors such as a percentage of net income, total assets, or revenue, and qualitative factors such as legal and regulatory requirements.

Q: What is qualitative materiality?

A: Qualitative materiality refers to the non-numerical aspects of a transaction or event that could influence the users' decisions, such as breaches of laws or conflicts of interest.

Q: What is quantitative materiality?

A: Quantitative materiality refers to the numerical or financial aspects of a transaction or event, often set as a percentage of a chosen benchmark such as total assets or revenue.

Q: What is the concept of relative materiality?

A: Relative materiality is the idea that the significance of an amount or event may vary depending on the context or entity's size and nature.

Q: How does materiality affect audit risk?

A: Materiality is inversely related to audit risk. The lower the materiality level, the lower the risk that the auditor will not detect a materially misstated item.

Q: What is the role of materiality in sampling?

A: Materiality helps in determining the sample size for audit procedures. A lower materiality level would require a larger sample size.

Q: What is performance materiality?

A: Performance materiality is a set amount less than overall materiality, used to reduce the risk that the aggregate of uncorrected and undetected misstatements exceeds materiality for the financial statements as a whole.

Q: Can materiality levels change during an audit?

A: Yes, materiality levels can change during an audit. If new information comes to light that impacts the auditor's assessment of materiality, the levels may need to be revised.

Q: How does materiality relate to audit evidence?

A: The concept of materiality guides the amount and type of audit evidence the auditor needs to collect. For more material areas, more persuasive or robust evidence is needed.

Q: How does materiality affect the auditor's report?

A: Any misstatements identified during the audit that are deemed material, either individually or in aggregate, need to be reported in the auditor's report.

Q: What is uncorrected misstatement?

A: Uncorrected misstatements are potential errors or discrepancies identified during the audit that, either individually or in aggregate, could be material but have not been corrected by the management.

Q: What is a material weakness in internal control?

A: A material weakness in internal control refers to a single or multiple deficiency in the internal control system. This weakness increases the likelihood of a significant error in the entity's financial statements either not being prevented or not being identified and rectified promptly.

Q: How does an auditor consider materiality in planning the audit?

A: In audit planning, the auditor sets a preliminary materiality level which guides the development of the audit strategy, including risk assessment and determination of nature, timing, and extent of audit procedures.

Q: Is materiality a fixed percentage in auditing?

A: No, materiality is not a fixed percentage. It is determined by the auditor based on their professional judgment and the specific circumstances of the entity.

Q: How is materiality related to professional judgment?

A: The concept of materiality heavily relies on the auditor's professional judgment. The auditor must use their experience and knowledge to determine what could be material to users of the financial statements.

Q: Can something be immaterial individually but material in aggregate?

A: Yes, individual items may be immaterial but could become material when aggregated with other misstatements.

Q: What is the relationship between materiality and the audit opinion?

A: If the auditor concludes that there are material misstatements in the financial statements, it may lead to a modified audit opinion.

Q: What is the benchmark in determining materiality?
A: The benchmark in determining materiality could be a percentage of total assets, revenue, or net income, among others. The choice of benchmark depends on the nature of the entity and its industry.
Q: How does materiality affect the scope of the audit?
A: Materiality influences the scope of the audit by helping to determine which areas to focus on and the extent of testing required in those areas.
Q: What is the role of materiality in evaluating audit findings?
A: Materiality helps in evaluating the significance of the audit findings and their potential impact on the financial statements.
Q: Can materiality be both qualitative and quantitative?
A: Yes, materiality has both qualitative and quantitative aspects. It considers not only the monetary value but also the nature and context of the item or event.
Q: How does materiality affect the determination of audit procedures?
A: The nature, timing, and intensity of audit procedures are impacted by materiality. For areas of greater materiality, more comprehensive and detailed procedures are typically necessary.
Q: What is the concept of triviality in relation to materiality?
A: Triviality refers to the threshold below which misstatements, either individually or in aggregate, are considered clearly trivial and not requiring consideration by the auditor.
Q: What is the difference between materiality at the financial statement level and at the individual account level?
A: Materiality at the financial statement level is the maximum amount by which the auditor believes the statements could be misstated without affecting the decisions of users. Materiality at the individual account level, or performance materiality, is lower

and is used to assess the risk of material misstatement at the account level.

Q: How is materiality reassessed during the audit?

A: Materiality may be reassessed during the audit if the auditor obtains new information that would have caused them to determine a different materiality level initially.

Q: How does materiality relate to fraud in auditing?

A: Even a small amount could be material if it involves fraud, particularly if it involves management or could have a significant impact on the entity's operations or reputation.

Q: What is the concept of 'clearly trivial' in relation to materiality?

A: 'Clearly trivial' is a concept related to materiality where certain misstatements are considered too small to reasonably influence the users' decisions, even when aggregated with other misstatements.

Q: How does an auditor communicate material misstatements to those charged with governance?

A: Material misstatements identified during the audit are typically communicated in a written report to those charged with governance, explaining their nature and potential impact on the financial statements.

Q: How does the auditor treat identified but uncorrected misstatements?

A: The auditor accumulates all identified but uncorrected misstatements throughout the audit.

At the end of the audit, the auditor considers whether these misstatements, in aggregate, could be material to the financial statements.

Q: How is materiality used in group audits?

A: In group audits, materiality is determined not only for the group financial statements as a whole but also at the component level, considering the size and complexity of the component and its significance to the group.

Q: How does a change in an entity's operations affect materiality?

A: A significant change in an entity's operations, such as a major acquisition or restructuring, could affect the assessment of materiality as it may alter the benchmarks or factors considered in determining materiality.

Q: What is the concept of 'tolerable misstatement' in relation to materiality?

A: Tolerable misstatement is a concept related to materiality, representing the maximum error in an account balance that the auditor would tolerate without modifying their audit opinion.

Q: How does an auditor document their consideration of materiality?

A: The auditor's consideration of materiality is typically documented in the audit planning memorandum or strategy, including the basis for determining materiality and any subsequent changes made during the audit.

Q: How can materiality be different for different stakeholders?

A: Different stakeholders may have different perspectives on what is material based on their interests and needs.

For example, regulators may be more concerned with compliance issues, while investors may focus more on profitability or financial stability.

Q: How does the auditor's understanding of the entity and its environment affect the assessment of materiality?

A: The auditor's understanding of the entity and its environment helps them to identify the factors that could influence the users' decisions and therefore should be considered in assessing materiality.

Q: How does materiality influence the evaluation of misstatements?

A: Materiality sets the threshold for evaluating whether the misstatements identified during the audit could materially misstate the financial statements and therefore require adjustment or disclosure.

Q: Can there be more than one level of materiality in an audit?

A: Yes, there can be more than one level of materiality in an audit. For example, there is overall materiality for the financial statements as a whole and performance materiality for individual accounts or transactions.

Q: How does materiality relate to the concept of 'true and fair' view in financial reporting?

A: Materiality aids in providing an accurate and honest perspective in financial reporting. It establishes the criteria for what needs to be reported and disclosed to portray a comprehensive and precise overview of the organization's financial health and performance.

Q: How does an auditor consider materiality in relation to related party transactions?

A: In relation to related party transactions, an auditor may consider lower materiality thresholds due to the higher risk of fraud or bias in these transactions.

Q: How does the concept of materiality apply to disclosures in the financial statements?

A: Materiality applies to disclosures in the financial statements in the same way as to the financial statement amounts. Disclosures that could influence the users' decisions should be considered material.

Q: How is materiality considered in the audit of estimates?

A: In the audit of estimates, materiality is considered in evaluating the reasonableness of the estimates and the related disclosures, including the potential for management bias.

Q: Can materiality be subjective in auditing?

A: Yes, materiality can be subjective as it relies on the auditor's professional judgment and understanding of the users' needs and expectations.

Q: How does the concept of materiality apply to the audit of non-financial information?

A: In the audit of non-financial information, materiality applies to the evaluation of the completeness and accuracy of the information and its consistency with the financial information.

Q: How does materiality relate to audit quality?

A: Materiality is a key aspect of audit quality as it guides the auditor's efforts and resources towards the areas that matter most to the users of the financial statements.

Q: How does materiality affect the auditor's communication with the entity's management?

A: The auditor communicates with the entity's management about the materiality levels set for the audit and any material misstatements identified during the audit.

Q: How does the concept of materiality apply to the audit of internal control?

A: In the audit of internal control, materiality is considered in evaluating the potential impact of control deficiencies on the reliability of the financial reporting process.

Q: Can materiality be reassessed after the audit?

A: Yes, materiality can be reassessed after the audit if new information comes to light that would have affected the auditor's assessment of materiality.

Q: How does materiality relate to the concept of 'fair presentation' in financial reporting?

A: Materiality helps to ensure a 'fair presentation' in financial reporting by setting the threshold for what must be reported and disclosed to present the financial position and performance of the entity accurately and completely.

Applications

Scenario 1: A global fashion retailer has started a new line of eco-friendly clothing. They have spent a considerable amount on R&D and marketing. The auditor, however, has deemed this expense as immaterial and excluded it from the financial statements.

Assessment: This approach is incorrect. Even though the expense might not be significant compared to the total revenue, it is a part of the company's operations and can impact the financial condition. The auditor should consider both qualitative and quantitative aspects of materiality.

Scenario 2: A small family-owned restaurant has not recorded a $500 expense for an event which was canceled due to unforeseen circumstances. The auditor, considering the materiality concept, decides to ignore the expense. Assessment: The auditor's decision is appropriate in this case, as the amount is relatively insignificant to the company's overall financial position. However, repeated instances of such omissions could potentially become material over time.

Scenario 3: A tech startup is raising funds for expansion. They have some minor legal issues which they did not disclose in their financial report. The auditor, applying the materiality concept, decides to let it pass since it is not a significant amount compared to their overall valuation.

Assessment: This could be a potentially risky situation. Even though the legal issues might not be significant monetarily, they can pose a major risk to the company's reputation and future operations. The auditor should consider the potential consequences and ensure appropriate disclosure.

Scenario 4: An online retail company has a policy of providing refunds for returned items. However, they have not recorded a liability for potential returns in their financial statements. The auditor, considering the materiality concept, decides to ignore it.

Assessment: This might not be the correct approach. Although the potential returns might not be significant in terms of the company's total sales, it is an inherent business risk and should be disclosed. The auditor should consider both the likelihood and the potential impact of the returns in their audit.

Scenario 5: A manufacturing company has some obsolete inventory which they have not written off in their financial statements. The auditor, applying the materiality concept, decides to ignore it.

Assessment: This is not an effective approach by the auditor. Even though the amount might not be significant, it is an inaccurate representation of the company's assets. The auditor should insist on writing off the obsolete inventory to provide a more accurate picture of the company's financial position.

Inherent Risk

Theoretical

What is inherent risk in auditing?

Inherent risk in auditing refers to the possibility of material misstatement of a financial statement element, assuming there are no related controls.

How is inherent risk assessed?

Inherent risk is typically assessed through a risk assessment which involves an understanding of the client's business, its industry, and the regulatory environment.

What factors increase inherent risk?

Factors such as complexity of transactions, susceptibility to theft or fraud, and the judgement involved in determining account balances can increase inherent risk.

What is the role of inherent risk in audit risk model? Inherent risk is one of the three components of the audit risk model, the other two being control risk and detection risk.

It impacts the overall audit risk. How does the auditor respond to high levels of inherent risk?

When inherent risk is high, auditors usually increase the extent of their substantive testing, perform more rigorous analytical procedures, or use more experienced staff for the audit. Does a high inherent risk always mean high audit risk? Not necessarily. While inherent risk is a component of audit risk, the overall audit risk also depends on control risk and detection risk. Can inherent risk be eliminated?

No, inherent risk cannot be eliminated as it is always present due to the inherent nature of business activities and transactions. How is inherent risk different from control risk?

Inherent risk exists independently of an audit of financial statements while control risk arises because of the potential failure of the control systems in place. Can auditors control inherent risk?

No, auditors cannot control inherent risk. They can, however, assess and respond to it. What elements of a financial statement have high inherent risk?

Elements such as cash, inventory, and accounts receivable usually have high inherent risk due to their susceptibility to theft and fraud.

How does industry affect inherent risk?

Different industries have different levels of inherent risks. For instance, industries with complex transactions or high levels of regulation may have higher inherent risk. How is inherent risk related to material misstatement? Inherent risk is the risk of material misstatement in the absence of any controls or interventions. How does the economic environment impact inherent risk? Changes in the economic environment, such as market volatility, can increase the inherent risk by causing fluctuations in asset values or changes in accounting estimates. How does inherent risk affect audit planning? The assessment of inherent risk helps in determining the nature, timing, and extent of audit procedures. What are the consequences of underestimating inherent risk? Underestimating inherent risk can lead to a less rigorous audit strategy, potentially missing material misstatements. What happens if inherent risk is overestimated? If inherent risk is overestimated, auditors may perform more extensive procedures than necessary, resulting in unnecessary costs. What role does management judgement play in inherent risk? The degree of management judgement involved in financial reporting impacts inherent risk. The more judgement, the higher the inherent risk.

Can inherent risk be quantified? Inherent risk is usually assessed qualitatively rather than quantitatively. It is evaluated based on auditor's judgement. How does inherent risk relate to fraud risk? Fraud risk is a part of inherent risk. High inherent risk may indicate high potential for fraudulent activities.

How does technology impact inherent risk?

Technology can both increase and decrease inherent risk. While it can improve accuracy and efficiency, it also introduces risks such as data breaches and system failures. Is inherent risk the same in every audit? No, inherent risk varies from audit to audit based on the client's business, industry, and other factors.

How does inherent risk relate to audit evidence?

The level of inherent risk impacts the quantity and quality of audit evidence required to express an opinion. How does an auditor assess inherent risk at the assertion level?

Auditors assess inherent risk at the assertion level by understanding and evaluating the susceptibility of an assertion to a material misstatement.

How do changes in laws and regulations impact inherent risk? Changes in laws and regulations can increase inherent risk by introducing new compliance requirements or changing existing ones. How does inherent risk affect the auditor's professional skepticism? High levels of inherent risk require auditors to exercise a higher degree of professional skepticism to identify potential misstatements. Can inherent risk be changed? Inherent risk cannot be changed as it is inherent to the entity's operations and environment. How does inherent risk relate to business risk? Business risk is a broader concept that includes inherent risk. It refers to the risks that could prevent the business from achieving its objectives. How does the complexity of transactions impact inherent risk?

The more complex a transaction, the higher the inherent risk due to the increased possibility of errors or misstatements. How does the use of estimates in financial reporting affect inherent risk? The use of estimates increases inherent risk as they involve a degree of uncertainty and judgement. Can auditors completely rely on their assessment of inherent risk? Auditors use their assessment of inherent risk as part of their audit strategy, but they also rely on other factors such as control risk and detection risk. How does inherent risk impact the audit opinion? If inherent risk is high and is not properly addressed during the audit, it could lead to a qualified or adverse audit opinion. Can the inherent risk be the same for all components of a financial statement? No, inherent risk can vary among different components of a financial statement based on their nature and complexity. How does the timing of transactions impact inherent risk? Transactions occurring at the end of the reporting period may have a higher inherent risk due to the rush to meet deadlines. How does inherent risk affect the audit risk model? The audit risk model consists of three components, one of which is inherent risk. An increase in inherent risk increases the overall audit risk, assuming all other factors remain constant. How does inherent risk relate to the going concern assumption? If there is a high inherent risk that the entity may not continue as a going concern, it affects the auditor's assessment of the financial statements.

How does inherent risk affect the materiality level?

A high level of inherent risk may lead to a lower materiality level, requiring the auditor to gather more evidence.

How does inherent risk impact the reliability of financial statements? High inherent risk may reduce the reliability of financial statements if not properly managed and controlled. Can inherent risk be completely mitigated? Inherent risk cannot be completely mitigated as it is inherent to the business and its environment. How do changes in the entity's operations affect inherent risk? Changes in the entity's operations can increase inherent risk by introducing new processes, products, or markets. How does the size of the entity impact inherent risk? Larger entities may have a higher inherent risk due to the complexity of their operations and transactions. How does the nature of the entity's business affect inherent risk? The nature of the business can impact inherent risk. Businesses with complex transactions or high levels of regulation may have higher inherent risk. How does the auditor's experience impact the assessment of inherent risk? An experienced auditor may be better able to assess inherent risk due to their knowledge and understanding of the business and industry. Can inherent risk be reduced? While inherent risk cannot be eliminated, it can be managed through effective internal controls and risk management practices. How does the entity's internal control system impact inherent risk? A strong internal control system can help manage inherent risk by preventing or detecting material misstatements. How does the auditor's understanding of the client's business impact their assessment of inherent risk? A better understanding of the client's business allows the auditor to more accurately assess inherent risk. How does inherent risk affect the auditor's reliance on internal controls? If inherent risk is high, the auditor may decide to rely less on internal controls and perform more substantive testing. How does inherent risk impact the nature of audit procedures? The level of inherent risk affects the nature of audit procedures. High inherent risk may warrant more detailed and rigorous audit procedures. How does inherent risk relate to the risk of fraud?

Inherent risk includes the risk of material misstatements due to fraud.
A high inherent risk may suggest a higher risk of fraud.
How is inherent risk related to the risk of error? Inherent risk includes the risk of material misstatements due to error. Increased inherent risk suggests a higher likelihood of errors. How does inherent risk affect the scope of the audit?
A high level of inherent risk may result in an expanded scope of the audit, requiring more detailed testing and review.

Applications

XYZ Ltd is a small manufacturing company that has recently decided to enter a foreign market. The inherent risks associated with this strategic move are high due to regulatory and cultural differences. What are some auditing processes that can help mitigate these risks? Effective auditing practices in this scenario would include conducting a thorough risk assessment to identify potential areas of concern. This might involve evaluating the company's understanding of the foreign market, examining its compliance with international trade laws, and assessing its preparation for cultural differences. Regular audits to monitor progress and ensure compliance would also be beneficial.
ABC Enterprises is a rapidly growing tech firm that has recently implemented a new accounting software system. The inherent risk of errors due to unfamiliarity with the new system is high. How should the auditors address this risk? In this case, the auditors should focus on understanding the new software and its potential pitfalls. They should conduct a thorough review of the system, including testing for accuracy and reliability. They should also assess the training provided to the employees and their comfort level with the new system. Ensuring adequate controls are in place to detect and correct errors will also be crucial.

DEF Pharmaceuticals is a company operating in a highly regulated industry. The inherent risk of non-compliance with industry regulations is high. How can an audit help manage this risk? An audit in this scenario should focus on regulatory compliance. This could include verifying that the company has a robust system for keeping abreast of regulatory changes, validating that it adheres to all current regulations, and checking that it has procedures in place to respond to any regulatory breaches. Regular audits can help ensure ongoing compliance and detect potential issues early.

GHI Retail is a company with a high turnover of staff. This increases the inherent risk of mistakes due to lack of familiarity with company procedures. How can an audit mitigate this risk? For GHI Retail, the auditors should examine the company's staff training and induction processes to ensure they are effective. They should also review the company's internal controls and procedures to ensure they are robust enough to withstand a high staff turnover. Regular audits can also help identify areas where additional training or controls may be needed.

JKL Construction has recently undertaken a large and complex project. The inherent risk of cost overruns and delays is high. How can an audit help manage this risk? In this situation, the audit should focus on project management practices. This could include reviewing the project's budget and timeline, checking the accuracy of cost and progress estimates, and verifying that adequate controls are in place to manage risks. An audit can also provide valuable insights into areas of concern and potential improvements.

Audit Risk

Theoretical

Q: What is audit risk?

A: Audit risk refers to the possibility that an auditor might unintentionally neglect to accurately adjust their view on financial statements that have significant errors.

Q: What are the three components of audit risk?

A: Inherent risk, control risk, and detection risk are the three elements that make up audit risk.

Q: What is inherent risk in auditing?

A: Inherent risk refers to the potential for a significant error in a claim, given there are no corresponding controls in place.

Q: What is control risk?

A: Control risk refers to the possibility of an assertion containing a potentially significant error—either on its own or when combined with other errors—that the entity's internal control system fails to prevent, identify, or correct promptly.

Q: What is detection risk?

A: Detection risk is the risk that the auditors' procedures will not detect a misstatement that exists in an assertion that could be material, either individually or when aggregated with other misstatements.

Q: How can auditors manage audit risk?

A: Auditors can manage audit risk by conducting thorough risk assessments, implementing strong internal controls, and performing comprehensive and effective audit procedures.

Q: Can audit risk be completely eliminated?
A: No, audit risk can never be completely eliminated due to the inherent limitations of an audit.
Q: How does the concept of materiality relate to audit risk?
A: Materiality is directly related to audit risk as it helps determine the extent of audit risk that is acceptable. Misstatements below the materiality threshold do not significantly impact the users' decision-making process, hence, auditors accept a higher level of audit risk for them.
Q: How are audit risk and audit evidence related?
A: The amount of audit evidence gathered is inversely proportional to the risk of an audit. The higher the audit risk, the more audit evidence the auditor should gather and vice versa.
Q: How does the inherent risk impact the audit strategy?
A: If an auditor determines that the inherent risk is high, they will need to perform more substantive testing to mitigate the risk.
Q: How does the auditor assess control risk?
A: The auditor assesses control risk by evaluating the effectiveness of the company's internal control system.
Q: How does the auditor manage detection risk?
A: The auditor manages detection risk by designing and implementing appropriate substantive procedures.
Q: What is the role of professional skepticism in managing audit risk?
A: Professional skepticism helps auditors to critically assess audit evidence and thus reduce audit risk.
Q: How does the complexity of a company's operations impact audit risk?
A: The more complex a company's operations, the higher the inherent risk and consequently the audit risk.
Q: Why is understanding the client's business environment crucial in managing audit risk?

A: Understanding the client's business environment helps the auditor in assessing the inherent risk and control risk, hence, managing the audit risk.

Q: How does fraud impact audit risk?

A: Fraud increases the audit risk as it could lead to material misstatements in the financial statements.

Q: How does the risk of material misstatement relate to audit risk?

A: The risk of material misstatement is a component of audit risk and consists of inherent risk and control risk.

Q: How do auditors respond to high levels of audit risk?

A: Auditors respond to high levels of audit risk by increasing the extent of audit procedures and gathering more audit evidence.

Q: How does the auditors' understanding of internal control impact detection risk?

A: The better the auditor's understanding of internal control, the lower the detection risk, as it helps them design effective audit procedures.

Q: How is audit risk used in determining the nature, timing, and extent of audit procedures?

A: The level of audit risk helps determine the nature (what procedures to perform), timing (when to perform them), and extent (how much work to do) of audit procedures.

Q: What is the audit risk model?

A: The audit risk model is a tool used by auditors to manage the overall risk of an audit. The typical formula for audit risk is represented as AR = IR x CR x DR, where AR stands for audit risk, IR for inherent risk, CR for control risk, and DR for detection risk.

Q: How can auditors mitigate inherent risk?

A: Auditors can't directly mitigate inherent risk as it is not within their control, but they can adjust their audit plan and procedures to address the areas of higher inherent risk.

Q: What is the impact of information technology on audit risk?

A: Information technology can both increase and decrease audit risk. It can increase audit risk due to the complexities and potential for error or fraud in IT systems, and it can decrease audit risk by enabling better data analysis and more effective audit procedures.

Q: How does the auditors' competence and capability impact audit risk?

A: The higher the auditors' competence and capability, the lower the detection risk and consequently the audit risk.

Q: How does the auditors' independence impact audit risk?

A: A lack of auditors' independence can increase audit risk as it may compromise their objectivity and professional skepticism.

Q: How can auditors mitigate control risk?

A: Auditors can't mitigate control risk directly as it relates to the client's internal controls. However, they can recommend improvements to the client's internal control system.

Q: How does the audit risk model help in audit planning?

A: The audit risk model helps auditors in determining the nature, timing, and extent of audit procedures to achieve an acceptable level of audit risk.

Q: Is there a relationship between audit risk and audit fees?

A: Yes, higher audit risk often results in higher audit fees because the auditor may need to perform more work to reduce the risk to an acceptable level.

Q: What is the impact of regulatory environment on audit risk?

A: A stringent regulatory environment can lower audit risk as it often results in better internal controls and more accurate financial reporting.

Q: How does the auditors' understanding of the client's industry impact audit risk?

A: A good understanding of the client's industry can reduce audit risk as it helps the auditor to better assess inherent risk and control risk.

Q: What is the role of audit risk in the auditors' report?

A: The auditor's report includes an opinion on the financial statements, which is based on the assessment of audit risk. The higher the audit risk, the more likely the auditor is to issue a qualified opinion or disclaimer of opinion.

Q: Can auditors completely eliminate detection risk?

A: No, detection risk cannot be completely eliminated because of the inherent limitations of an audit.

Q: How does the size of the company impact audit risk?

A: Larger companies often have more complex operations, which can increase inherent risk and hence audit risk.

Q: How do economic conditions impact audit risk?

A: Poor economic conditions can increase audit risk as companies may face financial difficulties, increasing the likelihood of material misstatements.

Q: How does the auditors' understanding of the client's accounting policies impact audit risk?

A: A good understanding of the client's accounting policies can reduce audit risk as it helps the auditor in assessing the appropriateness of those policies and the associated risks.

Q: What is the impact of the client's corporate governance on audit risk?

A: Good corporate governance can reduce audit risk as it often results in better internal controls and more accurate financial reporting.

Q: How do the auditors' professional judgment and experience impact audit risk?

A: The auditors' professional judgment and experience can significantly reduce audit risk as it improves their ability to identify and respond to potential risks.

Q: How does the complexity of the client's transactions impact audit risk?

A: More complex transactions increase inherent risk and consequently audit risk, as they are more prone to error or fraud.

Q: What is the role of audit risk in the auditors' decision to accept or continue a client engagement?

A: If the audit risk is too high and cannot be reduced to an acceptable level, the auditor may decide not to accept or continue the client engagement.

Q: How does the client's ethical values impact audit risk?

A: High ethical values can reduce audit risk as they often result in better internal controls and more accurate financial reporting.

Q: How does the client's financial stability impact audit risk?

A: Financial instability can increase audit risk as it increases the likelihood of material misstatements due to financial difficulties.

Q: How does the auditors' understanding of the client's objectives and strategies impact audit risk?

A: A good understanding of the client's objectives and strategies can reduce audit risk as it helps the auditor in assessing the business risks that may impact the financial statements.

Q: How does the client's risk management process impact audit risk?

A: An effective risk management process can reduce audit risk as it helps in identifying and managing risks that may lead to material misstatements.

Q: How does the auditors' use of audit assistants impact audit risk?

A: Proper supervision and review of the work of audit assistants can help in reducing detection risk and hence audit risk.

Q: How does the auditors' understanding of the client's operations impact audit risk?

A: A good understanding of the client's operations can reduce audit risk as it helps the auditor in assessing the inherent risk and control risk.

Q: How does the timing of the audit impact audit risk?

A: The timing of the audit can impact audit risk. For example, if the audit is rushed, it may increase detection risk.

Q: How does the auditors' knowledge of the applicable financial reporting framework impact audit risk?

A: A thorough knowledge of the applicable financial reporting framework can reduce audit risk as it helps the auditor in assessing the appropriateness of the client's accounting policies and disclosures.

Q: Can auditors completely eliminate inherent risk?

A: No, inherent risk cannot be completely eliminated as it is a function of the nature of the client's business and environment.

Q: How does the auditors' understanding of the client's system of internal control impact audit risk?

A: A good understanding of the client's system of internal control can reduce control risk and hence audit risk.

Q: How does the auditors' attitude towards risk impact audit risk?

A: If auditors are risk-averse, they may perform more extensive procedures and thereby reduce detection risk and hence audit risk. Conversely, if they are risk-tolerant, they may accept a higher level of audit risk.

Applications

Scenario 1: ABC Corp is a multinational company with different business units. The audit team has identified that there is a high audit risk associated with the inventory management of one of the business units. How can ABC Corp efficiently manage this audit risk?

In this scenario, ABC Corp can manage this audit risk by implementing an effective internal control system. This includes ensuring that the inventory is properly recorded and regularly checked. The use of software for inventory management can help reduce errors and discrepancies. The internal audit team should also perform regular audits of the inventory to identify any risks early on. The effectiveness of this solution can be evaluated by the decrease in the number of inventory-related audit issues.

Scenario 2: XYZ Inc. is a startup company that has not yet established an internal audit department. The management is concerned about the high audit risk due to lack of internal controls. What steps can XYZ Inc. take to address this audit risk?

XYZ Inc. can start by establishing a small internal audit team responsible for setting up internal controls. They can also hire external auditors for an independent review of their financial statements. Implementing a risk-based audit approach will help the company focus on areas with high audit risk. The effectiveness of this approach can be evaluated by the number of audit findings and the extent of their severity.

Scenario 3: PQR Ltd. is a manufacturing company with a decentralized operation. The audit team has identified a high audit risk due to lack of communication and coordination among different departments. How can PQR Ltd. mitigate this audit risk?

PQR Ltd. can mitigate this audit risk by implementing a centralized management system. This will improve communication and coordination among different departments. Regular meetings and updates among department heads can also help in identifying and addressing audit risks. The effectiveness of this solution can be evaluated by the decrease in the number of audit findings related to lack of coordination and communication.

Scenario 4: MNO Enterprises is a service-based company that has recently implemented a new IT system. The audit team has identified a high audit risk due to potential IT-related issues. What steps can MNO Enterprises take to manage this audit risk? MNO Enterprises can manage this audit risk by providing adequate training to its employees about the new IT system. They should also hire IT experts to regularly monitor and maintain the system. An IT audit can also be performed to identify any potential risks. The effectiveness of this solution can be evaluated by the number of IT-related audit issues and the smooth functioning of the IT system.

Business Risk

Theoretical

Q: What is business risk in the context of auditing?

A: Business risk in auditing refers to the potential that a company's operations or strategies will lead to financial loss, affecting the ability to achieve its objectives.

Q: How can auditors identify business risks?

A: Auditors identify business risks through risk assessment procedures such as interviews, observation, and review of the company's financial and non-financial information.

Q: What is the connection between business risk and audit risk?

A: Business risk impacts audit risk as it can affect the auditor's ability to gather sufficient appropriate evidence to draw a reasonable conclusion about the financial statements.

Q: What role does an auditor play in managing business risks?

A: An auditor does not directly manage business risks. However, they can provide valuable insights and recommendations after identifying and assessing these risks during the audit process.

Q: Why is understanding business risk essential for auditors?

A: Understanding business risk helps auditors design effective audit procedures, assess the likelihood of material misstatements, and provide valuable recommendations to the management.

Q: How does business risk impact the scope of an audit?

A: Higher levels of business risk may widen the scope of an audit, necessitating more in-depth investigations and additional audit procedures.

Q: What are some examples of business risks that an auditor might identify?

A: Examples of business risks include operational inefficiencies, market competition, regulatory changes, technological obsolescence, and financial instability.

Q: How does an auditor's understanding of a company's industry affect their assessment of business risk?

A: An understanding of the industry helps auditors identify potential business risks specific to that industry, which might not be evident in a general risk assessment.

Q: Can an auditor's assessment of business risk change during an audit?

A: Yes, an auditor's assessment of business risk can change during an audit as more information is gathered and different factors come to light.

Q: How does business risk impact an auditor's judgment on materiality?

A: Higher business risk could lead to lower materiality thresholds, as the potential for financial misstatements that could influence economic decisions increases.

Q: How does an auditor assess the management's strategy for managing business risks?

A: The auditor evaluates the management's approach by looking at their risk management policies, control activities, and monitoring mechanisms.

Q: What is the role of internal control in managing business risk?

A: Effective internal controls can help mitigate business risks by ensuring accurate financial reporting, efficient operations, and compliance with laws and regulations.

Q: How does business risk affect the nature, timing, and extent of audit procedures?

A: Higher levels of business risk may require more extensive audit procedures, performed at different times or focusing on different areas than initially planned.

Q: How does an auditor communicate identified business risks to the management?

A: The auditor communicates business risks identified during the audit to the management through the management letter or audit report.

Q: Can business risks completely be eliminated?

A: No, business risks cannot be completely eliminated. However, they can be managed and mitigated through effective risk management strategies and controls.

Q: How does the external environment affect a company's business risks?

A: The external environment, including economic conditions, industry trends, and regulatory changes, can introduce new business risks or exacerbate existing ones.

Q: What is the connection between business risk and going concern issues?

A: Significant business risks may raise doubts about a company's ability to continue as a going concern, which is a crucial consideration in an audit.

Q: How does an auditor consider a company's business model in assessing business risk?

A: The business model can reveal potential risks related to the company's operations, revenue generation, cost structure, and dependencies on specific resources or markets.

Q: What are some potential consequences of failing to identify significant business risks during an audit?

A: Failing to identify significant business risks can lead to an incorrect audit opinion, legal liability for the auditor, and potential financial loss for the company's stakeholders.

Q: How does technology impact business risk and the audit process?
A: Technology can both introduce new business risks, such as cyber threats, and provide new tools for auditors to identify and assess these risks more effectively.
Q: How can an understanding of a company's culture and values help in assessing business risk?
A: The company's culture and values can indicate its attitude towards risk-taking, which can influence the likelihood and potential impact of business risks.
Q: How does an auditor evaluate the effectiveness of a company's risk management system?
A: The auditor evaluates the risk management system's design, implementation, and operating effectiveness, often through techniques like walkthroughs and testing of controls.
Q: How does an auditor's professional skepticism relate to the assessment of business risks?
A: Professional skepticism helps auditors question the evidence and challenge management's assertions, which can lead to a more accurate and comprehensive assessment of business risks.
Q: Can business risks lead to fraud risk?
A: Yes, some business risks, especially those related to financial pressures or incentives, can increase the risk of fraud within the organization.
Q: How does an auditor's knowledge of a company's governance structure affect their assessment of business risk?
A: The governance structure can reveal the company's risk management capabilities, accountability mechanisms, and potential vulnerabilities to risks such as fraud or mismanagement.
Q: Should auditors consider business risks that are outside the company's control?

A: Yes, auditors should consider all significant business risks, including those outside the company's control, as they can still impact the financial statements.

Q: How does an auditor's understanding of a company's competitive position affect their assessment of business risk?

A: The competitive position can reveal risks related to market share, pricing power, and dependence on key customers or suppliers.

Q: What role does a company's strategy play in determining its business risks?

A: The company's strategy, including its growth plans, market focus, and competitive tactics, can create or amplify certain business risks.

Q: How do auditors use analytical procedures in assessing business risks?

A: Analytical procedures, such as ratio analysis and trend analysis, can help identify unusual patterns or changes that may indicate potential business risks.

Q: What is the connection between business risk and inherent risk in an audit?

A: Business risk contributes to inherent risk, which is the susceptibility of an assertion to a material misstatement, assuming there are no related controls.

Q: How does an auditor consider the impact of business risks on the company's future performance?

A: The auditor considers the potential impact of business risks on future performance by evaluating the company's plans, forecasts, and risk management strategies.

Q: How can an understanding of a company's supply chain help in assessing business risk?

A: The supply chain can reveal risks related to supplier reliability, cost fluctuations, and disruptions in the availability of key inputs.

Q: What is the role of a company's risk appetite in determining its business risks?
A: The company's risk appetite, or the level of risk it is willing to accept, can influence the nature and extent of its business risks.
Q: How does an auditor consider the impact of business risks on the company's cash flows?
A: The auditor considers the potential impact of business risks on cash flows by evaluating the company's liquidity, profitability, and financial stability.
Q: How does an understanding of a company's customer base help in assessing business risk?
A: The customer base can reveal risks related to customer concentration, demand fluctuations, and changes in consumer preferences or buying behavior.
Q: How do auditors use their knowledge of a company's past performance in assessing business risk?
A: Past performance can provide insights into the company's risk management capabilities, recurring issues, and potential vulnerabilities to future risks.
Q: How does an auditor evaluate the potential impact of business risks on the company's asset values?
A: The auditor evaluates the potential impact of business risks on asset values by considering factors like impairment, obsolescence, and depreciation.
Q: How does an auditor consider the impact of business risks on the company's liabilities?
A: The auditor considers the potential impact of business risks on liabilities by evaluating the company's debt levels, contingent liabilities, and financial commitments.
Q: How can an understanding of a company's operational processes help in assessing business risk?

A: Operational processes can reveal risks related to efficiency, quality control, and compliance with operational standards or regulations.

Q: How does an auditor consider the management's risk tolerance in assessing business risk?

A: The management's risk tolerance, or the level of risk they are comfortable with, can influence the company's risk-taking behavior and exposure to business risks.

Q: How does an understanding of a company's technology systems help in assessing business risk?

A: Technology systems can reveal risks related to data integrity, system reliability, and susceptibility to cyber threats.

Q: How does an auditor consider the impact of business risks on the company's equity?

A: The auditor considers the potential impact of business risks on equity by evaluating the company's retained earnings, dividends, and capital structure.

Q: How does an auditor consider the impact of business risks on the company's revenue?

A: The auditor considers the potential impact of business risks on revenue by evaluating the company's sales trends, pricing strategy, and market conditions.

Q: How does an auditor consider the impact of business risks on the company's expenses?

A: The auditor considers the potential impact of business risks on expenses by evaluating the company's cost structure, efficiency, and spending patterns.

Q: How does an understanding of a company's human resources help in assessing business risk?

A: Human resources can reveal risks related to employee turnover, labor relations, and compliance with labor laws or regulations.

Q: How does an auditor consider the impact of business risks on the company's investment activities?

A: The auditor considers the potential impact of business risks on investment activities by evaluating the company's investment strategy, portfolio, and market conditions.

Q: How does an understanding of a company's legal and regulatory environment help in assessing business risk?

A: The legal and regulatory environment can reveal risks related to compliance, litigation, and changes in laws or regulations.

Q: How does an auditor consider the impact of business risks on the company's financing activities?

A: The auditor considers the potential impact of business risks on financing activities by evaluating the company's borrowing costs, creditworthiness, and financial covenants.

Q: How can an understanding of a company's research and development activities help in assessing business risk?

A: Research and development activities can reveal risks related to innovation, intellectual property, and the success of new products or services.

Q: How does an understanding of a company's marketing and sales activities help in assessing business risk?

A: Marketing and sales activities can reveal risks related to market penetration, brand reputation, and customer satisfaction.

Applications

Scenario 1

A company in the retail industry has planned to introduce a new product line, but the market reaction is unpredictable. How does this affect the auditing process?

In this scenario, the inherent business risk is high due to market unpredictability. As an auditor, the focus should be on assessing the assumptions and projections made by the company in their financial statements. If the auditor finds that the company has been overly optimistic about the product's success, it could lead to material misstatements in the financial reports. This requires the auditor to perform more detailed testing and exercise professional skepticism.

Scenario 2

A manufacturing company has recently changed their supply chain process resulting in numerous delays and errors. How does this impact the auditing process and what steps should be taken? This change increases the operational risk. The auditor must assess the controls implemented to manage the new supply chain process. If the controls are weak or ineffective, it could result in misstatements in the inventory and cost of goods sold. The auditor should recommend the company to enhance their controls and conduct a thorough review of the inventory and related transactions.

Scenario 3

A financial institution has been flagged for potential fraudulent activities. How can this situation impact the auditing process and what approach should be taken?

This scenario introduces a high level of business risk due to potential legal and reputational damages. The auditor has to exercise extreme caution and carry out a rigorous audit focusing on areas susceptible to fraud. They should employ forensic auditing techniques, interview employees, and review internal controls. If any evidence of fraud is detected, it must be reported to the appropriate authorities.

Scenario 4

A tech startup is heavily reliant on a single customer for a significant portion of its revenue. What are the implications for the audit and what measures should be taken?

This situation presents a high business risk as the loss of the customer could significantly impact the company's revenue. The auditor should assess the company's ability to continue as a going concern and the impact on the revenue recognition. They should also confirm the existence of the customer and the accuracy of the revenue recorded from them.

Scenario 5

A pharmaceutical company is facing regulatory issues and potential lawsuits. How does this impact the auditing process? The regulatory issues and potential lawsuits introduce legal and compliance risks. The auditor needs to understand the nature of the regulatory issues and potential financial implications. They should also review the company's provision for legal claims and whether it is adequate. In this situation, obtaining a legal confirmation letter from the company's attorneys would be beneficial. The auditor should also assess the impact on the company's reputation and future earnings.

Control Risk

Theoretical

Q: What is control risk in auditing?

A: Control risk in auditing refers to the risk that a misstatement may occur in an account balance or class of transactions due to the absence or failure of internal controls.

Q: How does control risk impact an audit?

A: Control risk impacts an audit as it helps auditors determine the amount of substantive testing required. High control risk implies more substantive testing.

Q: What are the elements of control risk?

A: The elements of control risk include the design and implementation of internal controls and their effectiveness in preventing or detecting misstatements on a timely basis.

Q: How can auditors assess control risk?

A: Auditors assess control risk by understanding the client's internal control system, testing the controls, and evaluating their effectiveness.

Q: What is the difference between control risk and detection risk?

A: Control risk pertains to the effectiveness of a client's internal controls, while detection risk refers to the risk that an auditor will not detect a material misstatement.

Q: Can control risk be completely eliminated?

A: No, control risk cannot be completely eliminated as no internal control system can be entirely foolproof.

Q: What is the relationship between control risk and inherent risk?

A: Control risk and inherent risk are interrelated. If inherent risk is high, control risk must be kept low to maintain an acceptable audit risk level.

Q: What factors increase control risk?

A: Factors that increase control risk include weak internal controls, lack of segregation of duties, and lack of proper authorization procedures.

Q: Is control risk always assessed at a high level?

A: No, the level of control risk is assessed based on the auditor's judgment of the effectiveness of the client's internal controls.

Q: How can control risk be minimized?

A: Control risk can be minimized by implementing and maintaining effective internal controls, regular monitoring, and timely correction of identified control deficiencies.

Q: What role does control risk play in the audit risk model?

A: Control risk is one of the components of the audit risk model, which helps determine the acceptable level of audit risk.

Q: What is the impact of control risk on audit planning?

A: The level of control risk influences the nature, timing, and extent of audit procedures.

Q: How can auditors mitigate control risk?

A: Auditors can mitigate control risk by performing tests of controls and substantive tests to ensure the effectiveness of the client's internal controls.

Q: How is control risk related to material misstatement?

A: Control risk is directly related to the occurrence of material misstatements, as ineffective controls increase the likelihood of such misstatements.

Q: What is the impact of a high control risk on the auditor's opinion?

A: A high control risk may lead to a qualified or adverse auditor's opinion if the auditor believes that misstatements may exist that could be material and pervasive.

Q: What does a low control risk imply?

A: A low control risk implies that the client's internal control system is effective, reducing the likelihood of material misstatements.

Q: How does control risk affect audit fees?

A: High control risk may lead to higher audit fees as the auditor will need to perform more extensive tests and procedures to mitigate the risk.

Q: What is the role of internal audit in managing control risk?

A: The internal audit function helps manage control risk by regularly evaluating the effectiveness of internal controls and recommending improvements.

Q: Can control risk be negative?

A: No, control risk cannot be negative. It ranges from zero (no risk) to one (certainty of risk).

Q: How does control risk affect the reliability of financial statements?

A: High control risk may affect the reliability of financial statements as it increases the possibility of material misstatements.

Q: What are the consequences of ignoring control risk in an audit?

A: Ignoring control risk can lead to undetected material misstatements, resulting in an inaccurate audit opinion.

Q: How is control risk linked to fraud risk in an audit?

A: Ineffective controls increase control risk and provide opportunities for fraud, thereby increasing fraud risk.

Q: What is the significance of control risk in a financial statement audit?

A: The significance of control risk in a financial statement audit lies in its influence on the auditor's opinion of the fairness and accuracy of the financial statements.

Q: How does technology impact control risk?

A: Technology both reduces control risk by automating controls and increases it due to risks like cyber threats and system failures.

Q: How does control risk affect audit sampling?

A: A high control risk requires larger audit samples for testing, while a low control risk allows for smaller samples.

Q: How does the auditor document control risk?

A: The auditor documents control risk in audit working papers, documenting their understanding of the client's internal controls and the assessed level of control risk.

Q: Can auditors rely entirely on a client's internal controls to reduce control risk?

A: No, while effective internal controls can reduce control risk, auditors cannot solely rely on them and must perform their independent tests.

Q: How does control risk impact the audit risk model?

A: Control risk is a component of the audit risk model. A high control risk results in a lower detection risk to maintain a constant audit risk.

Q: How can management mitigate control risk?

A: Management can mitigate control risk by implementing robust internal controls, ensuring segregation of duties, and establishing effective monitoring and review processes.

Q: What is the role of the audit committee in managing control risk?

A: The audit committee oversees the effectiveness of internal controls and the audit process, thereby helping manage control risk.

Q: How does control risk affect the scope of an audit?

A: High control risk expands the scope of an audit, requiring more extensive testing, while low control risk narrows the scope.
Q: What is the relationship between control risk and audit evidence?
A: The level of control risk influences the amount and type of audit evidence the auditor needs to collect.
Q: Can control risk change over time?
A: Yes, control risk can change over time due to changes in the client's business environment, internal controls, and other factors.
Q: How can auditors reduce control risk?
A: Auditors cannot directly reduce control risk as it's managed by the client. However, they can advise the client on improving their internal controls.
Q: How does control risk affect the auditor's reliance on client representations?
A: High control risk reduces the auditor's reliance on client representations due to the increased possibility of material misstatements.
Q: How is control risk assessed in a computerized environment?
A: In a computerized environment, control risk is assessed by evaluating controls over data input, processing, output, and storage, including general and application controls.
Q: What is the role of control risk in determining materiality in an audit?
A: The level of control risk influences the determination of materiality in an audit. High control risk may require a lower materiality level.
Q: How does control risk impact the audit report?
A: A high control risk may lead to a modified audit report if the auditor believes that there are material misstatements due to weak controls.
Q: What is the role of control risk in substantive testing?

A: Control risk influences the extent of substantive testing. High control risk requires more extensive substantive testing.

Q: How does control risk affect the assessment of going concern in an audit?

A: High control risk may raise concerns about the client's ability to continue as a going concern if it indicates significant operational or financial issues.

Q: How is control risk related to audit judgment?

A: The assessment of control risk involves significant professional judgment to evaluate the design, implementation, and effectiveness of internal controls.

Q: How does an increase in control risk impact the audit strategy?

A: An increase in control risk may require a change in audit strategy, involving more extensive substantive testing and less reliance on the client's internal controls.

Q: How is control risk linked to audit quality?

A: Effective management of control risk contributes to higher audit quality by reducing the likelihood of undetected material misstatements.

Q: What is the impact of control risk on audit risk?

A: Control risk directly impacts audit risk. A high control risk increases audit risk unless counterbalanced by a decrease in inherent risk or detection risk.

Q: How does control risk affect the auditor's reliance on internal audit?

A: High control risk may reduce the auditor's reliance on the work of internal audit if it indicates weaknesses in the overall control environment.

Q: How does control risk impact the assessment of fraud risk?

A: Control risk impacts the assessment of fraud risk as weak controls increase the opportunity for fraud.

Q: How can control risk be monitored?

A: Control risk can be monitored through regular internal audits, management reviews, and external audits.

Q: Can control risk be quantified?

A: While control risk is typically assessed qualitatively, some auditors may use quantitative measures like statistical analysis to assess it.

Q: How does control risk affect the auditor's communication with management and those charged with governance?

A: The auditor's assessment of control risk forms part of their communication with management and those charged with governance, particularly regarding deficiencies in internal control.

Q: How does control risk impact the auditor's professional skepticism?

A: High control risk heightens the auditor's professional skepticism, requiring more rigorous questioning and testing of the information provided by the client.

Applications

Scenario: An online retail company has implemented a new inventory management system. The system is supposed to automatically update the inventory count whenever an item is sold. However, the auditors have noted discrepancies in the inventory counts during their audit.

Problem: The auditors suspect a control risk where the new system may not be updating the inventory correctly. They want to evaluate the effectiveness of the control measures put in place by the company to ensure the accuracy of inventory counts.

Solution: The auditors can test the system by randomly selecting transactions and comparing the system's inventory count against the physical count. If discrepancies are found, they can recommend improvements in the system or the implementation of additional control measures.

Scenario: A bank has outsourced its loan processing function to a third-party service provider. The service provider is responsible for verifying the creditworthiness of loan applicants and processing loan applications.

Problem: The auditors are concerned about the control risk that the service provider may not be adequately verifying the creditworthiness of loan applicants, which could lead to the bank approving loans to high-risk borrowers.

Solution: The auditors can evaluate the effectiveness of the bank's control measures by reviewing the service provider's procedures for verifying the creditworthiness of loan applicants. They can also review a sample of loan applications processed by the service provider to determine if the procedures were followed correctly.

Scenario: A pharmaceutical company has established a process for the approval and release of new drugs. This process includes several checks and balances to ensure that only safe and effective drugs are released.

Problem: The auditors have identified a control risk where the company's process for releasing new drugs may not be effective in preventing the release of unsafe or ineffective drugs.

Solution: The auditors can evaluate the effectiveness of the company's control measures by reviewing the process for releasing new drugs. They can also review a sample of new drugs released by the company to determine if the process was followed correctly.

Scenario: A global corporation has implemented a complex tax strategy to minimize its tax liability. This strategy involves several transactions that are designed to shift income to lower-tax jurisdictions.

Problem: The auditors are concerned about the control risk that the corporation may not be accurately reporting its income for tax purposes, which could lead to penalties and additional tax liabilities.

Solution: The auditors can evaluate the effectiveness of the corporation's control measures by reviewing the transactions involved in the tax strategy. They can also review the corporation's tax returns to determine if the income was reported correctly.

Scenario: A manufacturing company has a policy of conducting regular maintenance on its machinery to prevent breakdowns and ensure efficient production.

Problem: The auditors have identified a control risk where the company may not be conducting the regular maintenance as per its policy, which could lead to breakdowns and production losses.

Solution: The auditors can evaluate the effectiveness of the company's control measures by reviewing the maintenance records of the machinery. They can also physically inspect the machinery to determine if it is in good working condition.

Detection Risk

Theoretical

Q: What is the definition of detection risk in auditing?

A: Detection risk in auditing refers to the risk that an auditor will not detect a material misstatement that exists in an entity's financial statements.

Q: How does detection risk relate to audit risk?

A: Detection risk is a component of audit risk, along with inherent risk and control risk. Lowering detection risk reduces the overall audit risk.

Q: What factors could increase detection risk?

A: Factors that could increase detection risk include lack of auditor's competence, inadequate audit procedures, and time pressure during the audit process.

Q: How can an auditor reduce detection risk?

A: Detection risk can be reduced by implementing effective audit procedures, rigorous staff training, and careful review of audit evidence.

Q: Is detection risk directly or inversely related to inherent risk and control risk?

A: The relationship between detection risk and both inherent and control risk is inverse. When inherent and control risks are elevated, auditors are obligated to lower detection risk to keep the overall audit risk at an acceptable threshold.

Q: Why is the assessment of detection risk important in an audit?

A: Assessing detection risk helps the auditor to determine the extent of substantive testing needed to achieve an acceptable level of audit risk.

Q: What is the consequence of high detection risk?

A: High detection risk increases the chance that the auditor will not detect material misstatements in the financial statements, which could lead to an incorrect audit opinion.

Q: Can detection risk ever be eliminated entirely?

A: No, detection risk can never be entirely eliminated because of the inherent limitations of an audit, such as the use of sampling and the fact that most audit evidence is persuasive rather than conclusive.

Q: How is detection risk related to audit evidence?

A: The more persuasive the audit evidence, the lower the detection risk because the auditor has a higher level of assurance that the financial statements are free from material misstatement.

Q: How does the use of technology affect detection risk?

A: The use of technology in auditing, such as data analytics, can help to reduce detection risk by enabling more comprehensive analysis of data and identification of anomalies.

Q: What role does professional skepticism play in managing detection risk?

A: Professional skepticism helps auditors to critically assess audit evidence and reduces the likelihood of overlooking material misstatements, thereby reducing detection risk.

Q: Can materiality levels impact detection risk?

A: Yes, lower materiality levels increase the scope of audit procedures, which can help to reduce detection risk.

Q: What is the relationship between detection risk and audit assurance?

A: They are inversely related. As detection risk decreases, the level of audit assurance increases.

Q: How does an understanding of the client's business affect detection risk?

A: A deep understanding of the client's business can help an auditor identify areas of potential risk and design appropriate audit procedures, thereby reducing detection risk.

Q: How does the auditor's judgment impact detection risk?

A: An auditor's judgment can impact detection risk as it influences the design and selection of audit procedures as well as the interpretation of audit evidence.

Q: How does sampling risk contribute to detection risk?

A: The term sampling risk refers to the potential that an auditor's conclusion based on a sample might not align with the conclusion that would have been reached if the entire population had been evaluated. This risk is a component of detection risk.

Q: How does the nature, timing, and extent of audit procedures impact detection risk?

A: The nature, timing, and extent of audit procedures can significantly impact detection risk. More rigorous procedures, performed at the right time and to the appropriate extent, can help to reduce detection risk.

Q: How does detection risk relate to the concept of reasonable assurance in an audit?

A: Reasonable assurance is achieved when the auditor has reduced audit risk, including detection risk, to an acceptably low level.

Q: How does an error in the auditor's professional judgment affect detection risk?

A: Errors in the auditor's professional judgment can increase detection risk as they may lead to inappropriate audit procedures or misinterpretation of audit evidence.

Q: How does the use of specialists affect detection risk?

A: The use of specialists in areas where the auditor lacks expertise can help to reduce detection risk by providing more reliable audit evidence.

Q: How does the size and complexity of an entity affect detection risk?

A: Larger and more complex entities often have more complex transactions and higher volumes of data, which can increase detection risk if the auditor does not have the necessary resources or expertise to effectively audit such entities.

Q: How does management override of controls impact detection risk?

A: Management override of controls can significantly increase detection risk because it can lead to material misstatements that are not prevented or detected by the entity's internal controls.

Q: How does collusion among management or employees impact detection risk?

A: Collusion can increase detection risk as it can enable material misstatements to occur without being detected by the entity's internal controls or by the auditor.

Q: How does the auditor's understanding of internal control impact detection risk?

A: A thorough understanding of internal control can help the auditor to design effective audit procedures and reduce detection risk.

Q: Why is it necessary for an auditor to assess detection risk at both the financial statement level and the assertion level?

A: This is necessary because the risks and the audit procedures to address them may be different at these two levels.

Q: How does the concept of audit materiality relate to detection risk?

A: Audit materiality affects the level of detection risk that the auditor is willing to accept. Lower materiality levels generally result in lower acceptable levels of detection risk.

Q: How does detection risk impact the auditor's report?

A: If detection risk is high, the auditor may not have sufficient assurance to issue an unqualified opinion, which could affect the auditor's report.

Q: How do changes in an entity's industry or environment affect detection risk?

A: Changes in the entity's industry or environment can introduce new risks of material misstatement, which increases detection risk if the auditor does not appropriately adjust the audit approach.

Q: How does the competence of an entity's personnel affect detection risk?

A: The competence of an entity's personnel can affect the quality of the entity's accounting and internal control systems, which in turn affects detection risk.

Q: How does the complexity of transactions affect detection risk?

A: Complex transactions can be more difficult to audit and may increase the risk of material misstatement, thereby increasing detection risk.

Q: How does the use of estimates in financial reporting affect detection risk?

A: The use of estimates increases the risk of material misstatement due to estimation uncertainty, which in turn increases detection risk.

Q: How does the risk of fraud affect detection risk?

A: The risk of fraud increases detection risk because fraud often involves sophisticated schemes designed to evade detection.

Q: How does the volume of transactions affect detection risk?

A: A high volume of transactions can increase detection risk if the auditor does not have sufficient resources to adequately test all significant transactions.

Q: Can detection risk be managed through the use of analytics?

A: Yes, analytics can help the auditor to identify unusual patterns or trends that may indicate material misstatements, thereby reducing detection risk.

Q: Can an auditor's independence affect detection risk?

A: Yes, a lack of auditor independence can increase detection risk as it may impair the auditor's objectivity and professional skepticism.

Q: How does the timing of the auditor's tests affect detection risk?

A: The timing of the tests can affect detection risk. For example, year-end testing may reduce detection risk compared to interim testing because it covers the entire period.

Q: How does the nature of the auditor's tests affect detection risk?

A: The nature of the tests affects detection risk. For example, substantive tests of details generally reduce detection risk more than tests of controls or analytical procedures.

Q: How does the extent of the auditor's tests affect detection risk?

A: The extent of the tests affects detection risk. Larger sample sizes and more extensive procedures generally reduce detection risk.

Q: How does the risk of non-compliance with laws and regulations affect detection risk?

A: The risk of non-compliance increases detection risk because non-compliance may lead to material misstatements that are difficult to detect.

Q: How does the risk of related party transactions affect detection risk?

A: Related party transactions can increase detection risk because they may not be conducted at arm's length and may be more difficult to audit.

Q: How does the entity's use of IT systems affect detection risk?
A: The use of IT systems affects detection risk because it influences the nature and complexity of the entity's transactions and the effectiveness of its internal controls.
Q: Can the auditor's risk assessment procedures reduce detection risk?
A: Yes, effective risk assessment procedures can help the auditor to identify areas of high risk and design appropriate responses, thereby reducing detection risk.
Q: How does the entity's ethical culture affect detection risk?
A: An entity with a strong ethical culture is less likely to have material misstatements due to fraud, which can reduce detection risk.
Q: Can the auditor's understanding of the entity's operations reduce detection risk?
A: Yes, a deep understanding of the entity's operations can help the auditor to identify areas of potential risk and design effective audit procedures, thereby reducing detection risk.
Q: Can the use of audit software reduce detection risk?
A: Yes, audit software can help the auditor to perform more efficient and effective audit procedures, thereby reducing detection risk.
Q: How do changes in the entity's operations affect detection risk?
A: Changes in the entity's operations can introduce new risks of material misstatement, which increases detection risk if the auditor does not appropriately adjust the audit approach.
Q: How does the entity's financial stability affect detection risk?
A: An entity's financial stability can affect detection risk because financial instability can increase the risk of material misstatement due to fraud or error.

Q: How does the entity's governance structure affect detection risk?

A: The entity's governance structure can affect detection risk because it influences the effectiveness of the entity's internal controls and the likelihood of management override of controls.

Q: How does the use of group audits affect detection risk?

A: Group audits can increase detection risk because of the added complexity and the need to rely on the work of other auditors.

Q: How does the entity's business model affect detection risk?

A: The entity's business model can affect detection risk because it influences the nature and complexity of the entity's transactions and the risks of material misstatement.

Applications

Scenario: The auditors of a manufacturing company, ABC Ltd., are reviewing the company's inventory records. They are aware that there is a risk of not detecting errors or fraud in the inventory records. How do they evaluate and manage the detection risk?

Solution: The auditors can manage the detection risk by increasing the scope and intensity of their audit procedures. They could perform physical counts of the inventory, inspect the purchase and sales documents for irregularities, and scrutinize the inventory valuation methods used by the company. Effectiveness evaluation: This approach is effective in managing detection risk as it increases the auditors' chances of identifying errors or fraud.

Scenario: XYZ Bank's auditors are reviewing the bank's loan portfolio. They are conscious of the detection risk associated with the bank's loans potentially being overvalued or loans being given to uncreditworthy borrowers. How can they manage this detection risk?

Solution: The auditors could manage the detection risk by reviewing the bank's loan approval process, verifying the credentials and creditworthiness of the borrowers, and validating the valuation of the loans. They could also review the bank's loan loss reserves for adequacy. Effectiveness evaluation: This approach is effective as it provides a comprehensive assessment of the bank's loan portfolio and its associated risks.

Scenario: The auditors of a retail store, PQR Ltd., are examining the company's sales revenue records. They are aware of the detection risk associated with the overstatement of sales revenue or recording of fictitious sales. How can they mitigate this detection risk?

Solution: The auditors can mitigate the detection risk by reviewing the sales transactions for irregularities, validating the sales with the corresponding receipts and bank deposits, and scrutinizing the company's revenue recognition policies.

Effectiveness evaluation: This approach is effective as it ensures that the sales revenue is accurately recorded and any discrepancies are quickly identified.

Scenario: DEF Software's auditors are assessing the company's research and development expenses. They are conscious of the detection risk associated with the overstatement of these expenses. How can they manage this detection risk?

Solution: The auditors can manage the detection risk by reviewing the nature and classification of the research and development expenses, verifying the expenses with the corresponding invoices and contracts, and assessing the company's capitalization policies.

Effectiveness evaluation: This approach is effective as it ensures that the research and development expenses are appropriately recorded and any overstatements are swiftly identified.

Scenario: GHI Pharmaceuticals' auditors are reviewing the company's drug approval process. They are aware of the detection risk associated with the company not complying with the necessary regulatory approvals. How can they mitigate this detection risk?

Solution: The auditors can mitigate the detection risk by reviewing the drug approval documentation, verifying the approvals with the appropriate regulatory bodies, and assessing the company's compliance with the regulatory requirements. Effectiveness evaluation: This approach is effective as it ensures that the company is complying with the necessary regulations and any non-compliance is promptly identified.

Fraud Risk

Theoretical

Q: What is fraud risk in auditing?

A: Fraud risk in auditing refers to the potential threat of fraudulent activities occurring during the auditing process. This could involve manipulation of financial data, misrepresentation of information, or non-compliance with established procedures and standards.

Q: What are the types of fraud risks in auditing?

A: The types of fraud risks in auditing are typically categorized into three: fraudulent financial reporting, misappropriation of assets, and corruption.

Q: How does materiality relate to fraud risk in auditing?

A: Materiality is a concept in auditing that refers to the significance of an amount, transaction, or discrepancy. If a material misstatement due to fraud is present, it poses a significant fraud risk in an audit.

Q: What is the role of internal control in managing fraud risk?

A: Internal control systems help in managing fraud risk by setting up procedures and standards that prevent and detect fraudulent activities. This includes managing the control environment, assessing risks, controlling activities, disseminating information and communication, and overseeing everything.

Q: What is the importance of professional skepticism in fraud risk auditing?

A: Professional skepticism entails possessing an inquisitive mindset and conducting a thorough evaluation of audit evidence. It is important in fraud risk auditing as it enables auditors to identify and respond to potential fraud risks.

Q: How does management override of controls contribute to fraud risk?

A: Management override of controls can contribute to fraud risks as it can bypass established internal control systems, allowing fraudulent activities to occur.

Q: What is the significance of understanding the entity and its environment in fraud risk auditing?

A: Understanding the entity and its environment helps auditors identify areas where fraud risk might be high, it also informs the planning and execution of the audit.

Q: How does the auditor's risk assessment process relate to fraud risk?

A: The auditor's risk assessment process involves identifying and assessing the risks of material misstatement due to fraud. It guides the auditor in designing audit procedures to respond to the assessed risks.

Q: What is the role of audit evidence in fraud risk auditing?

A: Audit evidence is crucial in fraud risk auditing as it supports the auditor's findings and conclusions. The quality and sufficiency of audit evidence can affect the detection of fraud.

Q: How does an auditor communicate fraud risk findings?

A: Auditors communicate fraud risk findings through a detailed report that outlines the nature of the fraud, the extent of the risk, and the impact on the financial statements. They also offer recommendations to mitigate the risk.

Q: What is the impact of fraud risk on audit opinion?

A: If a fraud risk is significant and leads to a material misstatement in the financial statements, it could affect the auditor's opinion, possibly leading to a qualified or adverse opinion.

Q: How does the concept of 'significant risk' relate to fraud risk in auditing?

A: Significant risks are those that require special audit consideration due to their high risk of material misstatement. Fraud risk often falls into this category.

Q: What is the relationship between fraud risk factors and fraud risk?

A: Fraud risk factors are events or conditions that indicate an incentive or pressure to perpetrate fraud, or provide an opportunity to commit fraud. They increase the level of fraud risk.

Q: How can an auditor respond to assessed fraud risks?

A: Auditors can respond to assessed fraud risks through various methods such as enhancing their professional skepticism, obtaining more reliable evidence, and incorporating unpredictability in the selection of audit procedures.

Q: How does corporate governance influence fraud risk in auditing?

A: Corporate governance, through its oversight function, can influence fraud risk by promoting an ethical culture, implementing effective internal controls, and ensuring management's accountability.

Q: What is the role of forensic auditing in managing fraud risk?

A: Forensic auditing involves using investigative techniques to detect and prevent fraud. It can be a proactive approach to managing fraud risk.

Q: How does the use of technology impact fraud risk in auditing?

A: The use of technology can both increase and decrease fraud risk. It can increase risk through sophisticated fraudulent schemes, but it can also aid in detecting and preventing fraud through advanced analytical tools.

Q: How does the auditor's understanding of the entity's business model affect fraud risk assessment?

A: The auditor's understanding of the entity's business model can help identify areas where fraud risks may be high, and it can inform the design of audit procedures to respond to these risks.

Q: How does the complexity of transactions influence fraud risk in auditing?

A: The complexity of transactions can increase fraud risk as it provides more opportunities for concealing fraudulent activities.

Q: How can fraud risk be mitigated in an audit?

A: Fraud risk in an audit can be mitigated through effective internal controls, professional skepticism, understanding of the entity and its environment, and appropriate responses to assessed risks.

Q: How does an auditor's liability relate to fraud risk?

A: An auditor's liability increases if they fail to detect and report significant fraud risks, leading to material misstatements in the financial statements.

Q: How does the timing of audit procedures affect fraud risk detection?

A: The timing of audit procedures can affect the detection of fraud risk. Early procedures may allow for timely identification and response, while late procedures may not provide enough time for proper investigation and resolution.

Q: How does the concept of collusion impact fraud risk detection?

A: Collusion, where two or more individuals work together to commit fraud, can increase fraud risk and make detection more difficult due to the coordinated efforts to conceal the fraud.

Q: What is the relationship between the risk of material misstatement and fraud risk?

A: The risk of material misstatement refers to the risk that the financial statements are materially misstated due to error or fraud. Thus, fraud risk directly contributes to the risk of material misstatement.

Q: How does the auditor's independence impact fraud risk detection?

A: The auditor's independence can affect fraud risk detection. An independent auditor is more likely to maintain professional skepticism and uphold audit standards, leading to better detection of fraud risks.

Q: What is the role of an audit committee in managing fraud risk?

A: The audit committee plays a key role in overseeing the financial reporting process, internal controls, and the audit. Its involvement can help manage fraud risk by ensuring transparency and accountability.

Q: How does the size of the entity impact fraud risk in auditing?

A: The size of the entity can impact fraud risk. Larger entities may have more complex operations and transactions, providing more opportunities for fraud. However, they may also have more robust internal controls.

Q: What is the relationship between the auditor's professional judgment and fraud risk?

A: The auditor's professional judgment is crucial in identifying and assessing fraud risk. It involves the application of relevant knowledge and experience in making informed decisions during the audit.

Q: How does the concept of 'reasonable assurance' relate to fraud risk in auditing?

A: Reasonable assurance is the level of confidence that auditors aim to achieve in an audit. However, due to inherent limitations of an audit, absolute assurance of detecting fraud risk is not feasible.

Q: How does the nature of the entity's operations influence fraud risk?

A: The nature of the entity's operations can influence fraud risk. Operations involving cash transactions, high-value assets, or complex transactions can increase the risk of fraud.

Q: What is the role of risk assessment procedures in fraud risk auditing?

A: Risk assessment procedures help in identifying and assessing the risks of material misstatement due to fraud. They guide the auditor in designing and implementing responses to the assessed risks.

Q: How can an auditor use analytical procedures in fraud risk detection?

A: Analytical procedures entail assessing financial data by examining the potential relationships between financial and non-financial information. They can help detect unusual transactions or trends that may indicate fraud risk.

Q: How does the concept of 'fraud triangle' relate to fraud risk in auditing?

A: The fraud triangle is a model that describes three conditions generally present when fraud occurs: pressure, opportunity, and rationalization. It helps auditors identify and assess fraud risks.

Q: How does the auditor's responsibility for fraud detection relate to fraud risk?

A: The auditor has a responsibility to plan and perform the audit to obtain reasonable assurance about whether the financial statements are free from material misstatement, whether due to fraud or error. Thus, the detection of fraud risk is an integral part of the auditor's responsibility.

Q: How can the auditor use substantive procedures in responding to fraud risks?

A: Substantive procedures involve tests of details and analytical procedures. They help the auditor gather evidence to evaluate whether the financial statements are materially misstated due to fraud.

Q: What is the importance of documentation in fraud risk auditing?

A: Documentation is important in fraud risk auditing as it provides evidence of the auditor's findings and conclusions. It also serves as a record of the procedures performed, evidence obtained, and basis for the auditor's conclusions.

Q: How does the auditor's understanding of the entity's industry affect fraud risk assessment?

A: The auditor's understanding of the entity's industry can help identify industry-specific risks and practices that may contribute to fraud risk. It can also aid in understanding the entity's business model and operations.

Q: How does the use of specialists impact fraud risk detection?

A: Specialists, such as forensic auditors or IT auditors, can bring unique skills and expertise that can enhance fraud risk detection, especially in complex or specialized areas.

Q: What is the impact of fraud risk on other areas of the audit?

A: Fraud risk can affect other areas of the audit as it may influence the auditor's overall risk assessment, the design and performance of audit procedures, and the auditor's conclusions and reporting.

Q: How does the auditor's knowledge of the entity's internal audit function affect fraud risk assessment?

A: The auditor's knowledge of the entity's internal audit function can provide insights into the effectiveness of internal controls, which can affect the assessment of fraud risk.

Q: How does the concept of 'pervasive' relate to fraud risk in auditing?
A: Pervasive refers to the effects of misstatements or fraud risks that are not confined to specific elements, accounts, or items of the financial statements. If a fraud risk is pervasive, it could significantly affect the overall audit.
Q: How can the auditor use external confirmation procedures in fraud risk detection?
A: External confirmation procedures involve obtaining audit evidence directly from third parties. They can provide reliable evidence and help detect fraud risks, especially in areas such as receivables and payables.
Q: What is the role of management representation in fraud risk auditing?
A: Management representation is a form of audit evidence where management provides written assertions to the auditor. However, it is not sufficient alone to detect fraud risk as management may be involved in the fraud.
Q: How does the auditor's consideration of laws and regulations relate to fraud risk?
A: The auditor's consideration of laws and regulations is important as non-compliance may indicate fraud. It can also affect the auditor's assessment of fraud risks and the design of audit procedures.
Q: How does the concept of 'assertions' relate to fraud risk in auditing?
A: Assertions are claims made by management in the financial statements. Fraud risk relates to the risk that these assertions are not consistent with the underlying transactions and events due to intentional misstatements.
Q: How can an auditor use journal entry testing in fraud risk detection?

A: Journal entry testing involves examining the entity's journal entries for evidence of fraudulent financial reporting. It can help detect fraud risks, especially in areas such as revenue recognition and management override of controls.

Q: How does the auditor's understanding of the entity's accounting policies affect fraud risk assessment?

A: The auditor's understanding of the entity's accounting policies can help identify areas where management has significant judgment, which could be manipulated to commit fraud.

Q: What is the importance of group audits in managing fraud risk?

A: In group audits, the group auditor needs to consider the fraud risk at the group level and at the component level. Effective communication and coordination among the audit team can help manage fraud risk.

Q: How does the concept of 'related parties' relate to fraud risk in auditing?

A: Related parties and related party transactions can pose significant fraud risks as they may not be conducted under normal market conditions. They may be used to conceal fraud or manipulate financial results.

Q: How can the auditor use computer-assisted audit techniques (CAATs) in fraud risk detection?

A: CAATs can help detect fraud risks by analyzing large volumes of data, identifying unusual patterns or trends, and testing controls over automated systems.

Applications

Scenario 1: A large multinational corporation has recently been discovered to have a significant amount of false transactions and expenses, leading to inflated financial reports. The auditors had previously given a clean report. What could have been the possible lapses in auditing that led to this situation and how can it be rectified?

The auditors may have overlooked certain areas in their scrutiny or could have ignored some red flags due to negligence or collusion. To rectify this, an in-depth investigation must be conducted to identify the areas of failure. Additionally, the audit team must be trained in fraud detection techniques, and an audit plan must be developed that focuses on areas with high fraud risk.

Scenario 2: A retail company has been found to have inconsistencies in its inventory records, suggesting potential inventory fraud. What steps should an auditor take to investigate and prevent this?

The auditor should first confirm the discrepancies through a physical inventory count. Then, they should scrutinize the purchase and sales records to identify any irregularities. To prevent such issues, the auditor should establish a system of internal controls to monitor inventory and implement a segregation of duties to avoid conflicts of interest.

Scenario 3: A tech start-up is suspected to be overstating its revenue by recognizing it prematurely. How can an auditor verify this and what measures can be taken to prevent this?

An auditor can verify this by reviewing the company's revenue recognition policies and comparing it with the actual practices. They can also analyze the timing and pattern of revenue recognition for any anomalies. To prevent this, the auditor should recommend the implementation of robust internal controls, including a clear revenue recognition policy.

Scenario 4: A hospital is suspected of fraudulent billing practices. What steps should an auditor take in investigating this?

The auditor should first review the billing records and compare it with the service records to identify any discrepancies. They should also interview the staff involved in billing to understand the process and identify potential loopholes. To prevent this, the auditor should recommend a proper system of checks and balances in the billing process.

Scenario 5: A non-profit organization is suspected of diverting funds for personal use. How should an auditor respond to this situation?

The auditor must examine the organization's financial records in detail, tracing the flow of funds to identify any misappropriations. They should also review the internal controls in place and recommend improvements if necessary. Regular audits and transparent financial reporting can help prevent such situations.

Sampling Risk

Theoretical

Question: What is Sampling Risk in Auditing?

Answer: Sampling risk in auditing refers to the possibility that the auditor's conclusions, based on a sample of data, may be different from the conclusions they would reach if they examined all the data.

Question: What are the two types of sampling risks in auditing?

Answer: The two types of sampling risks are the risk of incorrect acceptance and the risk of incorrect rejection.

Question: What is the risk of incorrect acceptance in auditing?

Answer: The risk of incorrect acceptance refers to the possibility that the auditor may incorrectly determine that there isn't a significant error when in reality, there is.

Question: What is the risk of incorrect rejection in auditing?

Answer: The risk of incorrect rejection refers to the possibility that the auditor mistakenly determines there is a significant error when there actually isn't one.

Question: How can an auditor reduce sampling risk?

Answer: An auditor can reduce sampling risk by increasing the sample size or by using an appropriate sampling technique.

Question: How does increasing the sample size affect sampling risk?

Answer: Increasing the sample size generally reduces the sampling risk because it provides a more accurate representation of the population.

Question: What is the relationship between the confidence level and sampling risk?
Answer: The confidence level and sampling risk are inversely related. Increasing the confidence level decreases the sampling risk and vice versa.
Question: How does stratification affect sampling risk?
Answer: Stratification, or dividing the population into separate groups, can reduce sampling risk by ensuring that the sample is representative of the overall population.
Question: What role does judgment play in managing sampling risk?
Answer: Auditor's judgment is essential in managing sampling risk. It helps in determining the appropriate sample size and in selecting the most appropriate sampling method.
Question: How does the use of statistical sampling affect sampling risk?
Answer: Statistical sampling provides a measure of sampling risk and allows the auditor to quantify the risk and make more informed decisions.
Question: What is non-sampling risk?
Answer: Non-sampling risk is the risk that the auditor reaches an incorrect conclusion for any reason not related to sampling risk.
Question: How is sampling risk different from non-sampling risk?
Answer: While sampling risk arises from the use of a sample rather than a full population, non-sampling risk arises from factors such as lack of auditor competence, misinterpretation of data, and inappropriate audit procedures.
Question: Can sampling risk be eliminated?
Answer: Sampling risk can never be completely eliminated, but it can be managed and minimized through appropriate sample size and sampling techniques.
Question: What is the impact of sampling risk on audit quality?

Answer: High sampling risk can compromise audit quality as it may lead to incorrect conclusions and decisions.

Question: How can auditors manage sampling risk in the fieldwork stage?

Answer: Auditors can manage sampling risk in the fieldwork stage by using appropriate audit techniques, increasing the sample size, and using statistical sampling methods.

Question: What is the role of professional skepticism in managing sampling risk?

Answer: Professional skepticism allows auditors to critically assess audit evidence, reducing the chance of incorrect acceptance or rejection and thus managing sampling risk.

Question: How does materiality affect sampling risk?

Answer: The higher the materiality level, the higher the sampling risk as the auditor is willing to accept a higher risk of misstatement.

Question: How does inherent risk and control risk affect sampling risk?

Answer: If inherent and control risks are high, auditors will typically reduce the level of sampling risk they are willing to accept, meaning they may choose a larger sample size.

Question: How does the auditor's risk tolerance affect sampling risk?

Answer: The auditor's risk tolerance determines the acceptable level of sampling risk. A lower risk tolerance would require a larger sample size to reduce sampling risk.

Question: What is the role of audit evidence in managing sampling risk?

Answer: The quality and quantity of audit evidence collected can help manage sampling risk. Strong, relevant, and sufficient evidence reduces the likelihood of incorrect conclusions.

Question: How does the complexity of a population affect sampling risk?
Answer: The more complex a population, the greater the sampling risk. This is because it becomes more challenging to select a sample that is representative of the entire population.
Question: What is the relationship between audit risk and sampling risk?
Answer: Audit risk and sampling risk are directly related. A high level of sampling risk increases the overall audit risk.
Question: How does the use of technology impact sampling risk?
Answer: The use of technology can reduce sampling risk by enabling auditors to analyze larger data sets and make more accurate judgements.
Question: What is the role of internal controls in managing sampling risk?
Answer: Effective internal controls can reduce the likelihood of misstatements, thus helping to manage sampling risk.
Question: How does the concept of materiality relate to sampling risk?
Answer: Materiality is a threshold above which misstatements or omissions are considered to impact a user's decision. If misstatements below this threshold are accepted, it increases the sampling risk.
Question: How can an auditor mitigate the risk of incorrect acceptance?
Answer: An auditor can mitigate the risk of incorrect acceptance by increasing the sample size, using statistical sampling techniques, and applying professional skepticism when evaluating audit evidence.
Question: How can an auditor mitigate the risk of incorrect rejection?

Answer: The risk of incorrect rejection can be mitigated by thorough review and reevaluation of audit evidence, and by retesting the sample if necessary.
Question: Is sampling risk more significant in large or small populations?
Answer: The size of the population doesn't affect sampling risk. It's more about the representativeness of the sample selected.
Question: Can an auditor accept a certain level of sampling risk?
Answer: Yes, an auditor can accept a certain level of sampling risk. The acceptable level of risk is determined by the auditor's risk tolerance.
Question: How does sampling risk impact the auditor's opinion?
Answer: If sampling risk is high, it may lead to incorrect conclusions and incorrectly influence the auditor's opinion.
Question: What factors should an auditor consider when determining sample size to manage sampling risk?
Answer: The auditor should consider factors like the level of sampling risk they're willing to accept, the population characteristics, and the nature of the audit procedure.
Question: What is the role of substantive testing in managing sampling risk?
Answer: Substantive testing, which involves detailed testing of transactions and balances, can help manage sampling risk by providing additional evidence and assurance.
Question: How does sampling risk affect the reliability of audit evidence?
Answer: High levels of sampling risk can reduce the reliability of audit evidence, as the sample may not be representative of the entire population.
Question: How does systematic sampling impact sampling risk?
Answer: Systematic sampling can reduce sampling risk if the selection interval is not correlated with the occurrence of

misstatements. However, if such a correlation exists, it could increase the sampling risk.

Question: How can an auditor use their judgement to manage sampling risk?

Answer: An auditor can use their judgement to select appropriate sampling methods, determine the sample size, and interpret the results, all of which can help manage sampling risk.

Question: How can the risk of incorrect acceptance impact the financial statements?

Answer: The risk of incorrect acceptance can lead to material misstatements in the financial statements, which can mislead users of the financial statements.

Question: How is sampling risk related to audit assurance?

Answer: Sampling risk is inversely related to audit assurance. High sampling risk means lower audit assurance and vice versa.

Question: Can sampling risk be quantified?

Answer: Yes, sampling risk can be quantified, especially when statistical sampling methods are used.

Question: How does the auditor's understanding of the client's business affect sampling risk?

Answer: A deep understanding of the client's business can help the auditor make better judgements about sampling, potentially reducing sampling risk.

Question: How does the risk of incorrect acceptance differ from the risk of incorrect rejection in terms of their impact on the audit?

Answer: The risk of incorrect acceptance is more severe as it can lead to the auditor issuing an inappropriate audit opinion, while the risk of incorrect rejection leads to extra audit work but does not affect the audit opinion.

Question: How does the risk of material misstatement relate to sampling risk?

Answer: The risk of material misstatement is considered when determining the acceptable level of sampling risk. If the risk of material misstatement is high, the auditor would typically aim for a lower sampling risk.

Question: How does the use of audit software impact sampling risk?

Answer: Audit software can reduce sampling risk by facilitating data analysis, increasing the efficiency of sampling procedures, and allowing for larger sample sizes.

Question: How does the risk of incorrect rejection affect the audit process?

Answer: The risk of incorrect rejection may lead to additional audit work, as the auditor may decide to perform further tests to investigate the potential misstatement.

Question: How does the auditor's expectation of error affect sampling risk?

Answer: If the auditor expects a high level of errors, they may choose a larger sample size to reduce sampling risk.

Question: How do audit standards guide the management of sampling risk?

Answer: Audit standards provide guidelines on how to select sample sizes, choose appropriate sampling methods, and evaluate sampling results, all of which help manage sampling risk.

Question: How does the auditor's competence affect sampling risk?

Answer: An auditor's competence can greatly impact sampling risk. A competent auditor is more likely to select appropriate samples and correctly interpret results, thus reducing sampling risk.

Question: How does the nature of the audit procedure affect sampling risk?

Answer: The nature of the audit procedure affects the level of assurance it provides. Procedures providing higher assurance often involve lower sampling risk.

Question: How does the timing of the audit procedure affect sampling risk?

Answer: The timing of the audit procedure can affect sampling risk. For instance, performing procedures at year-end may involve lower sampling risk compared to interim procedures, as there is less time for misstatements to occur.

Question: What is the relationship between the tolerable error and sampling risk?

Answer: The tolerable error and sampling risk are inversely related. A lower tolerable error requires a lower sampling risk, which often means a larger sample size.

Question: How does the use of professional judgement in sample selection impact sampling risk?

Answer: The use of professional judgement in sample selection can help reduce sampling risk by ensuring that the sample is representative of the population.

Applications

Scenario 1: A small manufacturing company, Comet Inc., is under audit. The auditor randomly selects 100 invoices out of 10,000 to check for any discrepancies. If the auditor finds discrepancies in 5 invoices, what is the sampling risk and how effective is the audit?

In this scenario, the sampling risk can be described as the possibility that the auditor's findings, based on the sample, may not align with the results that would have been obtained if the whole population had been scrutinized. The auditor found discrepancies in 5% of the selected samples. However, as this is a sample, it might not represent the total population accurately. Therefore, the sampling risk is present. The effectiveness of the audit can be evaluated based on the discrepancy rate and the sampling risk. If the discrepancy rate is high in the population, the audit is not effective.

Scenario 2: Jewel Co. is a large jewellery store chain. The auditor selected every 10th sales transaction to be audited, from a total of 1,000 transactions. The auditor discovered that 20 out of 100 transactions had issues. What is the sampling risk, and how can we evaluate the audit's effectiveness?

The sampling risk here is the probability that the auditor's conclusion based on the sample of every 10th transaction might differ from the conclusion if all 1,000 transactions were audited. In this case, the auditor found that 20% of the audited transactions had issues, which renders a high sampling risk. To evaluate the audit's effectiveness, the auditor should consider the high discrepancy rate and the high sampling risk, and conclude that the audit might not be effective.

Scenario 3: Alpha Corp, a medium-sized tech company, is being audited. The auditor chose to audit 50% of the total transactions. After the audit, the auditor found discrepancies in 2% of the transactions. What is the sampling risk, and how effective was the audit?

In this scenario, the sampling risk is the risk that the auditor's conclusion, based on the 50% audited transactions, may differ from the conclusion if all transactions were audited. Given that discrepancies were found in only 2% of the audited transactions, the sampling risk is relatively low. The effectiveness of the audit can be considered high due to the low discrepancy rate and the low sampling risk.

Scenario 4: Zeta Ltd., a large pharmaceutical company, is under audit. The auditor decided to select 200 transactions randomly from a total of 5,000. The auditor found issues in 15 of the 200 transactions. What is the sampling risk, and how effective is this audit?

The sampling risk in this scenario is the risk that the auditor's conclusion, based on a random sample of 200 transactions, may differ from the conclusion if all 5,000 transactions were audited. The discrepancy rate is 7.5%, which means there is a moderate sampling risk. To evaluate the audit's effectiveness, the auditor should consider the discrepancy rate and the sampling risk. Given the moderate discrepancy rate and sampling risk, the audit is somewhat effective, but improvements can be made.

Strategic Risk

Theoretical

Q: What is strategic risk in auditing?

A: Strategic risk in auditing refers to the potential for loss due to a company's business strategies not panning out as expected.

Q: How can auditors identify strategic risks?

A: Auditors can identify strategic risks by analyzing a company's business model, internal and external environment, and strategic objectives.

Q: How does strategic risk affect the auditing process?

A: Strategic risk can affect the auditing process by introducing uncertainties that might impact the financial statements and the overall financial health of a company.

Q: How can auditors mitigate strategic risks?

A: Auditors can mitigate strategic risks by recommending risk management strategies and internal controls to the management.

Q: What is the role of internal audit in managing strategic risk?

A: The role of internal audit in managing strategic risk is to provide assurance on the effectiveness of risk management processes and internal controls.

Q: How can an organization's strategies impact its risk profile?

A: An organization's strategies can increase or decrease its risk exposure depending on the nature and extent of the risks involved in executing those strategies.

Q: How can strategic risk lead to financial misstatements?

A: Strategic risk can lead to financial misstatements if the company's strategies lead to financial losses that are not correctly reflected in the financial statements.

Q: How can auditors assess the impact of strategic risk on a company's financial performance?

A: Auditors can assess the impact of strategic risk on a company's financial performance by analyzing financial data and comparing actual results with the company's strategic objectives.

Q: What is the impact of strategic risk on the audit risk model?

A: The impact of strategic risk on the audit risk model is that it increases the inherent risk and overall audit risk.

Q: Can strategic risk be eliminated completely?

A: No, strategic risk cannot be eliminated completely. However, it can be managed and mitigated to acceptable levels.

Q: How can auditors help in strategic risk management?

A: Auditors can assist in strategic risk management by providing independent assurance on the effectiveness of risk management processes and internal controls.

Q: How does strategic risk differ from operational risk?

A: While strategic risk is related to a company's strategies, operational risk is related to the day-to-day operations of a company.

Q: How does strategic risk impact a company's reputation?

A: Strategic risk can impact a company's reputation if the company's strategies lead to negative outcomes such as financial losses or legal issues.

Q: How does strategic risk affect a company's competitive position?

A: Strategic risk can affect a company's competitive position if the company's strategies lead to loss of market share or competitive advantage.

Q: How can auditors evaluate the effectiveness of a company's strategic risk management?

A: Auditors can evaluate the effectiveness of a company's strategic risk management by assessing the alignment of strategic objectives with risk management processes and controls.

Q: What are the consequences of not managing strategic risk effectively?

A: The consequences of not managing strategic risk effectively can include financial losses, damage to reputation, loss of competitive advantage, and potential business failure.

Q: How can strategic risk influence the scope of an audit?

A: Strategic risk can influence the scope of an audit by determining the areas of high risk that need more attention during the audit.

Q: How does strategic risk relate to the concept of materiality in auditing?

A: Strategic risk relates to the concept of materiality in auditing as it can lead to material misstatements in the financial statements if not managed effectively.

Q: How does strategic risk affect a company's business continuity?

A: Strategic risk can affect a company's business continuity if the company's strategies lead to severe financial losses or operational disruptions.

Q: How can auditors help in the formulation of a company's strategic risk management policy?

A: Auditors can help in the formulation of a company's strategic risk management policy by providing insights on the potential risks associated with the company's strategies and recommending risk management measures.

Q: How does strategic risk affect the audit planning process?

A: Strategic risk affects the audit planning process by determining the risk areas that need to be included in the audit plan.

Q: How can auditors assess the impact of strategic risk on a company's profitability?

A: Auditors can assess the impact of strategic risk on a company's profitability by analyzing financial data and comparing actual profitability with the company's strategic objectives.

Q: How does strategic risk affect the audit risk assessment?

A: Strategic risk affects the audit risk assessment by influencing the inherent risk and overall audit risk.

Q: How can auditors use strategic risk information in their audit reports?

A: Auditors can use strategic risk information in their audit reports to highlight areas of high risk and recommend risk management measures.

Q: How can auditors help in improving a company's strategic risk management?

A: Auditors can help in improving a company's strategic risk management by providing recommendations for improving risk management processes and internal controls.

Q: Can strategic risk lead to audit failure?

A: Yes, unmanaged strategic risk can lead to audit failure if it results in material misstatements in the financial statements that are not detected during the audit.

Q: How does strategic risk relate to the concept of going concern in auditing?

A: Strategic risk relates to the concept of going concern in auditing as it can impact a company's ability to continue as a going concern if it leads to severe financial losses or operational disruptions.

Q: How does strategic risk affect the audit opinion?

A: Strategic risk can affect the audit opinion if it leads to material misstatements in the financial statements that are not detected and corrected.

Q: How can auditors consider strategic risk in their audit procedures?

A: Auditors can consider strategic risk in their audit procedures by focusing on areas of high risk and designing procedures to detect possible misstatements arising from strategic risk.

Q: How does strategic risk affect the auditor's professional skepticism?

A: Strategic risk can affect the auditor's professional skepticism by increasing the need for a skeptical mindset in assessing the risks associated with a company's strategies.

Q: How can auditors use strategic risk information in their communication with the audit committee?

A: Auditors can use strategic risk information in their communication with the audit committee to highlight areas of high risk and discuss risk management measures.

Q: How does strategic risk affect a company's risk appetite?

A: Strategic risk can affect a company's risk appetite by influencing the level of risk that the company is willing to take in pursuit of its strategic objectives.

Q: How does strategic risk affect the audit evidence collected by auditors?

A: Strategic risk can affect the audit evidence collected by auditors by influencing the nature, timing, and extent of audit procedures.

Q: How does strategic risk affect the auditor's assessment of control risk?

A: Strategic risk can affect the auditor's assessment of control risk by influencing the effectiveness of internal controls in managing strategic risk.

Q: How can auditors assess the impact of strategic risk on a company's cash flows?

A: Auditors can assess the impact of strategic risk on a company's cash flows by analyzing cash flow data and comparing actual cash flows with the company's strategic objectives.

Q: How does strategic risk affect the auditor's reliance on management's representations?

A: Strategic risk can affect the auditor's reliance on management's representations if it leads to misrepresentations about the company's strategies and their impact on the financial statements.

Q: How can auditors use strategic risk information in their risk assessment procedures?

A: Auditors can use strategic risk information in their risk assessment procedures to identify areas of high risk and design appropriate audit procedures.

Q: How does strategic risk affect the auditor's assessment of detection risk?

A: Strategic risk can affect the auditor's assessment of detection risk by influencing the likelihood of misstatements arising from strategic risk being detected during the audit.

Q: How can auditors use strategic risk information in their communication with management?

A: Auditors can use strategic risk information in their communication with management to discuss areas of high risk and recommend risk management measures.

Q: How does strategic risk affect a company's financial stability?

A: Strategic risk can affect a company's financial stability if the company's strategies lead to severe financial losses or operational disruptions.

Q: How can auditors assess the impact of strategic risk on a company's financial position?

A: Auditors can assess the impact of strategic risk on a company's financial position by analyzing financial data and comparing the company's actual financial position with its strategic objectives.

Q: How does strategic risk affect the auditor's assessment of inherent risk?

A: Strategic risk can affect the auditor's assessment of inherent risk by influencing the likelihood of misstatements arising from strategic risk.

Q: How can auditors use strategic risk information in their communication with stakeholders?

A: Auditors can use strategic risk information in their communication with stakeholders to provide information about the company's risk profile and the effectiveness of its risk management.

Q: How does strategic risk affect the auditor's understanding of the entity and its environment?

A: Strategic risk can affect the auditor's understanding of the entity and its environment, as it requires the auditor to consider the risks associated with the company's strategies and their impact on the company's financial and operational performance.

Q: How can auditors assess the impact of strategic risk on a company's operational performance?

A: Auditors can assess the impact of strategic risk on a company's operational performance by analyzing operational data and comparing actual performance with the company's strategic objectives.

Q: How does strategic risk affect the auditor's consideration of fraud risk?

A: Strategic risk can affect the auditor's consideration of fraud risk, as it can create incentives or pressures for management to commit fraud to achieve strategic objectives.

Q: How can auditors use strategic risk information in their audit documentation?

A: Auditors can use strategic risk information in their audit documentation to provide evidence of the audit procedures performed to address strategic risk and the audit findings related to strategic risk.

Q: How does strategic risk affect the auditor's assessment of the risk of material misstatement?

A: Strategic risk can affect the auditor's assessment of the risk of material misstatement by influencing the likelihood and potential impact of misstatements arising from strategic risk.

Q: How can auditors assess the impact of strategic risk on a company's growth prospects?

A: Auditors can assess the impact of strategic risk on a company's growth prospects by analyzing the company's growth projections and comparing them with the company's strategic objectives.

Q: How does strategic risk affect the auditor's evaluation of subsequent events?

A: Strategic risk can affect the auditor's evaluation of subsequent events, as it can influence the events occurring after the balance sheet date that may have a significant impact on the financial statements.

Applications

Question 1:

Scenario: A multinational corporation is considering expanding its operations to a politically unstable country. As an auditor, how would you assess this strategic risk?

Answer: The auditor should evaluate the potential political risks, such as changes in government, potential civil unrest, or changes in laws and regulations. They should also consider the corporation's contingency plans and risk mitigation strategies. The effectiveness of this approach is that it allows the auditor to highlight potential risks that the corporation may not have considered, thereby enabling more informed decision-making.

Question 2:

Scenario: An e-commerce company wants to launch a new product line but has not conducted adequate market research. What strategic risk does this pose and how would you as an auditor evaluate this?

Answer: The strategic risk is that the new product line may not meet customer needs or preferences, leading to financial losses. The auditor should evaluate this by reviewing the company's market research process, assessing whether adequate research has been undertaken, and considering the potential financial impact. This approach is effective because it can identify potential weaknesses in the company's strategic planning process.

Question 3:

Scenario: A manufacturing company is planning to adopt a new technology for its production process. As an auditor, how would you assess the strategic risk associated with this decision?

Answer: The auditor should analyze the potential technological risks, such as the reliability and security of the new technology, and the company's ability to adapt to technological changes. They should also assess the potential impact on the company's operations and financial performance. This approach is effective because it can highlight potential technological risks that may affect the company's strategic objectives.

Question 4:

Scenario: A financial institution is considering a merger with a smaller bank. As an auditor, how would you evaluate the strategic risk of this decision?

Answer: The auditor should review the financial stability of the smaller bank, assess the potential synergies and benefits of the merger, and consider the regulatory implications. They should also consider the potential impact on the financial institution's reputation and customer base. This approach is effective because it can highlight potential risks and benefits that may affect the success of the merger.

Question 5:

Scenario: A retail chain is planning to open stores in a new geographical market. As an auditor, how would you assess the strategic risk of this expansion?

Answer: The auditor should evaluate the potential market risks, such as competition, customer preferences, and economic conditions in the new market. They should also assess the company's market entry strategy and the potential impact on its overall financial performance. This approach is effective because it can identify potential risks that may affect the success of the company's expansion strategy.

Risk Assessment

Theoretical

Q: What is risk assessment in auditing?

A: Risk assessment in auditing is a systematic process where potential risks that may prevent an organization from achieving its objectives are identified and evaluated.

Q: Why is risk assessment important in auditing?

A: Risk assessment is important in auditing because it guides the auditors in determining areas where there is a high risk of material misstatement, thereby allowing them to focus their efforts on these areas.

Q: What are the key elements of risk assessment in auditing?

A: Key elements include identifying potential risks, assessing the likelihood and impact of risks, managing the risks, and monitoring and reviewing the process.

Q: How does an auditor perform a risk assessment?

A: An auditor performs a risk assessment by understanding the entity, its environment and its internal control, identifying and assessing risks of material misstatement, and responding to assessed risks.

Q: What is inherent risk in auditing?

A: Inherent risk is the susceptibility of an assertion to a material misstatement in the absence of any related controls.

Q: How does an auditor assess inherent risk?

A: An auditor assesses inherent risk by considering factors such as the nature of the business, the complexity of transactions, the susceptibility of the asset to theft, and the degree of judgment involved in determining account balances.

Q: What is control risk in auditing?

A: Control risk refers to the possibility that an error, which could potentially be significant on its own or when combined with other errors, might occur in a statement. This error may not be identified, prevented, or rectified in a timely manner by the organization's internal control system.

Q: How does an auditor assess control risk?

A: An auditor assesses control risk by evaluating the effectiveness of the entity's internal control system.

Q: What is detection risk in auditing?

A: The detection risk refers to the possibility that auditors' methods may fail to identify an existing error that could be significant, either on its own or when combined with other errors.

Q: How does an auditor manage detection risk?

A: An auditor manages detection risk by designing and implementing appropriate audit procedures.

Q: What is the relationship between inherent risk, control risk, and detection risk?

A: The relationship between these three risks is known as the audit risk model. The risk of material misstatement is the product of inherent risk and control risk, while audit risk is the product of the risk of material misstatement and detection risk.

Q: How do auditors use the audit risk model in risk assessment?

A: Auditors use the audit risk model to determine the nature, timing, and extent of audit procedures.

Q: What is the role of professional judgment in risk assessment?

A: Professional judgment is essential in risk assessment as auditors need to make informed decisions about the risks that could affect the financial statements and the effectiveness of the controls in place to mitigate these risks.

Q: How does an understanding of the entity and its environment contribute to risk assessment?

A: By comprehending the entity and its surroundings, the auditor can pinpoint possible risks and evaluate how they might affect the financial statements.

Q: What is materiality in auditing and how does it relate to risk assessment?

A: Materiality is a concept in auditing that refers to the significance of an amount, transaction, or discrepancy. It relates to risk assessment as it helps determine the level of risk that is acceptable.

Q: What is the role of internal control in risk assessment?

A: Internal control plays a crucial role in risk assessment as it helps prevent or detect misstatements. Effective internal controls reduce the risk of material misstatement.

Q: How does an auditor evaluate the effectiveness of internal control?

A: An auditor evaluates the effectiveness of internal control by testing control procedures, checking documentation, and making inquiries.

Q: What are some common risks in auditing?

A: Some common risks in auditing include the risk of fraud, the risk of error, and the risk of non-compliance with laws and regulations.

Q: How does an auditor respond to assessed risks?

A: An auditor responds to assessed risks by designing and implementing audit procedures that are responsive to the assessed risks.

Q: What is the role of risk assessment in planning an audit?

A: Risk assessment is key in planning an audit as it helps determine the areas of highest risk and guides the allocation of audit resources.

Q: What is a risk register in auditing?
A: A risk register is a document that lists potential risks, their likelihood, and impact, along with risk responses.
Q: How does an auditor use a risk register?
A: An auditor uses a risk register as a tool for identifying, assessing, and managing risks during the audit.
Q: What is the difference between a risk-based audit and a traditional audit?
A: In a risk-based audit, the focus is on understanding and assessing the risks that could affect the financial statements, and designing audit procedures to address these risks. In contrast, a traditional audit focuses on verifying transactions and balances.
Q: How can auditors mitigate the risk of fraud?
A: Auditors can mitigate the risk of fraud by implementing strong internal controls, conducting thorough risk assessments, and maintaining a high level of professional skepticism.
Q: What is the relationship between risk assessment and audit evidence?
A: The risk assessment guides the collection of audit evidence. The more significant the evaluated risk, the stronger the audit evidence must be.
Q: How does risk assessment affect the audit opinion?
A: The outcome of the risk assessment can impact the audit opinion. If the auditor concludes that there is a high risk of material misstatement that has not been adequately addressed, this could lead to a qualified or adverse opinion.
Q: What is a risk matrix in auditing?
A: A risk matrix is a tool used in risk assessment to visualize the level of risk by considering the likelihood of occurrence and the impact of each risk.
Q: How does an auditor use a risk matrix?

A: An auditor uses a risk matrix to prioritize risks and develop a response plan.

Q: How does risk assessment relate to the concept of professional skepticism in auditing?

A: Professional skepticism involves a questioning mind and a critical assessment of audit evidence. This attitude is key in risk assessment as it helps auditors identify potential risks and assess the adequacy of controls in place.

Q: What are some challenges in conducting a risk assessment in auditing?

A: Some challenges include understanding the complex business environment, assessing subjective elements like management integrity, and dealing with uncertainties.

Q: What is the role of risk assessment in auditing standards?

A: Risk assessment is a key component of auditing standards. It guides the auditors in the planning and execution of the audit.

Q: How does risk assessment contribute to audit quality?

A: Risk assessment contributes to audit quality by enabling auditors to focus their efforts on areas of highest risk and by guiding the collection of sufficient and appropriate audit evidence.

Q: What is the role of audit committees in risk assessment?

A: Audit committees play a key role in overseeing the risk assessment process. They review and approve the risk assessment and monitor its implementation.

Q: How does risk assessment affect the scope of an audit?

A: The risk assessment directly influences the scope of an audit. Higher risk areas will require more extensive testing and review, thereby expanding the scope of the audit.

Q: What is the difference between a quantitative and qualitative risk assessment in auditing?

A: A quantitative risk assessment uses numerical values to assess risk, while a qualitative risk assessment uses descriptive categories to evaluate risk.

Q: What is the role of risk assessment in the audit of financial statements?

A: Risk assessment in the audit of financial statements helps to identify areas where there is a high risk of material misstatement, thereby guiding the auditors in designing effective audit procedures.

Q: How does an auditor document the risk assessment process?

A: An auditor documents the risk assessment process through a variety of means, including risk registers, checklists, and audit working papers.

Q: How does an auditor assess the risk of non-compliance with laws and regulations?

A: An auditor assesses this risk by understanding the legal and regulatory framework applicable to the entity, evaluating the effectiveness of the entity's compliance procedures, and testing transactions and balances for compliance.

Q: What is a risk assessment procedure in auditing?

A: A risk assessment procedure is an action taken by the auditor to obtain the information necessary for identifying and assessing the risks of material misstatement.

Q: How does an auditor assess the risk of material misstatement due to fraud?

A: An auditor assesses this risk by understanding the entity's controls related to fraud, evaluating unusual or unexpected relationships identified in analytical procedures, and maintaining professional skepticism throughout the audit.

Q: What is the role of risk assessment in the audit of internal control?

A: Risk assessment in the audit of internal control helps to identify areas where the controls are weak and there is a high risk of control failure.

Q: How does an auditor assess the risk of management override of controls?

A: An auditor assesses this risk by understanding the entity's control environment, reviewing significant transactions for signs of management override, and maintaining professional skepticism.

Q: How does an auditor use analytical procedures in risk assessment?

A: An auditor uses analytical procedures in risk assessment to identify unusual or unexpected relationships that may indicate risks of material misstatement.

Q: How does risk assessment relate to the concept of materiality in auditing?

A: Risk assessment is influenced by the concept of materiality, as the auditors assess the risks of material misstatement in the financial statements.

Q: What are some common risk assessment techniques used in auditing?

A: Common risk assessment techniques include the use of checklists, risk matrices, and analytical procedures.

Q: How does risk assessment contribute to the efficiency of an audit?

A: By identifying and prioritizing risks, the auditors can focus their efforts on areas of greatest concern, thereby improving the efficiency of the audit.

Q: What is the role of risk assessment in the concept of audit evidence?

A: Risk assessment guides the collection of audit evidence. The higher the assessed risks, the more persuasive the audit evidence needs to be.

Q: What is the relationship between risk assessment and audit planning?

A: Risk assessment is a key component of audit planning. The outcomes of the risk assessment guide the development of the audit plan, including the nature, timing, and extent of audit procedures.

Q: How does an auditor assess the risk of misstatement due to error?

A: An auditor assesses this risk by understanding the entity's processes and controls, reviewing transactions and balances for accuracy, and maintaining professional skepticism.

Q: What is the role of risk assessment in the evaluation of audit findings?

A: Risk assessment plays a role in evaluating audit findings as it helps the auditor to determine the significance of the findings and their impact on the financial statements.

Applications

Scenario 1: A manufacturing company, XYZ Ltd., has just acquired its competitor, AB Corp. The audit team is tasked with assessing the investment risks involved. How should they go about it?

Answer: The audit team should initially evaluate the financial health of AB Corp. They should thoroughly review the financial records, revenue trends, and profitability margins. They should also assess the market value of AB Corp's assets and liabilities. Afterward, they should identify potential operational and strategic risks that can arise from the merger such as employee morale, cultural clashes or intellectual property disputes.

Scenario 2: A retail chain, DEF Stores, is planning to integrate a new POS system into its operations. The audit team has been instructed to perform a risk assessment of this new system. What factors should they consider?

Answer: The audit team should consider various factors such as the security of the new system, its compatibility with existing systems, and the reliability of the provider. They should also assess the potential impact on the company's operations if the system fails or becomes compromised.

Scenario 3: A financial services company, GHI Inc., is planning to expand its operations into a new geographical market. The audit team is required to assess the risks involved in this expansion. What steps should they take?

Answer: The audit team should start by understanding the new market demographics, the competition, the regulatory environment, and the economic conditions. They should also assess the company's readiness to tackle these new challenges and consider potential risks such as cultural differences, currency fluctuations, and changes in local laws.

Scenario 4: An IT firm, JKL Tech, is planning to outsource its customer service operations to a third-party provider. The audit team has been asked to evaluate the associated risks. How should they proceed?

Answer: The audit team should assess the provider's track record, financial stability, and data security measures. They should also consider the potential impact on customer satisfaction and the company's reputation in case of poor service from the provider.

Scenario 5: An e-commerce company, MNO Ecom, is planning to launch a new website. The audit team has been tasked to assess the risks associated with this launch. What should they look into?

Answer: The audit team should consider the reliability of the new website, its security features, its compatibility with different devices, and its user-friendliness. They should also assess the potential impact on the company's sales and customer satisfaction if the website crashes or has any other technical problems.

Risk Management

Theoretical

What is risk management in auditing?

Risk management in auditing is the process of identifying, assessing and prioritizing potential risks that could impact the audit process and implementing plans to mitigate these risks.

Why is risk management important in auditing?

Risk management is important in auditing because it helps to ensure that the audit is reliable, accurate, and free from material misstatement. It also helps to prevent any potential financial losses or legal issues.

What are the key components of audit risk?

The key components of audit risk include inherent risk, control risk, and detection risk.

What is inherent risk in auditing?

Inherent risk is the susceptibility of an assertion to a material misstatement, assuming there are no related controls.

What is control risk in auditing?

Control risk is the risk that a misstatement could occur in an assertion and that it will not be prevented or detected and corrected on a timely basis by the entity's internal control.

What is detection risk in auditing?

Detection risk is the risk that the auditors' procedures will not detect a misstatement that exists in an assertion that could be material, either individually or when aggregated with other misstatements.

How do auditors assess risk?

Auditors assess risk by understanding the entity and its environment, including its internal control, identifying and assessing the risks of material misstatement, and determining the responses to assessed risks.

What is the role of internal control in risk management?

Internal control plays a key role in risk management by helping to prevent, detect and correct potential risks that could impact the audit process.

How does risk management impact the audit process?

Risk management impacts the audit process by influencing the nature, timing, and extent of audit procedures.

What is audit risk model?

Audit risk model is a tool used by auditors to manage the risk that they may issue an inappropriate audit opinion.

What are the types of risks involved in auditing?

The types of risks involved in auditing include business risk, information risk, and audit risk.

How can auditors minimize audit risk?

Auditors can minimize audit risk by thoroughly understanding the client's business and environment, implementing a robust audit plan, and diligently executing audit procedures.

What is the difference between business risk and audit risk?

Business risk relates to the operations and outcomes of the organization, while audit risk relates to the risk of issuing an incorrect audit opinion.

What is the impact of risk assessment on audit planning?

Risk assessment impacts audit planning by determining the areas of highest risk which need to be focused on during the audit.

How does an auditor assess the effectiveness of internal controls?

An auditor assesses the effectiveness of internal controls by testing the design and implementation of controls, and by performing tests of controls to ensure they are operating effectively.

How is risk management linked to the quality of an audit?

Risk management is directly linked to the quality of an audit as effective risk management ensures that all potential risks are identified and mitigated, leading to a more accurate and reliable audit.

What are the steps involved in risk identification?

The steps involved in risk identification include understanding the entity and its environment, identifying the risks, and assessing the risks.

How does risk assessment influence the nature of audit evidence?

Risk assessment influences the nature of audit evidence as higher risk areas require more persuasive evidence.

What is the relationship between risk management and materiality in auditing?

The relationship between risk management and materiality in auditing is that higher risk areas may have lower materiality thresholds.

How can risk management help in fraud detection during audits?

Risk management can help in fraud detection during audits by identifying areas of high risk for fraud and implementing procedures to investigate these areas.

What is the difference between systematic and unsystematic risk in auditing?

Systematic risk is the risk inherent to the entire market or market segment, while unsystematic risk is specific to a particular entity.

How does an auditor's understanding of the client's industry affect risk management?

An auditor's understanding of the client's industry affects risk management as it helps in identifying industry-specific risks.

How do auditors manage risks related to the use of technology in audits?

Auditors manage risks related to the use of technology in audits by implementing controls over technology and by using specialized IT audit techniques.

How does risk management contribute to the reliability of financial statements?

Risk management contributes to the reliability of financial statements by ensuring that all material risks are identified and mitigated, leading to more accurate financial reporting.

What is the role of professional skepticism in risk management in auditing?

The role of professional skepticism in risk management in auditing is to question and critically assess audit evidence, which helps in identifying and assessing risks.

How can auditors manage risks associated with non-compliance with laws and regulations?

Auditors can manage risks associated with non-compliance with laws and regulations by understanding the applicable laws and regulations and by performing procedures to identify non-compliance.

What are the risks associated with related party transactions in auditing?

The risks associated with related party transactions in auditing include the risk of undisclosed related party transactions and the risk of misstatement of the terms and substance of the transactions.

How can auditors manage risks associated with estimates and judgments?

Auditors can manage risks associated with estimates and judgments by understanding the basis of the estimates and judgments and by testing the estimates and judgments for reasonableness.

What is the role of audit committees in risk management in auditing?

The role of audit committees in risk management in auditing is to oversee the risk management process and to provide independent oversight of the audit process.

How does the auditor's independence affect risk management?

The auditor's independence affects risk management as a lack of independence could increase the risk of an inappropriate audit opinion.

What is the impact of risk management on audit fees?

The impact of risk management on audit fees is that effective risk management can reduce the time and effort required for the audit, potentially reducing audit fees.

How can auditors manage risks associated with going concern issues?

Auditors can manage risks associated with going concern issues by understanding the entity's ability to continue as a going concern and by performing procedures to identify any going concern issues.

How does risk management impact communication with the client?

Risk management impacts communication with the client as it helps to ensure that all significant risks are communicated to the client in a timely manner.

What is the role of risk management in the audit of complex transactions?

The role of risk management in the audit of complex transactions is to identify and assess the risks associated with these transactions and to design appropriate audit responses.

How does risk management influence the selection of audit procedures?

Risk management influences the selection of audit procedures as higher risk areas require more detailed and extensive procedures.

How does risk management contribute to audit efficiency?

Risk management contributes to audit efficiency by focusing the audit effort on the areas of highest risk, which can reduce unnecessary work in low risk areas.

What is the role of risk management in the audit of fair value measurements?

The role of risk management in the audit of fair value measurements is to identify and assess the risks associated with these measurements and to design appropriate audit responses.

How can auditors manage risks associated with the use of experts in audits?

Auditors can manage risks associated with the use of experts in audits by understanding the qualifications and competence of the experts and by critically assessing the work of the experts.

What is the impact of risk management on the auditor's report?

The impact of risk management on the auditor's report is that effective risk management can contribute to a more accurate and reliable auditor's report.

How can auditors manage risks associated with group audits?

Auditors can manage risks associated with group audits by understanding the structure and activities of the group and by coordinating with the auditors of the group components.

What is the role of risk management in the audit of tax provisions?

The role of risk management in the audit of tax provisions is to identify and assess the risks associated with these provisions and to design appropriate audit responses.

How does risk management impact the audit of revenue recognition?
Risk management impacts the audit of revenue recognition by identifying and assessing the risks associated with revenue recognition and by designing appropriate audit responses.
What is the role of risk management in the audit of contingent liabilities?
The role of risk management in the audit of contingent liabilities is to identify and assess the risks associated with these liabilities and to design appropriate audit responses.
How can auditors manage risks associated with auditor rotation?
Auditors can manage risks associated with auditor rotation by ensuring a smooth transition of knowledge and by understanding the risks and issues identified by the previous auditor.
How does risk management impact the auditor's professional judgment?
Risk management impacts the auditor's professional judgment by providing a structured approach to identifying, assessing and responding to risks.
What is the role of risk management in the audit of financial instruments?
The role of risk management in the audit of financial instruments is to identify and assess the risks associated with these instruments and to design appropriate audit responses.
How can auditors manage risks associated with the use of audit software?
Auditors can manage risks associated with the use of audit software by understanding the functionality and limitations of the software and by implementing controls over the use of the software.
What is the impact of risk management on the audit of internal financial controls?

The impact of risk management on the audit of internal financial controls is that it helps to identify and assess the risks associated with these controls and to design appropriate audit responses.

How does risk management contribute to the auditor's understanding of the client's business?

Risk management contributes to the auditor's understanding of the client's business by identifying the risks associated with the business and its environment.

What is the role of risk management in the audit of intangible assets?

The role of risk management in the audit of intangible assets is to identify and assess the risks associated with these assets and to design appropriate audit responses.

Applications

Question 1:

A manufacturing company recently had a significant financial loss due to a fire in one of its factories. The auditor discovered that the company lacked sufficient insurance coverage for such events. How could the auditor have helped the company manage this risk?

Answer: Ideally, the auditor should have identified the potential risk of fire and other disasters during the risk assessment process. They could have recommended the company to have sufficient insurance coverage to mitigate the potential financial loss. The auditor's effectiveness in this scenario is questionable as they failed to identify a significant risk that eventually resulted in a considerable financial loss.

Question 2:

An IT services company is planning to expand its operations into a new country. However, the auditor warns of the potential legal and compliance risks associated with the new market. How should the company manage these risks?

Answer: The company should thoroughly research the laws and regulations of the new market, possibly with the help of a local legal team. They should also implement a robust compliance management system to ensure adherence to the new rules. The auditor plays a crucial role in this scenario by identifying the potential risks and recommending preventive measures, displaying their effectiveness in risk management.

Question 3:

A retail company is considering implementing a new inventory system. The auditor, however, identifies potential risks related to the system's integration with the current IT infrastructure and the employees' ability to use the new system effectively. How should the company address these risks?

Answer: The company should conduct a thorough cost-benefit analysis and feasibility study before implementing the new system. They should also provide extensive training to their employees to ensure they can adapt to the new system. The auditor's role in this scenario is vital as they highlighted potential risks that could have resulted in significant financial and operational issues later on.

Question 4:

A healthcare organization is in the process of digitizing all its patient records. The auditor, however, identifies potential risks related to data security and privacy. How could the organization manage these risks?

Answer: The organization should implement robust data security measures, such as encryption and secure storage, to protect patient data. They should also ensure compliance with all relevant privacy laws and regulations. The auditor's effectiveness in this scenario is evident as they identified critical risks related to data security and privacy, which are of paramount importance in the healthcare sector.

Question 5:

A logistics company is planning to acquire a smaller competitor. However, the auditor identifies potential financial and operational risks related to the acquisition. How should the company manage these risks?

Answer: The company should conduct thorough due diligence, including a review of the competitor's financial statements and operational processes. They should also formulate a detailed integration strategy to guarantee a seamless transition.

The auditor's effectiveness in this scenario is crucial as they helped the company understand the potential risks associated with the acquisition, allowing them to make an informed decision.

Sarbanes-Oxley Act

Theoretical

Q: What is the main purpose of the Sarbanes-Oxley Act in auditing?

A: The main purpose of the Sarbanes-Oxley Act in auditing is to improve the accuracy and reliability of corporate disclosures and prevent corporate fraud.

Q: Who does the Sarbanes-Oxley Act apply to?

A: The Sarbanes-Oxley Act applies to all public companies in the United States and international companies that have registered equity or debt securities with the Securities and Exchange Commission.

Q: What is the role of the auditor in relation to the Sarbanes-Oxley Act?

A: The role of the auditor is to audit the company's financial statements and provide an independent opinion on the fairness and accuracy of these statements in accordance with the Sarbanes-Oxley Act.

Q: How does the Sarbanes-Oxley Act affect the independence of auditors?

A: The Sarbanes-Oxley Act enhances auditor independence by restricting the types of non-audit services auditors can provide to their audit clients.

Q: What is Section 404 of the Sarbanes-Oxley Act?

A: Section 404 of the Sarbanes-Oxley Act requires management and auditors of public companies to establish internal controls and reporting methods on the adequacy of these controls.

Q: What penalties does the Sarbanes-Oxley Act impose for non-compliance?

A: The Sarbanes-Oxley Act imposes severe penalties for non-compliance, including fines and imprisonment for executives who knowingly certify false financial reports.

Q: Why is the Sarbanes-Oxley Act important in the auditing profession?

A: The Sarbanes-Oxley Act is important in the auditing profession because it sets standards for the integrity of the financial reporting process and holds executives accountable for the accuracy of financial statements.

Q: How does the Sarbanes-Oxley Act affect the audit committee of a company?

A: The Sarbanes-Oxley Act requires the audit committee to be directly responsible for the appointment, compensation, and oversight of the work of any registered public accounting firm employed by the company.

Q: What is the role of the Public Company Accounting Oversight Board (PCAOB) under the Sarbanes-Oxley Act?

A: The Sarbanes-Oxley Act created the PCAOB, a non-profit organization, to oversee public company audits and protect the interests of investors.

Q: How does the Sarbanes-Oxley Act promote transparency in financial reporting?

A: The Sarbanes-Oxley Act promotes transparency by requiring companies to disclose all material off-balance sheet liabilities, obligations, and transactions in their financial reports.

Q: What is the impact of the Sarbanes-Oxley Act on internal control?

A: The Sarbanes-Oxley Act has enhanced the importance of internal control in financial reporting and made it a central focus of corporate governance.

Q: How does the Sarbanes-Oxley Act define corporate responsibility for financial reports?

A: The Sarbanes-Oxley Act defines corporate responsibility for financial reports by requiring the CEO and CFO to certify the appropriateness of financial statements and the establishment of adequate internal controls for financial reporting.

Q: What provisions does the Sarbanes-Oxley Act have for whistleblower protection?

A: The Sarbanes-Oxley Act includes provisions for whistleblower protection, making it illegal for a company to discharge, demote, suspend, threaten, or harass an employee for providing information about fraudulent activities.

Q: How does the Sarbanes-Oxley Act impact the relationship between a company and its external auditors?

A: The Sarbanes-Oxley Act requires a greater level of independence between a company and its external auditors to prevent conflicts of interest and ensure unbiased financial reporting.

Q: How does the Sarbanes-Oxley Act affect a company's internal audit function?

A: The Sarbanes-Oxley Act enhances the role of the internal audit function by requiring it to evaluate the company's internal controls over financial reporting and identify any material weaknesses.

Q: How does the Sarbanes-Oxley Act contribute to ethical business behavior?

A: The Sarbanes-Oxley Act contributes to ethical business behavior by holding corporate officers accountable for the accuracy of financial statements and requiring the disclosure of any codes of ethics for senior financial officers.

Q: What is the impact of the Sarbanes-Oxley Act on corporate governance?

A: The Sarbanes-Oxley Act has significantly strengthened corporate governance by improving the accuracy and reliability of corporate disclosures, enhancing auditor independence, and increasing corporate accountability.

Q: How does the Sarbanes-Oxley Act affect the role of the CFO in a company?

A: The Sarbanes-Oxley Act increases the responsibilities of the CFO in ensuring the accuracy of the financial statements and the effectiveness of the internal controls over financial reporting.

Q: How does the Sarbanes-Oxley Act improve the quality of financial reporting?

A: The Sarbanes-Oxley Act improves the quality of financial reporting by setting higher standards for financial disclosures and internal controls, and requiring management to certify the accuracy of financial reports.

Q: How does the Sarbanes-Oxley Act impact the disclosure of off-balance sheet transactions?

A: The Sarbanes-Oxley Act mandates businesses to fully disclose any significant transactions, arrangements, and obligations not recorded on the balance sheet that could potentially have a substantial impact on their present or future financial status, fluctuations in financial condition, revenue or expenses, operational results, liquidity, capital outlays, or capital resources.

Q: What are the main components of the internal control framework as per the Sarbanes-Oxley Act?

A: The main components of the internal control framework as per the Sarbanes-Oxley Act are the control environment, risk assessment, control activities, information and communication, and monitoring activities.

Q: How does the Sarbanes-Oxley Act affect the audit report?

A: The Sarbanes-Oxley Act requires the auditor to attest to the management's assertion about the effectiveness of the company's internal control over financial reporting, which is included in the audit report.

Q: What is the role of the CEO under the Sarbanes-Oxley Act?

A: The role of the CEO under the Sarbanes-Oxley Act is to certify the appropriateness of financial statements and disclosures, and that these statements fairly present the financial condition and results of operations of the company.

Q: How does the Sarbanes-Oxley Act impact the reporting of material changes in financial condition or operations?

A: The Sarbanes-Oxley Act mandates companies to promptly and regularly reveal significant alterations in their financial status or operations.

Q: What is the impact of the Sarbanes-Oxley Act on the audit profession?

A: The Sarbanes-Oxley Act has significantly impacted the audit profession by enhancing auditor independence, increasing responsibilities for internal control assessments, and establishing the PCAOB to oversee the profession.

Q: How does the Sarbanes-Oxley Act protect investors?

A: The Sarbanes-Oxley Act protects investors by improving the accuracy and reliability of corporate disclosures, which are important for making investment decisions.

Q: How does the Sarbanes-Oxley Act affect the responsibility of a company's board of directors?

A: The Sarbanes-Oxley Act increases the responsibility of the board of directors in overseeing the company's financial reporting process and internal controls.

Q: What are the implications of the Sarbanes-Oxley Act on a company's risk management practices?
A: The Sarbanes-Oxley Act emphasizes the importance of risk management practices in a company, particularly in relation to financial reporting and disclosure risks.
Q: How does the Sarbanes-Oxley Act change the way public companies are audited?
A: The Sarbanes-Oxley Act changes the way public companies are audited by enhancing auditor independence, increasing the focus on internal control assessments, and establishing the PCAOB to oversee the audit profession.
Q: What is the significance of the Sarbanes-Oxley Act in corporate ethics?
A: The Sarbanes-Oxley Act plays a significant role in promoting corporate ethics by holding executives accountable for the accuracy and completeness of the financial reports and by requiring companies to disclose whether they have a code of ethics for senior financial officers.
Q: How does the Sarbanes-Oxley Act affect the role of the internal auditor in a company?
A: The Sarbanes-Oxley Act enhances the role of the internal auditor by requiring them to evaluate the company's internal controls over financial reporting and identify any material weaknesses.
Q: What is the significance of the Sarbanes-Oxley Act in relation to corporate fraud?
A: The Sarbanes-Oxley Act plays a significant role in preventing corporate fraud by improving the accuracy of corporate disclosures, enhancing auditor independence, and holding executives accountable for fraudulent financial reporting.
Q: How does the Sarbanes-Oxley Act impact a company's relationship with its shareholders?

A: The Sarbanes-Oxley Act enhances a company's relationship with its shareholders by improving the transparency and reliability of financial reporting and corporate disclosures.

Q: What is the relevance of the Sarbanes-Oxley Act in the context of accounting scandals?

A: The Sarbanes-Oxley Act is highly relevant in the context of accounting scandals as it was enacted in response to such scandals with the aim of improving corporate governance, enhancing auditor independence, and increasing the accuracy and transparency of financial reporting.

Q: How has the Sarbanes-Oxley Act influenced the accounting profession?

A: The Sarbanes-Oxley Act has significantly influenced the accounting profession by setting higher standards for financial reporting, enhancing the role of auditors, and establishing the PCAOB to oversee the profession.

Q: What is the role of the Securities and Exchange Commission (SEC) under the Sarbanes-Oxley Act?

A: The role of the SEC under the Sarbanes-Oxley Act is to enforce the act, oversee the PCAOB, and protect the interests of investors by ensuring the accuracy and reliability of corporate disclosures.

Q: How does the Sarbanes-Oxley Act affect the disclosure of related party transactions?

A: The Sarbanes-Oxley Act requires companies to disclose all material related party transactions in their financial reports.

Q: How does the Sarbanes-Oxley Act impact the due diligence process in mergers and acquisitions?

A: The Sarbanes-Oxley Act impacts the due diligence process in mergers and acquisitions by requiring companies to evaluate the target company's compliance with the act and the effectiveness of its internal controls.

Q: What are the implications of the Sarbanes-Oxley Act on a company's financial performance?
A: The Sarbanes-Oxley Act does not directly impact a company's financial performance, but it can indirectly affect it by improving the quality of financial reporting and increasing investor confidence.
Q: How does the Sarbanes-Oxley Act affect the accountability of corporate management?
A: The Sarbanes-Oxley Act increases the accountability of corporate management by requiring them to certify the accuracy of the financial statements and the effectiveness of the internal controls over financial reporting.
Q: How does the Sarbanes-Oxley Act ensure the reliability of financial information?
A: The Sarbanes-Oxley Act ensures the reliability of financial information by setting higher standards for financial reporting, enhancing auditor independence, and requiring management to certify the accuracy of financial reports.
Q: How does the Sarbanes-Oxley Act impact the responsibilities of a company's audit committee?
A: The Sarbanes-Oxley Act significantly increases the responsibilities of a company's audit committee in overseeing the financial reporting process and internal controls, and in appointing, compensating, and supervising the external auditors.
Q: How does the Sarbanes-Oxley Act improve corporate accountability and transparency?
A: The Sarbanes-Oxley Act improves corporate accountability and transparency by setting higher standards for financial reporting, enhancing auditor independence, requiring management to certify the accuracy of financial reports, and requiring companies to disclose material off-balance sheet transactions and related party transactions.

Q: What is the impact of the Sarbanes-Oxley Act on the disclosure of executive compensation?

A: The Sarbanes-Oxley Act requires companies to disclose all material aspects of executive compensation in their financial reports.

Q: How does the Sarbanes-Oxley Act address the issue of conflicts of interest in auditing?

A: The Sarbanes-Oxley Act addresses the issue of conflicts of interest in auditing by enhancing auditor independence, prohibiting auditors from providing certain non-audit services to their audit clients, and requiring the audit committee to pre-approve all audit and non-audit services.

Q: How does the Sarbanes-Oxley Act impact the financial reporting process?

A: The Sarbanes-Oxley Act impacts the financial reporting process by setting higher standards for financial reporting, enhancing auditor independence, requiring management to certify the accuracy of financial reports, and requiring companies to disclose material off-balance sheet transactions and related party transactions.

Q: How does the Sarbanes-Oxley Act affect the process of auditing internal controls?

A: The Sarbanes-Oxley Act requires auditors to audit the company's internal controls over financial reporting and provide an opinion on the effectiveness of these controls, thereby making internal control auditing a central part of the audit process.

Q: How does the Sarbanes-Oxley Act impact the role of the external auditor in a company?

A: The Sarbanes-Oxley Act enhances the role of the external auditor by increasing their responsibilities for auditing the company's financial statements and internal controls, and by requiring them to be more independent from the company.

Q: What are the consequences of non-compliance with the Sarbanes-Oxley Act?
A: Non-compliance with the Sarbanes-Oxley Act can result in severe penalties, including fines, imprisonment for executives who knowingly certify false financial reports, and loss of investor confidence.
Q: How does the Sarbanes-Oxley Act contribute to the integrity of the financial markets?
A: The Sarbanes-Oxley Act contributes to the integrity of the financial markets by improving the accuracy and reliability of corporate disclosures, which are essential for the functioning of the markets.

Applications

Scenario 1: A mid-sized corporation, "ABC Inc." is preparing for its first audit since the company went public. How does the Sarbanes-Oxley Act affect this audit and what steps should the auditors take to ensure compliance with the Act?
Answer: Sarbanes-Oxley Act (SOX) impacts the auditing process of ABC Inc. in several ways. First, Section 404 of SOX requires the company to provide an annual assessment of the effectiveness of their internal controls over financial reporting. The auditors must evaluate and report on the effectiveness of these controls. They should conduct a thorough review of the company's internal controls, assess their design and operating effectiveness, and report any material weaknesses. This will require collaboration with the management and may involve additional testing and documentation.
Effectiveness: This answer effectively captures the main requirements of SOX in auditing and provides a clear action plan for the auditors. However, it could be more effective if it outlines potential challenges and how to overcome them.

Scenario 2: A well-established multinational company, "XYZ Corp", is in the process of changing its auditors. What implications does the Sarbanes-Oxley Act have on this transition and what should the new auditors consider when taking over?

Answer: Under SOX, there are strict rules governing auditor independence. The new auditors of XYZ Corp need to ensure there are no conflicts of interest, such as financial or employment ties with the company. They should also review previous audit work to assess the effectiveness of the internal controls and financial reporting. If there are any issues identified, these should be communicated to the Audit Committee promptly.

Effectiveness: This answer effectively outlines the key considerations for the new auditors under SOX. However, it could be more effective if it includes a discussion on the role of the Public Company Accounting Oversight Board (PCAOB) in overseeing the transition.

Scenario 3: A tech start-up, "TechRise", has recently received significant investment and is considering going public. What role does the Sarbanes-Oxley Act play in this decision and what steps should TechRise take to prepare for potential audits?

Answer: SOX imposes significant compliance requirements on publicly traded companies, including mandatory internal control assessments and auditor attestations. TechRise must ensure they have robust internal controls and accurate financial reporting processes in place. They should engage external auditors early to help identify any potential weaknesses and start preparing for the increased scrutiny.

Effectiveness: This answer effectively highlights the importance of SOX in TechRise's decision to go public and provides practical steps for preparation. However, it would be more effective if it includes the potential penalties for non-compliance with SOX.

Risk-Based Audit

Theoretical

Q: What is the definition of risk-based audit?

A: Risk-based audit is an approach that focuses on evaluating the risks and vulnerabilities faced by an organization and establishing an audit strategy accordingly.

Q: How does risk-based auditing differ from traditional auditing?

A: While traditional auditing focuses on compliance and controls, risk-based auditing emphasizes the potential risks that could impact an organization's objectives.

Q: What are the main components of a risk-based audit?

A: The main components include: risk identification, risk assessment, risk mitigation strategies, and risk monitoring.

Q: What is the purpose of risk-based auditing?

A: The purpose is to help the organization identify and manage risks effectively, ensuring the achievement of its goals and objectives.

Q: Can risk-based auditing prevent all risks?

A: No, it can't prevent all risks. However, it helps in identifying potential risks and developing strategies to mitigate them.

Q: What is the first step in a risk-based audit?

A: The first step is risk identification, where potential risks facing the organization are identified.

Q: How are risks assessed in a risk-based audit?

A: Risks are assessed based on their potential impact on the organization's objectives and the likelihood of their occurrence.

Q: What is risk mitigation in the context of risk-based auditing?
A: Risk mitigation involves developing strategies to reduce the impact of identified risks.
Q: What role does risk monitoring play in a risk-based audit?
A: Risk monitoring ensures that risk mitigation strategies are effective and that new risks are identified and assessed promptly.
Q: Who is responsible for performing a risk-based audit?
A: Typically, internal auditors or external auditing firms carry out risk-based audits.
Q: How often should a risk-based audit be conducted?
A: The frequency of risk-based audits depends on the organization's risk profile and the industry in which it operates.
Q: What are the benefits of risk-based auditing?
A: Benefits include improved risk management, better decision-making, increased efficiency, and enhanced stakeholder confidence.
Q: What are the challenges of risk-based auditing?
A: Challenges may include lack of resources, inadequate risk assessment skills, and resistance from management.
Q: Is risk-based auditing a reactive or proactive approach?
A: Risk-based auditing is a proactive approach as it aims to identify and address risks before they materialize.
Q: How does risk-based auditing contribute to corporate governance?
A: It contributes by ensuring transparency and accountability in the organization's risk management processes.
Q: Can risk-based auditing be applied to any type of organization?
A: Yes, risk-based auditing can be applied to any organization, irrespective of its size or industry.
Q: How does risk-based auditing help in strategic planning?
A: By identifying and assessing risks, it provides valuable insights that can be used in strategic planning.

Q: What is the relationship between risk-based auditing and risk appetite?
A: Risk-based auditing helps determine whether the organization's risk appetite aligns with its strategic objectives.
Q: What skills are required for risk-based auditing?
A: Skills include risk assessment, analytical thinking, communication, and understanding of the organization's business.
Q: How does risk-based auditing add value to an organization?
A: It adds value by promoting effective risk management, enhancing operational efficiency, and improving decision-making.
Q: What is the role of technology in risk-based auditing?
A: Technology can aid in risk identification, assessment, and monitoring, making the audit process more efficient and effective.
Q: Can risk-based auditing eliminate all risks?
A: No, it can't eliminate all risks. Its purpose is to help manage risks effectively.
Q: What factors influence the success of risk-based auditing?
A: Factors include management support, adequate resources, and the skills and expertise of the audit team.
Q: How is a risk-based audit report prepared?
A: The report is prepared by documenting the audit findings, including the identified risks, their potential impact, and the proposed mitigation strategies.
Q: How do stakeholders benefit from risk-based auditing?
A: Stakeholders benefit as it provides assurance that the organization is effectively managing its risks, thus promoting confidence and trust.
Q: What is the difference between risk-based auditing and risk management?
A: While both involve dealing with risks, risk management is a continuous process carried out by the organization, while risk-based auditing is a periodic assessment conducted by auditors.

Q: How can risk-based auditing help in decision making?
A: By providing insights into the potential risks and their impact, it aids in making informed decisions.
Q: Can risk-based auditing be used as a tool for change management?
A: Yes, by identifying potential risks associated with proposed changes, it can contribute to effective change management.
Q: What is the role of communication in risk-based auditing?
A: Communication is crucial in conveying audit findings, recommendations, and risk mitigation strategies to the relevant stakeholders.
Q: How does risk-based auditing contribute to operational efficiency?
A: By identifying risks that could disrupt operations, it aids in maintaining operational efficiency.
Q: Is risk-based auditing a one-time process?
A: No, risk-based auditing is an ongoing process that should be conducted periodically to reflect changes in the organization's risk profile.
Q: Can risk-based auditing detect fraud?
A: While not its primary focus, risk-based auditing can help detect fraud by identifying unusual patterns or anomalies.
Q: What is the role of risk-based auditing in regulatory compliance?
A: It helps ensure that the organization is aware of and managing compliance-related risks effectively.
Q: Can risk-based auditing replace traditional auditing?
A: No, both types of auditing serve different purposes and should be used complementarily.
Q: What is the impact of organizational culture on risk-based auditing?

A: An organization's culture can influence the effectiveness of risk-based auditing, particularly in terms of risk perception and appetite.

Q: What is the relationship between risk-based auditing and internal control?

A: Risk-based auditing can evaluate the effectiveness of internal controls in managing identified risks.

Q: How does risk-based auditing contribute to financial stability?

A: By identifying and managing risks that could impact financial performance, it contributes to financial stability.

Q: What is the role of risk-based auditing in project management?

A: It can help identify and manage risks that could potentially derail a project.

Q: Can risk-based auditing be outsourced?

A: Yes, many organizations choose to outsource risk-based auditing to external firms for reasons such as objectivity and expertise.

Q: How does risk-based auditing relate to corporate social responsibility?

A: It can help identify risks related to social and environmental issues, thus contributing to corporate social responsibility efforts.

Q: What is the role of risk-based auditing in crisis management?

A: It can help identify potential crises and plan for their management.

Q: How can risk-based auditing improve customer satisfaction?

A: By identifying risks that could impact the quality of products or services, it can contribute to improving customer satisfaction.

Q: What is the relationship between risk-based auditing and business continuity planning?

A: Risk-based auditing can identify potential threats to business continuity and assess the effectiveness of the organization's business continuity plans.

Q: Can risk-based auditing predict future risks?
A: While not a prediction tool, risk-based auditing can provide insights into potential future risks based on current conditions and trends.
Q: How does risk-based auditing support innovation?
A: By managing risks associated with new initiatives, it can support innovation efforts.
Q: What is the relationship between risk-based auditing and corporate strategy?
A: Risk-based auditing helps ensure that the organization's strategy aligns with its risk appetite and that strategic risks are effectively managed.
Q: Can risk-based auditing provide a competitive advantage?
A: Yes, effective risk management through risk-based auditing can provide a competitive advantage by enhancing operational efficiency and decision-making.
Q: How does risk-based auditing impact employee performance?
A: By identifying risks related to human resources, it can contribute to improving employee performance and satisfaction.
Q: What is the role of risk-based auditing in supply chain management?
A: It can help identify and manage risks in the supply chain, thus ensuring its efficiency and reliability.
Q: Can risk-based auditing improve the organization's reputation?
A: Yes, by effectively managing risks, risk-based auditing can enhance the organization's reputation among stakeholders.

Applications

Problem Scenario 1:

You are an internal auditor for a large manufacturing company. The company recently implemented a new software system to manage their inventory. However, the implementation process was rushed, and there was not enough time for proper training. As a result, many employees are struggling to use the system effectively. How would you approach this situation from a risk-based audit perspective?

Answer: From a risk-based audit perspective, the first step would be to identify and assess the risk associated with the new software. The risk here is that incorrect use of the software could lead to inaccurate inventory records, which could result in financial misstatements. In order to mitigate this risk, I would recommend conducting training sessions for employees to ensure they understand how to use the software correctly. In addition, regular audits should be conducted to verify the accuracy of the inventory records.

Effectiveness: This approach is effective as it addresses the root cause of the problem, which is lack of proper training. By ensuring that employees are well-trained, the risk of errors is significantly reduced. Regular audits also ensure that any errors that do occur are caught and corrected in a timely manner.

Problem Scenario 2:

You are the head of an audit team for a bank. The bank has recently experienced a significant increase in loan defaults. The management is concerned about the impact this could have on the bank's financial stability. How would you approach this situation from a risk-based audit perspective?

Answer: The first step in a risk-based audit would be to identify the risks associated with the increase in loan defaults. This could be due to a variety of factors, such as poor credit risk assessment procedures, economic downturn, or a change in the bank's customer base. Once the risks have been identified, the audit team would need to assess the impact of these risks on the bank's financial stability. This could involve reviewing the bank's credit risk assessment procedures, analyzing economic trends, and examining the bank's customer base. Based on this assessment, the audit team could then recommend actions to mitigate these risks. Effectiveness: This approach is effective because it identifies the risks associated with the increase in loan defaults, assesses the impact of these risks, and recommends actions to mitigate these risks. By taking a proactive approach, the bank can minimize the impact of these risks on its financial stability.

Problem Scenario 3:

You are an auditor for a retail company. The company has recently expanded its online sales platform. However, there have been a number of customer complaints about the security of their personal information. How would you approach this situation from a risk-based audit perspective?

Answer: A risk-based audit would begin by identifying and assessing the risk associated with the security of customer information. In this case, the risk is that a data breach could lead to the loss of customer trust and potential legal ramifications. To mitigate this risk, I would recommend conducting a thorough review of the company's data security procedures. This could involve reviewing the company's IT infrastructure, examining the company's data protection policies, and assessing the company's readiness to respond to a data breach.

Effectiveness: This approach is effective as it addresses the root cause of the problem, which is the potential for a data breach. By ensuring that the company has robust data security procedures in place, the risk of a data breach is significantly reduced. In addition, by assessing the company's readiness to respond to a data breach, the company can ensure that it is prepared to respond quickly and effectively in the event of a data breach.

Compliance Audit

Theoretical

Q: What is a compliance audit?

A: A compliance audit is a comprehensive review of an organization's adherence to regulatory guidelines.

Q: What is the main aim of a compliance audit?

A: The main aim of a compliance audit is to ensure that a company is following the rules and regulations set forth by governing bodies and internal policies.

Q: Who usually performs a compliance audit?

A: Compliance audits are generally performed by an independent, third-party auditing firm or an internal auditor within the company.

Q: What areas can compliance audits cover?

A: Compliance audits can cover various areas such as financial, operational, IT, legal, or health and safety compliance.

Q: What is the output of a compliance audit?

A: The output of a compliance audit is usually a report that details the level of compliance and any areas of non-compliance.

Q: How often should a compliance audit be conducted?

A: The frequency of a compliance audit can vary depending on the industry and specific regulations. Some companies might require an annual compliance audit, while others might need more frequent checks.

Q: What is the significance of a compliance audit for a company?

A: A compliance audit helps a company to identify and address compliance issues, reduce risk, and maintain its reputation.

Q: What happens if a company fails a compliance audit?

A: If a company fails a compliance audit, it could face penalties, fines, legal consequences, and reputational damage.

Q: What role does management play in a compliance audit?

A: Management plays a crucial role in a compliance audit as they are responsible for ensuring the company meets all regulatory requirements.

Q: How does a compliance audit differ from a financial audit?

A: While a financial audit focuses on the accuracy of a company's financial statements, a compliance audit focuses on whether the company is following applicable laws, rules, and regulations.

Q: What are some common compliance audit procedures?

A: Some common compliance audit procedures include reviewing documents, interviewing staff, and observing operations.

Q: What is a compliance audit checklist?

A: A compliance audit checklist is a tool used to ensure all necessary areas are reviewed during the audit process.

Q: What are the steps involved in a compliance audit?

A: The steps involved in a compliance audit typically include planning, conducting the audit, reporting findings, and following up on corrective actions.

Q: How can a company prepare for a compliance audit?

A: A company can prepare for a compliance audit by conducting an internal review, ensuring all documentation is in order, and educating employees about compliance requirements.

Q: What skills are necessary for a compliance auditor?

A: A compliance auditor should have strong analytical skills, attention to detail, knowledge of relevant laws and regulations, and good communication skills.

Q: Can a compliance audit detect fraud?

A: A compliance audit can help detect fraud by identifying non-compliance with laws and regulations that may indicate fraudulent activities.

Q: What types of businesses need compliance audits?

A: All types of businesses, from small companies to large corporations, may need compliance audits depending on the industry and applicable regulations.

Q: What is the role of a compliance audit in corporate governance?

A: In corporate governance, a compliance audit ensures the company is adhering to ethical practices and legal requirements, thereby protecting shareholders' interests.

Q: Can a compliance audit lead to process improvement?

A: Yes, a compliance audit can lead to process improvement by identifying areas of non-compliance and recommending changes to improve compliance.

Q: Is a compliance audit mandatory?

A: Whether a compliance audit is mandatory or not depends on the industry, applicable laws, and regulations. In some cases, it is mandatory, while in others, it is optional but highly recommended.

Q: How does technology impact compliance audits?

A: Technology can make compliance audits more efficient and accurate by automating certain processes and providing tools for data analysis.

Q: What is the connection between a compliance audit and risk management?

A: A compliance audit is a part of risk management as it helps identify and mitigate compliance risks that can lead to legal and financial consequences.

Q: What can a company do to ensure a successful compliance audit?

A: To ensure a successful compliance audit, a company should maintain accurate and comprehensive records, stay updated with changes in regulations, and foster a culture of compliance among employees.

Q: What is the role of a compliance audit in maintaining a company's reputation?

A: A compliance audit helps maintain a company's reputation by demonstrating its commitment to operating ethically and legally.

Q: What are the potential consequences of non-compliance identified in a compliance audit?

A: Potential consequences of non-compliance identified in a compliance audit can include financial penalties, legal repercussions, operational disruptions, and damage to the company's reputation.

Q: How is a compliance audit report structured?

A: A compliance audit report is typically structured with an introduction, a summary of the audit's scope and objectives, a detailed account of the findings, and recommendations for improvement.

Q: How can a company ensure continuous compliance between audits?

A: A company can ensure continuous compliance between audits by implementing robust internal controls, providing regular training to employees, and conducting periodic internal audits.

Q: How does a compliance audit support decision-making within a company?

A: A compliance audit supports decision-making by providing insights into the company's compliance status, which can inform strategic planning and risk management.

Q: How does a compliance audit contribute to the overall health of a company?

A: A compliance audit contributes to the overall health of a company by ensuring it operates within the law, thereby reducing risks and fostering trust among stakeholders.

Q: What can a company do to mitigate the risks identified in a compliance audit?

A: A company can mitigate the risks identified in a compliance audit by implementing the auditor's recommendations, strengthening internal controls, and providing additional training to staff.

Q: How can a company use the findings of a compliance audit to improve its operations?

A: A company can use the findings of a compliance audit to identify areas for improvement, implement changes, and enhance its compliance processes.

Q: How does a compliance audit benefit a company's stakeholders?

A: A compliance audit benefits a company's stakeholders by providing assurance that the company is operating ethically and legally, thereby protecting their interests.

Q: What role does documentation play in a compliance audit?

A: Documentation plays a crucial role in a compliance audit as it provides evidence of the company's compliance efforts and supports the auditor's findings.

Q: How does a compliance audit enhance a company's transparency?

A: A compliance audit enhances a company's transparency by providing clear, documented evidence of its compliance with laws and regulations.

Q: How can a company's internal controls impact a compliance audit?

A: A company's internal controls can impact a compliance audit as strong internal controls can help ensure compliance, while weak controls can lead to non-compliance.

Q: What role does a company's culture play in a compliance audit?

A: A company's culture plays a significant role in a compliance audit as a culture of compliance can help ensure adherence to laws and regulations.

Q: How can a company respond to non-compliance issues identified in a compliance audit?

A: A company can respond to non-compliance issues identified in a compliance audit by taking corrective action, addressing the underlying causes, and implementing measures to prevent recurrence.

Q: How can a compliance audit help a company avoid legal issues?

A: A compliance audit can help a company avoid legal issues by identifying potential areas of non-compliance and recommending corrective actions.

Q: What is the role of a compliance audit in a company's strategic planning?

A: A compliance audit plays a role in a company's strategic planning by providing insights into compliance risks and opportunities, which can inform the company's strategic decisions.

Q: How does a compliance audit contribute to a company's sustainability?

A: A compliance audit contributes to a company's sustainability by ensuring it operates in a legal and ethical manner, which can help it maintain its operations in the long run.

Q: How can a company use a compliance audit to gain a competitive advantage?

A: A company can use a compliance audit to gain a competitive advantage by demonstrating its commitment to compliance, which can enhance its reputation and trust among customers and stakeholders.

Q: What is the relationship between a compliance audit and corporate social responsibility (CSR)?

A: A compliance audit can support a company's CSR efforts by ensuring it operates in a legal and ethical manner, which is a key aspect of CSR.

Q: How does a compliance audit help a company meet its objectives?

A: A compliance audit helps a company meet its objectives by identifying potential compliance issues that could hinder its progress and recommending corrective actions.

Q: How does a compliance audit impact a company's bottom line?

A: A compliance audit can positively impact a company's bottom line by reducing the risk of financial penalties and legal issues associated with non-compliance.

Q: How can a compliance audit support a company's growth?

A: A compliance audit can support a company's growth by ensuring it operates within the law, which can help it avoid disruptions and maintain its operations as it expands.

Q: How does a compliance audit contribute to a company's risk management strategy?

A: A compliance audit contributes to a company's risk management strategy by identifying compliance risks and recommending measures to mitigate them.

Q: How does a compliance audit relate to a company's operational efficiency?

A: A compliance audit can enhance a company's operational efficiency by identifying areas of non-compliance that could lead to disruptions or inefficiencies and recommending corrective actions.

Q: What role does communication play in a compliance audit?

A: Communication plays a critical role in a compliance audit as clear, effective communication can facilitate the audit process and ensure all relevant parties understand the audit's findings and recommendations.

Q: What is the impact of regulatory changes on a compliance audit?

A: Regulatory changes can significantly impact a compliance audit as they may introduce new compliance requirements that the company must meet.

Q: How can a company maintain its compliance status after a successful compliance audit?

A: A company can maintain its compliance status after a successful compliance audit by continuing to monitor its compliance efforts, staying updated with regulatory changes, and conducting regular internal audits.

Applications

Scenario 1:

A small-sized manufacturing company is implementing a new Enterprise Resource Planning (ERP) system to streamline their business processes. The internal audit department wants to verify whether the new system is compliant with the company's internal control procedures. What steps should the audit department take to ensure the system's compliance?

Answer: The audit department should start by reviewing the system's design and configuration, checking if it aligns with the company's internal control procedures. They should also run test transactions to ensure the ERP system captures the required data correctly and produces accurate reports. Once the system goes live, continuous monitoring should be carried out to detect any potential control breaches. This approach is proactive and should ensure the system's compliance, effectiveness, and efficiency.

Scenario 2:

A medium-sized retail chain has been noticing inconsistencies in their financial records. They suspect the problem might be due to non-compliance with their financial reporting standards. How can an auditor assess this situation?

Answer: The auditor should first review the company's financial policies and procedures. They should then trace some transactions from initiation to recording, comparing the process followed to the company's standard procedures. If deviations are found, these could be the root of the inconsistencies. The auditor should also check the financial reporting software for any configuration errors. By doing so, the auditor can identify lapses, provide recommendations and ensure adherence to financial reporting standards.

Scenario 3:

A rapidly expanding tech startup is struggling to remain compliant with industry regulations due to its rapid expansion. As an auditor, how would you assist the company in maintaining compliance?

Answer: The auditor should conduct a compliance audit to identify areas of non-compliance. They should review the company's compliance program, educate the team about relevant regulations, and assess the effectiveness of the controls in place. If necessary, they should recommend improvements or additions to the compliance program to ensure that the company stays compliant despite its rapid growth. This will help the company avoid legal penalties and maintain its reputation in the industry.

Scenario 4:

A pharmaceutical company is preparing for a compliance audit by the Food and Drug Administration (FDA). As an internal auditor, what steps should you take to ensure the company passes the audit?

Answer: The auditor should first familiarize themselves with FDA regulations and guidelines. Following this, they should conduct a mock audit to identify potential areas of non-compliance. They should also interview staff to assess their understanding of FDA regulations. By conducting a thorough review of the company's practices and procedures, the auditor can ensure that the company meets FDA standards before the actual audit.

Scenario 5:

A non-profit organization has received a large grant and needs to ensure that the funds are used compliantly. As an auditor, what steps would you take to ensure compliance?

Answer: The auditor should review the terms and conditions of the grant to understand the restrictions on its use. They should then assess the organization's internal controls to ensure that they are robust enough to prevent misuse of funds. This may involve reviewing financial reports, interviewing staff, and conducting spot checks on expenses. By doing so, the auditor can help ensure that the organization is using the grant funds appropriately and compliantly.

Forensic Audit

Theoretical

Q: What is a Forensic Audit?

A: A forensic audit involves scrutinizing and assessing an entity or individual's financial records to gather proof that can be utilized in a legal case or judicial process.

Q: What is the main purpose of a Forensic Audit?

A: The main purpose is to investigate fraud or financial misrepresentation and to provide evidence for legal proceedings if necessary.

Q: Who conducts a Forensic Audit?

A: A forensic audit is conducted by forensic auditors who are experts in accounting and legal proceedings.

Q: What is the difference between a traditional audit and a forensic audit?

A: Unlike a traditional audit which seeks to verify financial statements, a forensic audit is designed to uncover fraud, misconduct, or financial irregularities.

Q: What skills do forensic auditors need to possess?

A: They need to be knowledgeable in accounting, auditing, internal controls, fraud detection techniques, and legal proceedings.

Q: What are the phases of a Forensic Audit?

A: The phases include planning, data collection and analysis, reporting, and follow-up.

Q: What tools are used in a Forensic Audit?
A: Tools include data analysis software, fraud detection software, and legal databases.
Q: Can a Forensic Audit detect all fraud?
A: While it is a powerful tool for detecting fraud, it cannot guarantee the detection of all fraudulent activities due to the complexity and sophistication of some fraudulent schemes.
Q: What happens after a Forensic Audit is completed?
A: After completion, the forensic auditor prepares a report detailing the findings, which can be used in legal proceedings.
Q: What are some common types of fraud that a Forensic Audit can uncover?
A: Common types include misappropriation of assets, financial statement fraud, bribery, and corruption.
Q: What is the role of a Forensic Auditor in a court proceeding?
A: They may serve as an expert witness, presenting and explaining the evidence gathered during the audit.
Q: Can a Forensic Audit be performed on any type of organization?
A: Yes, it can be performed on any organization, regardless of its size or industry.
Q: Is a Forensic Audit a reactive or proactive process?
A: It can be both. It is reactive when responding to suspicions of fraud, and proactive when implemented as a preventative measure.
Q: What ethical standards should a Forensic Auditor adhere to?
A: They should adhere to the principles of integrity, objectivity, professional competence, confidentiality, and professional behavior.
Q: Can a Forensic Audit reveal errors in accounting procedures?
A: Yes, a forensic audit can uncover errors in accounting procedures which may have allowed fraud to occur.

Q: How can a Forensic Audit contribute to improving internal controls?

A: The findings from a forensic audit can identify weaknesses in internal controls, which can then be strengthened to prevent future fraud.

Q: What is the importance of a Forensic Audit in corporate governance?

A: It plays a crucial role in ensuring financial transparency, accountability, and the integrity of financial reports.

Q: Can a Forensic Audit be used as a deterrent to fraud?

A: Yes, the knowledge that a forensic audit could be conducted can act as a deterrent to potential fraudsters.

Q: Why should businesses consider having a forensic audit?

A: Businesses should consider it to ensure financial integrity, prevent and detect fraud, and to protect their assets and reputation.

Q: How long does it take to conduct a Forensic Audit?

A: The duration of a forensic audit depends on the complexity of the case and the number of transactions to be reviewed.

Q: Can a Forensic Audit be used to resolve disputes?

A: Yes, the findings from a forensic audit can be used to resolve disputes, particularly those relating to financial matters.

Q: What is the role of technology in a Forensic Audit?

A: Technology plays a key role in data collection and analysis, assisting in the detection of irregularities and fraudulent activities.

Q: How does a Forensic Audit contribute to risk management?

A: It aids in identifying financial risks and the areas where fraud could potentially occur, allowing for the implementation of preventative measures.

Q: What training is required to become a Forensic Auditor?

A: In addition to accounting and auditing knowledge, training in fraud detection, legal aspects, and the use of relevant software tools is required.

Q: What challenges can be faced during a Forensic Audit?

A: Challenges can include complex data analysis, difficulty in obtaining necessary information, and dealing with sophisticated fraud schemes.

Q: How is evidence collected during a Forensic Audit?

A: Evidence is collected through various means such as interviews, document reviews, and digital data analysis.

Q: Can a Forensic Auditor be held liable for not detecting fraud?

A: Yes, if it is proven that the auditor was negligent in their duties, they can be held liable.

Q: How is the scope of a Forensic Audit determined?

A: The scope is determined based on the purpose of the audit, the suspected fraud, and the areas of the organization to be covered.

Q: What is the significance of documentation in a Forensic Audit?

A: Documentation is important as it provides a record of the audit process, supports the findings, and serves as evidence in court.

Q: Are there any standards for conducting a Forensic Audit?

A: Yes, various professional bodies have issued standards and guidelines for conducting a forensic audit.

Q: What is the role of a Forensic Auditor in fraud prevention?

A: They play a key role by identifying areas of risk, recommending improvements in internal controls, and educating employees about fraud risks.

Q: How does a Forensic Audit differ from a fraud examination?

A: A forensic audit is broader and can include a fraud examination, but it also involves preparing evidence for court, which is not typically part of a fraud examination.

Q: What are the costs associated with a Forensic Audit?
A: The costs include the professional fees of the forensic auditor, the use of technology and software, and any additional resources required.
Q: Is it necessary to conduct a Forensic Audit annually?
A: It is not typically conducted annually but is done when there is a suspicion of fraud or as part of a periodic review of financial controls.
Q: Can a Forensic Audit be conducted remotely?
A: Yes, with advancements in technology, much of the data collection and analysis can be done remotely, though some aspects may require physical presence.
Q: What is the role of a Forensic Auditor in asset recovery?
A: They can assist in asset recovery by tracing misappropriated assets and providing evidence to support legal claims.
Q: How can a Forensic Audit enhance an organization's credibility?
A: It can enhance credibility by demonstrating a commitment to financial transparency and accountability.
Q: What qualities should a Forensic Auditor possess?
A: They should possess analytical skills, attention to detail, integrity, and the ability to communicate complex information clearly.
Q: Can a Forensic Audit result in criminal charges?
A: Yes, if the audit uncovers evidence of criminal activity, it can lead to criminal charges.
Q: Are Forensic Audits confidential?
A: Yes, the information gathered during a forensic audit is typically confidential and is only shared with authorized individuals.
Q: What is a Forensic Audit report?

A: A forensic audit report documents the findings of the audit, the evidence gathered, and the methodology used, and may include recommendations for action.

Q: Can a Forensic Audit be conducted by an internal audit team?

A: Yes, but it is often conducted by external specialists due to the specialized skills required and the need for objectivity.

Q: How does a Forensic Audit contribute to an organization's financial health?

A: By detecting and preventing fraud, it can help to protect the organization's assets and reputation, contributing to its financial health.

Q: Can a Forensic Audit be conducted on non-financial transactions?

A: Yes, it can be conducted on any area where there is a risk of fraud or misconduct.

Q: What is the relationship between a Forensic Audit and compliance?

A: A forensic audit can help to ensure compliance with financial regulations and standards, and can identify areas of non-compliance.

Q: Can the results of a Forensic Audit be challenged in court?

A: Yes, the results can be challenged, which is why it is important for the Forensic Auditor to ensure that their methodology is robust and the evidence is strong.

Q: Is a Forensic Audit the same as an investigation?

A: While they both involve an in-depth examination, a forensic audit is focused on financial transactions and is designed to produce evidence suitable for court.

Q: Can a Forensic Audit detect tax evasion?

A: Yes, a forensic audit can uncover evidence of tax evasion, such as underreported income or overstated deductions.

Q: How does a Forensic Audit support decision-making in an organization?

A: The findings from a forensic audit can provide valuable information for decision-making, such as identifying areas of risk and improving internal controls.

Q: Can the scope of a Forensic Audit change midway?

A: Yes, if the Forensic Auditor uncovers new information or risks during the audit, the scope may be adjusted accordingly.

Applications

Scenario 1: An employee in your firm has been accused of embezzling funds. You are tasked to conduct a forensic audit to determine if the allegations are true. What steps do you take in this audit?

The effectiveness of the answer lies in determining whether the auditor can correctly identify the necessary procedures, like investigating financial records, interviewing staff, and analyzing the employee's activities. If the auditor is able to provide concrete evidence of embezzlement, then the audit can be deemed successful.

Scenario 2: Your company has noticed discrepancies between the physical stock and the recorded inventory. How would you conduct a forensic audit to pinpoint the source of these discrepancies?

The key here is for the auditor to be able to identify the source of the discrepancies. This includes verifying inventory numbers, inspecting warehouses for any signs of theft or mismanagement, and scrutinizing the inventory management process for any flaws or loopholes. If the auditor can provide valid explanations for the discrepancies, the audit can be considered successful.

Scenario 3: The management of your company suspects that a business partner may have overstated their financial health in order to secure a contract. How do you approach this situation with a forensic audit?

The success of the audit here would depend on the auditor's ability to accurately assess the partner's financial health. This includes reviewing financial statements, investigating signs of fraud, and evaluating the company's overall financial stability. If the auditor discovers evidence of financial misrepresentation, it points to a successful audit.

Scenario 4: Your organization is considering acquiring another company but has concerns about potential financial irregularities in the target company's accounts. How do you conduct a forensic audit to identify any potential risks?

The effectiveness of the audit here would be based on the auditor's ability to identify potential financial risks. This would involve a thorough analysis of the target company's financial statements, identifying any patterns that may suggest fraud, and conducting interviews with key personnel. If the auditor identifies any significant risks that could affect the acquisition, the audit can be deemed successful.

Scenario 5: Your company has been accused of tax evasion and you are tasked with conducting a forensic audit to prove the company's innocence. How do you proceed?

The success of the audit would depend on the auditor's ability to provide proof of the company's tax compliance. This includes reviewing tax records, verifying the accuracy of tax calculations, and investigating any signs of tax evasion. If the auditor is able to prove that the company is tax compliant, the audit can be considered successful.

Financial Audit

Theoretical

Q: What is a financial audit?

A: A financial audit is an objective examination and evaluation of an organization's financial statements to make sure that the financial records are a fair and accurate representation of the transactions they claim to represent.

Q: What is the main objective of a financial audit?

A: The main objective of a financial audit is to provide an independent opinion to the stakeholders that the company's financial statements are accurate and complete.

Q: Who can perform a financial audit?

A: A financial audit can be conducted by an independent body outside of the organization, typically by a certified public accountant (CPA).

Q: What are the key components of a financial audit?

A: The key components of a financial audit include the balance sheet, income statement, cash flow statement, and statement of changes in equity.

Q: What are some common types of financial audit tests?

A: Common financial audit tests include analytical procedures, tests of details of transactions and balances, and tests of controls.

Q: What does the term 'materiality' mean in financial auditing?

A: Materiality in financial auditing refers to the significance of an amount, transaction, or discrepancy that might influence the decisions of a person relying on the financial statements.

Q: What is an internal audit?
A: An internal audit is an in-depth review of an organization's operations and procedures conducted by an entity within the organization. It aims at identifying potential risks and evaluating the effectiveness of risk management strategies.
Q: What is the difference between an internal audit and a financial audit?
A: A financial audit is focused on the financial statements and the transactions that form part of those statements, while an internal audit has a broader scope that includes the organization's operations and procedures.
Q: Why is risk assessment important in a financial audit?
A: Risk assessment helps auditors identify areas where there might be a significant risk of material misstatement, allowing them to focus their efforts on these areas.
Q: What is audit evidence?
A: Audit evidence refers to the information collected for the review of the company's financial transactions. This evidence may include bank statements, invoices, receipts, and other documents that support transactions.
Q: What is an audit opinion?
A: An audit opinion is a statement made by the auditor about whether the financial statements are presented fairly, in all material respects, in accordance with the applicable financial reporting framework.
Q: What is the role of an auditor in a financial audit?
A: The auditor's role in a financial audit is to objectively assess the financial statements of the organization, provide an opinion on their accuracy, and report this to the stakeholders.
Q: What is the significance of an unqualified audit opinion?

A: An unqualified audit opinion indicates that the financial statements give a true and fair view in accordance with the financial reporting framework.

Q: What does the term 'going concern' refer to in financial auditing?

A: Going concern in financial auditing refers to an assumption that the company will continue its operations and meet its obligations in the foreseeable future.

Q: What are some common financial auditing techniques?

A: Common financial auditing techniques include inspection, observation, inquiry, confirmation, and recalculation.

Q: What is an audit plan?

A: An audit plan lays out the strategy that will guide the audit, including the timing, nature, and extent of audit procedures to be performed.

Q: What is an audit failure?

A: An audit failure takes place when an auditor provides an incorrect audit opinion due to non-compliance with the standards of auditing.

Q: What is an audit risk?

A: Audit risk refers to the possibility that the auditor might inadvertently fail to correctly amend their opinion on financial statements that have significant inaccuracies.

Q: What is the difference between a statutory audit and a voluntary audit?

A: A statutory audit is a legally required review of the accuracy of a company's financial records, while a voluntary audit is not required by law but may be conducted for various purposes.

Q: What is a management letter in an audit?

A: A management letter is a by-product of the audit process and includes the auditor's findings and recommendations on improving the company's internal controls and efficiency.

Q: What are some common types of audit opinions?
A: The common types of audit opinions typically include unqualified opinion, qualified opinion, adverse opinion, and disclaimer of opinion.
Q: What is the aim of an audit of financial statements?
A: The aim of an audit of financial statements is to increase the trust and confidence of the intended users in these financial reports.
Q: What is audit sampling?
A: Audit sampling is the use of an audit procedure on a selection of items within an account balance or class of transactions.
Q: What is the importance of independence in financial auditing?
A: Independence is crucial in financial auditing to ensure that the auditor's opinion is objective and unbiased.
Q: What is the difference between a balance sheet audit and an income statement audit?
A: A balance sheet audit focuses on verifying the assets, liabilities, and equity at a specific point in time, while an income statement audit focuses on verifying the revenues, costs, and expenses over a period of time.
Q: What is a compliance audit?
A: A compliance audit is a review conducted to ascertain an organization's adherence to regulatory guidelines.
Q: What is a forensic audit?
A: A forensic audit is an examination and evaluation of an organization's financial information for use as evidence in court.
Q: What is the difference between a forensic audit and a financial audit?
A: A forensic audit is intended for legal use and is likely to be scrutinized by the court system, while a financial audit is conducted to provide confidence in the integrity of the financial statements.

Q: What is a performance audit?
A: A performance audit is an examination of a program, function, operation, or the management systems and procedures of a government or non-profit entity to assess whether the entity is achieving economy, efficiency, and effectiveness in the employment of available resources.
Q: What is an operational audit?
A: An operational audit is a review of an organization's operations to evaluate the efficiency, effectiveness, and economy of operations.
Q: What is the difference between a performance audit and an operational audit?
A: A performance audit focuses on the achievement of specific objectives related to economy, efficiency, and effectiveness, while an operational audit focuses on all aspects of operations to evaluate efficiency and effectiveness.
Q: What is an integrated audit?
A: An integrated audit is an audit that includes both a financial statement audit and an audit of internal control over financial reporting.
Q: What is a quality audit?
A: A quality audit is a process by which you review and evaluate an aspect of a project, system or process to ascertain how well it meets a set of predefined criteria or standards.
Q: What is the role of the audit committee in a financial audit?
A: The audit committee oversees the financial reporting process, selects the independent auditor, and receives the audit results both internal and external.
Q: What is an external audit?
A: An external audit is an independent examination of a company's financial statements and records by an outside party.

Q: What is the difference between an external audit and an internal audit?

A: An external audit is an independent review conducted by external auditors to express an opinion on whether the financial statements are free of material misstatements, while an internal audit is a function performed by the organization's own personnel to evaluate the internal control system.

Q: What is the role of audit working papers?

A Audit working papers function as a documentation of the audit procedures carried out, the proof acquired, and the determinations made by the auditor during the audit.

Q: What is audit risk assessment?

A: Audit risk assessment involves the identification and assessment of risks of material misstatement at the financial statement and assertion levels.

Q: What is the importance of professional skepticism in auditing?

A: The significance of professional skepticism in auditing lies in its ability to empower the auditor to detect and react to situations that could suggest potential inaccuracies.

Q: What is an audit procedure?

A: An audit procedure is a specific task performed by auditors to obtain audit evidence.

Q: What is substantive testing in auditing?

A: Substantive testing in auditing is a detailed testing of transactions, account balances, and disclosures to detect material misstatements in the financial statements.

Q: What is the difference between substantive testing and compliance testing?

A: Substantive testing involves direct verification of financial balances, transactions, and information, while compliance testing involves checking the effectiveness of internal controls in preventing or detecting material misstatements.

Q: What is the role of internal control in financial auditing?
A: Internal control plays a key role in financial auditing as it helps prevent or detect material misstatements in the financial statements.
Q: What is an audit report?
A: An audit report is a formal document where the auditor provides his opinion on whether the financial statements are free from material misstatements and are presented fairly in accordance with the applicable financial reporting framework.
Q: What is a qualified audit opinion?
A: An auditor issues a qualified audit opinion when they determine that aside from the impact of the specific issue related to the qualification, the financial statements accurately represent the company's financial standing in line with the financial reporting framework.
Q: What is an adverse audit opinion?
A: An adverse audit opinion is issued when the auditor concludes that the financial statements do not give a true and fair view in accordance with the financial reporting framework.
Q: What is a disclaimer of opinion?
A: When an auditor cannot gather enough suitable audit evidence to form an audit opinion, they may issue a disclaimer of opinion. This implies that the potential impacts on the financial statements might be significant and widespread.
Q: What is an auditor's responsibility regarding fraud in a financial audit?
A: An auditor's responsibility is to design audit procedures to identify material misstatements in the financial statements due to fraud, but it's not their responsibility to detect all frauds.
Q: What is a group audit?

A: A group audit is an audit of group financial statements, which include the financial information of more than one component (e.g., subsidiary, division, branch, etc.).

Q: What is a joint audit?

A: A joint audit is an audit of a single entity's financial statements by two or more auditors to share the responsibility of expressing an opinion on the financial statements.

Applications

Scenario 1: Unrecorded Liabilities

ABC Manufacturing has been experiencing a downturn in its financial performance. As an auditor, you noticed that the company has a significant amount of unrecorded liabilities. How would you evaluate this situation?

Answer: Unrecorded liabilities can distort the true financial position of a company. Auditors should conduct a thorough review of the company's transactions near the end of the reporting period. This may include a detailed review of invoices, purchase orders, and statements from suppliers. Additionally, auditors could consider conducting a subsequent disbursements review to identify any payments made for goods or services received but not recorded before year-end.

Effectiveness: This approach is effective as it provides a comprehensive view of the company's financial situation. It will help identify discrepancies and ensure liabilities are accurately reported.

Scenario 2: Related Party Transactions

You are auditing XYZ Company and discover that they have numerous transactions with related parties that are not disclosed in their financial statements. How would you address this issue?

Answer: The auditor should first understand the nature and purpose of these transactions. They should gather evidence to assess whether the transactions were conducted at arm's length and if they are appropriately disclosed. Auditors should also discuss with management the need for disclosing such transactions in the financial statements.

Effectiveness: This approach would ensure the company's financial statements provide a fair and transparent view of its financial performance and position. It would also help maintain the credibility of the company in the eyes of the stakeholders.

Scenario 3: Overstatement of Sales Revenue

While auditing DEF Tech, a software company, you found that the sales team was reporting contracts as sales before the software was delivered, leading to an overstatement of sales revenue. How would you handle this matter?

Answer: The auditor should review the company's revenue recognition policies and ensure they are in compliance with the applicable financial reporting framework. Any discrepancies should be highlighted and discussed with the management. The auditor should also recommend the company to revise its revenue recognition policy if necessary.

Effectiveness: This approach would ensure that the company's revenue is recognized correctly, providing a true and fair view of its financial performance. This would also enhance the company's credibility and reputation in the market.

Scenario 4: Inaccurate Inventory Valuation

During the audit of GHI Retail, you noticed discrepancies in the inventory valuation. The company has been using an outdated method to value its inventory which is leading to inaccurate financial statements. How would you address this?

Answer: The auditor should review the inventory valuation methodology used by the company. They should recommend the most suitable method as per industry standards and accounting principles. The auditor should also provide guidance on how to implement the changes and the impact it would have on the financial statements.

Effectiveness: This approach would ensure the company's inventory is valued accurately, thus providing a true and fair view of its financial position. It would also enhance the quality of the financial statements, making them more reliable for stakeholders.

Inventory Audit

Theoretical

What is an inventory audit?

An inventory audit is a process that confirms the accuracy of the quantity of items in a company's inventory through a physical count and comparison with recorded amounts.

What is the main purpose of an inventory audit?

The main purpose of an inventory audit is to verify the accuracy of the inventory records, prevent fraud, and ensure the company's financial statements are accurate.

What are the common types of inventory audit procedures?

The common types include physical inventory counts, cycle counting, and the use of perpetual inventory systems.

What is a physical inventory count?

It involves manually counting all inventory items and verifying the counts against the quantities reflected in the company's inventory records.

What is cycle counting?

Cycle counting is a process where a small subset of inventory, in a specified location, is counted on a specified day.

What is perpetual inventory system?

It is an inventory tracking system that records the sale or purchase of inventory immediately through the use of computerized point-of-sale systems and enterprise asset management systems.

What is the importance of an inventory audit for a business?

Inventory audits help in identifying discrepancies, preventing fraud, ensuring financial accuracy, and optimizing inventory management.

How often should inventory audits be conducted?

The frequency of inventory audits depends on the nature of the business and its operational needs. Some businesses may conduct audits annually, while others may do it quarterly or monthly.

What are the procedures to carry out an inventory audit?

The steps generally include planning the audit, conducting a physical count of inventory, comparing the physical count with the company's records, investigating any discrepancies, and making necessary adjustments.

How does an inventory audit contribute to financial accuracy?

By verifying the accuracy of the value and quantity of inventory, an inventory audit ensures that financial statements reflect the true financial position of a company.

How does an inventory audit help in preventing fraud?

Regular inventory audits can help detect any unusual activities or discrepancies which could be indicators of theft or fraud.

What skills are required to conduct an inventory audit?

Skills required include attention to detail, understanding of inventory management and auditing processes, ability to analyze data, and good communication skills.

How can technology aid in the inventory audit process?

Technology can automate the process of tracking and recording inventory movements, making the audit process more efficient and accurate.

What are the challenges involved in conducting an inventory audit?

Challenges can include incomplete records, inaccurate counts, large volume of inventory, and potential for fraud.

How can these challenges be mitigated?

These challenges can be mitigated through proper planning, use of technology, regular audits, and well-defined inventory management policies.

What role does documentation play in an inventory audit?

Documentation provides evidence of the audit process and findings, and helps in resolving discrepancies, and serves as a record for future audits.

What happens if discrepancies are found during an inventory audit?

If discrepancies are found, they need to be investigated to identify the root cause and adjustments need to be made to correct the inventory records.

Who should conduct an inventory audit?

Ideally, inventory audits should be conducted by an independent party, such as an external auditor, to ensure objectivity.

What is the role of an auditor in an inventory audit?

The auditor's role is to plan and execute the audit, verify the physical count of inventory, compare it with the company's records, identify discrepancies, and report the findings.

How can a company prepare for an inventory audit?

A company can prepare by ensuring all inventory records are up-to-date and accurate, organizing the inventory for easy counting, and coordinating with the auditor.

What happens after an inventory audit is completed?

After an audit, any necessary adjustments are made to the inventory records and the audit findings are reported to the management.

Can an inventory audit be conducted remotely?

Yes, with advancements in technology, remote inventory audits are possible through the use of video conferencing, drones, and other digital tools.

What is a cut-off analysis in inventory auditing?

A cut-off analysis involves checking transactions that occur at the end of a period to ensure they are recorded in the correct period.

How does an inventory audit impact a company's bottom line?

By ensuring accurate inventory records, a company can avoid overstocking or understocking, which can impact profit margins.

What is an obsolescence review in inventory auditing?

An obsolescence review involves identifying items in the inventory that are obsolete or slow-moving and may require valuation adjustments.

How can an inventory audit lead to improved inventory management?

Inventory audits can identify issues with inventory management processes, helping the company make necessary improvements.

What is the role of internal controls in inventory auditing?

Internal controls help ensure the integrity of the inventory count and records, and can help prevent fraud.

How does segregation of duties contribute to inventory audit effectiveness?

Segregation of duties ensures that no single individual has control over all aspects of the inventory process, reducing the risk of error or fraud.

What is the difference between a physical count and a cycle count?

A physical count involves counting all inventory items at once, while a cycle count involves counting a small subset of inventory at regular intervals.

Is it necessary to shut down operations during a physical count?

While it might not be necessary, it is often beneficial to shut down operations during a physical count to prevent confusion and ensure accuracy.

How can an inventory audit help in identifying theft or losses?

Regular audits can help identify discrepancies between physical counts and inventory records, which could indicate theft or losses.

How are discrepancies resolved during an inventory audit?

Discrepancies are usually resolved by investigating the cause, correcting errors in record keeping, and adjusting the inventory records.

What are the potential consequences of not conducting regular inventory audits?

Consequences can include financial inaccuracies, undetected fraud, poor inventory management, and potential losses.

Can you explain the distinction between a perpetual inventory system and a periodic inventory system?

A perpetual inventory system updates inventory records continuously, while a periodic inventory system updates inventory records at the end of a period.

How does an inventory audit contribute to operational efficiency?

An inventory audit can highlight inefficiencies and issues in the inventory management process, leading to improvements and increased operational efficiency.

What is a surprise inventory count?

A surprise inventory count is an unannounced count conducted to prevent employees from manipulating inventory figures.

What is a test count in inventory auditing?

A test count involves the auditor selecting a sample of items and verifying the count against the inventory records.

What factors should be considered when planning an inventory audit?

Factors to consider include the size and nature of the inventory, the inventory management system in place, and the resources available for the audit.

How is technology changing the way inventory audits are conducted?

Technology is making inventory audits more efficient and accurate by automating tracking and record keeping, and enabling remote audits.

How can inventory audit findings be used to improve business processes?

Findings from an inventory audit can identify areas of improvement in inventory management, leading to process improvements and cost savings.

What is shrinkage in the context of an inventory audit?

Shrinkage is the term used to describe inventory loss resulting from issues like theft, damage, or administrative mistakes.

How can an inventory audit help in identifying and reducing shrinkage?

Regular audits can help identify the causes of shrinkage, leading to measures to prevent such losses in the future.

What is the role of management in an inventory audit?

Management's role is to support the audit process, provide necessary information, and act on the audit findings.

How can the accuracy of an inventory audit be ensured?

The accuracy of an inventory audit can be ensured through thorough planning, use of reliable audit techniques, and verification of the audit findings.

What is a reconciliation process in an inventory audit?

The process of reconciliation includes matching the actual physical inventory count with the inventory records and addressing any mismatches.

What is a blind count in an inventory audit?

A blind count involves counting the inventory without having access to the quantity figures in the inventory records.

How can an inventory audit aid in decision making?

An inventory audit provides accurate information about the company's inventory, which can aid in decision making related to production, sales, and purchasing.

How does an inventory audit impact customer satisfaction?

By ensuring that inventory levels are accurate, a company can avoid stock-outs and delays, leading to improved customer satisfaction.

What is a movement analysis in an inventory audit?

A movement analysis involves tracking the movement of inventory items to identify any unusual or suspicious activity.

What is the relationship between an inventory audit and a company's profitability?

By ensuring accurate inventory records and efficient inventory management, an inventory audit can contribute to a company's profitability by reducing losses and improving operational efficiency.

Applications

Problem 1:

Company A is a large manufacturing firm that has a vast inventory of raw materials, semi-finished goods, and finished goods. However, auditors have noted inconsistencies in the inventory counts and the recorded numbers in the financial statements. It seems that the inventory turnover ratio is unusually low, suggesting potential obsolescence, miscounts, or theft. How should auditors approach this problem?

Solution:

Auditors should conduct a thorough physical count of the inventory to confirm the accuracy of the records. They should also review the company's procedures for recording inventory and check for any discrepancies. Additionally, they should examine the inventory turnover ratio in more detail to understand the cause of the low rate. If obsolescence is suspected, auditors should verify the valuation and adequacy of the allowance for obsolete inventory. If theft is suspected, auditors should investigate further to identify potential culprits. The effectiveness of the solution would depend on the accuracy of the physical count and the thoroughness of the review of the inventory recording procedures.

Problem 2:

Company B is a retail organization that uses the FIFO (First-In, First-Out) method for inventory costing. However, during an audit, it was discovered that some items were not being sold in the order they were purchased, leading to inaccurate cost of goods sold. How can auditors resolve this issue?

Solution:

The auditors should first confirm that the company is indeed not following the FIFO method accurately. They can do this by tracking a sample of items from purchase to sale. If the issue is confirmed, auditors should recommend that the company either adhere strictly to the FIFO method or switch to an inventory costing method that better fits their practices, such as LIFO (Last-In, First-Out) or Average Cost. The effectiveness of this solution depends on how accurately the company can implement the recommended changes and whether these changes result in more accurate financial statements.

Problem 3:

Company C is a technology firm that maintains a large inventory of high-value items. In a recent audit, it was discovered that the company had been significantly overvaluing its inventory, leading to inflated profit margins. How should auditors address this problem?

Solution:

Auditors should reassess the valuation of the inventory using accepted accounting principles. They should check the invoices and delivery notes of the purchases and sales to verify the costs recorded. They should also recommend that the company implement stricter controls over inventory valuation to prevent such issues in the future. The effectiveness of the solution would depend on how well the company implements these new controls and whether this leads to more accurate and reliable financial reporting.

IT Audit

Theoretical

Q: What is an IT audit?

A: An IT audit refers to the procedure of gathering and analyzing proof of an organization's information systems, operations, and practices. Its purpose is to ascertain if the systems effectively protect assets, uphold data integrity, and function efficiently to fulfill the organization's objectives.

Q: What is the objective of an IT audit?

A: The purpose of an IT audit is to assess the systems and processes that are in place to secure the integrity of information systems and data.

Q: What are the types of IT audits?

A: The types of IT audits include systems and applications audit, information processing facilities audit, systems development audit, management of IT and enterprise architecture audit, and client/server, telecommunication, intranets, and extranets audit.

Q: What is a systems and applications audit?

A: A systems and applications audit is an audit to verify that systems and applications are appropriate, efficient, and adequately controlled to ensure valid, reliable, timely, and secure input, processing, and output at all levels of a system's activity.

Q: What is an information processing facilities audit?

A: An audit of the information processing facilities is conducted to confirm that the facility is well-managed to guarantee prompt, precise, and effective processing of applications, even under normal and potentially unstable situations.

Q: What is a systems development audit?

A: An audit of systems development is conducted to confirm that the systems being created align with the organization's objectives and that they're being developed following the universally accepted standards for systems development.

Q: What is a management of IT and enterprise architecture audit?

A: A management of IT and enterprise architecture audit is an audit to verify that IT management has developed an organizational structure and procedures to ensure a controlled and efficient environment for information processing.

Q: What is a client/server, telecommunication, intranets, and extranets audit?

A: An audit of client/server, telecommunication, intranets, and extranets is carried out to ensure that there are controls in place on the client's computer (the one receiving services), the server, and the network that links the clients and servers.

Q: What are the key stages of an IT audit process?

A: The key stages of an IT audit process are planning, studying and evaluating controls, testing and analyzing controls, reporting, and follow-up.

Q: What happens in the planning stage of an IT audit?

A: In the planning stage, the auditor outlines the audit objectives, identifies the systems and network environments, and determines the audit procedures to be used.

Q: What happens in the studying and evaluating controls stage of an IT audit?

A: In this stage, the auditor identifies the controls in operation and assesses their adequacy and effectiveness.

Q: What happens in the testing and analyzing controls stage of an IT audit?

A: In this stage, the auditor tests the controls to verify that they are working as described and are effective in managing risks.

Q: What happens in the reporting stage of an IT audit?

A: In this stage, the auditor documents the results of the audit, highlighting any issues or weaknesses identified and recommending corrective actions.

Q: What happens in the follow-up stage of an IT audit?

A: In the follow-up stage, the auditor verifies that the recommended actions have been implemented and are working effectively.

Q: Can you explain the responsibilities of an IT auditor?

A: An IT auditor is tasked with the duty of assessing and examining an organization's IT infrastructure, procedures, and operations.

Q: What are the skills required for an IT auditor?

A: The skills required for an IT auditor include a strong understanding of IT systems and processes, analytical thinking, attention to detail, and excellent communication skills.

Q: What is the difference between an IT audit and a financial audit?

A: An IT audit focuses on assessing the systems and processes that support financial data and information, while a financial audit focuses on the accuracy of financial statements.

Q: What is risk assessment in IT audit?

A: Risk assessment in IT audit involves identifying and evaluating risks associated with the IT environment to determine the impact on the organization's operations and objectives.

Q: What is a control in the context of an IT audit?

A: A control in the context of an IT audit is a procedure or policy that provides a reasonable assurance that the IT environment operates as intended and that data is reliable.

Q: What are the key components of an IT audit report?

A: The key components of an IT audit report include an executive summary, scope and objectives of the audit, methodology, findings and recommendations, and a conclusion.

Q: How can an organization prepare for an IT audit?

A: An organization can prepare for an IT audit by understanding the scope of the audit, reviewing previous audit reports, documenting IT processes and controls, and ensuring that all systems and data are accessible to the auditor.

Q: What are some common issues found in IT audits?

A: Some common issues found in IT audits include lack of sufficient controls, outdated systems, poor data management practices, and non-compliance with regulations.

Q: What is the role of IT governance in an IT audit?

A: IT governance plays a crucial role in an IT audit as it sets the direction and establishes the controls for the IT environment. The effectiveness of IT governance is often a key focus of an IT audit.

Q: How is data privacy considered in an IT audit?

A: Data privacy is a key consideration in an IT audit. The auditor assesses whether the organization has appropriate controls in place to protect sensitive data and comply with relevant regulations.

Q: What is the relationship between IT audit and cybersecurity?

A: IT audit and cybersecurity are closely related. A key part of an IT audit is assessing the organization's cybersecurity controls and practices to ensure that data and systems are protected from threats.

Q: How often should an IT audit be conducted?

A: The frequency of IT audits can vary depending on the organization's size, complexity, and industry. However, it's generally recommended to conduct an IT audit at least once a year.

Q: What is the role of internal audit in IT audit?

A: The role of internal audit in IT audit is to provide an independent assessment of the organization's IT controls, processes, and policies. They help identify risks and recommend improvements.

Q: What is the role of external audit in IT audit?

A: The role of external audit in IT audit is to provide an independent and objective assessment of the organization's IT environment, often as part of a financial audit or regulatory compliance audit.

Q: What is the difference between IT audit and IT compliance?

A: IT audit involves assessing the effectiveness of IT controls and processes, while IT compliance focuses on ensuring that the organization is adhering to relevant laws, regulations, and standards.

Q: What is SOX compliance in the context of an IT audit?

A: SOX compliance refers to adherence to the Sarbanes-Oxley Act, which requires organizations to implement certain controls and processes to ensure the accuracy and reliability of financial reporting. An IT audit would assess the effectiveness of these controls.

Q: What is the role of an IT audit in disaster recovery planning?

A: An IT audit plays a crucial role in disaster recovery planning by assessing the effectiveness of the organization's disaster recovery processes and controls, and recommending improvements to ensure business continuity in the event of a disaster.

Q: How does an IT audit contribute to an organization's strategic planning?

A: An IT audit can contribute to an organization's strategic planning by providing insights into the effectiveness and efficiency of IT operations, identifying areas for improvement, and supporting decision-making on IT investments.

Q: What is a vulnerability assessment in an IT audit?

A: An IT audit's vulnerability assessment entails detecting, measuring, and ranking vulnerabilities in a system, network, or infrastructure.

Q: What is a penetration test in an IT audit?

A: A penetration test in an IT audit is a simulated attack on a system or network to evaluate its security and identify vulnerabilities that could be exploited by hackers.

Q: What is the role of data analytics in an IT audit?

A: Data analytics can play a significant role in an IT audit by enabling auditors to analyze large volumes of data quickly and accurately, identify patterns and trends, and provide evidence to support audit findings.

Q: What is an IT audit checklist?

A: An IT audit checklist is a tool used by auditors to guide the audit process. It typically includes key areas to review, questions to ask, and documentation to obtain.

Q: What is the importance of documentation in an IT audit?

A: Documentation is essential in an IT audit as it provides evidence of the controls and processes in place and supports the auditor's findings and recommendations.

Q: How does an IT audit support risk management?

A: An IT audit supports risk management by identifying and assessing risks in the IT environment, evaluating the effectiveness of controls to mitigate these risks, and recommending improvements.

Q: What is the role of change management in an IT audit?

A: Change management plays a key role in an IT audit as it involves monitoring and controlling changes to the IT environment to ensure they do not introduce new risks or vulnerabilities.

Q: How can an IT audit support operational efficiency?

A: An IT audit can support operational efficiency by identifying inefficiencies in IT processes and systems, and recommending improvements to increase productivity and reduce costs.

Q: What is the role of IT audit in project management?

A: IT audit plays a role in project management by evaluating the controls and processes in place for managing IT projects, assessing project risks, and ensuring that projects are delivered on time and within budget.

Q: What is the role of IT audit in IT service management?

A: IT audit plays a role in IT service management by evaluating the effectiveness and efficiency of IT services, assessing service risks, and recommending improvements to enhance service delivery and customer satisfaction.

Q: What is the role of IT audit in data governance?

A: IT audit plays a role in data governance by assessing the controls and processes for managing and protecting data, ensuring data quality, and ensuring compliance with data regulations.

Q: What is the role of IT audit in IT asset management?

A: IT audit plays a role in IT asset management by assessing the controls and processes for managing and tracking IT assets, ensuring optimal utilization of assets, and ensuring compliance with asset management policies and regulations.

Q: What is the role of IT audit in IT performance management?

A: IT audit plays a role in IT performance management by assessing the processes for measuring and managing IT performance, ensuring alignment with business objectives, and recommending improvements to enhance IT performance.

Q: What is the role of IT audit in IT security management?

A: IT audit plays a crucial role in IT security management by assessing the controls and processes for managing IT security, identifying security risks, and recommending improvements to enhance IT security.

Q: What is the role of IT audit in IT financial management?
A: IT audit plays a role in IT financial management by assessing the controls and processes for managing IT finances, ensuring alignment with financial goals, and recommending improvements to enhance financial performance.
Q: What is the role of IT audit in IT strategy management?
A: IT audit plays a role in IT strategy management by assessing the processes for developing and implementing IT strategy, ensuring alignment with business strategy, and recommending improvements to enhance strategic performance.
Q: What is the role of IT audit in IT vendor management?
A: IT audit plays a role in IT vendor management by assessing the controls and processes for managing IT vendors, ensuring alignment with vendor management goals, and recommending improvements to enhance vendor performance.
Q: What is the role of IT audit in IT service delivery?
A: IT audit plays a role in IT service delivery by assessing the effectiveness and efficiency of IT services, evaluating service risks, and recommending improvements to enhance service delivery and customer satisfaction.

Applications

Scenario 1:

A company named AlphaTech has recently implemented a new software system to streamline its operations. As an IT auditor, you are tasked with ensuring that the new system is secure and compliant with regulations. You perform an audit and discover that the system has multiple security vulnerabilities that could potentially expose sensitive data.

Solution: The IT auditor should recommend immediate patches for the identified vulnerabilities, followed by regular system updates. They should also suggest a comprehensive review of the system's security features, and the implementation of stronger access controls and encryption methods.

Effectiveness: This solution is effective as it addresses the immediate security threats, while also laying the groundwork for ongoing system maintenance and enhancement.

Scenario 2:

BetaCorp, a financial institution, has experienced a significant system outage that lasted several hours, causing a loss of data and disruption of services. As an IT auditor, you are asked to investigate the incident.

Solution: The IT auditor should conduct a thorough analysis of the incident, including a review of system logs and interviews with IT staff. They should recommend implementing a robust data backup and recovery plan, and improving system redundancy to avoid similar incidents in the future.

Effectiveness: This solution is effective as it not only identifies the root cause of the problem, but also provides a proactive approach to prevent the recurrence of such issues.

Scenario 3:

A retail chain, GammaStores, has recently launched its e-commerce platform. However, they do not have a cybersecurity policy in place. As an IT auditor, your job is to assess the risk.

Solution: The IT auditor should insist on the creation and implementation of a comprehensive cybersecurity policy. This should include rules on password management, use of firewalls, encryption, and regular system updates. Regular cybersecurity training for employees should also be recommended.

Effectiveness: The solution is effective as it not only addresses the immediate risk but also ensures that the company is better prepared to handle future cyber threats.

Scenario 4:

DeltaHealth, a healthcare provider, uses a system that frequently crashes. As an IT auditor, you need to assess the situation.

Solution: The IT auditor should conduct a thorough investigation to determine the cause of the frequent crashes. They should recommend system upgrades or replacement if necessary. They should also suggest regular system maintenance to prevent future crashes.

Effectiveness: This solution is effective because it addresses the immediate problem and suggests ways to prevent future system crashes.

Management Audit

Theoretical

Q: What is a management audit?

A: A management audit is a systematic evaluation of managerial activities to assess the efficiency and effectiveness of management and to ensure that the organization's objectives are achieved.

Q: What is the primary purpose of a management audit?

A: The primary purpose of a management audit is to identify areas of inefficiency, redundancy, or outdated procedures in an organization's management processes.

Q: How does a management audit differ from a financial audit?

A: While a financial audit focuses on the accuracy of financial records, a management audit focuses on the effectiveness and efficiency of management processes.

Q: What are the key components of a management audit?

A: The key components of a management audit include an assessment of management policies, practices, control procedures, and decision-making processes.

Q: What is the role of an auditor in a management audit?

A: The auditor's role in a management audit is to evaluate the efficiency and effectiveness of management processes, identify areas for improvement, and provide recommendations to enhance performance.

Q: Why is a management audit necessary?

A: A management audit is necessary to ensure that an organization's management processes are functioning effectively, to identify areas for improvement, and to support decision-making processes.

Q: Can a management audit identify potential risks?

A: Yes, a management audit can identify potential risks associated with inefficiencies in management processes, which can then be mitigated to prevent future problems.

Q: How can a management audit improve organizational performance?

A: A management audit can improve organizational performance by identifying areas of inefficiency and providing recommendations for improvement.

Q: What skills are necessary for conducting a management audit?

A: Skills necessary for conducting a management audit include analytical thinking, problem-solving, communication, and a deep understanding of management processes and practices.

Q: How often should a management audit be conducted?

A: The frequency of a management audit can vary depending on the organization's needs, but it is generally conducted annually to ensure continuous improvement.

Q: What is the outcome of a successful management audit?

A: The outcome of a successful management audit is improved efficiency and effectiveness of management processes, reduced risk, and enhanced decision-making capabilities.

Q: How does a management audit contribute to strategic planning?

A: A management audit contributes to strategic planning by providing valuable information about the effectiveness of management processes, which can be used to inform strategic decisions.

Q: What are the steps involved in a management audit?

A: The steps involved in a management audit include planning, data collection, analysis, reporting, and follow-up.

Q: What challenges can arise during a management audit?
A: Challenges can arise during a management audit, such as resistance from management, lack of data, and difficulties in measuring management effectiveness.
Q: What tools can be used to conduct a management audit?
A: Tools such as questionnaires, interviews, document reviews, and observation can be used to conduct a management audit.
Q: How can the results of a management audit be communicated effectively?
A: The results of a management audit can be communicated effectively through a detailed report that includes findings, recommendations, and an action plan.
Q: What role does management play in facilitating a management audit?
A: Management plays a crucial role in facilitating a management audit, as they provide necessary information, support the audit process, and implement recommendations.
Q: What is the relationship between a management audit and corporate governance?
A: A management audit supports corporate governance by ensuring that management processes are effective and aligned with the organization's objectives.
Q: Can a management audit be conducted internally?
A: Yes, a management audit can be conducted internally by an organization's own audit team, or externally by a third-party auditor.
Q: How is a management audit scope defined?
A: The scope of a management audit is defined based on the organization's objectives, the areas of management to be evaluated, and the resources available.
Q: What is the importance of impartiality in a management audit?

A: Impartiality is important in a management audit to ensure that findings and recommendations are objective and free from bias.

Q: How can a management audit support continuous improvement?

A: A management audit supports continuous improvement by identifying areas for improvement and providing recommendations for enhancing management processes.

Q: Who can request a management audit?

A: A management audit can be requested by the board of directors, senior management, or any stakeholder who has an interest in the efficiency and effectiveness of the organization's management processes.

Q: What is the role of a management audit in risk management?

A: A management audit plays a role in risk management by identifying and assessing potential risks associated with management processes.

Q: How can the findings of a management audit inform decision-making processes?

A: The findings of a management audit can inform decision-making processes by providing valuable insights into the effectiveness of management processes and areas for improvement.

Q: What types of organizations can benefit from a management audit?

A: All types of organizations, regardless of their size or industry, can benefit from a management audit.

Q: What is the role of a management audit in change management?

A: A management audit can play a role in change management by identifying the need for change in management processes and providing recommendations for implementing change.

Q: How can a management audit enhance accountability?

A: A management audit enhances accountability by evaluating the effectiveness of management processes and holding management responsible for implementing recommendations for improvement.
Q: Can a management audit be used to evaluate the performance of individual managers?
A: While a management audit primarily focuses on management processes, it can also be used to evaluate the performance of individual managers.
Q: How can a management audit contribute to organizational learning?
A: A management audit contributes to organizational learning by providing valuable insights into the effectiveness of management processes, which can be used to inform future practices.
Q: What is the role of documentation in a management audit?
A: Documentation plays a crucial role in a management audit, as it provides evidence of management processes and supports the audit findings.
Q: How can a management audit support innovation?
A: A management audit can support innovation by identifying outdated or inefficient management processes and providing recommendations for new and improved processes.
Q: How can resistance to a management audit be managed?
A: Resistance to a management audit can be managed through effective communication, involving management in the audit process, and demonstrating the benefits of the audit.
Q: What is the role of a management audit in quality management?
A: A management audit plays a role in quality management by ensuring that management processes meet quality standards and contribute to the achievement of the organization's objectives.
Q: How can a management audit support transparency?

A: A management audit supports transparency by providing an objective evaluation of management processes and making the findings available to stakeholders.

Q: What is the relationship between a management audit and performance management?

A: A management audit supports performance management by evaluating the effectiveness of management processes and providing recommendations for enhancing performance.

Q: Can a management audit be used to evaluate the effectiveness of strategic initiatives?

A: Yes, a management audit can be used to evaluate the effectiveness of strategic initiatives by assessing whether they are being managed effectively.

Q: How does a management audit support compliance with regulations?

A: A management audit supports compliance with regulations by ensuring that management processes are in line with legal and regulatory requirements.

Q: What is the role of a management audit in crisis management?

A: A management audit can play a role in crisis management by identifying potential risks and providing recommendations for mitigating them.

Q: How can the recommendations of a management audit be implemented effectively?

A: The recommendations of a management audit can be implemented effectively through a detailed action plan, management support, and continuous monitoring.

Q: Can a management audit evaluate the effectiveness of communication processes?

A: Yes, a management audit can evaluate the effectiveness of communication processes as part of the overall assessment of management effectiveness.

Q: How can a management audit support stakeholder engagement?
A: A management audit can support stakeholder engagement by providing transparent information about the effectiveness of management processes and involving stakeholders in the audit process.
Q: What is the role of a management audit in resource management?
A: A management audit can play a role in resource management by evaluating the efficiency and effectiveness of resource allocation and utilization.
Q: How can a management audit support sustainability initiatives?
A: A management audit can support sustainability initiatives by assessing the effectiveness of management processes in achieving sustainability objectives.
Q: What is the role of a management audit in performance measurement?
A: A management audit plays a role in performance measurement by providing an objective assessment of the effectiveness of management processes.
Q: How can a management audit support organizational culture?
A: A management audit can support organizational culture by assessing the alignment of management processes with the organization's values and norms.
Q: What is the role of a management audit in project management?
A: A management audit can play a role in project management by evaluating the effectiveness of project management processes and providing recommendations for improvement.
Q: Can a management audit be used to evaluate the effectiveness of decision-making processes?

A: Yes, a management audit can be used to evaluate the effectiveness of decision-making processes as part of the overall assessment of management effectiveness.

Q: How can a management audit support employee engagement?

A: A management audit can support employee engagement by identifying areas for improvement in management practices and processes that affect employee motivation and satisfaction.

Q: What is the role of a management audit in operational efficiency?

A: A management audit plays a key role in operational efficiency by identifying inefficiencies in management processes and providing recommendations for improvement.

Applications

Scenario 1:

John is an auditor for a multi-national corporation. He is tasked with conducting a management audit for a smaller subsidiary company. The subsidiary company has been experiencing frequent changes in managerial personnel. John's task is to ascertain whether these changes have affected the efficiency of the company. He notices that the frequent changes have led to inconsistencies in decision-making and execution of tasks. The management audit reveals a lack of continuity and coherence in the company's operations. This, John concludes, has negatively impacted the company's efficiency.

Scenario 2:

Mary is a seasoned auditor in a manufacturing firm tasked with conducting a management audit. She is looking into the company's production unit that has seen a decline in productivity over the recent quarters. Her audit reveals that the decline is due to poor supervision and inefficient management of resources. The managers have not been effectively coordinating the workflow, leading to a lack of synergy among the employees. Mary recommends a retraining of managers to improve their supervisory skills and better manage resources.

Scenario 3:

Peter, an auditor for a chain of retail stores, is carrying out a management audit on one of their poorly performing stores. He discovers that the store's poor performance is due to the ineffective communication between the management and the staff. The staff are not fully aware of the store's objectives and goals, leading to poor performance. Peter suggests that the management should improve communication channels and ensure that all staff members are aware of the store's goals.

Scenario 4:

Jane is an auditor in a software company. She is tasked with conducting a management audit on the company's software development department. She notices that the department has been consistently missing deadlines. Jane's audit reveals a lack of proper project management. The projects are not effectively planned, and the department lacks a system to track the progress of each project. Jane concludes that the department needs to adopt a project management tool to improve efficiency.

Scenario 5:

Mark, an auditor in a logistics company, is conducting a management audit on the company's delivery department. The department has been receiving numerous customer complaints regarding late deliveries. Mark's audit reveals that the department is understaffed and the current staff are overworked. He suggests that the company should hire more delivery personnel to meet the increasing demand for their services.

Operational Audit

Theoretical

Q: What is an operational audit?

A: An operational audit is a detailed analysis conducted to evaluate the efficiency, effectiveness, and economy of operations within an organization.

Q: What is the main goal of an operational audit?

A: The main goal of an operational audit is to improve operational efficiency within an organization.

Q: What are the key elements assessed during an operational audit?

A: Key elements assessed during an operational audit include organizational structure, information systems, policies and procedures, and operational processes.

Q: Who usually conducts an operational audit?

A: An operational audit is typically conducted by internal auditors or an external consulting firm.

Q: How does an operational audit differ from a financial audit?

A: While a financial audit focuses on the accuracy of financial statements, an operational audit evaluates the effectiveness and efficiency of operations.

Q: What are the main stages of an operational audit?

A: The main stages of an operational audit are planning, fieldwork, reporting, and follow-up.

Q: How does an operational audit benefit an organization?

A: An operational audit can identify inefficiencies, reduce costs, improve productivity, and help an organization meet its strategic goals.

Q: What is the role of management in an operational audit?

A: Management is responsible for implementing the recommendations made during an operational audit.

Q: How often should an operational audit be conducted?

A: The frequency of operational audits depends on the size and complexity of the organization, but they are typically done annually.

Q: What is the first step in an operational audit?

A: The first step in an operational audit is planning, which includes defining the scope and objectives of the audit.

Q: What types of businesses benefit from operational audits?

A: All types of businesses can benefit from operational audits, from small companies to large corporations.

Q: What is the role of a risk assessment in an operational audit?

A: A risk assessment helps auditors identify the areas of operation that pose the greatest risk and need to be audited.

Q: What is the purpose of the fieldwork stage in an operational audit?

A: The fieldwork stage involves collecting and analyzing data to assess the operations against the audit objectives.

Q: How are the results of an operational audit reported?

A: The results of an operational audit are typically reported in a written document, which outlines the findings, recommendations, and any necessary action plans.

Q: What happens during the follow-up stage of an operational audit?

A: During the follow-up stage, auditors check whether the recommended changes have been implemented and are having the desired effect.

Q: What skills are necessary for an operational auditor?
A: An operational auditor needs analytical skills, communication skills, knowledge of the industry and business operations, and understanding of audit principles and procedures.
Q: What is a process map in the context of an operational audit?
A: A process map is a visual tool used by auditors to understand and analyze the steps involved in a process.
Q: How can an operational audit improve customer satisfaction?
A: An operational audit can identify areas of inefficiency that may be impacting customer service and recommend improvements.
Q: What is the role of benchmarking in an operational audit?
A: Benchmarking involves comparing an organization's operations to industry standards or best practices to identify areas for improvement.
Q: How can an operational audit contribute to strategic planning?
A: An operational audit can provide valuable insights into the effectiveness and efficiency of operations, which can inform strategic planning.
Q: Can an operational audit help with regulatory compliance?
A: Yes, an operational audit can identify areas of non-compliance and recommend measures to ensure regulatory compliance.
Q: What is the relationship between operational audit and performance management?
A: An operational audit can provide insights into performance and recommend improvements, contributing to effective performance management.
Q: What is the role of internal controls in an operational audit?
A: Internal controls are assessed during an operational audit to ensure they are effectively managing risks and promoting efficient operations.
Q: Can operational audits identify fraud?

A: While not their primary purpose, operational audits can identify signs of fraud, such as irregularities in processes or controls.

Q: How does an operational audit align with an organization's objectives?

A: An operational audit helps ensure that operations are conducted effectively and efficiently, helping the organization achieve its objectives.

Q: What is the role of documentation in an operational audit?

A: Documentation is crucial in an operational audit to provide evidence of the audit process and findings.

Q: Can an operational audit help in decision making?

A: Yes, the insights and recommendations from an operational audit can inform strategic decision making.

Q: What is a SWOT analysis in the context of an operational audit?

A: A SWOT analysis is a tool used in operational audits to identify strengths, weaknesses, opportunities, and threats in the organization's operations.

Q: How does an operational audit address operational risks?

A: An operational audit identifies operational risks and recommends measures to mitigate them.

Q: What is the role of communication in an operational audit?

A: Effective communication is crucial in an operational audit to ensure all stakeholders understand the audit process, findings, and recommendations.

Q: How can operational audits improve productivity?

A: Operational audits can identify inefficiencies and recommend improvements, leading to increased productivity.

Q: What is an audit trail in the context of an operational audit?

A: An audit trail is a record of the audit process, including the data collected, analysis conducted, and conclusions reached.

Q: How does an operational audit contribute to continuous improvement?
A: An operational audit identifies areas for improvement and recommends changes, contributing to continuous improvement in operations.
Q: What is the role of technology in operational audits?
A: Technology can facilitate data collection, analysis, and reporting in operational audits.
Q: Can operational audits identify cost-saving opportunities?
A: Yes, operational audits can identify inefficiencies and unnecessary expenses, leading to cost savings.
Q: How does an operational audit address quality issues?
A: An operational audit can identify quality issues and recommend measures to improve quality.
Q: Can operational audits help with change management?
A: Yes, the insights and recommendations from operational audits can inform and support change management.
Q: What is the role of performance indicators in an operational audit?
A: Performance indicators are used in operational audits to measure the effectiveness and efficiency of operations.
Q: How do operational audits contribute to risk management?
A: Operational audits identify operational risks and recommend measures to mitigate them, contributing to effective risk management.
Q: What is the relationship between operational audits and corporate governance?
A: Operational audits contribute to effective corporate governance by ensuring operations are conducted efficiently, effectively, and in compliance with regulations.
Q: What is the role of an operational audit committee?

A: An operational audit committee provides oversight of the operational audit process and ensures the implementation of audit recommendations.

Q: Can operational audits improve operational resilience?

A: Yes, operational audits can identify vulnerabilities and recommend measures to enhance operational resilience.

Q: What is the role of data analysis in operational audits?

A: Data analysis is used in operational audits to assess the effectiveness and efficiency of operations.

Q: Can operational audits contribute to innovation?

A: Yes, the insights from operational audits can inform and inspire innovation in operations.

Q: How do operational audits support sustainability efforts?

A: Operational audits can identify opportunities to improve efficiency and reduce waste, supporting sustainability efforts.

Q: What is the role of stakeholder engagement in operational audits?

A: Stakeholder engagement is important in operational audits to ensure all relevant perspectives are considered and to build support for the implementation of audit recommendations.

Q: Can operational audits improve supply chain management?

A: Yes, operational audits can identify inefficiencies and risks in the supply chain and recommend improvements.

Q: What is the role of operational audits in mergers and acquisitions?

A: Operational audits can provide valuable insights into the operations of a target company in a merger or acquisition.

Q: What is the relationship between operational audits and business continuity planning?

A: Operational audits can identify vulnerabilities and recommend measures to enhance resilience, informing business continuity planning.

Q: How do operational audits support ethical business practices?
A: Operational audits can identify unethical practices and recommend measures to promote ethical operations.

Applications

Scenario 1:

At XYZ Corporation, an operational audit was conducted and the audit team discovered that the company's IT systems were outdated and were not fully capable of supporting business operations. The audit team also found a lack of standard operating procedures (SOPs) for various processes in the company.

Question: As an operational auditor, how would you address these challenges?

Answer: As an operational auditor, I would recommend the management to update the company's IT system to ensure it supports the business processes effectively. I would also suggest the development and implementation of SOPs for all processes within the organization. This would improve efficiency, reduce errors, and ensure consistency in operations.

Scenario 2:

In ABC Manufacturing Company, an operational audit revealed that the company was not effectively utilizing its production capacity. The audit also found a high rate of product defects which was impacting the company's profitability.

Question: As an operational auditor, what steps would you take to improve the situation?

Answer: As an operational auditor, I would recommend strategies to optimize the use of production capacity. This could include techniques like lean manufacturing or just-in-time production. To address the high defect rate, I would suggest implementing a robust quality control system, and possibly investing in better training for workers.

Scenario 3:

During an operational audit at PQR Tech, it was found that the company had a high employee turnover rate. The audit also revealed that there were no effective performance appraisal systems in place.

Question: As an operational auditor, how would you propose to rectify these issues?

Answer: As an operational auditor, I would propose the implementation of a comprehensive performance appraisal system that rewards good performance and encourages employee retention. I would also suggest the management to look into the reasons for high employee turnover and take corrective actions accordingly. This could include improving the work environment, offering competitive salaries, or providing better growth opportunities.

Scenario 4:

In an operational audit at LMN Retail, the audit team found that the company's inventory management system was not efficient, leading to frequent stock outs and overstocking of certain items.

Question: As an operational auditor, what would be your advice to the management?

Answer: I would suggest the management to invest in an advanced inventory management system that can accurately forecast demand and manage inventory levels efficiently. This would help reduce stock-outs and overstocking, thus improving the company's profitability.

Scenario 5:

During an operational audit at EFG Services, it was found that the company's customer service was not up to the mark, leading to a high number of customer complaints.

Question: As an operational auditor, how would you address this issue?

Answer: I would recommend the management to focus on improving customer service by providing proper training to the customer service staff. The company could also implement a customer feedback system to understand the areas of improvement and take appropriate corrective actions.

In all these scenarios, the effectiveness of the auditor's recommendations would be evaluated based on the improvement in the respective areas after their implementation.

Performance Audit

Theoretical

Q: What is a performance audit?

A: A performance audit is an independent examination of a program, function, operation or the management systems and procedures of a governmental or non-profit entity to assess whether the entity is achieving economy, efficiency and effectiveness in the employment of available resources.

Q: Who conducts the performance audit?

A: Performance audits are usually carried out by internal or external auditors.

Q: What is the main purpose of a performance audit?

A: The primary goal of a performance audit is to supply information that enhances public accountability and aids decision-making for those tasked with supervising or implementing remedial measures.

Q: What are the steps involved in a performance audit?

A: The steps involved in a performance audit include planning, conducting, reporting and follow-up.

Q: What is the planning phase in a performance audit?

A: The planning phase involves identifying the audit objectives and scope, understanding the auditee's operations, and developing an audit plan.

Q: What happens during the conducting phase of a performance audit?

A: During the conducting phase, auditors gather evidence through various methods such as interviews, observations, and document reviews to assess the auditee's performance against the audit objectives.

Q: What is included in the reporting phase of a performance audit?

A: The reporting phase involves preparing an audit report that presents the audit findings, conclusions, and recommendations.

Q: What is the follow-up phase in a performance audit?

A: The follow-up phase involves monitoring the auditee's actions to address the audit recommendations.

Q: What is the role of performance audit in improving accountability?

A: Performance audit enhances accountability by providing objective and independent assessments of whether government programs and operations are implemented effectively, efficiently, and in compliance with applicable laws and regulations.

Q: How does a performance audit differ from a financial audit?

A: While a financial audit focuses on whether financial statements are presented fairly in accordance with generally accepted accounting principles, a performance audit focuses on assessing the performance of an organization, program, activity or function in order to provide recommendations for improvement.

Q: What is the concept of materiality in a performance audit?

A: Materiality in a performance audit refers to the significance of an issue or event that could impact the auditee's ability to achieve its objectives.

Q: What is the role of risk assessment in a performance audit?

A: Risk assessment in a performance audit helps in identifying areas of high risk that need more focus during the audit.

Q: What is the importance of evidence in a performance audit?

A: Evidence in a performance audit is crucial as it provides the basis for the auditors' findings, conclusions, and recommendations.

Q: How does a performance audit contribute to decision-making?

A: A performance audit provides vital information that can be used by management and other decision-makers to make informed decisions about the operations and performance of their organization.

Q: What skills are required for conducting a performance audit?

A: Conducting a performance audit requires skills like analytical thinking, critical evaluation, effective communication, and a thorough understanding of the auditee's operations.

Q: What is the relevance of performance audit in the public sector?

A: Performance audit in the public sector helps in enhancing public accountability, improving service delivery, and promoting efficient use of public resources.

Q: How can the findings of a performance audit be used?

A: The findings of a performance audit can be used by the auditee to improve their operations and performance, and by oversight bodies and other stakeholders to hold the auditee accountable.

Q: What is the role of performance audit in promoting transparency?

A: Performance audit promotes transparency by providing an independent and objective assessment of the auditee's operations and performance.

Q: What are some challenges encountered in conducting a performance audit?

A: Some challenges in conducting a performance audit include lack of access to necessary information, resistance from the auditee, and limitations in the auditors' skills and knowledge.

Q: What is the relationship between performance audit and governance?
A: Performance audit contributes to good governance by promoting accountability, transparency, effectiveness, and efficiency in the management of public resources.
Q: What is the impact of a performance audit on internal controls?
A: A performance audit can help in identifying weaknesses in internal controls and provide recommendations for improvement.
Q: How does a performance audit support strategic planning?
A: A performance audit provides valuable insights on the effectiveness, efficiency, and economy of operations that can be used in strategic planning.
Q: What is the role of communication in a performance audit?
A: Communication is vital in a performance audit as it facilitates understanding between the auditors and the auditee, and ensures that the audit findings, conclusions, and recommendations are clearly conveyed.
Q: What is the relevance of a performance audit in a non-profit organization?
A: In a non-profit organization, a performance audit can help in assessing whether the organization is effectively achieving its mission and making efficient use of its resources.
Q: What are the ethical considerations in conducting a performance audit?
A: Some ethical considerations in conducting a performance audit include maintaining independence and objectivity, ensuring confidentiality of information, and performing the audit with integrity and professionalism.
Q: What is the role of performance audit in promoting efficiency?

A: Performance audit promotes efficiency by identifying areas of waste, inefficiency, and ineffectiveness in the auditee's operations and providing recommendations for improvement.

Q: How does a performance audit support continuous improvement?

A: A performance audit supports continuous improvement by providing regular assessments of the auditee's performance and recommending actions for improvement.

Q: What is the impact of a performance audit on risk management?

A: A performance audit can help in identifying and assessing risks, and contribute to the effectiveness of the auditee's risk management processes.

Q: What is the importance of stakeholder engagement in a performance audit?

A: Stakeholder engagement is important in a performance audit as it helps in understanding the perspectives of different stakeholders and ensuring that their concerns and expectations are considered in the audit.

Q: What is the role of performance audit in promoting economy?

A: Performance audit promotes economy by assessing whether resources are being used in the most cost-effective manner.

Q: How does a performance audit contribute to public trust?

A: Performance audit contributes to public trust by providing independent and objective assessments of the performance of public entities, and promoting transparency and accountability.

Q: What is the importance of a performance audit plan?

A: A performance audit plan provides a roadmap for the audit, outlining the audit objectives, scope, methodology, and timeline.

Q: How is the effectiveness of a performance audit measured?

A: The effectiveness of a performance audit can be measured by the extent to which its findings and recommendations have been implemented by the auditee and led to improvements in performance.

Q: What is the role of performance audit in promoting value for money?

A: Performance audit promotes value for money by assessing whether resources are being used effectively, efficiently, and economically.

Q: How can performance audit contribute to service delivery?

A: Performance audit can contribute to service delivery by identifying areas for improvement and recommending actions to enhance the quality, efficiency, and effectiveness of services.

Q: What is the importance of performance indicators in a performance audit?

A: Performance indicators are important in a performance audit as they provide a basis for assessing the auditee's performance against the audit objectives.

Q: What is the role of performance audit in promoting accountability?

A: Performance audit promotes accountability by providing an independent and objective assessment of the performance of an organization, program, activity or function, and recommending actions for improvement.

Q: How does a performance audit contribute to operational efficiency?

A: A performance audit contributes to operational efficiency by identifying areas for improvement in the auditee's operations and recommending actions for improvement.

Q: What is the importance of objectivity in a performance audit?

A: Objectivity is vital in a performance audit as it ensures that the audit findings and conclusions are based on unbiased analysis of evidence.

Q: How can a performance audit contribute to policy development?

A: A performance audit can contribute to policy development by providing evidence-based information that can be used in formulating and revising policies.

Q: What is the role of performance audit in promoting effectiveness?

A: Performance audit promotes effectiveness by assessing whether the auditee is achieving its objectives and providing recommendations for improvement.

Q: How does a performance audit contribute to resource management?

A: A performance audit contributes to resource management by identifying areas of waste and inefficiency, and recommending actions for more effective and efficient use of resources.

Q: What is the importance of independence in a performance audit?

A: Independence is vital in a performance audit as it ensures that the auditors are free from any influence that could compromise their judgement or objectivity.

Q: How can a performance audit contribute to organizational learning?

A: A performance audit can contribute to organizational learning by providing valuable insights on the organization's performance and operations, and recommending actions for improvement.

Q: What is the role of performance audit in promoting transparency?

A: Performance audit promotes transparency by providing an independent and objective assessment of the auditee's performance and operations, and making the audit findings and recommendations public.

Q: What is the importance of a performance audit report?

A: A performance audit report is important as it communicates the audit findings, conclusions, and recommendations to the auditee and other stakeholders.

Q: How does a performance audit contribute to decision-making?

A: A performance audit contributes to decision-making by providing objective and evidence-based information that can be used in making informed decisions.

Q: What is the role of performance audit in promoting accountability?

A: Performance audit promotes accountability by providing an independent and objective assessment of the auditee's performance and operations, and recommending actions for improvement.

Q: How does a performance audit contribute to risk management?

A: A performance audit contributes to risk management by identifying and assessing risks, and recommending actions for managing those risks.

Q: What is the importance of follow-up in a performance audit?

A: Follow-up is important in a performance audit as it ensures that the auditee has taken appropriate actions to address the audit recommendations.

Applications

Scenario 1: ABC Manufacturing Company recently underwent an internal performance audit, and the results were not satisfactory. The audit report showed a significant deviation in the company's production processes, with a substantial number of defective products being produced. How would you assess the effectiveness of the performance audit?

Evaluation: A performance audit's effectiveness can be determined by its ability to identify areas of inefficiency or non-compliance in an organization's operations and to recommend corrective actions.

In this scenario, the audit was effective as it identified a significant issue in the production process. The next step is to implement the recommendations provided in the audit report to improve the quality of the products.

Scenario 2: XYZ Corporation hired an external auditor to conduct a performance audit. However, the auditor's report lacked clarity and depth in its findings. The corporation's management is unsure of what actions to take based on the report. How can the effectiveness of this audit be evaluated?

Evaluation: The effectiveness of a performance audit can also be measured by the clarity and usability of its findings and recommendations. In this case, the audit was ineffective as it failed to provide clear, actionable findings. The auditor should have provided detailed suggestions for improvement based on identified issues.

Scenario 3: DEF Construction, a large construction company, underwent a performance audit that highlighted several safety violations at their worksites. The audit report provided suggestions for improving safety measures and mitigating risks. However, no improvements have been noticed in the subsequent months. How would you evaluate the effectiveness of this audit?

Evaluation: Despite the audit identifying safety violations and providing recommendations, its effectiveness is questionable if no changes are implemented. An effective performance audit should not only identify problems but should also lead to improvements in operations. Therefore, it is crucial for DEF Construction to act upon the recommendations provided in the audit report.

Scenario 4: GHI Retail, a supermarket chain, conducted a performance audit to assess their inventory management process. The audit revealed several inefficiencies in their current system and recommended a restructuring of the process. Following the audit, the company implemented the recommendations, which led to significant improvements. How can the effectiveness of this audit be gauged?

Evaluation: The audit's effectiveness can be determined by the positive changes it brings about in the company's operations. In this scenario, the audit was successful as it identified inefficiencies, provided actionable recommendations, and those recommendations were implemented, leading to noticeable improvements in inventory management.

Scenario 5: JKL Tech, a software development company, had a performance audit that focused on their project management practices. The audit report pointed out that projects were frequently delivered late and over budget. However, no specific recommendations were provided for improvement. How would you assess the audit's effectiveness?

Evaluation: While the audit identified key issues in project management, its lack of specific recommendations limits its effectiveness. An effective performance audit should provide concrete, actionable recommendations for improvement, to guide the organization towards better performance. In this case, the auditor should have suggested ways to improve project management practices to ensure timely and within budget delivery.

External Audit

Theoretical

Q: What is an external audit?

A: An external audit is a review of financial statements and procedures conducted by an independent auditor to ensure compliance with laws, regulations and industry standards.

Q: What is the main objective of an external audit?

A: The main objective of an external audit is to provide an independent assessment of the financial statements accuracy and the effectiveness of internal controls in an organization.

Q: Who are the key stakeholders in an external audit?

A: Key stakeholders in an external audit include shareholders, investors, regulatory authorities, and the organization's management.

Q: How is an external auditor different from an internal auditor?

A: An external auditor is independent from the organization being audited, whereas an internal auditor is an employee of the organization.

Q: What are the key steps involved in an external audit process?

A: The key steps include planning, testing, evaluating, and reporting.

Q: What is the role of external auditors in fraud detection?

A: While their main role is not to detect fraud, external auditors can help uncover fraud during their review of the financial statements and internal controls.

Q: What qualifications are required for an external auditor?
A: External auditors typically have a bachelor's degree in accounting or finance, along with certifications like the Certified Public Accountant (CPA).
Q: What is the importance of auditor independence?
A: Auditor independence is important to ensure the audit results are unbiased and objective.
Q: How does an external audit improve financial transparency?
A: An external audit provides an unbiased review of an organization's financial statements, thereby enhancing its credibility and transparency.
Q: What is an audit report?
A: An audit report is a formal document where the auditor provides their opinion on the financial statements' accuracy and the effectiveness of internal controls in an organization.
Q: What is a qualified audit report?
A: A qualified audit report indicates that the auditor has reservations about the financial statements' accuracy or the effectiveness of internal controls.
Q: What is an unqualified audit report?
A: An unqualified audit report indicates that the auditor has no reservations about the financial statements' accuracy or the internal controls' effectiveness.
Q: What factors may influence the scope of an external audit?
A: Factors could include the size of the organization, the complexity of its operations, and the industry in which it operates.
Q: How can an external audit add value to an organization?
A: An external audit can add value by identifying areas for improvement and providing reassurance to stakeholders about the organization's financial health.
Q: What challenges can external auditors face during an audit?

A: Challenges can include lack of cooperation from the auditee, complex accounting issues, and time constraints.

Q: What is the role of external auditors in corporate governance?

A: External auditors play a key role in corporate governance by providing an independent assessment of the organization's financial statements and internal controls.

Q: How often should an external audit be conducted?

A: An external audit is typically conducted annually, but the exact frequency can depend on regulatory requirements and the organization's needs.

Q: What is the difference between a statutory and a non-statutory audit?

A: A statutory audit is required by law, while a non-statutory audit is not legally required and may be conducted for internal purposes.

Q: What are the different types of audit opinions?

A: Audit opinions include unqualified (clean), qualified, adverse, and disclaimer of opinion.

Q: How do external auditors assess the risk of material misstatement?

A: Auditors assess this risk by examining the organization's internal controls, understanding its operations and industry, and performing substantive testing on the financial statements.

Q: What does the term 'going concern' mean in auditing?

A: The term 'Going concern' implies the presumption that the organization will persist in conducting its activities in the near future.

Q: How do external auditors test internal controls?

A: Auditors test internal controls by observing operations, reviewing documentation, and performing walk-throughs and substantive tests.

Q: What is the difference between a financial audit and a performance audit?
A: A financial audit focuses on the accuracy of financial statements, while a performance audit evaluates the effectiveness and efficiency of operations.
Q: What is materiality in the context of an audit?
A: Materiality refers to the threshold above which misstatements or omissions in the financial statements are considered to influence the decisions of users.
Q: What is the role of audit evidence in an external audit?
A: Audit evidence provides the basis for the auditor's opinion on the financial statements' accuracy and the effectiveness of internal controls.
Q: How do external auditors maintain their independence?
A: Auditors maintain their independence by avoiding conflicts of interest, not taking on management roles within the auditee, and adhering to professional standards and ethics.
Q: What are the consequences of a poor audit?
A: A poor audit can lead to inaccurate financial reporting, loss of stakeholder trust, regulatory penalties, and potential legal repercussions.
Q: What is an audit risk?
A: Audit risk is the risk that the auditor may unknowingly fail to appropriately modify their opinion on financial statements that are materially misstated.
Q: How can technology aid in the external audit process?
A: Technology can aid in data analysis, risk assessment, and the effective and efficient execution of audit procedures.
Q: What is an integrated audit?
A: An integrated audit involves evaluating both the financial statements and the effectiveness of internal controls over financial reporting.

Q: What is the role of an engagement letter in an external audit?
A: An engagement letter outlines the scope of the audit, the auditor's responsibilities, and the terms of the engagement.
Q: How does an external audit contribute to accountability in an organization?
A: An external audit contributes to accountability by providing an independent assessment of the organization's financial accuracy and adherence to laws and regulations.
Q: What is the difference between a compliance audit and a financial audit?
A: A compliance audit checks the organization's adherence to laws and regulations, while a financial audit reviews the accuracy of financial statements.
Q: What is the 'audit trail' in an external audit?
A: An audit trail is a set of documents that provide evidence of the transactions and events examined during the audit.
Q: What is an audit sampling?
A: Audit sampling is the process of selecting a subset of transactions or data for examination, to provide a basis for conclusions about the entire data set.
Q: What role does professional skepticism play in an external audit?
A: Professional skepticism involves maintaining an attitude of questioning and critical assessment throughout the audit, which helps identify potential misstatements or issues.
Q: Why is confidentiality important in an external audit?
A: Confidentiality is important to protect sensitive information about the organization and to maintain trust between the auditor and the auditee.
Q: What distinguishes an audit from a review?

A: An audit provides a high level of assurance through in-depth examination and testing, while a review provides a moderate level of assurance through analytical procedures and inquiries.

Q: How can an external audit support decision-making in an organization?

A: The findings from an external audit can inform strategic decisions, guide improvements in internal controls, and enhance financial planning and management.

Q: What is the importance of communication in an external audit?

A: Effective communication ensures that all parties understand the audit scope, findings, and recommendations, and promotes transparency and collaboration.

Q: What is the difference between substantive testing and compliance testing in an audit?

A: Substantive testing verifies the accuracy of transactions and balances in the financial statements, while compliance testing checks the effectiveness of internal controls.

Q: How does an external audit support risk management in an organization?

A: An external audit can identify potential financial risks and assess the effectiveness of the organization's risk management strategies and controls.

Q: What are the key qualities of an effective external auditor?

A: Key qualities include analytical skills, attention to detail, integrity, independence, and strong communication skills.

Q: What is the role of management representation in an external audit?

A: Management representation is a written statement from the organization's management confirming the accuracy of the information provided to the auditor.

Q: How do external auditors ensure the reliability of audit evidence?

A: Auditors ensure the reliability of audit evidence through procedures like cross-checking, corroborating with independent sources, and assessing the quality and relevance of the evidence.

Q: What is a joint audit?

A: A joint audit is an audit conducted by two or more auditing firms, typically for large or complex organizations.

Q: What is the auditor's responsibility regarding subsequent events?

A: The auditor is responsible for considering any events or transactions that occur after the balance sheet date but before the audit report is issued, as they may affect the financial statements.

Q: How do external auditors deal with disagreements with management during an audit?

A: Disagreements are typically resolved through discussions, consultations, and if necessary, escalation to the audit committee or board of directors.

Q: What is the difference between an interim audit and a final audit?

A: An interim audit is conducted during the organization's fiscal year, while a final audit is conducted at the end of the fiscal year.

Q: What is the importance of continuous learning and professional development for external auditors?

A: Continuous learning and professional development help auditors stay updated with changes in laws, regulations, and industry standards, and enhance their skills and knowledge for effective auditing.

Applications

Scenario 1: A rapidly growing tech start-up has decided to undertake an external audit for the first time. The company is unsure about how to prepare for this process. What steps should they take to ensure a smooth and effective audit?

Solution: Firstly, the company needs to maintain clear and organized financial records, including all transactions and contracts. They should also familiarize themselves with auditing standards, as this will help them understand what auditors look for during the process. Furthermore, they should have internal controls in place to minimize errors and fraud. Lastly, open communication between the auditor and the company is crucial to address any issues that may arise during the audit.

Scenario 2: A medium-sized manufacturing company has been conducting external audits for several years. However, the company is not satisfied with the auditors' effectiveness as they feel the auditors are too lenient and do not identify significant issues in the financial statements. How can the company ensure a more effective audit?

Solution: The company can request a more thorough audit or switch to a different audit firm with a reputation for rigorous auditing. They should clearly communicate their expectations to the auditors and regularly meet with them to discuss any concerns. They could also consider hiring an audit quality assurance service to review the auditors' work.

Scenario 3: A retail company is planning to expand into international markets. They are unsure if their current external audit process, which is suited for domestic operations, would be effective for international operations. What changes, if any, should the company make to its audit process?

Solution: The company needs to ensure that their auditors understand international auditing standards and are familiar with the legal requirements of the countries they are expanding into. They should also ensure that the auditors have the necessary language skills to effectively communicate with international branches. Furthermore, they might need to adjust their audit schedule to account for different time zones and business practices.

Scenario 4: A non-profit organization has been accused of financial mismanagement and fraud. The organization wants to regain public trust by conducting an external audit. However, they are worried that the audit might uncover more issues, further damaging their reputation. What should the non-profit do?

Solution: While an audit might uncover more issues, it's a crucial step towards transparency and accountability. The non-profit should cooperate fully with the auditors and take immediate steps to rectify any issues identified. They should also communicate openly with the public about the steps they are taking to address their financial management issues.

Scenario 5: A large corporation is facing a lawsuit related to financial misrepresentation. The corporation's external auditors had given the financial statements a clean audit report. Is it possible that the auditors were ineffective, and if so, how?

Solution: Auditors might miss issues due to fraud, error, or their own negligence. The corporation should review the audit process and consider whether the auditors had access to all necessary information. If the auditors were at fault, the corporation could consider legal action against them or switch to a different audit firm.

Internal Audit

Theoretical

Q: What is the primary objective of an internal audit?

A: The primary objective of an internal audit is to evaluate the effectiveness of an organization's internal controls, corporate governance, and accounting processes.

Q: What is the role of an internal auditor?

A: An internal auditor's role involves examining the effectiveness of an organization's internal controls, including its corporate governance and accounting processes.

Q: What is the difference between an internal audit and an external audit?

A: An internal audit is conducted by an organization's own employees to identify internal control inefficiencies. An external audit is performed by an independent entity to validate financial statements.

Q: How does the internal audit add value to an organization?

A: Internal audit adds value by identifying risks and suggesting improvements to enhance the efficiency and effectiveness of an organization's operations.

Q: What are the key components of an internal audit?

A: Key components of an internal audit include planning, fieldwork, reporting findings, and follow-up reviews.

Q: What does an internal audit report include?

A: An internal audit report usually includes an executive summary, scope and objectives, methodology, key findings, and recommendations.

Q: Why is risk assessment crucial in an internal audit?

A: Risk assessment helps to prioritize the areas that pose the highest potential risk to an organization, ensuring the audit focuses on these areas.

Q: What is the role of internal audit in corporate governance?

A: Internal audit plays a crucial role in corporate governance by ensuring compliance with laws and regulations, and assessing the effectiveness of internal controls.

Q: What is the significance of independence in internal auditing?

A: Independence allows internal auditors to objectively assess the organization's processes and controls without any bias or influence.

Q: What are the types of internal audits?

A: The types of internal audits include operational audits, financial audits, IT audits, and compliance audits.

Q: How does an internal audit support the management?

A: Internal audit supports management by providing unbiased insights into the organization's operations and making recommendations for improvements.

Q: What is meant by internal control in the context of an internal audit?

A: Internal control refers to the procedures and policies implemented by an organization to ensure business operations are effective, efficient, and compliant with laws and regulations.

Q: How does an internal audit enhance an organization's accountability?

A: An internal audit enhances accountability by regularly evaluating the effectiveness of controls, thereby ensuring transparency and integrity in an organization's processes.

Q: What is the role of an audit committee in an internal audit?
A: An audit committee oversees the internal audit function, reviews audit findings, and ensures necessary actions are taken.
Q: What skills should an effective internal auditor possess?
A: An effective internal auditor should possess strong analytical skills, attention to detail, integrity, communication skills, and knowledge of auditing standards and procedures.
Q: What is the purpose of a follow-up review in an internal audit?
A: A follow-up review is conducted to check if the recommended actions have been implemented effectively.
Q: How does an internal audit contribute to risk management?
A: An internal audit contributes to risk management by identifying and assessing risks that could affect the organization's objectives.
Q: What are the ethical considerations for an internal auditor?
A: Ethical considerations for an internal auditor include integrity, objectivity, confidentiality, and competency.
Q: What is a risk-based audit approach in internal auditing?
A: A risk-based audit approach focuses on the areas of highest risk to the organization's objectives.
Q: How does technology impact internal auditing?
A: Technology can improve the efficiency and effectiveness of internal auditing by enabling data analysis, automating processes, and facilitating real-time tracking and reporting.
Q: What is the importance of continuous auditing in an internal audit?
A: Continuous auditing allows for real-time evaluation of an organization's operations, which can lead to timely identification and mitigation of risks.
Q: How does an internal audit ensure compliance?

A: An internal audit ensures compliance by checking whether the organization's processes and controls are in line with applicable laws, regulations, and standards.

Q: What is the difference between a compliance audit and an operational audit in internal auditing?

A: A compliance audit checks for adherence to laws and regulations, while an operational audit assesses the efficiency and effectiveness of operations.

Q: What is the significance of an internal audit charter?

A: An internal audit charter formally defines the internal audit's purpose, authority, and responsibility within the organization.

Q: How can an internal audit support an organization's strategic objectives?

A: An internal audit can support strategic objectives by assessing the effectiveness of processes and controls related to those objectives and recommending improvements.

Q: What is the role of internal audit in fraud detection?

A: Internal audit plays a role in fraud detection by assessing the effectiveness of controls designed to prevent and detect fraud.

Q: What are the steps involved in conducting an internal audit?

A: The steps involved in conducting an internal audit typically include planning, conducting fieldwork, analyzing findings, and reporting and follow-up.

Q: What is the relationship between internal audit and the board of directors?

A: The internal audit function usually reports to the board of directors, specifically to the audit committee, to maintain its independence.

Q: What is internal audit's role in the financial reporting process?

A: Internal audit's role in the financial reporting process is to ensure the accuracy and reliability of the financial information by assessing the effectiveness of financial controls.

Q: How does internal audit contribute to organizational learning?
A: Internal audit contributes to organizational learning by sharing insights and recommendations that can lead to improvements in processes and controls.
Q: What is the significance of materiality in internal auditing?
A: Materiality refers to the significance of an item or error that could influence the decisions of the users of financial information.
Q: How does internal audit relate to corporate social responsibility?
A: Internal audit can assess how well the organization adheres to its corporate social responsibility commitments and recommend improvements.
Q: What is the role of internal audit in business continuity planning?
A: Internal audit can assess the effectiveness of the organization's business continuity plans and suggest improvements.
Q: How does internal audit help in improving operational efficiency?
A: Internal audit identifies inefficiencies in operations and suggests improvements, thereby helping to improve operational efficiency.
Q: What is the importance of communication skills in internal auditing?
A: Communication skills are vital in internal auditing as auditors need to clearly convey their findings and recommendations to management and other stakeholders.
Q: What is the role of internal audit in the budgeting process?
A: Internal audit can examine the budgeting process for fairness, accuracy, and compliance with organizational policies.
Q: How does internal audit help in identifying business risks?

A: Internal audit helps in identifying business risks by assessing the effectiveness of controls and processes designed to mitigate those risks.

Q: What is the role of internal audit in a merger or acquisition?

A: Internal audit can assess the risks associated with a merger or acquisition and provide insights to help management make informed decisions.

Q: What is the importance of professional skepticism in internal auditing?

A: Professional skepticism allows internal auditors to conduct their work with an unbiased and questioning mindset, which is essential for effective auditing.

Q: How can internal audit contribute to cost savings?

A: By identifying inefficiencies and suggesting improvements, internal audit can help the organization reduce waste and save costs.

Q: What is the role of internal audit in the procurement process?

A: Internal audit can examine the procurement process for compliance with policies and efficiency.

Q: How can internal audit help to improve customer satisfaction?

A: By assessing and improving the organization's processes and controls, internal audit can indirectly contribute to better customer satisfaction.

Q: What are the challenges faced by internal auditors?

A: Challenges faced by internal auditors may include resistance from staff, maintaining independence, keeping up with changes in regulations and technology, and managing a broad scope of responsibilities.

Q: What is the role of internal audit in project management?

A: Internal audit can assess the effectiveness of project management controls and provide insights to help improve project outcomes.

Q: How does internal audit interact with external auditors?
A: Internal audit and external auditors often collaborate and share information to improve the overall audit process, while maintaining their separate roles and responsibilities.
Q: What is the importance of an audit trail in internal auditing?
A: An audit trail is important as it provides a record of the auditor's work, which can be reviewed for quality assurance and used as evidence of the audit process.
Q: How does internal audit assess the control environment of an organization?
A: Internal audit assesses the control environment by examining the organization's culture, structure, policies, and procedures.
Q: What is the impact of regulatory changes on internal auditing?
A: Regulatory changes can impact the scope and focus of internal auditing, requiring auditors to stay updated and ensure the organization remains compliant.
Q: What is the role of internal audit in data privacy and protection?
A: Internal audit can assess the effectiveness of controls related to data privacy and protection, ensuring compliance with relevant laws and regulations.
Q: How can internal audit contribute to an organization's sustainability efforts?
A: Internal audit can assess the effectiveness of the organization's sustainability initiatives and suggest improvements, contributing to the organization's long-term sustainability efforts.

Applications

Scenario 1: A manufacturing company has an internal audit department that has not been following the Generally Accepted Auditing Standards (GAAS) while conducting their audits. As a result, the audit reports have several inaccuracies and omissions.

In this case, the effectiveness of the internal audit is compromised due to non-compliance with GAAS. The auditors must be trained on these standards and be made to understand their importance. The company can also consider hiring a third-party audit firm to conduct an independent audit as a means of comparison and validation.

Scenario 2: An e-commerce company has noticed discrepancies between their inventory records and actual inventory count. The internal audit team is tasked with investigating and determining the cause of this issue.

This scenario calls for effective internal audit procedures to identify the source of the discrepancy. The audit team needs to meticulously review the inventory management process, identify any loopholes or errors, and recommend corrective actions. This will not only solve the current issue but also prevent similar occurrences in the future.

Scenario 3: A financial institution has an internal audit team that focuses only on financial audits, ignoring the operational aspects of the business.

The lack of an operational audit can lead to inefficiencies and risks in the business operations. The internal audit team should expand its scope to include operational audits, which would entail evaluating the effectiveness of operations and suggesting improvements. This will ensure a holistic and comprehensive audit for the entire organization.

Scenario 4: The internal audit team of a healthcare organization has discovered fraudulent activities related to insurance claims. However, the audit reports have not been communicated effectively to the management, leading to delayed action.

This scenario highlights the importance of effective communication in internal auditing. The audit team should present the findings in a clear, concise manner, highlighting the risks and implications. They should also suggest actionable steps to address the identified fraud, thereby enabling the management to take prompt action.

Scenario 5: A retail chain conducts internal audits but fails to follow up on the audit findings, leading to recurring issues.

The internal audit's effectiveness is undermined if there is no follow-up or implementation of the audit recommendations. The auditors should have a system to track the implementation of their recommendations and hold the concerned departments accountable. This will help in resolving the identified issues and improving the overall business operations.

Internal Control

Theoretical

Q: What is the purpose of internal controls in auditing?

A: The purpose of internal controls in auditing is to provide reasonable assurance about the achievement of operational efficiency, reliability of financial reporting, and compliance with laws and regulations.

Q: How does segregation of duties contribute to effective internal control?

A: Segregation of duties reduces the risk of errors and fraud by ensuring that no single individual is in a position to initiate, approve, record, and review financial transactions.

Q: What does the term 'control environment' refer to in the context of internal controls?

A: The control environment is defined by the collective awareness, attitude, and actions of the organization's directors and management regarding the importance of control within the organization.

Q: How does risk assessment contribute to effective internal control?

A: Risk assessment helps in identifying and analyzing risks to the achievement of the organization's objectives and determining how those risks should be managed.

Q: What are preventive controls in internal auditing?

A: Preventive controls are structured to deter mistakes or inconsistencies from happening. They are proactive measures that assist in guaranteeing departmental goals are accomplished.
Q: What are detective controls in internal auditing?
A: Detective controls are designed to identify an error or irregularity that has already occurred. They provide evidence that a mistake or fraud has taken place.
Q: How does a strong internal control system contribute to an organization's operational efficiency?
A: A strong internal control system can reduce waste, inefficiency, and fraud, thus improving the organization's operational efficiency.
Q: What is the role of the auditor in evaluating an organization's internal control system?
A: The auditor's role is to assess the effectiveness of the internal control system in preventing or detecting errors and fraud.
Q: How do information and communication contribute to effective internal control?
A: Information and communication systems enable the organization's people to capture and exchange the information needed to conduct, manage, and control its operations.
Q: How does monitoring contribute to effective internal control?
A: The process of monitoring evaluates the performance quality of internal control over a period of time. It includes timely examination of the controls' design and operation, followed by implementing necessary corrective measures.
Q: What are compensating controls in internal auditing?
A: When primary controls are not suitable or available, compensating controls are utilized as an alternative. They are designed to offer a reasonable assurance level in such situations.
Q: How does internal control contribute to reliable financial reporting?

A: Internal control guarantees that transactions are documented as required to allow the creation of financial statements following universally accepted accounting principles.

Q: How does internal control contribute to compliance with laws and regulations?

A: Internal control ensures that transactions are executed in accordance with management's general or specific authorization, and recorded as necessary to maintain accountability for assets.

Q: What is the relationship between internal control and corporate governance?

A: Internal control is a key element of corporate governance. It provides a framework for the organization to achieve its objectives and manage its risks.

Q: How does the use of technology impact internal controls?

A: Technology can enhance internal controls by automating controls and reducing the risk of human error. However, it can also introduce new risks such as system failures or cyber threats.

Q: What are the limitations of internal controls in auditing?

A: Internal controls cannot prevent collusion between employees, management override, or errors in judgement. They can only provide reasonable, not absolute, assurance.

Q: How do auditors test the effectiveness of internal controls?

A: Auditors test internal controls by evaluating the design of the controls, and then testing the operating effectiveness of the controls.

Q: What is the role of an internal auditor in relation to internal controls?

A: The internal auditor evaluates the effectiveness of internal controls, identifies areas of risk, and makes recommendations for improvement.

Q: What is the difference between a control deficiency and a material weakness in internal control?

A: A control deficiency exists when the design or operation of a control does not allow management to prevent or detect misstatements. A material weakness is a deficiency, or combination of deficiencies, in internal control that significantly increases the risk of a material misstatement in the financial statements.

Q: What is the difference between internal control over financial reporting and internal control over operations?

A: Internal control over financial reporting ensures the reliability of financial statements, while internal control over operations focuses on the effectiveness and efficiency of operations.

Q: How do auditors document their understanding of an entity's internal control?

A: Auditors document their understanding of an entity's internal control through narratives, flowcharts, internal control questionnaires, or a combination of these methods.

Q: What are the key components of an internal control system?

A: The fundamental elements of an internal control system include the control environment, assessment of risk, control activities, communication and information, as well as monitoring.

Q: What is the role of management in establishing and maintaining internal controls?

A: Management is responsible for establishing and maintaining an adequate system of internal control within the organization.

Q: What is the relationship between the level of risk and the strength of internal controls?

A: The higher the level of risk, the stronger the internal controls should be to mitigate those risks.

Q: Why is it important for auditors to consider the possibility of management override of controls?

A: It's important because management override of controls can lead to material misstatements in the financial statements.

Q: How do auditors assess the risk of material misstatement due to fraud?
A: Auditors evaluate the likelihood of significant inaccuracies due to fraud by taking into account factors that increase fraud risk. They also analyze the structure and application of internal controls designed to prevent and identify fraud.
Q: What is the difference between a control activity and a control procedure in internal auditing?
A: A control activity is a specific action taken to help ensure management's directives are carried out, while a control procedure is a specific method used to apply a control activity.
Q: How do auditors evaluate the appropriateness of an entity's use of the going concern assumption?
A: Auditors evaluate the appropriateness of the going concern assumption by considering factors such as the entity's ability to generate adequate cash flows, its financial condition, and the economic environment in which it operates.
Q: What is the role of the audit committee in relation to internal controls?
A: The audit committee is responsible for overseeing the financial reporting process and internal controls, as well as the audit process.
Q: How does an understanding of an entity's internal control assist the auditor in planning the audit?
A: An understanding of an entity's internal control helps the auditor to identify the areas of highest risk of material misstatement and to design appropriate audit procedures.
Q: What is the difference between a substantive audit approach and a controls reliance audit approach?
A: In a substantive audit approach, the auditor primarily relies on substantive procedures to detect material misstatements. In a

controls reliance approach, the auditor relies on the effectiveness of the entity's internal controls.

Q: What is the role of internal control in preventing and detecting fraud?

A: Internal control plays a crucial role in preventing and detecting fraud by establishing procedures and controls that deter fraudulent activities and by detecting any fraudulent transactions that do occur.

Q: What are the potential consequences of a failure in internal control?

A: A failure in internal control can lead to financial loss, damage to reputation, non-compliance with laws and regulations, and potentially even the failure of the organization.

Q: What is the relationship between materiality and internal control?

A: Materiality is a concept that refers to the significance of an amount, transaction, or discrepancy. If a control failure could lead to a material misstatement, the control is considered to be important to the audit.

Q: How does the concept of reasonable assurance relate to internal control?

A: Reasonable assurance refers to the level of assurance that internal controls are operating effectively. It acknowledges that there are limitations in internal control and that not all errors and fraud can be prevented or detected.

Q: What are some common types of control activities?

A: Common types of control activities include authorization of transactions, reconciliations, reviews of operating performance, security of assets, and segregation of duties.

Q: How does the auditor's assessment of control risk impact the nature, timing, and extent of audit procedures?

A: The higher the auditor's assessment of control risk, the more substantive testing the auditor will need to perform and the less they will rely on the entity's internal controls.

Q: What is the difference between an inherent limitation and a control deficiency in internal control?

A: An inherent limitation is a limitation that exists due to the nature of internal control, such as the possibility of collusion or management override. A control deficiency is a shortcoming in the design or operation of internal control that prevents it from achieving its objectives.

Q: What are some indicators of a material weakness in internal control?

A: Some indicators of a material weakness in internal control include identification of fraud by senior management, restatement of previously issued financial statements, and identification of a material misstatement by the auditor that was not initially identified by the entity's internal controls.

Q: How do auditors communicate internal control deficiencies to those charged with governance?

A: Auditors communicate internal control deficiencies to those charged with governance through a written report, which details the nature of the deficiencies and the potential impact on the financial statements.

Q: What role does professional skepticism play in the auditor's evaluation of internal control?

A: Professional skepticism involves a questioning mind and a critical assessment of audit evidence. It is crucial in the auditor's evaluation of internal control, as it helps the auditor to identify weaknesses and assess the risk of material misstatement.

Q: What is the difference between a direct control and an indirect control in internal auditing?

A: A direct control is a control that directly prevents or detects material misstatements. An indirect control, also known as a monitoring control, is a control that ensures direct controls are functioning as intended.

Q: How can an organization's control environment be strengthened?

A: An organization's control environment can be strengthened by promoting ethical values, setting a strong tone at the top, maintaining effective oversight by the board of directors, and holding management accountable for the design and operation of internal controls.

Applications

Scenario 1: ABC Ltd is a multinational corporation with a diverse portfolio of businesses. The company's internal audit discovered that there were multiple instances of fraud in one of their departments. The auditors identified a clear lack of internal controls over the department's financial reporting process. How should the auditors address this issue?

Solution: The auditors should develop a plan to review and improve the existing internal controls. This might involve installing new software to track financial transactions, training staff on the importance of adhering to company policies, and implementing a stricter review process to identify and correct errors.

Scenario 2: XYZ Inc. is a technology company that recently underwent a significant expansion. During the internal audit, it was discovered that the IT department lacked proper internal controls over their data management processes, which resulted in several data breaches. What steps should the auditors take to mitigate this problem?

Solution: Firstly, auditors should recommend the implementation of a robust data management system with strict access controls.

Additionally, it would be beneficial to conduct regular data audits, provide staff training on data protection, and establish a clear protocol for reporting and handling data breaches.

Scenario 3: DEF Corporation, a retail company, has been experiencing inventory shortages. The internal audit revealed that the company lacked efficient internal controls over its inventory management process. How can the auditors help to solve this problem?

Solution: Auditors can recommend the introduction of an inventory management software to monitor stock levels accurately. They can also suggest conducting regular stock counts, setting reorder levels, and establishing a system for timely reporting of discrepancies.

Scenario 4: GHI Pharmaceuticals has been cited by regulatory authorities for non-compliance with industry standards. The internal audit identified a lack of internal controls over the company's compliance management process. What corrective actions should the auditors recommend?

Solution: The auditors should suggest the creation of a compliance team responsible for ensuring adherence to all regulatory standards. This team should regularly review and update the company's policies and procedures, conduct compliance training for employees, and establish a system for reporting and addressing non-compliance issues.

Scenario 5: JKL Manufacturing has been facing quality issues with its products. The internal audit revealed insufficient internal controls over the company's quality management system. How can the auditors help to rectify this situation?

Solution: The auditors should recommend the implementation of a comprehensive quality management system. This could include regular product inspections, setting quality standards, providing training on quality control procedures, and establishing a mechanism for reporting and resolving quality issues.

Physical Audit

Theoretical

Q: What is a physical audit in the context of auditing?

A: A physical audit is a process of examining an organization's tangible assets to verify their existence, condition, and value.

Q: What is the primary reason for conducting a physical audit?

A: The primary reason is to ensure the accuracy of an organization's financial statements, especially those related to tangible assets.

Q: What are some examples of tangible assets that can be audited physically?

A: These can include buildings, equipment, inventory, and other physical assets owned by the organization.

Q: What are the steps involved in conducting a physical audit?

A: It typically involves planning, gathering data, examining the assets, and reporting the findings.

Q: Who is responsible for conducting a physical audit?

A: It is usually conducted by an internal or external auditor or a team of auditors.

Q: Why is planning important in a physical audit?

A: Planning helps to determine the scope, objectives, and procedures of the audit, ensuring it is conducted efficiently and effectively.

Q: How is data gathered during a physical audit?

A: Data is gathered through various methods such as physical inspection, observation, and document review.

Q: What types of documents are reviewed during a physical audit?
A: These can include purchase invoices, receipts, asset registers, and depreciation schedules.
Q: What happens during the examination phase of a physical audit?
A: The auditor physically inspects the assets, verifies their existence, checks their condition, and compares them with the recorded data.
Q: What is the outcome of a physical audit?
A: The outcome is a report that presents the findings of the audit, which can be used to correct discrepancies, improve asset management, and ensure accurate financial reporting.
Q: How does a physical audit contribute to accurate financial reporting?
A: It verifies the existence and value of tangible assets, which are essential components of an organization's balance sheet.
Q: How does a physical audit improve asset management?
A: It can identify discrepancies, losses, and inefficiencies, enabling the organization to address them and improve its asset management practices.
Q: What skills are required to conduct a physical audit?
A: These include analytical skills, attention to detail, knowledge of auditing standards, and familiarity with the organization's assets and operations.
Q: What challenges can arise during a physical audit?
A: Challenges can include access to assets, incomplete or inaccurate records, time constraints, and resistance from staff.
Q: How can these challenges be addressed?
A: They can be addressed through effective planning, clear communication, cooperation from staff, and adherence to auditing standards.

Q: What role does technology play in physical audit?
A: Technology can facilitate data gathering, analysis, and reporting, making the audit more efficient and accurate.
Q: How often should a physical audit be conducted?
A: The frequency depends on the organization's size, nature of assets, and risk factors. It could be annual, bi-annual, or more frequent.
Q: Can a physical audit be outsourced?
A: Yes, many organizations hire external auditors to conduct their physical audits.
Q: What is the role of internal auditors in a physical audit?
A: Internal auditors may conduct the audit or assist external auditors by providing information and facilitating access to assets.
Q: What is the role of management in a physical audit?
A: Management is responsible for maintaining accurate records, facilitating the audit, and addressing the findings.
Q: Can a physical audit detect fraud?
A: Yes, a physical audit can detect discrepancies that may indicate fraud, such as missing or unrecorded assets.
Q: What happens if discrepancies are found during a physical audit?
A: Discrepancies should be investigated, corrected, and reported to management. They may also lead to adjustments in the financial statements.
Q: How can a physical audit enhance accountability?
A: By verifying the existence and value of assets, a physical audit can hold managers accountable for their stewardship of the organization's resources.
Q: Can a physical audit be conducted remotely?
A: While some aspects can be done remotely, such as document review, other aspects like physical inspection require on-site presence.

Q: Can a physical audit be conducted for intangible assets?
A: No, a physical audit is typically used for tangible assets. Intangible assets are audited through other methods.
Q: Why is a physical audit important for inventory control?
A: It verifies the existence and condition of inventory, helping to ensure accurate record-keeping and prevent losses.
Q: How can a physical audit contribute to cost control?
A: By identifying inefficiencies and losses, a physical audit can help the organization to reduce costs and improve profitability.
Q: What is the relationship between a physical audit and risk management?
A: A physical audit can identify risks related to tangible assets, such as theft, damage, and depreciation, enabling the organization to manage these risks.
Q: How can a physical audit contribute to strategic planning?
A: The findings of a physical audit can inform strategic decisions about asset acquisition, disposal, maintenance, and utilization.
Q: What is the role of physical audit in corporate governance?
A: By enhancing transparency and accountability, a physical audit supports good corporate governance.
Q: How does a physical audit relate to sustainability?
A: A physical audit can assess the condition and lifespan of assets, contributing to sustainability by promoting efficient use and maintenance of resources.
Q: What is the relevance of a physical audit in a digital economy?
A: Even in a digital economy, organizations still rely on tangible assets, making physical audits relevant for verifying their existence and value.
Q: How does a physical audit support decision-making?
A: The findings of a physical audit provide reliable information for decision-making regarding asset management, financial reporting, and strategic planning.

Q: What is the impact of a physical audit on stakeholders' confidence?
A: A successful physical audit can enhance stakeholders' confidence in the organization's management and financial reporting.
Q: What is the connection between a physical audit and regulatory compliance?
A: A physical audit can help to ensure compliance with regulations regarding asset management and financial reporting.
Q: How can a physical audit support business continuity?
A: By identifying risks and inefficiencies, a physical audit can contribute to business continuity planning.
Q: What is the role of a physical audit in corporate social responsibility?
A: By promoting efficient use and maintenance of assets, a physical audit can contribute to the organization's corporate social responsibility.
Q: Can a physical audit detect tax evasion?
A: While not its primary purpose, a physical audit can detect discrepancies that may indicate tax evasion, such as unrecorded or undervalued assets.
Q: What is the role of a physical audit in merger and acquisition transactions?
A: A physical audit can verify the existence and value of the target company's tangible assets, supporting due diligence in merger and acquisition transactions.
Q: How can a physical audit contribute to innovation?
A: The findings of a physical audit can inspire innovative solutions for asset management, cost control, and risk management.
Q: Can a physical audit be conducted in a non-profit organization?

A: Yes, a physical audit can be conducted in any organization that owns tangible assets, including non-profit organizations.

Q: What is the relationship between a physical audit and organizational performance?

A: By improving asset management, cost control, and risk management, a physical audit can enhance organizational performance.

Q: Can a physical audit improve customer satisfaction?

A: Indirectly, a physical audit can contribute to customer satisfaction by enhancing the organization's efficiency, reliability, and financial stability.

Q: What is the connection between a physical audit and organizational culture?

A: A physical audit can promote a culture of accountability, transparency, and continuous improvement.

Q: How does a physical audit relate to ethical business practices?

A: By enhancing transparency and accountability, a physical audit can support ethical business practices.

Q: Can a physical audit improve supplier relationships?

A: By ensuring accurate record-keeping and prompt payment for assets acquired, a physical audit can contribute to positive supplier relationships.

Q: What is the role of a physical audit in crisis management?

A: A physical audit can identify risks and vulnerabilities related to tangible assets, supporting crisis management planning.

Q: Can a physical audit contribute to employee morale?

A: By promoting fairness, accountability, and job security, a physical audit can contribute to positive employee morale.

Q: What is the connection between a physical audit and corporate reputation?

A: A successful physical audit can enhance the organization's reputation for honesty, responsibility, and good management.

Q: How does a physical audit contribute to organizational resilience?
A: By identifying and addressing risks and inefficiencies, a physical audit can enhance the organization's ability to withstand and recover from challenges.

Applications

Scenario 1: A manufacturing company, XYZ Corp, has been reporting consistent profits over the last five years. However, the company's physical inventory count has been decreasing year after year. The auditing team has been assigned the task to investigate this discrepancy. Upon conducting a physical audit, the team discovers that the company has been selling off its old machinery without updating its asset records. The company was advised to regularly update their asset records to avoid such discrepancies in the future.

Scenario 2: ABC Retail, a supermarket chain, has noticed discrepancies in its inventory records. The records show that there are more items in stock than what is physically present in the stores. The auditors conduct a physical audit and discover that the company's point-of-sale system has a glitch that fails to update the inventory records upon a sale. The problem was fixed by the IT department and a recount of the inventory was conducted to update the records accurately.

Scenario 3: DEF Ltd., a real estate company, has reported in its financial statements that it owns a property in a prime location. However, during a physical audit, the auditors were unable to locate the property. Upon further investigation, it was discovered that the property was sold two years ago but the sale was not recorded in the company's books. The auditors recommended

DEF Ltd. to update their records and implement a stronger internal control system to prevent such issues.

Scenario 4: GHI Inc., a tech company, has reported an increase in its computer equipment. However, during a physical audit, the auditors found that the number of computers in the office was less than what was reported. GHI Inc. explained that many of their employees work remotely and have company laptops at home. The auditors advised the company to keep better track of their equipment and to establish a check-out system for employees with company property.

Scenario 5: JKL Industries, a construction company, claims to have large quantities of construction materials in their warehouses. However, during a physical audit, the auditors found the warehouses to be nearly empty. When questioned, the company admitted to having supply chain issues and not updating their records. The auditors recommended JKL Industries to improve their inventory management system and regularly update their records.

Quality Audit

Theoretical

Q: What is a Quality Audit?

A: A Quality Audit is a systematic review of an organization's quality management system. It is aimed at improving the overall quality of goods or services.

Q: Who typically conducts a Quality Audit?

A: Quality Audits are generally conducted by an internal or external auditor or a team of auditors.

Q: What is the purpose of a Quality Audit?

A: The primary purpose of a Quality Audit is to assess the effectiveness of a company's quality management system and to identify areas for improvement.

Q: What are the types of Quality Audits?

A: There are three main types of Quality Audits: system audits, process audits, and product audits.

Q: What is a system audit?

A: A system audit involves examining the management of the system, to verify if it has been effectively implemented and maintained.

Q: What is a process audit?

A: An audit of a process is an analysis of outcomes to ascertain if the associated activities and resources are being managed effectively.

Q: What is a product audit?

A: A product audit is a detailed inspection of the product itself, or of a product component, subassembly, or final assembly, to check it against predetermined standards.

Q: What are the main steps in a Quality Audit?

A: The main steps in a Quality Audit are planning, execution, reporting, and follow-up.

Q: What is the importance of planning in a Quality Audit?

A: Planning involves identifying the objectives of the audit, the areas to be audited, and the personnel involved. It helps to ensure that the audit is effective and efficient.

Q: What happens during the execution phase of a Quality Audit?

A: During the execution phase, the auditor gathers information by observing processes, interviewing personnel, and reviewing documents.

Q: What is included in the audit report?

A: The audit report contains a summary of the findings, including any nonconformities, and recommendations for improvements.

Q: What happens during the follow-up phase of a Quality Audit?

A: During the follow-up phase, the auditor verifies that the recommendations have been implemented and that they are effective.

Q: What are the benefits of a Quality Audit?

A: Benefits of a Quality Audit include improved efficiency, reduced waste, increased customer satisfaction, and compliance with regulatory requirements.

Q: What is a nonconformity in a Quality Audit?

A: A nonconformity is a failure to meet a requirement. This could be a failure to follow a procedure, or a failure to meet a customer requirement.

Q: What is the role of the auditor in a Quality Audit?

A: The auditor's role is to objectively assess the quality management system or process being audited, identify nonconformities and areas for improvement, and provide a report of the findings.

Q: What qualities should a good auditor possess?

A: A good auditor should be objective, fair, knowledgeable about the organization and its processes, and able to communicate effectively.

Q: How can an organization prepare for a Quality Audit?

A: An organization can prepare for a Quality Audit by reviewing its quality management system, ensuring that procedures are followed, and training personnel on the audit process.

Q: What are the consequences of not conducting a Quality Audit?

A: Without regular Quality Audits, an organization may not identify nonconformities or areas for improvement, which could lead to decreased customer satisfaction, increased waste, and non-compliance with regulatory requirements.

Q: How often should a Quality Audit be conducted?

A: The frequency of Quality Audits can vary depending on the organization, but they should be conducted regularly to ensure ongoing compliance and continuous improvement.

Q: What is the difference between an internal and external audit?

A: An internal audit is conducted by personnel within the organization, while an external audit is conducted by an independent third party.

Q: What is the role of management in a Quality Audit?

A: Management's role in a Quality Audit includes setting the objectives of the audit, providing resources, and acting on the recommendations.

Q: Can a Quality Audit be conducted remotely?

A: Yes, with advancements in technology, Quality Audits can be conducted remotely. This is known as a virtual audit.

Q: What is a virtual audit?

A: A virtual audit is a Quality Audit that is conducted using technology such as video conferencing, rather than in person.

Q: What are the challenges of conducting a virtual audit?

A: Challenges of conducting a virtual audit include technological issues, such as poor internet connection, and the inability to physically observe processes or products.

Q: What is an audit checklist?

A: An audit checklist is a tool used by auditors to help ensure that they cover all necessary areas during the audit.

Q: What is included in an audit checklist?

A: An audit checklist typically includes the areas to be audited, the information to be gathered, and the criteria against which the areas will be assessed.

Q: What is the difference between a compliance audit and a Quality Audit?

A: A compliance audit checks for adherence to regulations and standards, while a Quality Audit checks for adherence to the organization's quality management system.

Q: What is a corrective action in a Quality Audit?

A: A corrective action is a step taken to remove the source of a discovered discrepancy or any other unfavorable situation.

Q: What is preventive action in a Quality Audit?

A: Taking preventive action is a step initiated to eradicate the source of a potential nonconformity or any other unfavorable circumstance.

Q: What is the difference between corrective action and preventive action?

A: Corrective action is reactive and taken after a nonconformity is detected, while preventive action is proactive and taken to prevent potential nonconformities.

Q: What are the key elements of a Quality Audit?

A: The key elements of a Quality Audit are planning, execution, reporting, and follow-up.

Q: What is a Quality Management System?

A: A Quality Management System is a set of policies, procedures, and processes used by an organization to deliver products or services that meet customer and regulatory requirements.

Q: How does a Quality Audit support a Quality Management System?

A: A Quality Audit supports a Quality Management System by providing feedback on its effectiveness and identifying areas for improvement.

Q: Can a Quality Audit be used to achieve certification to a quality standard?

A: Yes, a Quality Audit is a key part of the process of achieving certification to a quality standard such as ISO 9001.

Q: What is ISO 9001?

A: ISO 9001 is an international standard for quality management systems. It sets out the criteria for a quality management system and is based on a number of quality management principles including a strong customer focus, the involvement of top management, a process approach, and continual improvement.

Q: How does a Quality Audit support continuous improvement?

A: A Quality Audit supports continuous improvement by identifying nonconformities and areas for improvement, and by monitoring the effectiveness of corrective and preventive actions.

Q: What is the role of documentation in a Quality Audit?

A: Documentation plays a key role in a Quality Audit, as it provides evidence that processes have been followed and that the quality management system is effective.

Q: What is risk-based auditing?

A: Risk-based auditing is an approach that focuses on the risks that are most likely to impact an organization's objectives.

Q: How can risk-based auditing be used in a Quality Audit?
A: In a Quality Audit, risk-based auditing can be used to prioritize areas for audit based on their potential impact on product or service quality.
Q: What is the relationship between quality and customer satisfaction?
A: High-quality products and services are more likely to meet or exceed customer expectations, leading to higher customer satisfaction.
Q: How can a Quality Audit improve customer satisfaction?
A: A Quality Audit can improve customer satisfaction by identifying and addressing issues that may impact product or service quality.
Q: What is a third-party audit?
A: A third-party audit is an audit conducted by an independent organization, typically to verify compliance with a standard or regulation.
Q: How does a third-party audit differ from an internal audit?
A: A third-party audit is conducted by an external organization, while an internal audit is conducted by personnel within the organization.
Q: What is the role of evidence in a Quality Audit?
A: Evidence plays a crucial role in a Quality Audit, as it provides support for the auditor's findings and recommendations.
Q: What types of evidence might an auditor look for in a Quality Audit?
A: In a Quality Audit, an auditor might look for evidence such as records, documents, and data, as well as evidence gathered through observation and interviews.
Q: What is the purpose of an exit meeting in a Quality Audit?

A: The purpose of an exit meeting in a Quality Audit is to present the findings of the audit to management and to discuss any necessary corrective actions.

Q: What is the difference between a conformance and a nonconformance in a Quality Audit?

A: A conformance is when a requirement has been met, while a nonconformance is when a requirement has not been met.

Q: What is an audit scope?

A: The audit scope defines the boundaries of the audit, including the areas to be audited and the time period covered.

Q: What is an audit objective?

A: The audit objective is what the audit is intended to achieve. This could be to verify compliance with a standard, to identify areas for improvement, or to assess the effectiveness of a process.

Q: How does a Quality Audit contribute to an organization's success?

A: A Quality Audit contributes to an organization's success by identifying areas for improvement, reducing waste, improving efficiency, and increasing customer satisfaction.

Applications

Scenario 1:

In a manufacturing company, the quality manager reports that the company is consistently meeting the standards set by the ISO 9001. However, customer complaints about the product's quality have been increasing. You have been brought in as an external auditor to conduct a quality audit.

To address this scenario, I would first review the quality management system documentation to understand the company's quality control standards and procedures. Then, I'll interview employees to gauge their understanding and application of the quality standards. I'll also examine the company's records of customer complaints and responses. If discrepancies are found, recommendations for improvement will be made, including staff training, updating procedures, or increasing quality control checks.

Scenario 2:

A software development company has recently adopted Agile methodologies. Management has noticed some inconsistencies in the quality of the delivered products. You are appointed as a quality auditor to assess the situation.

As a quality auditor, I would evaluate how well the Agile methodologies have been implemented and are followed. I would examine the team's understanding of Agile principles, their use of Agile tools, and their responses to customer feedback. I would also analyze the quality of the software being produced in terms of bug rates, customer satisfaction, and delivery times. If the Agile methodologies aren't being correctly applied, I would suggest improvements like training, changes in work processes, or better use of Agile tools.

Scenario 3:

A healthcare organization has been receiving complaints about long wait times and poor patient care. The organization claims to be following all the healthcare quality standards. You are hired to perform a quality audit.

In this scenario, I would review the organization's patient care procedures and compare them to the healthcare quality standards that they should be following. I would interview staff and observe their work practices to understand the reasons for the long wait times and poor patient care. I would also review patient complaints and the organization's responses. Possible solutions could include increasing staffing levels, improving work processes, or providing additional training to staff.

Scenario 4:

A food processing company has been flagged for potential health and safety violations. As a quality auditor, you are tasked to investigate.

In such a case, I would examine the company's safety procedures, equipment maintenance records, and employee training records. I would also conduct onsite inspections to observe the company's operations. If the company is found to be violating health and safety standards, I would recommend corrective actions like improving safety procedures, maintaining equipment, and training employees on safety practices.

In each of these scenarios, the quality audit aims to identify gaps in the organization's quality standards and practices, and suggest improvements to ensure compliance with the required standards.

Procedure Audit

Theoretical

Question: What is a procedure audit?

Answer: A procedure audit is an examination of company operations to evaluate if procedures are being followed as stated and if they are effective in achieving the company's objectives.

Question: What is the main goal of a procedure audit?

Answer: The main goal of a procedure audit is to assess the efficiency, effectiveness, and compliance of an organization's procedures.

Question: Who typically conducts procedure audits?

Answer: Procedure audits are usually conducted by internal or external auditors, or sometimes by third-party professionals.

Question: Why is a procedure audit important?

Answer: A procedure audit is important as it helps to identify weaknesses in the procedures, improve efficiency, and ensure compliance with regulatory standards.

Question: What are the key stages in a procedure audit?

Answer: The key stages in a procedure audit include planning, execution, reporting, and follow-up.

Question: What does the planning stage of a procedure audit involve?

Answer: The planning stage involves defining the scope of the audit, identifying the procedures to be audited, and preparing an audit plan.

Question: What happens during the execution stage of a procedure audit?
Answer: During the execution stage, the auditor conducts the audit according to the plan, gathering evidence about the implementation and effectiveness of the procedures.
Question: What is the purpose of the reporting stage in a procedure audit?
Answer: The reporting stage involves presenting the audit findings, including any non-compliance or inefficiencies, and making recommendations for improvement.
Question: What does the follow-up stage of a procedure audit involve?
Answer: The follow-up stage involves checking whether the recommended improvements have been implemented and if they have been effective in addressing the identified issues.
Question: How can a procedure audit improve operational efficiency?
Answer: A procedure audit can identify inefficiencies in procedures and suggest improvements, leading to better use of resources and increased operational efficiency.
Question: How can a procedure audit help in risk management?
Answer: By identifying procedural weaknesses and non-compliance, a procedure audit can help manage risks associated with financial loss, legal problems, or damage to the company's reputation.
Question: What kind of skills does a procedure auditor need?
Answer: A procedure auditor needs strong analytical skills to interpret complex information, attention to detail to identify issues, and communication skills to report the findings clearly.
Question: How often should a procedure audit be conducted?

Answer: The frequency of a procedure audit depends on the company's needs, but it is generally recommended to conduct one at least annually.

Question: Can a procedure audit lead to cost savings for a company?

Answer: Yes, by identifying inefficiencies and suggesting improvements, a procedure audit can lead to cost savings in the long run.

Question: How does a procedure audit support quality management in a company?

Answer: A procedure audit can ensure that the company's procedures are aligned with its quality standards and goals, supporting the company's quality management efforts.

Question: What is a corrective action in the context of a procedure audit?

Answer: A corrective action is a measure taken to fix an identified non-compliance or inefficiency in a procedure.

Question: How is evidence collected during a procedure audit?

Answer: Evidence can be collected through various methods, such as interviews, observation, document review, and testing of procedures.

Question: What is the role of documentation in a procedure audit?

Answer: Documentation provides evidence of the procedures being followed and their effectiveness, and it is also used to record the audit findings and recommendations.

Question: What is an audit report in a procedure audit?

Answer: An audit report is a formal document that presents the audit findings, including any non-compliance or inefficiencies, and provides recommendations for improvement.

Question: How can a procedure audit contribute to continuous improvement in a company?

Answer: A procedure audit can identify areas for improvement and monitor the effectiveness of implemented changes, supporting the company's continuous improvement efforts.

Question: What is the difference between a procedure audit and a process audit?

Answer: A procedure audit focuses on evaluating whether procedures are being followed as stated, while a process audit evaluates the efficiency and effectiveness of a process.

Question: Can a procedure audit identify training needs in a company?

Answer: Yes, a procedure audit can identify if employees are not following procedures correctly due to lack of knowledge or skills, indicating a need for training.

Question: What are some examples of non-compliance that a procedure audit might find?

Answer: Non-compliance in a procedure audit could include failure to follow procedures, inadequate documentation, or not meeting regulatory requirements.

Question: What is a procedural control in the context of a procedure audit?

Answer: A procedural control is a mechanism that ensures procedures are being followed correctly and consistently.

Question: Can a procedure audit be used to prepare for an external audit?

Answer: Yes, a procedure audit can help a company prepare for an external audit by identifying and addressing issues in advance.

Question: What is a procedural deviation in a procedure audit?

Answer: A procedural deviation is a departure from the stated procedures, which can be identified in a procedure audit.

Question: What are some challenges in conducting a procedure audit?

Answer: Challenges can include resistance from employees, lack of resources, and difficulty in interpreting complex information.
Question: How can a procedure audit help in decision making?
Answer: By providing reliable information about the effectiveness of procedures, a procedure audit can support informed decision making.
Question: Can a procedure audit be used to evaluate the performance of employees?
Answer: While a procedure audit is not a performance evaluation, it can provide insight into whether employees are following procedures correctly.
Question: How can a procedure audit contribute to customer satisfaction?
Answer: By ensuring that procedures are effective and efficient, a procedure audit can contribute to the delivery of high-quality products or services, leading to customer satisfaction.
Question: Can a procedure audit be used to evaluate the effectiveness of a company's internal controls?
Answer: Yes, a procedure audit can evaluate the effectiveness of internal controls by checking if they are being followed and if they are effective in managing risks.
Question: What is a procedural risk in a procedure audit?
Answer: A procedural risk is the possibility that a procedure is not effective in achieving its intended purpose, which can be identified in a procedure audit.
Question: How can a procedure audit support innovation in a company?
Answer: A procedure audit can identify areas for improvement and suggest new ways of doing things, supporting innovation.
Question: Can a procedure audit be used to evaluate the effectiveness of a company's management system?

Answer: Yes, a procedure audit can evaluate the effectiveness of a management system by assessing the procedures that support it.

Question: How can a procedure audit contribute to the reliability of a company's financial reporting?

Answer: By ensuring that financial procedures are being followed correctly, a procedure audit can contribute to the reliability of financial reporting.

Question: What is a procedural deficiency in a procedure audit?

Answer: A procedural deficiency is a weakness in a procedure that reduces its effectiveness, which can be identified in a procedure audit.

Question: How can a procedure audit contribute to regulatory compliance?

Answer: A procedure audit can help ensure that company procedures are compliant with relevant laws and regulations.

Question: Can a procedure audit be used to evaluate the effectiveness of a company's IT systems?

Answer: Yes, a procedure audit can evaluate the effectiveness of IT systems by assessing the procedures related to IT operations and security.

Question: Can a procedure audit be used to evaluate the effectiveness of a company's supply chain management?

Answer: Yes, a procedure audit can evaluate the effectiveness of supply chain management by assessing the procedures related to procurement, inventory management, and logistics.

Question: How can a procedure audit contribute to a company's strategic planning?

Answer: By providing insights into the effectiveness of procedures, a procedure audit can support strategic planning by informing decisions about process improvements and resource allocation.

Question: How can a procedure audit contribute to a company's environmental sustainability efforts?

Answer: A procedure audit can evaluate the effectiveness of environmental procedures and suggest improvements, contributing to the company's sustainability efforts.

Question: Can a procedure audit be conducted remotely?

Answer: Yes, with the use of technology, a procedure audit can be conducted remotely, although this may present some challenges in terms of data access and communication.

Question: What is a procedural objective in a procedure audit?

Answer: A procedural objective is the intended outcome of a procedure, which is evaluated in a procedure audit to determine if the procedure is effective.

Question: Can a procedure audit be used to evaluate the effectiveness of a company's human resource management?

Answer: Yes, a procedure audit can evaluate the effectiveness of human resource management by assessing the procedures related to recruitment, training, performance management, and employee relations.

Question: How can a procedure audit help in crisis management?

Answer: A procedure audit can identify procedural weaknesses that could lead to a crisis and suggest improvements to prevent such situations.

Question: Can a procedure audit be used to evaluate the effectiveness of a company's safety procedures?

Answer: Yes, a procedure audit can evaluate the effectiveness of safety procedures by checking if they are being followed correctly and if they are effective in preventing accidents.

Question: How can a procedure audit support a company's corporate social responsibility efforts?

Answer: A procedure audit can evaluate the effectiveness of procedures related to corporate social responsibility, such as community engagement and environmental sustainability.

Question: Can a procedure audit be used to evaluate the effectiveness of a company's customer service procedures?
Answer: Yes, a procedure audit can evaluate the effectiveness of customer service procedures by assessing their impact on customer satisfaction and loyalty.
Question: What is a procedural standard in a procedure audit?
Answer: A procedural standard is a benchmark or criterion against which the procedures are evaluated in a procedure audit.
Question: Can a procedure audit contribute to a company's competitive advantage?
Answer: Yes, by identifying and addressing procedural inefficiencies, a procedure audit can contribute to a company's competitive advantage by improving operational efficiency and customer satisfaction.

Applications

Scenario 1:

A newly established business, XYZ Corp., has just completed its first year of operations. As a proactive measure, the management wants to initiate an internal audit to ensure all procedures have been correctly followed. However, they are confused about how to proceed with auditing their procedures. How can they effectively audit their procedures?

Solution:

The first step is to determine which procedures need auditing. This could be based on the risk level, importance to the business, or regulatory requirements. Once the procedures are identified, XYZ Corp. should design an audit plan that outlines the objectives, scope, and methodology of the audit. It should also assign responsibilities and timelines. Next, they should execute the audit plan, collecting and analyzing evidence to assess the effectiveness of the procedures. Finally, the findings should be reported to the management with recommendations for improvement.

Scenario 2:

ABC Ltd. recently underwent an external audit which highlighted several procedural inefficiencies. The company is now looking to rectify these issues. However, they are unsure how to monitor whether the rectifications are effective. How can they ensure that these changes are implemented and are working effectively?

Solution:

ABC Ltd. can use procedure audit to track the implementation of changes. They can start by defining the new procedures clearly and communicating them to the relevant personnel. Next, they should establish key performance indicators (KPIs) to measure the effectiveness of the new procedures. Regular audits should be conducted to monitor adherence to these procedures and the KPIs should be tracked to measure their effectiveness. Any deviations should be immediately addressed to ensure continuous improvement.

Scenario 3:

DEF Inc. is a large organization with multiple departments. They have a centralized procedure for procurement, but each department seems to have developed its own way of following it. The management is concerned that this could lead to inconsistencies and inefficiencies. How can they ensure that the same procedure is uniformly followed across the organization?

Solution:

DEF Inc. should initiate a procedure audit across all departments. This includes reviewing the existing procedure, interviewing employees, and observing how the procedure is followed in each department. The audit will help identify any variations in how the procedure is implemented. Based on the findings, the company can then standardize the procedure across all departments, provide training where necessary, and institute regular audits to ensure consistent application.

Scenario 4:

GHI Co. has a well-established procedure for customer service. However, despite this, they have been receiving numerous customer complaints. The management suspects that the procedure may not be followed correctly. How can they investigate this issue?

Solution:

GHI Co. can use a procedure audit to investigate the issue. They should review the customer service procedure and compare it with the actual practices being followed. This could involve interviewing customer service representatives, observing their interactions with customers, and reviewing customer complaints. If the audit reveals deviations from the procedure, corrective actions should be taken. This might involve retraining staff, modifying the procedure, or implementing stricter monitoring measures.

Tax Audit

Theoretical

Q: What is a tax audit?

A: A tax audit is a formal examination conducted by the government or a tax authority to verify the accuracy of a tax return filed by an individual or business.

Q: What is the main purpose of a tax audit?

A: The main purpose of a tax audit is to ensure compliance with tax laws and to verify that taxpayers are accurately reporting their income and deductions.

Q: What prompts a tax audit?

A: Several factors may prompt a tax audit, including discrepancies in reported income, excessive deductions, high-value transactions, and random selection by the tax authority.

Q: Who can perform a tax audit?

A: A tax audit can be performed by authorized tax officials from the government or a tax authority.

Q: What are the types of tax audits?

A: The types of tax audits include correspondence audits, office audits, field audits, and taxpayer compliance measurement program audits.

Q: What happens during a tax audit?

A: During a tax audit, the auditor examines the taxpayer's financial records, receipts, and other documents to verify the accuracy of the tax return.

Q: What are the potential outcomes of a tax audit?
A: The potential outcomes of a tax audit can range from no change to the tax return to additional taxes, penalties, and interest being assessed.
Q: What rights do taxpayers have during a tax audit?
A: Taxpayers have the right to representation, the right to appeal the auditor's decision, and the right to confidentiality during a tax audit.
Q: How long does a tax audit usually take?
A: The length of a tax audit can vary widely, depending on the complexity of the case and the cooperation of the taxpayer.
Q: What are the possible consequences of a negative tax audit outcome?
A: The possible consequences of a negative tax audit outcome include additional tax liabilities, penalties, interest charges, and in severe cases, legal action.
Q: What is the role of a tax auditor?
A: The role of a tax auditor is to examine financial records, verify the accuracy of tax returns, identify any discrepancies, and ensure compliance with tax laws.
Q: What skills are necessary for a tax auditor?
A: A tax auditor needs to have strong analytical skills, attention to detail, knowledge of tax laws and regulations, and excellent communication skills.
Q: How can a taxpayer prepare for a tax audit?
A: A taxpayer can prepare for a tax audit by organizing their financial records, reviewing their tax return, and consulting with a tax professional.
Q: Can a tax audit result in a refund?
A: Yes, a tax audit can result in a refund if the auditor determines that the taxpayer overpaid their taxes.
Q: How can a taxpayer reduce their chances of being audited?

A: A taxpayer can reduce their chances of being audited by accurately reporting their income, only claiming legitimate deductions, keeping detailed records, and seeking professional tax advice.

Q: Can a tax audit be avoided?

A: While there's no surefire way to avoid a tax audit, the likelihood can be reduced by following tax laws, accurately reporting income and deductions, and maintaining thorough records.

Q: What is the difference between a tax audit and a financial audit?

A: A tax audit focuses solely on a taxpayer's compliance with tax laws, while a financial audit examines a company's financial statements to ensure they are accurate and comply with accounting standards.

Q: Can a tax audit lead to criminal charges?

A: Yes, if a tax audit uncovers evidence of tax evasion or fraud, it could potentially lead to criminal charges.

Q: Do all businesses get audited?

A: No, not all businesses get audited. The likelihood of an audit depends on various factors such as the size of the business, the industry, and the complexity of the tax return.

Q: Can individuals be audited?

A: Yes, individuals can be audited. The likelihood of an individual audit depends on various factors such as the level of income, the types of deductions claimed, and the accuracy of the tax return.

Q: What does a tax auditor look for?

A: A tax auditor looks for discrepancies between the tax return and the taxpayer's financial records, evidence of unreported income, and illegitimate deductions.

Q: What is an IRS tax audit?

A: An IRS tax audit is the process of examining an individual's or organization's financial records and accounts. This is done to confirm that the information provided aligns with the tax laws and to ensure that the amount of tax reported is accurate.

Q: How often does a tax audit occur?

A: The frequency of a tax audit can vary widely. Some taxpayers may never experience an audit, while others may be audited regularly due to the nature of their business or income.

Q: What are the benefits of a tax audit for the government?

A: The benefits of a tax audit for the government include increased tax revenue, improved compliance with tax laws, and deterrence of tax evasion.

Q: What are the benefits of a tax audit for the taxpayer?

A: The benefits of a tax audit for the taxpayer can include a better understanding of tax laws, correction of errors on the tax return, and in some cases, a refund of overpaid taxes.

Q: Is a tax audit confidential?

A: Yes, information disclosed during a tax audit is confidential and can only be shared with authorized individuals.

Q: Can a tax audit be appealed?

A: Yes, if a taxpayer disagrees with the outcome of a tax audit, they have the right to appeal the decision.

Q: How is a tax audit conducted?

A: A tax audit is conducted through a thorough examination of the taxpayer's financial records, interviews with the taxpayer, and comparison of the tax return with the taxpayer's actual financial situation.

Q: Can a tax audit be conducted remotely?

A: Yes, some types of tax audits, such as correspondence audits, can be conducted remotely through the exchange of documents and communication via mail or email.

Q: What can trigger an IRS audit?

A: Several factors can trigger an IRS audit, including discrepancies in reported income, excessive deductions, high-value transactions, and random selection.

Q: Who is most likely to be audited by the IRS?

A: Individuals with high income, self-employed individuals, and businesses with large, complex tax returns are most likely to be audited by the IRS.

Q: What is the difference between a tax audit and a tax investigation?

A: A tax audit is a routine check to ensure compliance with tax laws, while a tax investigation is a more in-depth examination triggered by suspicion of tax evasion or fraud.

Q: What are the stages of a tax audit?

A: The stages of a tax audit include notification, preparation, examination, outcome, and potentially, appeal.

Q: How long does the IRS have to audit a tax return?

A: Generally, the IRS has three years from the date a tax return is filed to initiate an audit.

Q: What happens if a taxpayer cannot pay the additional tax assessed after an audit?

A: If a taxpayer cannot pay the additional tax assessed after an audit, they may be able to arrange a payment plan with the tax authority.

Q: What documents are needed for a tax audit?

A: The documents needed for a tax audit can include income statements, expense receipts, bank statements, property records, and other financial documents.

Q: What is a tax audit report?

A: A tax audit report is a document that summarizes the findings of a tax audit, including any discrepancies found and the resulting changes to the tax liability.

Q: What is a tax audit defense?

A: A tax audit defense is the process of defending a taxpayer's position during a tax audit, often with the assistance of a tax professional.

Q: How does a tax audit affect a taxpayer?

A: A tax audit can affect a taxpayer by resulting in additional tax liabilities, penalties, and interest. It can also cause stress and require a significant amount of time and effort.

Q: What happens if a taxpayer disagrees with the result of a tax audit?

A: If a taxpayer disagrees with the result of a tax audit, they have the right to appeal the decision through the tax authority's appeals process.

Q: What happens if a taxpayer refuses to participate in a tax audit?

A: If a taxpayer refuses to participate in a tax audit, the tax authority may make a determination based on the information available, which could result in additional tax, penalties, and interest.

Q: Can a tax audit be conducted after a tax return has been accepted?

A: Yes, a tax audit can be conducted after a tax return has been accepted if the tax authority identifies potential issues with the return.

Q: How can a taxpayer protect themselves during a tax audit?

A: A taxpayer can protect themselves during a tax audit by keeping thorough records, seeking professional advice, knowing their rights, and cooperating with the tax auditor.

Q: What is the role of a tax attorney in a tax audit?

A: A tax attorney can provide legal advice, represent the taxpayer during the audit, help prepare documents, negotiate with the tax authority, and potentially, appeal the audit decision.

Q: What is a desk audit in tax terms?

A: A desk audit is a type of tax audit that is conducted through correspondence rather than in-person meetings. The taxpayer sends the requested documents to the tax authority for review.

Q: What is an audit reconsideration in tax terms?

A: An audit reconsideration is a process where a taxpayer can request that the tax authority reevaluate the results of a tax audit if they believe there has been an error.

Q: What is a field audit in tax terms?

A: A field audit refers to a tax audit performed at the taxpayer's residence, business location, or the office of their accountant. This form of audit is usually more extensive compared to other audit types.

Q: What is a correspondence audit in tax terms?

A: A correspondence audit is a type of tax audit that is conducted through the mail. The taxpayer is asked to send specific documents and information to the tax authority for review.

Q: What is an office audit in tax terms?

A: An office audit is a type of tax audit that is conducted at a local IRS office. The taxpayer is asked to bring specific documents and information for review.

Q: What is a random audit in tax terms?

A: A random audit is a type of tax audit that is conducted without a specific reason. The tax return is selected at random for review.

Applications

Scenario 1:

John is the owner of a small manufacturing firm. His business has been growing steadily over the year, and he has recently crossed the revenue threshold of $1 million. As a result, he is now required to undergo a tax audit. However, John has been managing his accounts himself and is not sure if he has maintained them correctly.

Solution:

John should first hire a professional tax auditor. The auditor will begin by reviewing his financial statements, accounting books, and tax returns to identify any discrepancies. They will also check if the tax calculations are accurate and if all the necessary documents are in order. Once any issues are identified, they will work with John to rectify them and ensure his accounts are compliant with tax laws.

Scenario 2:

Sara owns a chain of restaurants. She has always been diligent about keeping her books in order and has never faced any issues with tax audits. However, this year, she expanded her business and opened new outlets in different states. Now, she's confused about the different state taxes and is worried about the upcoming tax audit.

Solution:

To deal with interstate tax issues, Sara should consider hiring a tax professional who specializes in state taxes. This specialist will know the different tax laws of each state and can guide Sara in ensuring compliance with all of them. The tax auditor will also help her understand her tax obligations in each state and help her prepare for the tax audit.

Scenario 3:

Peter, a freelance graphic designer, has recently crossed the revenue mark that requires him to undergo a tax audit. Being a freelancer, he never felt the need to keep his financial books in order. Now, he's worried about the audit as he doesn't have a clear financial record.

Solution:

Peter needs to hire a tax auditor immediately. The first step would be to gather and organize all financial information, including invoices, bank statements, and receipts. The tax auditor can then work with Peter to create a financial record and identify any missing information. They will also guide Peter on how to maintain his records in the future to simplify tax audits.

Scenario 4:

Emily runs an online clothing store. She has always managed her taxes herself using online tax software. However, this year, due to a glitch in the software, some of her financial data was lost, and now she's unable to prepare for the tax audit.

Solution:

In this case, Emily should immediately contact a tax auditor and explain the situation. The auditor will help reconstruct the lost data from other sources like bank statements and sales records. They will also manually check all the tax calculations to ensure accuracy. It would also be advisable for Emily to consider hiring a professional for her taxes in the future to avoid such issues.

Statutory Audit

Theoretical

Q: What is a statutory audit?

A: A statutory audit is a legally required review of the accuracy of a company's or government's financial statements and records.

Q: What is the main purpose of a statutory audit?

A: The primary objective is to assess if an organization offers a just and precise depiction of its financial status by scrutinizing data like bank balances, accounting records, and financial dealings.

Q: Who conducts the statutory audit?

A: A statutory audit is conducted by a qualified external auditor or a firm of auditors who are independent of the organization.

Q: What is the role of an auditor in a statutory audit?

A: The auditor's role is to check the accuracy and fairness of the financial statements, ensuring they comply with the applicable laws and standards.

Q: What are the key stages in a statutory audit process?

A: The key stages include planning, testing, evaluation, and reporting.

Q: What is the difference between a statutory audit and an internal audit?

A: A statutory audit is a legally required audit performed by external auditors, while an internal audit is performed by employees within the organization to help improve its operations and systems.

Q: What are the outcomes of a statutory audit?
A: The outcomes include a detailed report outlining the accuracy of the financial statements, areas of concern, and recommendations for improvement.
Q: How often is a statutory audit conducted?
A: Statutory audits are typically conducted annually, but can be done more frequently if necessary.
Q: What are the penalties for not conducting a statutory audit?
A: Penalties can include heavy fines, legal action, and damage to the company's reputation.
Q: What benefits can a company gain from a statutory audit?
A: Benefits include increased credibility with stakeholders, improved financial management, and detection of errors or fraud.
Q: What documents are required for a statutory audit?
A: Documents include financial statements, invoices, bank statements, and other financial records.
Q: What skills are required by an auditor to conduct a statutory audit?
A: Skills include knowledge of accounting principles, attention to detail, strong analytical skills, and a thorough understanding of business processes.
Q: What is the role of management in a statutory audit?
A: Management is responsible for providing all necessary documents and information to the auditor, and implementing any recommendations following the audit.
Q: How is the scope of a statutory audit determined?
A: The scope is determined by the legal requirements and the objectives of the audit.
Q: What are the key principles guiding a statutory audit?
A: Key principles include objectivity, integrity, independence, confidentiality, and professional competence.
Q: Can an auditor be held liable for errors in a statutory audit?

A: Yes, an auditor can be held liable for professional negligence if they fail to detect material errors or fraud.

Q: How long does a statutory audit typically take?

A: The length varies depending on the size and complexity of the organization, but it typically takes several weeks.

Q: How is the quality of a statutory audit ensured?

A: Quality is ensured through rigorous planning, testing, and review processes, and by adhering to professional auditing standards.

Q: What factors can influence the effectiveness of a statutory audit?

A: Factors include the skill and experience of the auditor, the cooperation of management, and the quality of the organization's financial systems and controls.

Q: How is a statutory audit report structured?

A: The report typically includes an introduction, a statement of responsibilities, a description of the scope of the audit, the auditor's opinion, and any significant issues identified.

Q: What is the importance of audit evidence in a statutory audit?

A: Audit evidence provides the basis for the auditor's opinion and helps ensure the audit is thorough and accurate.

Q: How are materiality levels determined in a statutory audit?

A: Materiality levels are determined based on the size and nature of the organization, and the potential impact of errors or misstatements on the financial statements.

Q: What is the role of risk assessment in a statutory audit?

A: Risk assessment helps the auditor identify areas of potential concern and determine the extent of testing required.

Q: How does an auditor verify the accuracy of a company's financial statements?

A: The auditor verifies accuracy by checking original documents, reconciling balances, and testing transactions.

Q: What is the impact of technology on statutory audits?
A: Technology can improve efficiency, accuracy, and speed of audits by automating routine tasks and providing sophisticated analysis tools.
Q: What is the relationship between a statutory audit and corporate governance?
A: A statutory audit contributes to good corporate governance by promoting transparency, accountability, and effective financial management.
Q: Why is professional skepticism important in a statutory audit?
A: Professional skepticism helps auditors identify potential errors or fraud, question assumptions, and ensure the accuracy of financial statements.
Q: What is the auditor's opinion in a statutory audit?
A: The auditor's opinion is a statement about whether the financial statements are free from material misstatements and fairly represent the company's financial position.
Q: How can a statutory audit help detect fraud?
A: A statutory audit can help detect fraud by identifying inconsistencies or irregularities in the financial statements.
Q: What are the limitations of a statutory audit?
A: Limitations can include time and resource constraints, the possibility of management deception, and the inherent limitations of financial statements.
Q: What is the role of audit sampling in a statutory audit?
A: The process of audit sampling entails reviewing a portion of transactions or data in order to form conclusions about the whole population.
Q: How does an auditor evaluate internal controls in a statutory audit?

A: The auditor evaluates internal controls by reviewing policies and procedures, testing controls, and assessing the risk of control failure.

Q: What is the difference between a qualified and unqualified audit opinion?

A: A qualified opinion indicates there are issues with the financial statements, while an unqualified opinion indicates the auditor believes the statements are accurate and complete.

Q: What is the role of communication in a statutory audit?

A: Communication is vital for ensuring all parties understand the audit process, the findings, and any recommendations.

Q: How does a statutory audit contribute to public trust in a company?

A: A statutory audit contributes to public trust by providing independent assurance that the company's financial statements are accurate and reliable.

Q: Can a statutory audit be voluntary?

A: While some audits are legally required, a company can choose to have a statutory audit voluntarily for added assurance.

Q: What is the difference between a statutory audit and a tax audit?

A: A statutory audit is an examination of all financial records of an organization, while a tax audit focuses specifically on tax returns and compliance with tax laws.

Q: What is the role of judgment in a statutory audit?

A: Judgment is used to interpret audit evidence, assess risks, and draw conclusions about the fairness and accuracy of financial statements.

Q: What are the challenges faced by auditors in conducting a statutory audit?

A: Challenges can include complex accounting issues, time pressures, risk of litigation, and maintaining independence.

Q: How is auditor independence maintained in a statutory audit?
A: Independence is maintained by avoiding conflicts of interest, not providing consulting services to audit clients, and rotating audit partners.
Q: What is an audit risk in the context of a statutory audit?
A: Audit risk is the risk that the auditor may unknowingly fail to appropriately modify their opinion on financial statements that are materially misstated.
Q: How does a statutory audit add value to a business?
A: A statutory audit adds value by identifying areas for improvement, enhancing credibility with stakeholders, and supporting strategic decision making.
Q: What is the difference between a statutory audit and a compliance audit?
A: A statutory audit verifies the accuracy of financial statements, while a compliance audit checks whether an organization is following relevant laws, policies, and regulations.
Q: How do auditors maintain confidentiality during a statutory audit?
A: Auditors maintain confidentiality by securing data, not disclosing information to third parties without permission, and adhering to professional ethical standards.
Q: How are discrepancies addressed in a statutory audit?
A: Discrepancies are typically discussed with management, investigated further, and reported in the audit findings.
Q: How does a statutory audit impact a company's financial reporting process?
A: A statutory audit can improve the financial reporting process by identifying errors, suggesting improvements, and ensuring compliance with accounting standards.
Q: What is the role of audit planning in a statutory audit?

A: Audit planning involves understanding the business, assessing risks, and determining the scope and approach of the audit.

Q: What is the difference between a statutory audit and a forensic audit?

A: A statutory audit is a regular review of financial statements, while a forensic audit is a detailed investigation typically conducted in response to suspected fraud or legal issues.

Q: How is the audit fee determined in a statutory audit?

A: The audit fee is typically based on the size and complexity of the organization, the time required, and the level of expertise needed.

Q: What is the impact of regulatory changes on a statutory audit?

A: Regulatory changes can affect the scope, approach, and findings of a statutory audit, and require auditors to stay up-to-date with the latest laws and standards.

Applications

Scenario 1:

Suppose a business named XYZ Ltd. has recently conducted a statutory audit, and the auditor has highlighted inconsistencies in the inventory levels reported by the company. The management is unsure about how to resolve this issue. How should the management approach this problem?

Solution: The management should conduct an internal investigation to understand the reason behind the inconsistencies. They should also review their inventory tracking systems and processes. If required, they should consider implementing a more robust system. In addition, they should communicate with the statutory auditor to gain a better understanding of the issue and make necessary corrections.

Scenario 2:

Consider a situation where Alpha Enterprises has hired a new statutory auditor. This auditor has identified several discrepancies in the company's financial statements, which the previous auditor had overlooked. How should Alpha Enterprises address this situation?

Solution: Alpha Enterprises should review the discrepancies pointed out by the new auditor with utmost seriousness. They should conduct a meeting with the previous auditor to discuss these issues. If the previous auditor's negligence or incompetence is proven, they might need to take legal action against them. Meanwhile, they should work with the new auditor to rectify the discrepancies and ensure the accuracy of their financial statements.

Scenario 3:

Imagine a situation where a statutory auditor for a company named Beta Corp discovers that the company has been avoiding taxes by underreporting their profits.

What should be the next step for the auditor?

Solution: The statutory auditor has a legal and ethical obligation to report such fraudulent activities. They should immediately bring this matter to the attention of the company's management. If the management does not take appropriate action, the auditor should report the issue to the relevant tax authorities.

Scenario 4:

Suppose a statutory auditor of a firm, Gamma Inc., discovers that the company's management has been misusing funds for personal expenses. How should the auditor react to this situation?

Solution: The auditor should immediately report this to the company's board of directors. They should provide detailed evidence supporting their claims. If the board does not take appropriate action, the auditor should report the matter to the relevant regulatory bodies. They should also suggest ways to improve the internal control systems to prevent such instances in the future.

Scenario 5:

Consider a scenario where Delta Co. has misrepresented its financial health to attract investors. This was discovered during a statutory audit. How should this situation be handled? Solution: The statutory auditor should report this to the company's management and board of directors. They should recommend immediate corrective measures to rectify the misrepresentation. If the company fails to take action, the auditor should inform the investors and the relevant regulatory bodies about this misleading information.

Audit Sampling

Theoretical

Question: What is audit sampling?

Answer: Audit sampling is a technique used by auditors to test a portion of a population to make inferences about the entire population. It's used when it's impractical or unnecessary to examine all items in a population.

Question: What are the main types of audit sampling?

Answer: There are two main types of audit sampling: statistical and non-statistical. Statistical sampling involves the use of statistical techniques, while non-statistical sampling is based on the auditor's judgement.

Question: What is the purpose of audit sampling?

Answer: The purpose of audit sampling is to provide a reasonable basis for the auditor to draw conclusions about the population from which the sample is selected.

Question: What factors influence the sample size in audit sampling?

Answer: Factors that influence the sample size in audit sampling include the risk of material misstatement, the tolerable misstatement, and the expected misstatement.

Question: Can you explain the distinction between statistical and non-statistical sampling?

Answer: Statistical sampling uses mathematical rules to select the sample and evaluate the results, while non-statistical sampling relies on the auditor's judgement and expertise.

Question: What is the risk of incorrect acceptance in audit sampling?

Answer: The risk of incorrect acceptance refers to the possibility that the auditor might incorrectly determine that a population is not significantly misrepresented when in fact, it is.

Question: What is stratified sampling in auditing?

Answer: Stratified sampling is a method where the population is divided into subgroups, or strata, and a sample is selected from each stratum.

Question: What is the role of professional judgment in audit sampling?

Answer: Professional judgment plays a critical role in determining the appropriate sample size, selecting the sample items, and evaluating the sample results.

Question: What is a sampling error in auditing?

Answer: Sampling error refers to the discrepancy between a characteristic of the population from which a sample is drawn and the same characteristic in the sample itself.

Question: What is the risk of incorrect rejection in audit sampling?

Answer: The risk of incorrect rejection refers to the possibility that the auditor incorrectly determines that a population is significantly misrepresented when in fact it isn't.

Question: How does the auditor decide the appropriate sample size in audit sampling?

Answer: The auditor determines the sample size based on the level of sampling risk, the tolerable error, and the expected error.

Question: What is the concept of materiality in audit sampling?

Answer: Materiality in audit sampling refers to the maximum amount of misstatement that could exist in a population without affecting the auditor's opinion.

Question: What is systematic sampling in auditing?

Answer: Systematic sampling is a method where items are selected at regular intervals from the population.

Question: What is the concept of precision in audit sampling?

Answer: Precision in audit sampling refers to the range within which the true value of the population characteristic is likely to lie.

Question: How does the auditor evaluate the results of the audit sample?

Answer: The auditor evaluates the results of the audit sample by comparing the actual misstatements found in the sample with the tolerable misstatement.

Question: What is the risk of assessing control risk too low in audit sampling?

Answer: The risk of assessing control risk too low is the risk that the auditor concludes that the controls are more effective than they actually are.

Question: What is the risk of assessing control risk too high in audit sampling?

Answer: The risk of assessing control risk too high is the risk that the auditor concludes that the controls are less effective than they actually are.

Question: What is haphazard sampling in auditing?

Answer: Haphazard sampling is a non-statistical sampling method where items are selected randomly without any specific plan.

Question: What is the concept of confidence level in audit sampling?

Answer: Confidence level in audit sampling refers to the degree of certainty that the sample results represent the population.

Question: What is the concept of tolerable error in audit sampling?

Answer: Tolerable error in audit sampling is the maximum error in the population that the auditor is willing to accept.

Question: What is the concept of expected error in audit sampling?

Answer: Expected error in audit sampling is the amount of error that the auditor expects to find in the population.

Question: What is the concept of sampling risk in audit sampling?

Answer: Sampling risk in audit sampling is the risk that the auditor's conclusion based on a sample may be different from the conclusion if the entire population was examined.

Question: What is block sampling in auditing?

Answer: Block sampling is a non-statistical sampling method where a continuous series of items from the population are selected.

Question: What is the concept of representativeness in audit sampling?

Answer: Representativeness in audit sampling refers to the extent to which the sample mirrors the characteristics of the population.

Question: What is the concept of population in audit sampling?

Answer: Population in audit sampling refers to the entire set of data from which the auditor wishes to draw a conclusion.

Question: How does the auditor select the sample in audit sampling?

Answer: The auditor selects the sample in audit sampling using techniques such as random selection, systematic selection, haphazard selection, or block selection.

Question: What is the concept of sample selection in audit sampling?

Answer: Sample selection in audit sampling refers to the process of choosing a subset of the population for examination.

Question: What is the concept of sample evaluation in audit sampling?

Answer: Sample evaluation in audit sampling refers to the process of analyzing the results of the sample and drawing conclusions about the population.

Question: What is monetary unit sampling in auditing?

Answer: Monetary unit sampling is a statistical sampling method where each dollar in the population has an equal chance of being selected.

Question: What is the concept of attribute sampling in audit sampling?

Answer: Attribute sampling in audit sampling is a method used to estimate the rate of occurrence of a specific characteristic in the population.

Question: How does the auditor deal with deviations found in the sample in audit sampling?

Answer: The auditor deals with deviations found in the sample by projecting the deviations to the population and comparing the projected misstatement with the tolerable misstatement.

Question: What is the concept of projection of errors in audit sampling?

Answer: Projection of errors in audit sampling is the process of estimating the total misstatement in the population based on the misstatement found in the sample.

Question: What is the concept of allowance for sampling risk in audit sampling?

Answer: Allowance for sampling risk in audit sampling is the amount that is added to the projected misstatement to allow for the possibility that the actual misstatement in the population may be greater than the projected misstatement.

Question: What is the concept of upper limit of misstatement in audit sampling?
Answer: Upper limit of misstatement in audit sampling is the sum of the projected misstatement and the allowance for sampling risk.
Question: What is the concept of lower limit of misstatement in audit sampling?
Answer: Lower limit of misstatement in audit sampling is the sum of the projected misstatement and the allowance for negative sampling risk.
Question: What is the concept of negative sampling risk in audit sampling?
Answer: Negative sampling risk in audit sampling is the risk that the actual misstatement in the population may be less than the projected misstatement.
Question: What is the concept of detection risk in audit sampling?
Answer: Detection risk in audit sampling is the risk that the auditor will not detect a material misstatement that exists in the population.
Question: What is the concept of inherent risk in audit sampling?
Answer: The inherent risk in audit sampling refers to the potential for a significant error in a claim, given that there are no corresponding controls in place.
Question: What is the concept of control risk in audit sampling?
Answer: Control risk in audit sampling is the risk that a misstatement could occur and not be prevented or detected and corrected on a timely basis by the entity's internal control.
Question: What is the concept of audit risk in audit sampling?
Answer: The risk in audit sampling, known as audit risk, refers to the possibility of the auditor giving an incorrect audit opinion when there are significant errors in the financial statements.

Question: What is the concept of risk of material misstatement in audit sampling?
Answer: The risk of material misstatement in audit sampling refers to the possibility that the financial records have significant inaccuracies before the audit is conducted.
Question: What is the concept of audit evidence in audit sampling?
Answer: The audit opinion is based on conclusions derived from information utilized by the auditor, known as audit evidence in audit sampling.
Question: What is the concept of assertion in audit sampling?
Answer: Assertion in audit sampling is a representation by management, explicit or otherwise, that is embodied in the financial statements.
Question: What is the concept of test of controls in audit sampling?
Answer: Test of controls in audit sampling is a procedure designed to evaluate the operating effectiveness of controls in preventing, or detecting and correcting, material misstatements at the assertion level.
Question: What is the concept of test of details in audit sampling?
Answer: Test of details in audit sampling is a procedure to test for error or fraud in individual transactions, account balances, and disclosures.
Question: What is the concept of substantive procedures in audit sampling?
Answer: Substantive procedures in audit sampling are tests designed to detect material misstatements at the assertion level.
Question: What is the concept of audit procedure in audit sampling?

Answer: The audit sampling procedure in auditing is a detailed guide that outlines the audit evidence to be collected during the audit process.

Question: What is the concept of audit program in audit sampling?

Answer: Audit program in audit sampling is a list of audit procedures to be performed, specified in an audit plan, which sets out the nature, timing, and extent of planned further audit procedures.

Question: What is the concept of audit plan in audit sampling?

Answer: Audit plan in audit sampling is a detailed strategy of the audit work to be performed, the procedures to be followed, the timing of the work, and the resources required.

Question: What is the concept of audit strategy in audit sampling?

Answer: Audit strategy in audit sampling is the approach intended to respond to assessed risks of material misstatement at the financial statement level, and the nature, timing and extent of further audit procedures to be performed.

Applications

Scenario 1:

An auditor, Sarah, is auditing a large manufacturing company. She randomly selects 100 invoices out of 10,000 to check for discrepancies. Out of 100 invoices, she found 4 with errors. Sarah extrapolates this error rate across the entire population of invoices. Does this indicate a significant issue?

Solution:

Sarah identified a 4% error rate. If she extrapolates this across 10,000 invoices, it implies that 400 invoices may contain errors. Whether this is significant or not depends on the company's error threshold. If the company has a threshold of 5%, then this error rate wouldn't be considered significant. However, if the threshold was 2%, then this error rate would indicate a significant issue.

Scenario 2:

John is auditing a retail company with a large inventory. He decides to use systematic sampling, selecting every 10th item for inspection. Out of 100 items, he found 5 defective items. What can John infer about the total population of the inventory?

Solution:

John's sampling revealed a 5% defect rate. If he extrapolates this to the entire inventory, he can assume approximately 5% of the inventory may be defective. However, he must also consider the risk of sampling error as systematic sampling can lead to over or underestimation of the defect rate if the defects are clustered.

Scenario 3:

Emma, an auditor for a financial institution, uses stratified sampling to audit the loan files. She divides the loan files into three strata based on loan amounts: small, medium, and large. After auditing a proportionate number of files from each stratum, she finds that the error rate in the large loan file stratum is significantly higher than the other two. What should Emma do next?

Solution:

Emma has discovered an anomaly in the large loan file stratum which requires further investigation. The high error rate could indicate a systemic issue in processing large loans. Emma should conduct a more intensive audit of the large loan file stratum to identify and rectify the cause of the errors.

Scenario 4:

James, an auditor, is auditing a pharmaceutical company. He uses cluster sampling and divides the company's drugs into clusters based on their types. After auditing, he finds that one cluster has a significantly higher error rate than others. What should James infer from this?

Solution:

The high error rate in one cluster may indicate a problem specific to that type of drug. James should investigate further to determine the cause of this discrepancy. However, he should also consider the risk of sampling error and the potential for the error rate to be different if another sample was chosen.

Scenario 5:

Lisa, an auditor, is auditing a service company. She uses haphazard sampling to select a sample. After auditing, she finds a high error rate. What should Lisa infer from this?

Solution:

Haphazard sampling can sometimes lead to non-representative samples. The high error rate may be due to this non-representativeness. Lisa should consider using a more systematic sampling method to ensure the representativeness of her sample before making any inferences about the entire population.

Balance Sheet Audit

Theoretical

Q: What is a balance sheet audit?

A: A balance sheet audit is a process where an auditor or audit firm reviews the financial statements of a company, particularly its balance sheet, to verify its accuracy and compliance with financial reporting standards.

Q: Why is a balance sheet audit important?

A: A balance sheet audit is important because it ensures the accuracy of a company's financial information, which is crucial for decision-making by investors, creditors, and other stakeholders.

Q: What does an auditor look for in a balance sheet audit?

A: An auditor looks for discrepancies, inaccuracies, and non-compliance with financial reporting standards in a balance sheet audit.

Q: What are the main components of a balance sheet that are audited?

A: The main components of a balance sheet that are audited are assets, liabilities, and equity.

Q: What is the role of an auditor in a balance sheet audit?

A: The role of an auditor in a balance sheet audit is to verify the accuracy of the financial statements, identify any discrepancies, and provide an opinion on the financial position of the company.

Q: How does an auditor verify the assets in a balance sheet audit?

A: An auditor verifies the assets in a balance sheet audit by reviewing the documentation related to the assets, such as purchase invoices, depreciation schedules, and physical verification.

Q: How does an auditor verify the liabilities in a balance sheet audit?

A: An auditor verifies the liabilities in a balance sheet audit by reviewing the supporting documentation for the liabilities, such as loan agreements, lease contracts, and legal claims.

Q: How does an auditor verify the equity in a balance sheet audit?

A: An auditor verifies the equity in a balance sheet audit by reviewing the company's share capital records, retained earnings, and other components of equity.

Q: What are some common issues encountered in a balance sheet audit?

A: Some common issues encountered in a balance sheet audit include inaccurate recording of assets or liabilities, non-compliance with financial reporting standards, and inadequate documentation.

Q: What is the outcome of a balance sheet audit?

A: The outcome of a balance sheet audit is an audit report where the auditor provides an opinion on the fairness and accuracy of the company's balance sheet.

Q: What skills are required for conducting a balance sheet audit?

A: Skills required for conducting a balance sheet audit include analytical skills, attention to detail, knowledge of financial reporting standards, and strong understanding of accounting principles.

Q: How does a balance sheet audit differ from an income statement audit?

A: A balance sheet audit focuses on the company's assets, liabilities, and equity at a particular point in time, while an income statement audit focuses on the company's revenues, expenses, and net income over a period of time.

Q: What are the steps involved in a balance sheet audit?

A: The steps involved in a balance sheet audit include planning, understanding the company's business and industry, risk assessment, testing of balance sheet items, and audit reporting.

Q: What is the role of internal control in a balance sheet audit?

A: The role of internal control in a balance sheet audit is to ensure the accuracy and reliability of the financial statements, detect and prevent fraud, and ensure compliance with laws and regulations.

Q: What is the difference between a balance sheet audit and a financial statement audit?

A: A balance sheet audit is a part of a financial statement audit. While a financial statement audit reviews all the financial statements of a company, a balance sheet audit specifically focuses on the balance sheet.

Q: How does an auditor use sampling in a balance sheet audit?

A: An auditor uses sampling in a balance sheet audit to select a representative group of items from the balance sheet for detailed testing, reducing the amount of work while still obtaining a reasonable assurance.

Q: What is materiality in a balance sheet audit?

A: Materiality in a balance sheet audit refers to the significance of an error or omission in the financial statements that could affect the decisions of users.

Q: How does an auditor handle fraud in a balance sheet audit?

A: If an auditor suspects or detects fraud during a balance sheet audit, they are required to gather evidence, discuss with management, and report to the appropriate level of management or those charged with governance.

Q: What are the consequences of a poor balance sheet audit?

A: The consequences of a poor balance sheet audit may include inaccurate financial reporting, loss of investor confidence, regulatory penalties, and potential legal repercussions.

Q: How can a balance sheet audit add value to a company?

A: A balance sheet audit can add value to a company by identifying errors or issues in its financial reporting, improving its internal controls, enhancing its credibility with stakeholders, and providing insights for decision-making.

Q: What is the difference between a statutory audit and a balance sheet audit?

A: A statutory audit is a legally required review of a company's financial statements, while a balance sheet audit is a specific type of audit that focuses on the company's balance sheet.

Q: How does an auditor determine the scope of a balance sheet audit?

A: The scope of a balance sheet audit is determined based on the size and complexity of the company, the risks associated with its financial reporting, and the auditor's professional judgment.

Q: What role does professional skepticism play in a balance sheet audit?

A: Professional skepticism in a balance sheet audit involves the auditor having a questioning mind and a critical assessment of audit evidence, which helps in identifying discrepancies and potential fraud.

Q: How does an auditor document their work in a balance sheet audit?

A: An auditor documents their work in a balance sheet audit through working papers, which include a record of the audit procedures performed, the audit evidence obtained, and the conclusions reached.

Q: What are some key risk areas in a balance sheet audit?

A: Some key risk areas in a balance sheet audit include valuation of assets and liabilities, recognition of revenue and expenses, and completeness and accuracy of the financial statements.

Q: What is the significance of an audit opinion in a balance sheet audit?

A: An audit opinion in a balance sheet audit provides assurance to the users of the financial statements about the fairness and accuracy of the company's balance sheet.

Q: How does an auditor communicate the results of a balance sheet audit?

A: An auditor communicates the results of a balance sheet audit through an audit report, which includes the auditor's opinion, the basis for the opinion, and any other significant findings.

Q: What is the difference between substantive testing and control testing in a balance sheet audit?

A: Substantive testing in a balance sheet audit involves verification of the transactions and balances, while control testing involves evaluation of the company's internal control system.

Q: What is the relevance of audit evidence in a balance sheet audit?

A: Audit evidence in a balance sheet audit provides the basis for the auditor's opinion and helps in identifying any discrepancies or issues in the financial statements.

Q: How does an auditor assess the going concern assumption in a balance sheet audit?

A: An auditor assesses the going concern assumption in a balance sheet audit by evaluating the company's ability to continue its operations in the foreseeable future based on its financial condition and other relevant factors.

Q: What is the purpose of an engagement letter in a balance sheet audit?

A: The purpose of an engagement letter in a balance sheet audit is to establish the terms of the audit engagement, including the scope of the audit, the responsibilities of the auditor and the management, and the expected deliverables.

Q: How does an auditor use analytical procedures in a balance sheet audit?

A: An auditor uses analytical procedures in a balance sheet audit to understand the relationships between different items in the financial statements and identify any unusual trends or fluctuations.

Q: What is the difference between a qualified and unqualified opinion in a balance sheet audit?

A: A qualified opinion in a balance sheet audit means that the auditor has reservations about the fairness of the financial statements, while an unqualified opinion means that the auditor believes the financial statements are fairly presented.

Q: What is the auditor's responsibility regarding fraud in a balance sheet audit?

A: The auditor's responsibility regarding fraud in a balance sheet audit is to design and implement audit procedures that can reasonably detect material misstatements due to fraud.

Q: How does an auditor evaluate estimates in a balance sheet audit?

A: An auditor evaluates estimates in a balance sheet audit by reviewing the basis of the estimates, checking the consistency with prior periods, and comparing with industry averages or other benchmarks.

Q: What is the role of audit software in a balance sheet audit?

A: Audit software in a balance sheet audit helps in automating the audit procedures, analyzing large amounts of data, and generating audit reports.

Q: How does an auditor handle disagreements with management in a balance sheet audit?

A: If an auditor disagrees with management in a balance sheet audit, they should communicate their concerns, seek to resolve the disagreement through discussion, and if necessary, escalate the issue to the audit committee or the board of directors.

Q: What is the role of the audit committee in a balance sheet audit?

A: The role of the audit committee in a balance sheet audit is to oversee the audit process, review the audit findings, and ensure the independence and integrity of the audit.

Q: How does an auditor assess the risks of material misstatement in a balance sheet audit?

A: An auditor assesses the risks of material misstatement in a balance sheet audit by understanding the company's business and industry, evaluating its internal control system, and performing risk assessment procedures.

Q: How does an auditor verify the cash balances in a balance sheet audit?

A: An auditor verifies the cash balances in a balance sheet audit by reviewing the bank statements, reconciling the bank balances with the cash book, and confirming the balances with the banks.

Q: How does an auditor verify the inventory balances in a balance sheet audit?

A: An auditor verifies the inventory balances in a balance sheet audit by observing the physical count of inventory, reviewing the inventory records, and testing the valuation of inventory.

Q: How does an auditor verify the accounts receivable balances in a balance sheet audit?

A: An auditor verifies the accounts receivable balances in a balance sheet audit by reviewing the aged receivables report, confirming the balances with the customers, and testing the allowance for doubtful debts.

Q: How does an auditor verify the accounts payable balances in a balance sheet audit?

A: An auditor verifies the accounts payable balances in a balance sheet audit by reviewing the aged payables report, confirming the balances with the suppliers, and testing the completeness of the payables.

Q: How does an auditor verify the fixed assets in a balance sheet audit?

A: An auditor verifies the fixed assets in a balance sheet audit by reviewing the fixed assets register, observing the physical existence of the assets, and testing the depreciation calculations.

Q: How does an auditor verify the long-term liabilities in a balance sheet audit?

A: An auditor verifies the long-term liabilities in a balance sheet audit by reviewing the loan agreements, confirming the balances with the lenders, and testing the interest and principal repayment calculations.

Q: How does an auditor verify the share capital in a balance sheet audit?

A: An auditor verifies the share capital in a balance sheet audit by reviewing the share register, confirming the number of shares issued with the company's registrar, and testing the share premium calculations.

Q: What is the significance of the auditor's independence in a balance sheet audit?

A: The auditor's independence in a balance sheet audit is crucial to ensure the objectivity and credibility of the audit, as it prevents any conflict of interest that could compromise the audit findings.

Q: How does an auditor use a confirmation letter in a balance sheet audit?

A: An auditor uses a confirmation letter in a balance sheet audit to obtain a direct confirmation from a third party, such as a bank or a customer, about a specific balance or transaction.

Q: How does an auditor handle subsequent events in a balance sheet audit?

A: An auditor handles subsequent events in a balance sheet audit by reviewing the events occurring after the balance sheet date and determining their impact on the financial statements.

Q: What is the impact of changes in accounting policies on a balance sheet audit?

A: Changes in accounting policies can significantly impact a balance sheet audit, as the auditor needs to review the appropriateness of the changes, assess their impact on the financial statements, and ensure their proper disclosure.

Applications

Scenario 1: ABC Company has recently procured a large parcel of land to expand their operations. The land acquisition has been recorded in the balance sheet but the audit team finds that the value of the land has been overstated.

Solution: In this case, the audit team should determine the correct value of the land. They should review the purchase agreement, assess the market value of similar properties, and determine if any improvements were made to the land. Once the correct value is determined, the balance sheet should be adjusted accordingly.

Scenario 2: During the audit of XYZ Corp, auditors find out that the accounts payable section of the balance sheet does not match with the company's purchase records and invoices. It appears that some of the invoices were not recorded.

Solution: The auditors need to reconcile the accounts payable with the purchase records and invoices. They need to ensure that all invoices have been recorded accurately and the balance sheet reflects the correct amount of accounts payable. Any discrepancies should be corrected and the necessary adjustments should be made in the company's accounting system.

Scenario 3: While auditing DEF Inc, auditors realize that the company has not recorded the depreciation of its fixed assets on the balance sheet.

Solution: The auditors need to calculate the depreciation for the period and adjust the value of the fixed assets on the balance sheet. They should also review the company's policy for recording depreciation to ensure that it complies with the relevant accounting standards.

Scenario 4: GHI Ltd has recently sold a part of its business. This sale has not been reflected in the company's balance sheet causing an overstatement of assets and an understatement of liabilities.

Solution: The auditors should review the sale agreement and calculate the impact of the sale on the company's assets and liabilities. They should then adjust the balance sheet to reflect the sale. They should also ensure that the company has a process in place to update the balance sheet for such transactions in the future.

Scenario 5: JKL Corp has recently issued bonds. The auditors find that the bonds payable are not recorded in the balance sheet.

Solution: The auditors should review the bond issuance documents and calculate the value of the bonds payable. They should then adjust the balance sheet to reflect the bonds payable. They should also ensure that the company has a process in place to record such transactions in the future.

Income Statement Audit

Theoretical

Q: What is an income statement audit?

A: An income statement audit is a thorough review of a company's income statement by an external auditor to validate the accuracy and fairness of the financial information presented.

Q: What is the primary purpose of an income statement audit?

A: The primary purpose of an income statement audit is to provide assurance that the financial statements are free from material misstatement and accurately represent the company's financial position.

Q: What does an auditor look for in an income statement?

A: An auditor looks for irregularities or discrepancies, such as unrecorded revenue or expenses, inconsistencies in the recording of transactions, or incorrect application of accounting principles.

Q: What are the main components of an income statement that auditors pay attention to?

A: The main components include revenue, cost of goods sold, operating expenses, net income, and any extraordinary items.

Q: How does an auditor verify revenues on the income statement?

A: Auditors verify revenues through various methods such as examining invoices, contracts, and other supporting documents, and by comparing recorded revenues with actual cash receipts.

Q: How does an auditor verify expenses on the income statement?

A: Auditors verify expenses by examining invoices, purchase orders, and other supporting documentation, and by comparing recorded expenses with actual cash payments.

Q: How does an auditor determine if the cost of goods sold on the income statement is accurate?

A: Auditors review the company's inventory procedures, verify the cost of individual items, and ensure that costs are properly allocated between inventory and cost of goods sold.

Q: How does an auditor handle extraordinary items on the income statement?

A: Extraordinary items are scrutinized to ensure their nature and amount are properly disclosed and are not part of the company's regular operations.

Q: What are some common errors an auditor might find on an income statement?

A: Common errors include incorrect revenue recognition, misclassification of expenses, incorrect calculation of cost of goods sold, and omission of extraordinary items.

Q: What happens if an auditor finds a material misstatement on the income statement?

A: If a material misstatement is found, the auditor will require the company to correct the misstatement. If the company refuses, the auditor may issue a qualified or adverse audit opinion.

Q: How does an income statement audit contribute to financial transparency?

A: It ensures that the company's financial information is accurate, reliable, and compliant with accounting standards, thereby boosting investor confidence and financial transparency.

Q: How does an auditor determine whether the income statement complies with Generally Accepted Accounting Principles (GAAP)?

A: The auditor checks for adherence to GAAP principles such as revenue recognition, expense matching, and proper classification of items.

Q: What is the difference between auditing an income statement and a balance sheet?

A: An income statement audit focuses on verifying the income and expenses for a specific period, while a balance sheet audit verifies the assets, liabilities, and equity at a specific point in time.

Q: What is the role of internal controls in an income statement audit?

A: Internal controls help ensure the accuracy and reliability of financial reporting. Auditors assess these controls to see if they are effective in preventing or detecting errors in the income statement.

Q: What is the role of professional skepticism in an income statement audit?

A: Professional skepticism involves the auditor having a questioning mind and a critical assessment of the evidence. It's essential in identifying potential misstatements or fraud in the income statement.

Q: How can an auditor detect fraud in an income statement?

A: Auditors can detect fraud by identifying unusual patterns or discrepancies, such as unusually high revenues or low expenses, and by assessing the company's internal controls.

Q: What is the difference between a qualified and an unqualified audit opinion?

A: An unqualified opinion is given when the auditor believes the income statement is fairly presented in accordance with GAAP, while a qualified opinion is given when there are material misstatements or the statement does not fully comply with GAAP.

Q: What is the significance of an adverse audit opinion?

A: An adverse audit opinion indicates that the income statement contains material misstatements and does not present a fair view of the company's financial performance, which could have severe implications for the company's reputation and investor confidence.

Q: What is the impact of an income statement audit on stakeholders?

A: It assures stakeholders that the financial information is reliable, which aids in decision-making related to investments, loans, or other business decisions.

Q: How does an auditor confirm the completeness of revenues and expenses on the income statement?

A: The auditor may trace transactions from the original documents to the income statement, and perform analytical procedures such as comparing current year revenues and expenses with previous years.

Q: How does an auditor test for the accuracy of the income statement?

A: Accuracy can be tested through procedures such as reconciling the income statement to underlying accounting records, and verifying calculations and amounts.

Q: What is the relationship between risk assessment and the audit of an income statement?

A: Risk assessment helps the auditor identify areas in the income statement that have a high risk of material misstatement, and guides the nature, timing, and extent of audit procedures.

Q: How does an auditor evaluate the reasonableness of estimates in the income statement?

A: The auditor evaluates the method used to make the estimate, compares the estimate to actual results, and assesses whether the estimate is consistent with industry norms.

Q: How does an auditor verify the correct classification of items on the income statement?

A: The auditor ensures that revenues, expenses, and extraordinary items are properly classified according to their nature, and in accordance with relevant accounting standards.

Q: How does an auditor evaluate the presentation and disclosure of the income statement?

A: The auditor checks that the income statement is presented in a clear and understandable manner, and that all required disclosures are included and appropriately described.

Q: What is the role of materiality in an income statement audit?

A: Materiality helps the auditor determine the significance of misstatements or omissions. If a misstatement or omission could influence the economic decisions of users, it is considered material.

Q: How does an auditor use analytical procedures in an income statement audit?

A: Analytical procedures involve evaluating financial information by studying plausible relationships among financial and non-financial data. These can help identify unusual transactions or trends that may indicate misstatements.

Q: What is the importance of understanding the client's business in an income statement audit?

A: Understanding the client's business helps the auditor identify key income and expense items, assess the risk of material misstatement, and design appropriate audit procedures.

Q: What is the impact of changes in accounting policies on the audit of an income statement?

A: Changes in accounting policies can affect the comparability of the income statement over time. The auditor must ensure that any changes are properly disclosed and applied consistently.

Q: What is the role of audit evidence in an income statement audit?

A: Audit evidence provides the basis for the auditor's opinion. It is obtained through inspection, observation, inquiry, confirmation, and analytical procedures.

Q: What does it mean if an auditor issues a disclaimer of opinion on the income statement?

A: A disclaimer of opinion means that the auditor is unable to form an opinion on the fairness of the income statement, possibly due to a lack of sufficient audit evidence or significant uncertainties.

Q: What is the concept of "true and fair view" in the context of an income statement audit?

A: "True and fair view" means that the income statement presents an accurate and honest picture of the company's financial performance, in accordance with GAAP.

Q: How does the auditor assess the going concern assumption in an income statement audit?

A: The auditor assesses whether there are significant doubts about the company's ability to continue as a going concern. If there are, these must be disclosed in the income statement.

Q: How does the auditor handle related party transactions in an income statement audit?

A: The auditor ensures that related party transactions are properly disclosed and accounted for, and that they are conducted at arm's length.

Q: What is the objective of substantive procedures in an income statement audit?

A: Substantive procedures aim to detect material misstatements in the income statement, and provide evidence about the completeness, accuracy, and validity of the data.

Q: How does the auditor address contingencies in an income statement audit?

A: The auditor assesses whether contingencies are properly disclosed and accounted for in accordance with accounting standards.

Q: What is the role of professional judgement in an income statement audit?

A: Professional judgement allows the auditor to make informed decisions about the nature, timing, and extent of audit procedures, and the evaluation of audit evidence.

Q: How does the auditor handle subsequent events in an income statement audit?

A: The auditor checks whether subsequent events that occur after the end of the reporting period but before the issuance of the financial statements are properly accounted for and disclosed.

Q: What is the significance of an emphasis of matter paragraph in the auditor's report?

A: A paragraph that emphasizes a matter is designed to highlight an issue that is suitably disclosed or presented in the financial statements. However, the auditor deems this issue to be of significant importance that it warrants emphasis.

Q: How does the auditor handle uncertainties in an income statement audit?

A: The auditor evaluates whether uncertainties are properly disclosed and accounted for, and considers their impact on the overall fairness of the income statement.

Q: What is the role of assertions in an income statement audit?

A: Assertions are claims made by management about the recognition, measurement, presentation, and disclosure of items in the income statement. The auditor tests these assertions to gather evidence.

Q: How does an auditor use sampling in an income statement audit?

A: Sampling involves selecting a subset of transactions for testing, to draw conclusions about the entire population. It allows the auditor to conduct the audit more efficiently.

Q: What is the concept of "sufficient appropriate audit evidence" in an income statement audit?

A: This idea pertains to the volume and merit of proof required by the auditor to establish a sound foundation for their viewpoint. Sufficiency is about the quantity of the evidence, and appropriateness deals with its pertinence and dependability.

Q: How does the auditor handle the issue of fraud in an income statement audit?

A: It is the auditor's duty to strategize and execute the audit in order to achieve a reasonable level of certainty that the financial statements do not contain significant inaccuracies, whether these inaccuracies are due to fraud or error.

Q: What is the difference between a financial statement audit and an operational audit?

A: A financial statement audit focuses on verifying the accuracy and completeness of the financial statements, while an operational audit evaluates the efficiency and effectiveness of operations.

Q: What is the impact of information technology on an income statement audit?

A: Information technology affects how transactions are processed and controls are implemented. The auditor needs to understand the IT systems and assess the risks associated with them.

Q: How does the auditor evaluate the company's accounting estimates?

A: The auditor evaluates whether the accounting estimates are reasonable, based on the available information and in accordance with the applicable financial reporting framework.

Q: How does the auditor test the cut-off of transactions in an income statement audit?

A: The auditor tests whether transactions are recorded in the correct accounting period, by examining documents and records around the year-end.

Q: How does the auditor handle a disagreement with management in an income statement audit?

A: The auditor discusses the matter with management, and if no agreement is reached, escalates the issue to those charged with governance or seeks legal advice.

Q: What are the ethical requirements for an auditor conducting an income statement audit?

A: The auditor must comply with ethical requirements such as independence, integrity, objectivity, professional competence, confidentiality, professional behavior, and technical standards.

Applications

Scenario 1: XYZ Corporation has reported an increase in its revenue by 25% in its annual income statement. However, the audit team has noticed a discrepancy in the reported revenue and the actual revenue recorded in the sales ledger. The audit team needs to address this issue.

Solution: The audit team must first assess the sales transactions recorded in the sales ledger and compare them to the figures reported on the income statement. They must then identify any discrepancies and understand the reasons behind them. If the discrepancies are due to errors or oversights, the audit team should recommend a restatement of the income statement. If fraudulent activity is detected, the audit team should report it to the senior management and suggest appropriate actions.

Scenario 2: ABC Enterprises has reported a significant decrease in its cost of goods sold (COGS) on its income statement, leading to an increase in gross profit. The audit team suspects that the company might have capitalized certain costs that should have been expensed.

Solution: The audit team should review the company's inventory valuation methods and its capitalization policy. They should also review the invoices and purchase orders related to the inventory to validate the costs recorded. If the suspicions are found to be true, the audit team should recommend that the company correct the error and restate its income statement. Scenario 3: DEF Industries has reported a large amount of bad debts expense on its income statement. The audit team, however, believes that the company's allowance for doubtful accounts is not sufficient.

Solution: The audit team should review DEF's policy for estimating its allowance for doubtful accounts. They should also examine the aging schedule of accounts receivable and the historical data on bad debts. If the allowance is indeed found to be insufficient, the audit team should recommend that DEF increase its allowance for doubtful accounts and restate its income statement.

Scenario 4: GHI Inc. has reported a significant increase in its research and development (R&D) expenses on its income statement. The audit team is unsure whether all these costs qualify to be categorized as R&D costs.

Solution: The audit team should review the company's policy for classifying its R&D costs. They should also review the details of the costs included under the R&D heading on the income statement. If any costs are found to be incorrectly classified, the audit team should recommend that GHI reclassify these costs and restate its income statement. Scenario 5: JKL Company has reported a large loss from discontinued operations on its income statement. The audit team believes that some of these losses relate to the company's ongoing operations.

Solution: The audit team should review the company's policy for classifying its losses from discontinued operations. They should also review the details of the losses included under this heading on the income statement. If any losses are found to be incorrectly classified, the audit team should recommend that JKL reclassify these losses and restate its income statement.

Cash Flow Statement Audit

Theoretical

Q: What is a cash flow statement audit?

A: A cash flow statement audit is a process where an auditor examines a company's cash flow statement to verify that it accurately reflects the company's cash inflows and outflows during a specific period.

Q: Why is cash flow statement audit necessary?

A: A cash flow statement audit is necessary to ensure the accuracy and completeness of the information presented in the statement. It helps prevent financial fraud and misrepresentation.

Q: How is a cash flow statement audit conducted?

A: It is conducted through various means such as examining receipts, invoices, bank statements, and other documents that reflect the company's cash transactions.

Q: What are the main sections of a cash flow statement that are audited?

A: The main sections are operating activities, investing activities, and financing activities.

Q: What are the key elements auditors look for in a cash flow statement audit?

A: They look for the accuracy of cash inflows and outflows, proper classification of cash flows into the correct categories, and compliance with accounting standards.

Q: How does an auditor verify the cash inflows from operating activities?

A: The auditor verifies it by checking receipts, sales invoices, and contracts, and comparing them with the recorded amounts.

Q: How does an auditor check the cash outflows in investing activities?

A: The auditor checks the outflows by examining purchase invoices, contracts, or other documents related to investments made by the company.

Q: How does an auditor verify the cash inflows and outflows from financing activities?

A: The auditor verifies it by examining loan agreements, share issuance documents, or repayment schedules.

Q: What happens if discrepancies are found in a cash flow statement audit?

A: If discrepancies are found, the auditor will investigate the cause and may suggest adjustments or corrections to the cash flow statement.

Q: Who is responsible for the accuracy of a cash flow statement?

A: The company's management is responsible for the accuracy of the cash flow statement.

Q: How does an auditor conclude a cash flow statement audit?

A: The auditor concludes by preparing an audit report, stating whether the cash flow statement is fairly presented, in all material respects, in accordance with the applicable financial reporting framework.

Q: What is the importance of cash flow statement audit for stakeholders?

A: It provides assurance to stakeholders about the company's financial health and its ability to generate cash flows.

Q: What is the role of internal controls in cash flow statement audit?

A: Internal controls help ensure the accuracy and reliability of the cash flow statement. The auditor evaluates these controls as part of the audit process.

Q: What are some common errors that can be identified during a cash flow statement audit?
A: Common errors include incorrect classification of cash flows, mathematical errors, incomplete recording of transactions, and non-compliance with accounting standards.
Q: How does an auditor determine the scope of a cash flow statement audit?
A: The scope is determined based on the size and complexity of the company's operations, the nature of its transactions, and the quality of its internal controls.
Q: What are the challenges in auditing a cash flow statement?
A: Challenges include the complexity of transactions, lack of documentation, weak internal controls, and the possibility of fraud.
Q: How can an auditor mitigate the risks in cash flow statement audit?
A: The auditor can mitigate risks by thoroughly understanding the company's business, developing a robust audit plan, and applying professional skepticism.
Q: What skills are required for auditing a cash flow statement?
A: Skills required include a strong understanding of accounting principles, analytical skills, attention to detail, and the ability to understand complex financial transactions.
Q: How does an auditor use analytical procedures in a cash flow statement audit?
A: Analytical procedures involve comparing the company's cash flows with its past performance or with industry norms to identify unusual trends or inconsistencies.
Q: What is the relationship between the cash flow statement and other financial statements in an audit?
A: The cash flow statement is interconnected with the balance sheet and income statement. Changes in these statements are

reflected in the cash flow statement, so the auditor must consider these relationships during the audit.

Q: What are the consequences of a poorly conducted cash flow statement audit?

A: A poorly conducted audit can lead to inaccurate financial reporting, which can mislead investors and other stakeholders, and potentially lead to legal and regulatory consequences for the company.

Q: What tools can auditors use to facilitate a cash flow statement audit?

A: Auditors can use software tools for data analysis, document management, and workflow automation to facilitate the audit process.

Q: What is the importance of professional skepticism in cash flow statement audit?

A: Professional skepticism helps the auditor to not accept information at face value, but to question and verify the information to ensure its accuracy.

Q: How does an auditor deal with non-compliance in a cash flow statement audit?

A: In case of non-compliance, the auditor will report the issue to the management and may suggest adjustments or corrections. If the issue is not resolved, it may lead to a qualified or adverse audit opinion.

Q: How does an auditor communicate the results of a cash flow statement audit?

A: The auditor communicates the results through an audit report, which includes the auditor's opinion on the fairness of the cash flow statement.

Q: How often is a cash flow statement audit conducted?

A: A cash flow statement audit is typically conducted annually as part of the company's annual audit.

Q: What is the difference between a cash flow statement audit and a balance sheet audit?

A: Both are components of the financial statement audit, however, the focus of a cash flow statement audit is the cash movement, while a balance sheet audit concentrates on the company's equity, liabilities, and assets at a particular moment in time.

Q: Can a company have a positive cash flow but still be in financial trouble?

A: Yes, a company can have positive cash flow from operations but still be in financial trouble if it's not able to meet its long-term debt obligations or if it's not investing in its future growth.

Q: How does an auditor handle missing documentation during a cash flow statement audit?

A: If documentation is missing, the auditor may use alternative procedures to verify the transactions, such as third-party confirmations or analytical procedures.

Q: Can an auditor rely solely on the internal audit function for a cash flow statement audit?

A: While an internal audit function can provide valuable input, an external auditor must independently verify the information and cannot solely rely on the work of internal auditors.

Q: What is the role of an audit committee in a cash flow statement audit?

A: The audit committee oversees the audit process, ensures the independence of the auditor, and reviews the audit findings.

Q: What is the difference between a direct method and an indirect method cash flow statement in an audit?

A: The direct method showcases cash flows from operating activities as cash inflows and outflows, while the indirect method begins with net income and makes adjustments for non-cash transactions and variations in operating assets and liabilities.

Q: How does an auditor evaluate the reasonableness of estimates in a cash flow statement audit?

A: The auditor evaluates the reasonableness of estimates by considering the company's estimation process, the assumptions used, and comparing the estimates with actual results or industry norms.

Q: How does an auditor handle disagreement with management during a cash flow statement audit?

A: In case of disagreements, the auditor discusses the issue with management to understand their viewpoint. If the disagreement persists, the auditor may seek legal or other professional advice.

Q: How can a cash flow statement audit help identify fraud?

A: A cash flow statement audit can help identify fraud by detecting unusual or suspicious transactions, such as large cash inflows or outflows without a plausible explanation.

Q: What is the impact of changes in accounting policies on a cash flow statement audit?

A: Changes in accounting policies can affect the presentation and classification of cash flows. The auditor needs to understand and assess the impact of these changes.

Q: How does an auditor assess the going concern assumption in a cash flow statement audit?

A: The auditor assesses the going concern assumption by considering the company's ability to generate sufficient cash flows to meet its obligations in the foreseeable future.

Q: Can a cash flow statement audit be conducted remotely?

A: Yes, with the use of technology and digital tools, a cash flow statement audit can be conducted remotely, although it may require additional procedures for document verification.

Q: What is the role of judgment in a cash flow statement audit?

A: Judgment plays a crucial role in areas such as assessing the adequacy of disclosures, evaluating the reasonableness of estimates, and forming an overall audit opinion.

Q: How does an auditor assess the risk of material misstatement in a cash flow statement audit?

A: The auditor assesses the risk by considering factors such as the complexity of transactions, the effectiveness of internal controls, and the integrity of management.

Q: Can a cash flow statement audit detect tax evasion?

A: While it's not its primary purpose, a cash flow statement audit can potentially detect signs of tax evasion, such as unreported income or overstated expenses.

Q: Can an auditor change the classification of cash flows during a cash flow statement audit?

A: The classification of cash flows is determined by the company's management. However, if the auditor believes that a classification is incorrect, they may suggest a reclassification.

Q: What is the impact of foreign currency transactions on a cash flow statement audit?

A: Foreign currency transactions can create complexities in a cash flow statement audit due to exchange rate fluctuations and the need to translate foreign currency amounts.

Q: How does an auditor handle related party transactions in a cash flow statement audit?

A: The auditor scrutinizes related party transactions closely to ensure they are at arm's length and properly disclosed.

Q: How does an auditor evaluate the consistency of a cash flow statement?

A: The auditor evaluates the consistency by comparing the current statement with previous periods to identify significant changes or trends.

Q: Can a cash flow statement be audited without auditing the other financial statements?
A: No, a cash flow statement cannot be audited in isolation as it is interconnected with the balance sheet and income statement.
Q: How does an auditor handle contingencies in a cash flow statement audit?
A: The auditor evaluates the likelihood and potential impact of contingencies and ensures they are adequately disclosed in the cash flow statement.
Q: Can a cash flow statement audit reveal operational inefficiencies?
A: Yes, a cash flow statement audit can reveal operational inefficiencies, such as excessive cash tied up in inventory or receivables.
Q: What is the relationship between a cash flow statement audit and a company's liquidity?
A: A cash flow statement audit provides an insight into a company's liquidity by examining its ability to generate cash to meet its short-term obligations.
Q: How does an auditor ensure the objectivity of a cash flow statement audit?
A: The auditor ensures objectivity by maintaining professional skepticism, avoiding conflicts of interest, and adhering to auditing standards and ethical guidelines.

Applications

Scenario 1: A company named Techtronics Ltd. is experiencing a significant decrease in its net income. However, the CFO insists that the company is doing well because it has a strong operating cash flow. As an auditor, you need to verify this claim.
Solution: Review the cash flow statement and divide the operating cash flow by the net income. If this ratio is considerably high, it suggests that the company's earnings quality is low. This is because

companies can manipulate earnings more easily than cash flow. If the ratio is close to 1, the CFO's claim can be considered accurate.

Scenario 2: A retail company, Shop-n-Save, has reported increased profits for the year. However, the company's cash and cash equivalents have declined. As an auditor, you are asked to investigate this anomaly.

Solution: A detailed review of the cash flow statement reveals that the company has been investing heavily in inventory and has also paid off a significant amount of debt. This explains why, despite increased profits, the cash and cash equivalents have decreased.

Scenario 3: An IT company, WebWorld, has reported a significant increase in its cash flow from operations. However, the company's revenues have been declining. As an auditor, you are asked to review the cash flow statement.

Solution: In this scenario, you should focus on the changes in working capital. If the company has been delaying payments to its suppliers or collecting receivables quicker, it would result in an increase in cash flow from operations. However, this does not reflect an improvement in the company's operations but rather a change in cash management.

Scenario 4: A manufacturing firm, Build-n-Grow, shows a high positive cash flow from investing activities. As an auditor, you need to understand the reason behind this.

Solution: The cash flow statement reveals that the company sold off a considerable part of its long-term investments. While this explains the high positive cash flow from investing activities, it may not be a positive indicator for the company's growth as it may signify a lack of profitable investment opportunities.

Scenario 5: A pharmaceutical company, MedCure, shows a consistent increase in cash flow from financing activities over the past three years. As an auditor, you need to analyze this trend.

Solution: The cash flow statement indicates that MedCure has been raising money through debt. While this increases the cash flow from financing activities, it also increases the company's debt load. Therefore, the increase in cash flow from financing activities may not necessarily be a positive sign.

Internal Control System

Theoretical

Q: What is an internal control system in auditing?

A: An internal control system in auditing is a process implemented by a company to ensure the integrity of financial and accounting information, meet operational and profitability targets, and transmit management policies throughout the organization.

Q: What are the main objectives of internal control systems?

A: The objectives of internal control systems are to safeguard assets, ensure financial information accuracy, promote operational efficiency, and ensure compliance with laws and regulations.

Q: What five elements make up an internal control system?

A: The five components are control environment, risk assessment, control activities, information and communication, and monitoring.

Q: What is the control environment in an internal control system?

A: The control environment is the set of standards, processes, and structures that provide the basis for carrying out internal control across the organization.

Q: What role does risk assessment play in an internal control system?

A: Risk assessment involves identifying and analyzing risks that could prevent the organization from achieving its objectives.

Q: What are control activities in an internal control system?

A: Control activities refer to the measures put in place by policies and procedures to guarantee the execution of management directives.

Q: What is the significance of information and communication in an internal control system?

A: Ensuring all pertinent information is identified, captured, and disseminated promptly allows staff to fulfill their duties effectively, highlighting the importance of information and communication.

Q: What is the role of monitoring in an internal control system?

A: Monitoring involves ongoing evaluations to ascertain whether each component of the internal control system is functioning as intended.

Q: What is the importance of an internal control system in auditing?

A: An internal control system is essential in auditing as it helps detect and prevent errors, fraud, and compliance issues.

Q: Who is responsible for implementing an internal control system?

A: The management of an organization is responsible for implementing an internal control system.

Q: How does an auditor evaluate an internal control system?

A: Auditors evaluate an internal control system by testing the design and operation of controls, checking compliance with policies and procedures, and assessing the system's effectiveness in managing risks.

Q: What is a preventive control in an internal control system?

A: Preventive controls are established to deter mistakes or inconsistencies from happening. These are anticipatory controls that aid in avoiding losses.

Q: What is a detective control in an internal control system?

A: Controls designed as detectives aim to identify mistakes or discrepancies after they have taken place.

Q: What is a corrective control in an internal control system?
A: Corrective controls are actions taken to reverse the effects of errors detected.
Q: Can an internal control system completely eliminate the risk of errors and fraud?
A: No, an internal control system can reduce the risk of errors and fraud but cannot completely eliminate them.
Q: What is segregation of duties in an internal control system?
A: Segregation of duties is a concept in an internal control system where no single individual has control over all aspects of any financial transaction.
Q: What is the purpose of internal control over financial reporting?
A: The purpose is to provide reasonable assurance regarding the reliability of financial reporting and the preparation of financial statements.
Q: What are compensating controls in an internal control system?
A: Compensating controls are alternative controls that are put in place to counteract weaknesses in other control areas.
Q: How does an internal control system aid in decision making?
A: An internal control system aids in decision making by providing accurate and timely information, ensuring compliance with laws and regulations, and minimizing the risk of unexpected losses.
Q: What is the role of the internal auditor in an internal control system?
A: The internal auditor assesses the effectiveness of the internal control system, identifies areas of risk, and makes recommendations for improvement.
Q: How often should an internal control system be reviewed?
A: An internal control system should be reviewed regularly, at least annually, to ensure its continued effectiveness.

Q: What factors can affect the effectiveness of an internal control system?

A: Factors that can affect the effectiveness include changes in management, employee turnover, rapid growth, new technology, and regulatory changes.

Q: How does an internal control system help in risk management?

A: An internal control system helps in risk management by identifying potential risks and implementing controls to mitigate those risks.

Q: What is the role of the audit committee in an internal control system?

A: The audit committee oversees the effectiveness of the internal control system and ensures that management is taking appropriate steps to address identified control deficiencies.

Q: What is the difference between a manual and automated internal control system?

A: A manual control system involves human intervention, while an automated control system uses technology to monitor and control business activities.

Q: What is a control deficiency in an internal control system?

A: A control deficiency arises when a control's design or function does not enable management or employees to promptly prevent or identify mistakes.

Q: What impact does a weak internal control system have on an audit?

A: A weak internal control system can increase the risk of material misstatement in the financial statements, leading to more extensive substantive testing by the auditor.

Q: What role does corporate governance play in an internal control system?

A: Corporate governance plays a crucial role in establishing the organization's control environment by setting the tone and ethical values of the company, which forms the foundation of the internal control system.

Q: How does an internal control system support operational efficiency?

A: An internal control system supports operational efficiency by establishing clear policies and procedures, promoting accountability, and facilitating timely decision making.

Q: What role does technology play in an internal control system?

A: Technology can enhance the effectiveness and efficiency of an internal control system by automating control activities, improving information quality, and enabling real-time monitoring.

Q: What is a test of controls in an audit of an internal control system?

A: A test of controls is an audit procedure to evaluate the effectiveness of a control in preventing or detecting errors.

Q: What is the impact of an ineffective internal control system on a company's reputation?

A: An ineffective internal control system can lead to financial misstatements, regulatory non-compliance, or fraud, which can damage a company's reputation.

Q: How can an internal control system help in fraud detection?

A: An internal control system can help in fraud detection by implementing effective control activities such as segregation of duties, regular reconciliations, and stringent approval processes.

Q: Can an internal control system be too strict?

A: Yes, an overly strict control system can stifle innovation, reduce operational efficiency, and lead to employee dissatisfaction.

Q: What is an integrated internal control system?

A: An integrated internal control system is one that coordinates the activities of different departments or functions within the organization to achieve common control objectives.

Q: What is the role of management's philosophy and operating style in an internal control system?
A: Management's philosophy and operating style influence the control environment, which forms the foundation of an internal control system.
Q: What are internal controls over cash in an internal control system?
A: Internal controls over cash include segregation of duties, authorization of transactions, independent checks, and physical safeguards.
Q: How does an internal control system contribute to business success?
A: An internal control system contributes to business success by ensuring accurate financial reporting, promoting operational efficiency, detecting and preventing fraud, and ensuring compliance with laws and regulations.
Q: What is the significance of an internal control questionnaire in an audit?
A: An internal control questionnaire is a tool used by auditors to understand and evaluate the client's internal control system.
Q: What are the consequences of not having an internal control system?
A: The absence of an internal control system can lead to financial misstatements, fraud, inefficiency, and non-compliance with laws and regulations.
Q: What are the steps in the internal control process?
A: The steps include establishing control objectives, identifying risks, designing control activities, implementing the controls, and monitoring their effectiveness.
Q: What is the relationship between internal control and external audit?

A: The external auditor depends on the internal control system to decide the scope of their audit processes. If the internal control system is robust, it can decrease the need for extensive substantive testing.

Q: What is the connection between an internal control system and ethical business practices?

A: An internal control system promotes ethical business practices by enforcing compliance with laws and regulations, preventing fraud, and ensuring accurate financial reporting.

Q: What is an internal control report in an audit?

A: An internal control report is a document prepared by the auditor that describes the scope of the audit, the auditor's assessment of the client's internal control system, and any identified control deficiencies.

Q: What is the role of an internal control system in financial statement preparation?

A: An internal control system ensures that financial statements are prepared accurately and in accordance with applicable accounting standards.

Q: How does an internal control system help in managing business risks?

A: An internal control system helps in managing business risks by identifying potential risks and implementing controls to mitigate those risks.

Q: What is the role of an internal control system in ensuring data integrity?

A: An internal control system ensures data integrity by implementing controls over data input, processing, storage, and output.

Q: What is the role of an internal control system in regulatory compliance?

A: An internal control system ensures regulatory compliance by enforcing adherence to applicable laws and regulations.

Q: What is the difference between internal control and internal audit?

A: Internal control is a system implemented by management to ensure the organization's objectives are achieved, while internal audit is an independent function that evaluates the effectiveness of the internal control system.

Q: What are the limitations of an internal control system?

A: Limitations of an internal control system include human error, collusion among employees, management override, and the cost of implementing controls exceeding their benefits.

Applications

Scenario 1:

Company A conducts an annual audit process. The internal control system indicates a discrepancy in the accounting records. The investigation reveals a significant number of unauthorized transactions. How can the company address this issue?

Solution: The company needs to strengthen its internal control system. This can be achieved by implementing robust authorization procedures. For instance, dual approval for transactions above a certain limit can be set up. Also, access to sensitive information should be restricted to relevant personnel only.

Scenario 2:

A retail company, B, discovered during an audit that there were recurring discrepancies between the inventory records and the actual stock in the warehouse. The internal control system failed to flag these discrepancies. What measures can Company B take to rectify the situation?

Solution: Company B should enhance its internal control system to include a real-time tracking mechanism of its inventory. This could involve integrating an inventory management software that syncs with the sales and purchasing systems. Regular physical stock counts should also be conducted as a control measure.

Scenario 3:

Company C, a manufacturing firm, found during an audit that their production costs were significantly higher than what was reported in the financial statements. The internal control system did not identify this discrepancy. What should the company do to avoid such issues in the future?

Solution: To address this issue, company C should improve its cost accounting system. The internal control system should be configured to accurately record production costs, including direct materials, direct labor, and manufacturing overheads. It is also crucial to regularly review and update the system to reflect changes in production processes and costs.

Scenario 4:

During an audit, IT Company D discovered that there was a high rate of resource wastage in its projects. The internal control system was not effective in monitoring resource utilization. How can the company rectify this?

Solution: Company D needs to incorporate a resource management module in its internal control system. This would help in tracking and optimizing resource allocation, thereby reducing wastage. The company should also consider implementing a project management software to monitor project timelines and resource use effectively.

Scenario 5:

Bank E identified during an audit that its loan approval process was not consistent, leading to high default rates. The internal control system did not detect this issue. What steps can bank E take to improve its loan approval process?

Solution: Bank E should enhance its internal control system to include a comprehensive credit scoring model. This would ensure that loans are only approved to creditworthy customers. The bank should also consider automating the loan approval process to ensure consistency and limit human error.

Due Diligence

Theoretical

What is due diligence in auditing?

Due diligence in auditing is a comprehensive appraisal of a business undertaken by an auditor to establish its assets and liabilities and evaluate its commercial potential.

Why is due diligence important in auditing?

Due diligence is important in auditing because it helps to identify potential financial risks and liabilities, assess the business's sustainability and profitability, and ensure that the company is in compliance with relevant laws and regulations.

What is the main purpose of conducting a due diligence audit?

The main purpose of conducting a due diligence audit is to confirm all material facts in regards to a sale and to verify all financial information.

What are some components of due diligence in auditing?

Some components of due diligence in auditing include financial due diligence, legal due diligence, operational due diligence, and strategic due diligence.

What is financial due diligence in auditing?

Financial due diligence in auditing involves a thorough examination and analysis of a company's financial statements, accounting practices, and overall financial health.

What is legal due diligence in auditing?

Legal due diligence in auditing involves verifying the legality of business operations, examining legal documents, and checking for any pending or potential legal issues.

What is the difference between due diligence and an audit?

While both involve a thorough examination of a company's financials, an audit is typically a more standardized and formal process, while due diligence tends to be more flexible and focused on areas of concern identified during preliminary investigation.

How does due diligence add value to an audit?

Due diligence adds value to an audit by providing a deeper understanding of the company's financial health, identifying potential risks and liabilities, and offering insights into the company's operations and strategic direction.

How is due diligence conducted in auditing?

Due diligence in auditing is conducted through a process of data collection and analysis, interviews with key personnel, site visits, and review of financial and operational records.

What are the key steps involved in due diligence in auditing?

Key steps involved in due diligence in auditing include planning and preparation, data collection and analysis, report preparation, and presentation of findings.

What does an auditor look for during due diligence?

During due diligence, an auditor looks for any inconsistencies or discrepancies in the financial statements, reviews the company's compliance with laws and regulations, and assesses the company's risk management strategies.

Who performs due diligence in auditing?

Due diligence in auditing is usually performed by a team of auditors or due diligence professionals who have expertise in the company's industry and the specific areas being reviewed.

When is due diligence performed in the auditing process?

Due diligence is usually performed after preliminary financial analysis and before the finalization of a transaction or agreement.

What are the potential outcomes of due diligence in auditing?

Potential outcomes of due diligence in auditing include the identification of potential risks and liabilities, recommendations for changes in business operations, and insights into the company's financial health and strategic direction.

What are the risks associated with not conducting due diligence in auditing?

Risks associated with not conducting due diligence in auditing include financial loss, legal issues, and damage to the company's reputation.

How long does the due diligence process in auditing typically take?

The due diligence process in auditing typically takes several weeks to several months, depending on the size and complexity of the company being audited.

Can an auditor refuse to perform due diligence?

An auditor can refuse to perform due diligence if they believe that there is a conflict of interest, if they do not have the necessary resources or expertise, or if the scope of the due diligence is not clearly defined.

What are the costs involved in due diligence in auditing?

Costs involved in due diligence in auditing can include fees for the auditing team, expenses related to data collection and analysis, and costs associated with implementing recommended changes.

How can a company prepare for due diligence in auditing?

A company can prepare for due diligence in auditing by maintaining accurate and up-to-date financial records, ensuring compliance with relevant laws and regulations, and having a clear understanding of its business operations and strategic direction.

What role does technology play in due diligence in auditing?

Technology plays a key role in due diligence in auditing by facilitating data collection and analysis, improving the efficiency and accuracy of the audit process, and enabling better communication and collaboration among the audit team.

Can due diligence in auditing be outsourced?

Yes, due diligence in auditing can be outsourced to a professional auditing firm or a team of due diligence specialists.

What are some challenges faced during due diligence in auditing?

Some challenges faced during due diligence in auditing include difficulties in accessing or verifying data, resistance from the company being audited, and complexities in interpreting legal and financial information.

What are the consequences of inadequate due diligence in auditing?

Inadequate due diligence in auditing can result in missed red flags, incorrect assessments of the company's financial health, and potential legal issues.

How can the results of due diligence in auditing be used?

The results of due diligence in auditing can be used to make informed business decisions, develop risk management strategies, and implement changes to business operations.

What is the role of due diligence in mergers and acquisitions?

In mergers and acquisitions, due diligence is used to assess the financial health, legal status, and strategic fit of the target company, helping to identify potential risks and benefits of the transaction.

How does due diligence in auditing differ across industries?

Due diligence in auditing can differ across industries due to variations in regulatory requirements, business practices, and risk factors.

What is the role of due diligence in corporate governance?

In corporate governance, due diligence is used to ensure that the company is being managed in a way that protects the interests of shareholders and meets regulatory requirements.

Can due diligence in auditing detect fraud?

While due diligence in auditing is not specifically designed to detect fraud, a thorough and well-conducted audit can often uncover signs of fraudulent activity.

How does due diligence in auditing relate to risk management?

Due diligence in auditing is a key part of risk management, as it helps to identify potential financial and operational risks, assess their potential impact, and develop strategies to mitigate them.

What is the relationship between due diligence and financial reporting?

Due diligence and financial reporting are closely related, as the findings of a due diligence audit are often used to inform financial reports and disclosures.

Can due diligence in auditing be automated?

While certain aspects of due diligence in auditing can be automated, such as data collection and analysis, other aspects, like interviews and site visits, still require human involvement.

What is the impact of globalization on due diligence in auditing?

Globalization has increased the complexity of due diligence in auditing by introducing new regulatory requirements, increasing the diversity of business practices, and making it more difficult to verify information across different jurisdictions.

How can a company demonstrate due diligence in auditing to stakeholders?

A company can demonstrate due diligence in auditing to stakeholders by conducting regular audits, being transparent about the audit process and findings, and taking action to address any identified issues.

What is the role of ethics in due diligence in auditing?

Ethics plays a crucial role in due diligence in auditing, as auditors must act with integrity, maintain confidentiality, and avoid conflicts of interest.

How has due diligence in auditing evolved over time?

Due diligence in auditing has evolved over time to become more comprehensive, incorporating areas like operational and strategic due diligence, and has also been impacted by technological advancements.

What is the relationship between due diligence in auditing and corporate social responsibility?

Due diligence in auditing can help to ensure that a company is meeting its corporate social responsibility commitments, by examining areas like environmental impact, labor practices, and community engagement.

Can due diligence in auditing predict future performance?

While due diligence in auditing can provide valuable insights into a company's current financial health and operational efficiency, it is not designed to predict future performance.

How does due diligence in auditing affect investor confidence?

Due diligence in auditing can have a positive impact on investor confidence, by providing assurance that the company's financial reports are accurate and that it is in compliance with relevant laws and regulations.

What is the role of due diligence in auditing in preventing corporate scandals?

Due diligence in auditing can play a critical role in preventing corporate scandals, by identifying potential issues early on and ensuring that they are addressed promptly and appropriately.

How can the effectiveness of due diligence in auditing be measured?

The effectiveness of due diligence in auditing can be measured in terms of the accuracy of the audit findings, the identification of potential risks and liabilities, and the impact of the audit on business operations and decision-making.

What skills are required for conducting due diligence in auditing?

Skills required for conducting due diligence in auditing include financial analysis, legal knowledge, attention to detail, critical thinking, and effective communication.

How does due diligence in auditing impact the valuation of a company?

Due diligence in auditing can impact the valuation of a company by revealing information about its financial health, business operations, and risk profile that can affect its perceived value.

Can due diligence in auditing be conducted remotely?

With advancements in technology, many aspects of due diligence in auditing can be conducted remotely, although some elements may still require in-person engagement.

What happens if discrepancies are found during due diligence in auditing?

If discrepancies are found during due diligence in auditing, these are usually discussed with the company for clarification or correction, and may lead to adjustments in the company's financial statements or business practices.

Is there a standard format for reporting the results of due diligence in auditing?

While there is no standard format for reporting the results of due diligence in auditing, most reports include sections on financial analysis, legal review, operational assessment, and strategic evaluation.

How can due diligence in auditing help in decision making?

Due diligence in auditing can support decision making by providing reliable and in-depth information about a company's financial health, operations, and risk profile.

What factors can influence the scope of due diligence in auditing?

Factors that can influence the scope of due diligence in auditing include the size and complexity of the company, the purpose of the audit, and the specific areas of concern or interest.

How does due diligence in auditing support transparency and accountability?

Due diligence in auditing supports transparency and accountability by providing an independent and thorough examination of a company's financial and operational activities.

Can due diligence in auditing be skipped for smaller businesses?

While the extent and depth of due diligence may vary, it is generally recommended for all businesses, regardless of size, as it can help to identify potential risks and ensure financial accuracy.

How does due diligence in auditing contribute to a company's overall success?

Due diligence in auditing contributes to a company's overall success by helping to prevent financial and legal issues, supporting informed decision-making, and promoting transparency and accountability.

Applications

Scenario 1:

A company named "Fresh Farm Ltd." is planning to acquire "Green Groceries Ltd.", a small scale grocery store. The management of Fresh Farm Ltd. has hired an audit firm to perform due diligence. The auditors have found some discrepancies in the financial statements of Green Groceries Ltd.

Solution: The auditors should report these findings to Fresh Farm Ltd. and suggest them to reconsider the deal. If Fresh Farm Ltd. still decides to go ahead with the acquisition, they should negotiate the price based on the financial discrepancies found during the due diligence process.

Scenario 2:

"Tech Titans Ltd." is planning to merge with "Innovative Minds Ltd.", a software development company. During the due diligence process performed by the auditors, it was found that Innovative Minds Ltd. has several pending lawsuits related to copyright infringement.

Solution: The auditors should advise Tech Titans Ltd. to either postpone the merger until the lawsuits are settled or to consider the potential financial implications of these lawsuits in the merger deal. Tech Titans Ltd. could also negotiate a lower price to account for the potential liabilities from the lawsuits.

Scenario 3:

"Golden Real Estate Ltd." is considering investing in "Skyhigh Constructions Ltd.", a construction company. During the due diligence process, the auditors found that Skyhigh Constructions Ltd. has several incomplete projects and has been consistently missing project deadlines.

Solution: The auditors should suggest Golden Real Estate Ltd. to either reconsider the investment or negotiate for a lower investment amount. If Golden Real Estate Ltd. still decides to invest, they should insist on stricter project deadlines and penalties for missing them in the investment agreement.

Scenario 4:

"Health First Ltd.", a pharmaceutical company, is planning to acquire "Life Saver Drugs Ltd." During the due diligence process, the auditors found that Life Saver Drugs Ltd. has not been adhering to certain regulatory standards in their manufacturing process.

Solution: The auditors should advise Health First Ltd. to postpone the acquisition until Life Saver Drugs Ltd. complies with all the regulatory standards. They should also propose a lower acquisition price to account for the potential fines and penalties that could arise from the regulatory non-compliance.

Scenario 5:

"Fast Forward Logistics Ltd." is planning to invest in "Zoom Delivery Ltd." The auditors performing the due diligence found that Zoom Delivery Ltd. has a high employee turnover rate and low employee morale.

Solution: The auditors should advise Fast Forward Logistics Ltd. to either reconsider the investment or negotiate for a lower investment amount. If they still decide to invest, they should suggest implementing measures to improve employee morale and retention at Zoom Delivery Ltd. as part of the investment agreement.

Audit Evidence

Theoretical

Q: What is audit evidence?

A: Audit evidence refers to the data collected or analyzed by an auditor to form an opinion on the accuracy of the entity's financial statements and operations.

Q: Why is audit evidence important?

A: Audit evidence is crucial as it forms the basis of the auditor's report. Without appropriate evidence, the auditor cannot form a valid opinion about the financial statements.

Q: What constitutes strong audit evidence?

A: Strong audit evidence is relevant, reliable, and sufficient. It should directly relate to the audit objective and should be sufficient in quantity to support the auditor's opinion.

Q: What are the different types of audit evidence?

A: Audit evidence types can include physical evidence, documentary evidence, testimonial evidence, analytical evidence, and electronic evidence.

Q: What is physical audit evidence?

A: Physical audit evidence refers to tangible items or assets that an auditor can physically verify, such as inventory or fixed assets.

Q: What is documentary audit evidence?

A: Documentary audit evidence refers to written or printed information, like invoices, contracts, or bank statements, supporting the transactions recorded in the financial statements.

Q: What is testimonial audit evidence?

A: Testimonial audit evidence refers to the information obtained from the entity's personnel or third parties through inquiries or interviews.

Q: What is analytical audit evidence?

A: Analytical audit evidence involves the analysis of significant ratios and trends, including the investigation of fluctuations and inconsistencies.

Q: What is electronic audit evidence?

A: Electronic audit evidence refers to digital data or transactions stored in the entity's information systems that are relevant to the audit.

Q: What is the relevance of audit evidence?

A: Relevance refers to the connection or pertinence of the audit evidence to the audit objective or assertion being tested.

Q: What does sufficiency in audit evidence imply?

A: Sufficiency refers to the quantity of audit evidence. The auditor needs to collect enough evidence to convincingly support their opinion.

Q: What is the reliability of audit evidence?

A: Reliability refers to the trustworthiness or credibility of the audit evidence. The more reliable the evidence, the more assurance it provides to the auditor.

Q: How can an auditor ensure the reliability of audit evidence?

A: The auditor can ensure the reliability of audit evidence by using multiple sources, using appropriate audit procedures, and evaluating the credibility of the information source.

Q: What are some factors that affect the reliability of audit evidence?

A: Factors affecting reliability can include the source of the evidence, the nature and quality of the evidence, and the circumstances under which it is obtained.

Q: What role does professional judgment play in audit evidence?

A: Professional judgment is vital in determining the nature, timing, and extent of audit procedures to obtain sufficient and appropriate audit evidence.

Q: How is audit evidence used in forming an audit opinion?

A: Audit evidence is analyzed and evaluated to determine if the financial statements are free from material misstatement and if they present a true and fair view of the entity's financial position.

Q: What is the relationship between audit risk and audit evidence?

A: The relationship is inverse. The higher the audit risk, the more audit evidence the auditor needs to collect, and vice versa.

Q: What is the role of internal control in audit evidence?

A: The effectiveness of internal controls affects the nature, timing, and extent of audit procedures, and hence the amount and type of audit evidence needed.

Q: How does documentary evidence differ from testimonial evidence in terms of reliability?

A: Documentary evidence is generally more reliable than testimonial evidence because it can be independently verified, while testimonial evidence depends on the individual's memory and honesty.

Q: Can an auditor rely solely on analytical evidence?

A: No, analytical evidence is only a part of the audit evidence and should be used in conjunction with other types of evidence.

Q: What is the objective of audit procedures?

A: The objective of audit procedures is to obtain sufficient and appropriate audit evidence to support the auditor's opinion.

Q: What is the difference between audit evidence and audit procedures?

A: Audit evidence is the information used by the auditor, while audit procedures are the methods used to gather this information.

Q: What is the importance of documenting audit evidence?

A: Documenting audit evidence is important to provide a record of the auditor's work, show compliance with auditing standards, and support the audit opinion.

Q: Can audit evidence be both quantitative and qualitative?

A: Yes, audit evidence can be both quantitative, such as numerical data, and qualitative, such as system controls or personnel competence.

Q: What is the concept of materiality in relation to audit evidence?

A: Materiality relates to the significance of an item or error that could influence the decisions of users. The auditor considers materiality when planning the audit and evaluating the audit evidence.

Q: Are there any limitations to obtaining audit evidence?

A: Yes, limitations can exist due to the inherent limitations of auditing, such as the use of judgment, the concept of materiality, and the nature of audit procedures.

Q: How does an auditor obtain audit evidence from third parties?

A: An auditor can obtain evidence from third parties through confirmations, inquiries, or reviewing external documents or reports.

Q: What is audit sampling?

A: Audit sampling involves applying audit procedures to a portion of items within a group rather than all of them. This allows the auditor to gather and assess audit evidence.

Q: What is substantive testing in auditing?

A: Substantive testing is the collection of audit evidence to detect material misstatements in the financial statements. It involves detailed testing of transactions, balances, and procedures.

Q: How does substantive testing contribute to audit evidence?

A: Substantive testing provides direct evidence about the completeness, accuracy, and validity of data in the financial statements.
Q: What is the difference between compliance testing and substantive testing?
A: Compliance testing checks the operating effectiveness of internal controls, while substantive testing checks for material misstatements in the financial statements.
Q: How does compliance testing contribute to audit evidence?
A: Compliance testing provides evidence about the effectiveness of internal controls, which influences the nature, timing, and extent of substantive testing.
Q: What is negative confirmation in audit evidence?
A: Negative confirmation is a type of audit evidence where the auditor assumes the information is correct unless the third party responds with a disagreement.
Q: What is positive confirmation in audit evidence?
A: Positive confirmation is a type of audit evidence where the auditor asks the third party to respond whether the information is correct or not.
Q: What is the hierarchy of audit evidence?
A: The hierarchy of audit evidence, from most reliable to least, is usually: auditor's direct personal knowledge, external evidence, internal evidence, and verbal evidence.
Q: What are some challenges in obtaining audit evidence?
A: Challenges can include access to information, time constraints, complex transactions, non-responsive third parties, or limitations imposed by the entity.
Q: What is audit evidence in electronic form?
A: Audit evidence in electronic form refers to digital data or transactions stored in the entity's information systems, such as electronic invoices, emails, or digital signatures.

Q: How does an auditor evaluate audit evidence?
A: The auditor evaluates audit evidence by considering its relevance and reliability, assessing its consistency with other evidence, and drawing conclusions based on professional judgment.
Q: What is the role of skepticism in audit evidence?
A: Professional skepticism involves a questioning mind and a critical assessment of audit evidence, which helps the auditor identify inconsistencies, inaccuracies, or fraud.
Q: What is contradictory audit evidence?
A: Contradictory audit evidence is information that contradicts or conflicts with other audit evidence, which may indicate a material misstatement or fraud.
Q: What is corroborative audit evidence?
A: Corroborative audit evidence is information that supports or confirms other audit evidence, enhancing its reliability.
Q: What is the importance of third-party confirmations in audit evidence?
A: Third-party confirmations can provide highly reliable external evidence about certain assertions, such as existence, rights, and obligations.
Q: What is the difference between direct and indirect audit evidence?
A: Direct evidence is obtained through the auditor's own work and senses, while indirect evidence is obtained through the work of others.
Q: What is the role of assertions in audit evidence?
A: Assertions are the representations made by management that are embodied in the financial statements. The auditor collects audit evidence to verify these assertions.
Q: How does the auditor use professional judgment in evaluating audit evidence?

A: The auditor uses professional judgment to assess the relevance and reliability of audit evidence, identify inconsistencies or anomalies, and draw conclusions.

Q: What is the difference between persuasive and conclusive audit evidence?

A: Persuasive audit evidence provides a reasonable basis for the auditor's opinion, while conclusive audit evidence provides absolute assurance, which is not attainable in an audit due to its inherent limitations.

Q: What is the role of audit evidence in detecting fraud?

A: The auditor collects and evaluates audit evidence to identify any indications of fraud, such as inconsistencies, unusual transactions, or deviations from normal patterns.

Q: What is the concept of "audit trail" in relation to audit evidence?

A: An audit trail refers to the sequence of documents and records that allow the auditor to trace a transaction from its origin through its processing cycle to its final inclusion in the financial statements.

Q: Can an auditor rely on audit evidence obtained in previous audits?

A: While some information from previous audits may be relevant, the auditor should obtain current audit evidence in each audit because the conditions may have changed.

Q: What is the relationship between audit evidence and the auditor's report?

A: The audit evidence forms the basis for the auditor's report. The auditor evaluates the audit evidence to determine whether the financial statements are presented fairly in all material respects.

Applications

Scenario 1: ABC Company is a manufacturing unit. The audit team reviewed the purchase invoices and found inconsistencies in the amount invoiced and the actual amount paid. How can the auditors collect audit evidence to verify the accuracy of the transactions?

Solution: To validate the accuracy of the transactions, auditors can cross-verify the purchase orders, receiving reports, and payment vouchers. Also, they can perform a reconciliation of suppliers' statements with the ledger accounts. This will provide them with sufficient audit evidence to conclude on the accuracy of the transactions.

Scenario 2: XYZ is a service-providing company. The company's financial statements show an increase in revenues. However, the auditors suspect that the revenue might be overstated. How can they gather audit evidence in this scenario?

Solution: To gather audit evidence, auditors can test the revenue transactions by matching them with the service agreements and customer invoices. They can also confirm the revenues by directly communicating with the customers. Further, they can perform an analytical procedure by comparing the current year's revenue with the prior years' figures and industry trends.

Scenario 3: DEF Ltd. has recently acquired a property. The auditors need to verify the existence and ownership of the property. What audit evidence can they collect in this situation?

Solution: The auditors can inspect the title deeds and other legal documents to confirm the ownership. They can also physically inspect the property to verify its existence. Moreover, they can review the minutes of the board meeting where the decision of the acquisition was taken.

Scenario 4: PQR Ltd. has reported significant bad debts in the current financial year. The auditors need to ascertain the correctness of this reporting. How can they collect audit evidence to validate this?

Solution: The auditors can review the company's credit policy and procedure for recognizing bad debts. They can also analyze the age-wise analysis of receivables to assess the recoverability of the debts. Moreover, they can discuss with the management about the steps taken for the recovery of the debts.

Scenario 5: MNO is a trading company. The auditors found discrepancies in the inventory count. How can they collect audit evidence to verify the existence and valuation of the inventory?

Solution: The auditors can physically verify the inventory to confirm its existence. They can also review the inventory records and perform a reconciliation with the general ledger. Moreover, they can assess the methodology used by the company for the valuation of the inventory to ensure it's in compliance with the applicable accounting standards.

Compliance Testing

Theoretical

Q: What is Compliance testing in auditing?

A: Compliance testing in auditing is a procedure where auditors review an organization's financial records to ensure they are in compliance with regulatory standards, laws, and policies.

Q: Why is compliance testing important in auditing?

A: Compliance testing is essential in auditing as it helps to identify any deviations from established regulations and standards, which could result in legal penalties for the organization.

Q: What is the main purpose of compliance testing?

A: The main purpose of compliance testing is to ensure that an organization's financial records and operations adhere to the relevant laws, standards, and regulations.

Q: How is compliance testing conducted?

A: Compliance testing is conducted through a systematic review and examination of an organization's financial records, practices, and operations.

Q: What are the consequences of non-compliance in auditing?

A: Non-compliance in auditing can result in legal penalties, fines, and could potentially damage the organization's reputation.

Q: What is the role of an auditor in compliance testing?

A: An auditor's role in compliance testing is to review and examine the organization's financial records and operations, and report any non-compliance to the relevant authorities.

Q: What skills are required for compliance testing in auditing?
A: Compliance testing in auditing requires skills such as attention to detail, analytical thinking, knowledge of regulatory standards and laws, and strong ethical standards.
Q: What are the different types of compliance testing?
A: The different types of compliance testing include transaction testing, walkthrough testing, and control testing.
Q: What is transaction testing in compliance auditing?
A: Transaction testing in compliance auditing involves reviewing a sample of transactions to ensure they comply with the relevant rules and regulations.
Q: What is walkthrough testing in compliance auditing?
A: Walkthrough testing in compliance auditing involves tracing a transaction from its initiation to its final recording in the financial statements, to ensure it has been properly authorized and recorded.
Q: What is control testing in compliance auditing?
A: Control testing in compliance auditing involves reviewing an organization's internal controls to ensure they are effective in preventing or detecting non-compliance.
Q: How does compliance testing differ from substantive testing?
A: While compliance testing focuses on checking the effectiveness of controls and adherence to regulations, substantive testing focuses on the accuracy of financial records and statements.
Q: What is the relationship between compliance testing and risk assessment?
A: Compliance testing is a part of risk assessment, as it helps to identify any potential risks of non-compliance that could impact the organization.
Q: What are the steps involved in compliance testing?
A: The steps involved in compliance testing include planning, execution, analysis, and reporting.

Q: Who is responsible for compliance in an organization?
A: The responsibility for compliance in an organization typically lies with the management team, but the implementation and monitoring are often carried out by a compliance officer or team.
Q: How often should compliance testing be conducted?
A: The frequency of compliance testing can vary depending on the organization's risk profile, but it is typically conducted on an annual basis.
Q: What factors are considered in planning compliance testing?
A: Factors considered in planning compliance testing include the organization's risk profile, the nature of its operations, and the regulatory environment in which it operates.
Q: What role does technology play in compliance testing?
A: Technology can significantly aid compliance testing by automating routine checks, improving accuracy, and providing real-time monitoring capabilities.
Q: How does compliance testing contribute to the overall audit process?
A: Compliance testing forms a crucial part of the audit process as it helps to identify any potential risks or issues related to regulatory non-compliance.
Q: How can non-compliance be mitigated?
A: Non-compliance can be mitigated through regular testing, effective internal controls, and continuous monitoring and review.
Q: What are the common challenges encountered in compliance testing?
A: Common challenges in compliance testing include resource constraints, technological limitations, and the complexity of regulatory requirements.
Q: How is the effectiveness of compliance testing measured?
A: The effectiveness of compliance testing is measured through the rate of non-compliance detected, the effectiveness of controls

in preventing non-compliance, and the organization's ability to address identified issues.

Q: What are the ethical considerations in compliance testing?

A: Ethical considerations in compliance testing include maintaining objectivity and confidentiality, avoiding conflicts of interest, and reporting any non-compliance without bias.

Q: How can an organization improve its compliance testing process?

A: An organization can improve its compliance testing process by investing in training and technology, regularly reviewing and updating its compliance policies, and fostering a culture of compliance.

Q: What impact does a positive compliance testing result have on an organization?

A: A positive compliance testing result can enhance an organization's reputation, reduce legal and financial risks, and increase trust among stakeholders.

Q: Can compliance testing be outsourced?

A: Yes, compliance testing can be outsourced to external auditors who have specialized knowledge and expertise in regulatory compliance.

Q: What should be included in a compliance testing report?

A: A compliance testing report should include details of the tests conducted, the results, any non-compliance found, recommendations for improvement, and a plan of action.

Q: How does compliance testing help in decision-making processes?

A: Compliance testing provides valuable information that can guide decision-making processes, such as risk management, strategic planning, and operational improvements.

Q: Is compliance testing only applicable to financial organizations?

A: No, compliance testing is applicable to any organization that needs to comply with regulatory standards and laws, regardless of the industry.

Q: How does the size of an organization affect its compliance testing procedures?

A: The size of an organization may affect the complexity and scope of its compliance testing procedures, with larger organizations typically requiring more extensive testing.

Q: What role does documentation play in compliance testing?

A: Documentation plays a crucial role in compliance testing as it provides evidence of the tests conducted, the results, and any corrective actions taken.

Q: What is the difference between proactive and reactive compliance testing?

A: Proactive compliance testing involves regular testing and monitoring to prevent non-compliance, while reactive compliance testing involves responding to identified instances of non-compliance.

Q: How does compliance testing relate to corporate governance?

A: Compliance testing is a key component of corporate governance, as it helps to ensure that the organization is operating within the bounds of the law and upholding its responsibilities to stakeholders.

Q: What is the role of internal audit in compliance testing?

A: The internal audit function plays a crucial role in compliance testing by conducting regular checks, identifying potential compliance risks, and recommending corrective actions.

Q: How does compliance testing contribute to an organization's financial stability?

A: By ensuring regulatory compliance, compliance testing can help to prevent fines and penalties that could impact an organization's financial stability.

Q: How can technology be leveraged to improve compliance testing procedures?
A: Technology can be leveraged to automate routine checks, improve the accuracy of testing, and provide real-time monitoring and reporting capabilities.
Q: Can compliance testing be skipped if an organization has strong internal controls?
A: Even with strong internal controls, compliance testing is still necessary to ensure that the controls are functioning as intended and that the organization remains in compliance with relevant laws and regulations.
Q: What are the potential consequences of inadequate compliance testing?
A: Inadequate compliance testing can result in undetected non-compliance, which could lead to legal penalties, financial loss, and damage to the organization's reputation.
Q: How does compliance testing help to promote transparency within an organization?
A: Compliance testing promotes transparency by ensuring that the organization's operations and financial records are in accordance with the law and regulatory standards, and by providing a clear report of the testing results.
Q: How does compliance testing contribute to stakeholder trust?
A: Compliance testing contributes to stakeholder trust by demonstrating the organization's commitment to lawful and ethical operations.
Q: How can the results of compliance testing be communicated to stakeholders?
A: The results of compliance testing can be communicated to stakeholders through a comprehensive report, which details the tests conducted, the results, and any corrective actions taken.
Q: What are some best practices for effective compliance testing?

A: Best practices for effective compliance testing include regular testing, thorough documentation, strong internal controls, and continuous monitoring and review.

Q: How does compliance testing relate to ethical business practices?

A: Compliance testing is a key aspect of ethical business practices, as it helps to ensure that the organization is operating within the bounds of the law and upholding its responsibilities to stakeholders.

Q: What is the impact of regulatory changes on compliance testing?

A: Regulatory changes can impact compliance testing by necessitating updates to the testing procedures and potentially increasing the complexity of the testing process.

Q: How can an organization prepare for a compliance audit?

A: An organization can prepare for a compliance audit by conducting regular self-audits, ensuring thorough documentation, and addressing any identified issues promptly.

Q: How can compliance testing contribute to an organization's competitive advantage?

A: Compliance testing can contribute to an organization's competitive advantage by demonstrating its commitment to lawful and ethical practices, which can enhance its reputation and trust among stakeholders.

Q: What are the likely consequences of failing a compliance audit?

A: Failing a compliance audit can result in legal penalties, financial loss, and damage to the organization's reputation.

Q: How should an organization respond to a negative compliance testing result?

A: An organization should respond to a negative compliance testing result by promptly addressing the identified issues, improving its internal controls, and conducting further testing to ensure compliance.

Q: How does compliance testing help to identify operational inefficiencies?

A: Compliance testing can help to identify operational inefficiencies by highlighting areas where the organization's practices are not in line with regulatory standards, which can often indicate areas for improvement.

Q: Is compliance testing only relevant to organizations in regulated industries?

A: While compliance testing is particularly important for organizations in regulated industries, it is relevant to any organization that needs to comply with legal and ethical standards.

Applications

Scenario 1:

A manufacturing company has implemented a new accounting system. The audit team needs to check whether the system complies with the regulatory requirements and company policies. The team performs a compliance test by checking the system's access controls, data integrity, and backup process. They discovered that although the system has strong access controls and data integrity, it lacks an efficient backup process, making the company vulnerable to data loss. The auditor recommends the company to enhance their backup process to ensure complete compliance.

Scenario 2:

An online retail company is being audited for compliance with data protection laws. The auditor checks their data handling and storage processes, encryption methods, and consent mechanisms for data collection. The auditor finds that while their data handling and storage processes are compliant, the consent mechanism does not fully meet the requirements of the law, as it does not clearly inform customers about third-party data sharing. The auditor advises the company to revise their consent mechanism to ensure full compliance with the data protection laws.

Scenario 3:

A pharmaceutical company is being audited for compliance with Good Manufacturing Practices (GMP). The auditor checks the cleanliness and hygiene practices, staff training, and record-keeping practices. The auditor identifies that the company has excellent cleanliness and hygiene practices and staff training, but their record-keeping practices need improvement, as they do not adequately document all the necessary information. The auditor suggests the company to improve their record-keeping practices to meet the GMP standards.

Scenario 4:

A bank is being audited for compliance with anti-money laundering regulations. The auditor reviews the bank's customer due diligence processes, transaction monitoring systems, and reporting procedures. The auditor discovers that the bank's customer due diligence process is not thorough enough, which could allow potential money launderers to open accounts. The auditor recommends the bank to strengthen their customer due diligence process to ensure compliance with anti-money laundering regulations.

Scenario 5:

A restaurant chain is being audited for compliance with food safety regulations. The auditor checks the restaurant's food handling practices, storage conditions, and staff training. The auditor finds that the restaurant chain's food handling practices and storage conditions are excellent, but the staff training on food safety is not sufficient. The auditor suggests the restaurant chain to provide comprehensive food safety training to all staff to ensure compliance with food safety regulations.

Scope Limitation

Theoretical

Q: What is scope limitation in auditing?

A: Scope limitation in auditing refers to the constraints or restrictions on the auditor's ability to gather necessary evidence to draw a conclusion or make an opinion about an entity's financial statements.

Q: What are some common causes of scope limitation in auditing?

A: Some common causes include the client's refusal to provide necessary information, circumstances beyond the control of the auditor such as natural disasters, and restrictions imposed by laws or regulations.

Q: How does scope limitation impact an auditor's report?

A: Depending on the severity of the scope limitation, the auditor may modify their audit opinion, issue a disclaimer of opinion, or even withdraw from the engagement.

Q: What is the difference between a scope limitation and a qualified opinion?

A: A scope limitation refers to the inability to obtain necessary audit evidence, while a qualified opinion is the auditor's conclusion that the financial statements are not fully in accordance with the applicable financial reporting framework.

Q: Can auditors accept an engagement with a known scope limitation?

A: Generally, auditors should not accept an engagement if they know beforehand that there will be a significant scope limitation. However, there might be exceptions under certain circumstances.

Q: Can scope limitations be resolved?

A: In some cases, auditors can resolve scope limitations by implementing alternative audit procedures or by obtaining the required information from other sources.

Q: What is a disclaimer of opinion due to a scope limitation?

A: A disclaimer of opinion due to a scope limitation is a type of audit report where the auditor states that they cannot form an opinion on the financial statements due to a significant scope limitation.

Q: How does scope limitation affect the credibility of an audit?

A: Scope limitation can undermine the credibility of an audit as it may imply that the auditor did not have complete access to the necessary information to form an opinion.

Q: What is the role of management in preventing scope limitations?

A: Management has a responsibility to provide auditors with the necessary information and access to perform their audit. Any refusal or restriction by management can lead to a scope limitation.

Q: How can auditors communicate scope limitations to the users of financial statements?

A: Auditors can communicate scope limitations through their audit report, specifically in the section where they explain the basis for their audit opinion.

Q: What is an inherent limitation in auditing?

A: An inherent limitation in auditing refers to limitations that arise from the nature of financial reporting itself, such as the use of judgment and estimation.

Q: How does an inherent limitation differ from a scope limitation?
A: While an inherent limitation is unavoidable and arises from the nature of the audit itself, a scope limitation is a restriction on the auditor's ability to gather necessary audit evidence.
Q: What could be the possible consequences of scope limitation for an audited organization?
A: Consequences can include a modification of the audit opinion, loss of credibility, or potential legal ramifications if the scope limitation leads to material misstatements in the financial statements.
Q: Can auditors refuse to sign off on accounts due to a scope limitation?
A: Yes, auditors can refuse to sign off on accounts if they believe that a significant scope limitation has prevented them from obtaining sufficient audit evidence.
Q: What is a material scope limitation?
A: A material scope limitation is one that, in the auditor's judgment, could potentially have a significant impact on the financial statements and the auditor's opinion.
Q: How can the risk of scope limitations be minimized?
A: The risk of scope limitations can be minimized by ensuring open communication between the auditors and management, planning the audit carefully, and using alternative audit procedures where necessary.
Q: What is the difference between a scope limitation and an audit risk?
A: A scope limitation is a restriction on the auditor's ability to gather evidence, while an audit risk is the risk that the auditor may unknowingly fail to appropriately modify their opinion when the financial statements are materially misstated.
Q: How does a scope limitation affect the audit process?

A: A scope limitation may require the auditor to modify their audit plan, use alternative audit procedures, or even withdraw from the engagement.

Q: What is the relationship between scope limitation and materiality in auditing?

A: The concept of materiality in auditing helps determine the significance of a scope limitation. If the auditor believes that a scope limitation could lead to material misstatements in the financial statements, then it is considered a significant issue.

Q: How does the auditor determine the severity of a scope limitation?

A: The severity of a scope limitation is determined by the auditor's judgment, based on the potential impact of the limitation on the auditor's ability to obtain sufficient audit evidence and the potential impact on the financial statements.

Q: What is the auditor's responsibility if a scope limitation is identified?

A: If a scope limitation is identified, the auditor's responsibility is to attempt to perform alternative audit procedures to obtain the necessary evidence. If this is not possible, the auditor may need to modify their audit opinion or withdraw from the engagement.

Q: Can a scope limitation be ignored if it is not material?

A: If a scope limitation is not material, it may not significantly impact the auditor's opinion. However, it should not be completely ignored as it may still affect certain aspects of the audit.

Q: What is an example of a scope limitation in an audit?

A: An example of a scope limitation is when the client refuses to provide certain information or when certain documents or records are not available for review.

Q: How does a scope limitation affect the auditor's independence?

A: A scope limitation does not directly affect the auditor's independence. However, if the scope limitation is caused by the client's actions, such as refusal to provide necessary information, it may raise questions about the auditor's ability to conduct an independent audit.

Q: Can an auditor be held liable for not identifying a scope limitation?

A: While auditors are expected to identify and address scope limitations in their audit, they may not be held liable if they have acted in accordance with applicable auditing standards and professional judgment.

Q: What are the types of scope limitations in auditing?

A: Scope limitations can be either client-imposed (e.g., the client refuses to provide necessary information) or circumstances-imposed (e.g., certain records are destroyed by a natural disaster).

Q: How does a scope limitation affect the audit risk?

A: A scope limitation increases the audit risk as it constrains the auditor's ability to gather necessary evidence and form a reliable opinion on the financial statements.

Q: What is the impact of a scope limitation on the audit conclusion?

A: A scope limitation may lead to a modification of the audit conclusion, a disclaimer of opinion, or in severe cases, withdrawal from the engagement.

Q: How does a scope limitation relate to the concept of professional skepticism in auditing?

A: Professional skepticism involves questioning and verifying the information obtained during an audit. A scope limitation may challenge this process, as it restricts the auditor's ability to gather and verify information.

Q: What steps should an auditor take when a scope limitation is identified?
A: When a scope limitation is identified, the auditor should try to resolve it, perform alternative audit procedures if possible, communicate the issue with the client, and consider the impact on the audit opinion.
Q: How does a scope limitation affect the audit planning process?
A: If a scope limitation is identified during the audit planning process, the auditor may need to revise the audit plan, consider the use of alternative audit procedures, or reconsider the feasibility of the audit engagement.
Q: What is the difference between a scope limitation and an audit exception?
A: A scope limitation refers to a restriction on the auditor's ability to obtain necessary evidence, while an audit exception is a deviation from the applicable financial reporting framework identified during the audit.
Q: Can an auditor issue an unqualified opinion if there is a scope limitation?
A: If the scope limitation is not material and the auditor has been able to obtain sufficient audit evidence, an unqualified opinion might still be issued. However, if the scope limitation is significant, it may lead to a qualified opinion, a disclaimer of opinion, or withdrawal from the engagement.
Q: How does a scope limitation affect the auditor's judgment?
A: A scope limitation may challenge the auditor's judgment as it restricts the auditor's ability to gather necessary evidence and form a reliable opinion on the financial statements.
Q: Can a scope limitation be considered a weakness in internal control?

A: While a scope limitation itself is not a weakness in internal control, it might be a symptom of underlying weaknesses in the entity's internal control system.

Q: What is the role of the audit committee in addressing scope limitations?

A: The audit committee has a role in ensuring that the auditor has unrestricted access to necessary information and in resolving any potential scope limitations.

Q: Can a scope limitation lead to a modified audit report?

A: Yes, a scope limitation can lead to a modified audit report, where the auditor provides a qualified opinion, an adverse opinion, or a disclaimer of opinion.

Q: What is the difference between a scope limitation and a going concern issue?

A: A scope limitation refers to a restriction on the auditor's ability to obtain necessary evidence, while a going concern issue refers to doubts about the entity's ability to continue as a going concern.

Q: How does a scope limitation affect the auditor's responsibility to detect fraud?

A: A scope limitation may hinder the auditor's ability to detect fraud, as it restricts the auditor's access to necessary information and evidence.

Q: Can a scope limitation be a red flag for potential fraud?

A: While a scope limitation itself is not necessarily a sign of fraud, it may raise suspicion if it appears that the client is intentionally restricting the auditor's access to information.

Q: What is the impact of a scope limitation on the audit engagement letter?

A: The engagement letter should clarify the auditor's right to access necessary information. If a scope limitation arises, it may indicate a breach of the terms of the engagement letter.

Q: Can a scope limitation affect the auditor's assessment of materiality?
A: Yes, a scope limitation can affect the auditor's assessment of materiality, as it may restrict the auditor's ability to identify and evaluate material misstatements.
Q: How does a scope limitation relate to the audit evidence?
A: A scope limitation restricts the auditor's ability to gather necessary audit evidence, which forms the basis for the auditor's opinion on the financial statements.
Q: How can a scope limitation affect the timing of the audit?
A: A scope limitation may delay the audit process, as the auditor may need additional time to perform alternative audit procedures or to resolve the limitation.
Q: What is the difference between a scope limitation and an uncertainty in an audit?
A: A scope limitation is a restriction on the auditor's ability to obtain necessary evidence, while an uncertainty refers to a lack of clarity or predictability about a matter affecting the financial statements.
Q: Can a scope limitation be an audit finding?
A: Yes, a scope limitation can be an audit finding, and it should be communicated in the auditor's report.
Q: How does a scope limitation affect the audit fee?
A: A scope limitation may increase the audit fee, as the auditor may need to spend additional time and resources to address the limitation.
Q: Can a scope limitation influence the audit strategy?
A: Yes, a scope limitation can influence the audit strategy, as the auditor may need to revise the audit plan or consider alternative audit procedures.
Q: Can a scope limitation affect the auditor's understanding of the entity and its environment?

A: Yes, a scope limitation can affect the auditor's understanding of the entity and its environment, as it may restrict the auditor's access to necessary information.

Q: Can a scope limitation affect the auditor's risk assessment?

A: Yes, a scope limitation can affect the auditor's risk assessment, as it may increase the risk of material misstatement in the financial statements.

Applications

Scenario 1: Audit of an International Business Corporation

Problem: An international business corporation, XYZ Ltd, hired an audit firm for the audit of their financial statements. The audit team faced challenges due to language barriers and differences in accounting standards in different countries where the corporation operates. This limited the audit's scope.

Solution: The audit firm could hire local auditors or translators to overcome the language barrier. They could also educate themselves about the accounting standards of the different countries where the business operates.

Scenario 2: Audit of a Company with Incomplete Records

Problem: ABC, a manufacturing company, hired an auditor to inspect its financial records. However, the auditor discovered that the company had incomplete records for a specific period due to a system crash. This resulted in a scope limitation in auditing.

Solution: The auditor could use alternative auditing procedures to gather evidence for the period with missing records. For instance, they could compare the financial data of the same period from previous years or use industry averages.

Scenario 3: Audit with Time Constraints

Problem: An audit firm was hired to audit the financial statements of a healthcare provider, DEF Ltd. However, the firm was given a very short period to complete the audit, restricting their ability to conduct a thorough audit.

Solution: The audit firm could request an extension of the deadline. If this is not possible, they could prioritize the key areas for the audit, such as revenue and expenses, to ensure the most critical areas are reviewed.

Scenario 4: Audit of a Company with Limited Access to Information

Problem: An audit firm was hired to audit a tech startup, GHI Inc. However, GHI Inc. refused to provide access to certain confidential information, which was crucial for the audit. This resulted in a scope limitation.

Solution: The audit firm could explain the importance of complete transparency during an audit and ensure them that all sensitive information will be kept confidential. If the client still refuses to provide the information, the auditor may need to qualify their opinion due to the scope limitation.

Scenario 5: Audit of a Company with Complex Transactions

Problem: A financial services company, JKL Corp, hired an audit firm. The firm found it challenging to audit certain complex transactions such as derivative contracts and hedge accounting. This limited the scope of their audit.

Solution: The audit firm could hire or consult with experts in these areas to understand and audit the complex transactions. The audit team could also receive additional training to increase their knowledge about these transactions.

Substantive Procedures

Theoretical

Q: What is the primary purpose of substantive procedures in auditing?

A: The primary purpose of substantive procedures is to detect material misstatements in the financial statements.

Q: What are the two types of substantive procedures?

A: The two types of substantive procedures are tests of details and analytical procedures.

Q: Can you explain what tests of details are in substantive procedures?

A: Tests of details involve checking the accuracy and validity of the transactions and balances in the financial statements.

Q: What is the goal of analytical procedures in substantive procedures?

A: The goal of analytical procedures is to identify inconsistencies, fluctuations, or trends that might indicate a material misstatement.

Q: What is the relationship between substantive procedures and audit risk?

A: Substantive procedures are used to mitigate audit risk by detecting material misstatements that could cause the financial statements to be misleading.

Q: How does the auditor determine which substantive procedures to use?

A: The auditor determines which substantive procedures to use based on their assessment of the risks of material misstatement in the financial statements.

Q: Why is understanding the client's business important in substantive procedures?

A: Understanding the client's business helps the auditor to identify where material misstatements are likely to occur, and therefore which substantive procedures are needed.

Q: How do substantive procedures relate to audit evidence?

A: Substantive procedures are used to gather audit evidence to support the auditor's opinion on the financial statements.

Q: Why are substantive procedures performed at the end of the audit?

A: Substantive procedures are performed at the end of the audit to ensure that any changes in the financial statements during the audit period are identified and assessed.

Q: Can you explain the concept of materiality in relation to substantive procedures?

A: Materiality is a key concept in auditing. It refers to the point at which misstatements in the financial statements would influence a user's decision. Substantive procedures are designed to detect such material misstatements.

Q: How do auditors use sampling in substantive procedures?

A: Auditors use sampling in substantive procedures to check a representative selection of transactions or balances, rather than checking every single one.

Q: Why are confirmations from third parties used in substantive procedures?

A: Confirmations from third parties are used to independently verify information in the financial statements.

Q: How do auditors use cut-off tests in substantive procedures?

A: Cut-off tests are used to ensure that transactions are recorded in the correct accounting period.

Q: What is the role of analytical procedures in the evaluation of audit results?

A: Analytical procedures help auditors understand the relationships among different pieces of financial information and identify any unusual or unexpected relationships that may indicate a material misstatement.

Q: What is the purpose of vouching in substantive procedures?

A: The purpose of vouching is to verify that transactions recorded in the financial statements actually occurred.

Q: How do auditors use reconciliation in substantive procedures?

A: Auditors use reconciliation to check the consistency of different sets of records or documents.

Q: How are substantive procedures used in the audit of inventories?

A: Substantive procedures for inventories might include physical checks of inventory quantities, valuation tests, and cut-off tests for inventory transactions.

Q: How are substantive procedures used in the audit of accounts receivable?

A: Substantive procedures for accounts receivable might include confirmations from customers, ageing analysis, and tests of controls over the recording and collection of receivables.

Q: How are substantive procedures used in the audit of fixed assets?

A: Substantive procedures for fixed assets might include physical inspection of assets, verification of ownership documents, and tests of depreciation calculations.

Q: How are substantive procedures used in the audit of accounts payable?

A: Substantive procedures for accounts payable might include confirmation from suppliers, reconciliation of supplier statements to ledger balances, and cut-off tests for payable transactions.

Q: How do substantive procedures help in detecting fraud?

A: Substantive procedures help to detect fraud by identifying transactions or balances that are inconsistent, unusual, or not supported by appropriate evidence.

Q: Can you explain the concept of professional skepticism in relation to substantive procedures?

A: Professional skepticism means that the auditor does not accept evidence at face value but investigates further if something seems unusual or inconsistent. This is a key part of performing substantive procedures.

Q: How does the auditor use judgement in deciding on substantive procedures?

A: The auditor uses judgement in deciding which substantive procedures to perform, based on their understanding of the business and their assessment of the risks of material misstatement.

Q: How does the auditor document substantive procedures?

A: The auditor documents substantive procedures in the audit working papers, including the nature, timing, and extent of the procedures, and the conclusions drawn.

Q: What is the role of the audit team in substantive procedures?

A: The audit team carries out the substantive procedures under the direction of the audit manager or partner, and their work is reviewed to ensure it is sufficient and appropriate.

Q: How do substantive procedures differ in a small business audit compared to a large business audit?
A: In a small business audit, there may be fewer transactions and less complexity, so the substantive procedures may be less extensive. However, the basic principles and objectives are the same.
Q: Can an audit be completed without substantive procedures?
A: No, substantive procedures are a key part of the audit process. Without them, the auditor would not have sufficient appropriate evidence to support their opinion on the financial statements.
Q: How do substantive procedures contribute to the auditor's opinion?
A: Substantive procedures provide the evidence that the auditor needs to form an opinion on whether the financial statements are free from material misstatement.
Q: Can substantive procedures be automated?
A: Some substantive procedures can be automated, such as data analysis techniques used in analytical procedures. However, many substantive procedures require human judgement and cannot be fully automated.
Q: How do auditors use data analytics in substantive procedures?
A: Data analytics can be used in substantive procedures to analyze large volumes of data and identify unusual or inconsistent patterns that may indicate a material misstatement.
Q: Why is timing important in substantive procedures?
A: Timing is important in substantive procedures to ensure that the auditor has sufficient time to perform the procedures and deal with any issues that arise, and that any changes in the financial statements during the audit period are identified.
Q: How do auditors use observation in substantive procedures?

A: Observation can be used in substantive procedures to check physical assets or processes, such as the client's inventory counting process.

Q: Why are substantive procedures necessary even if the client has strong internal controls?

A: Even if the client has strong internal controls, substantive procedures are still necessary because controls can fail or be overridden, and they cannot prevent all misstatements.

Q: How do auditors use inquiry in substantive procedures?

A: Inquiry can be used in substantive procedures to obtain information from the client or third parties, such as explanations of unusual transactions or balances.

Q: How do auditors use inspection in substantive procedures?

A: Inspection can be used in substantive procedures to examine documents, records, or physical assets.

Q: How does the auditor decide on the extent of substantive procedures?

A: The auditor decides on the extent of substantive procedures based on their assessment of the risks of material misstatement and the quality of the client's internal controls.

Q: How does the auditor evaluate the results of substantive procedures?

A: The auditor evaluates the results of substantive procedures by considering whether the evidence obtained supports the financial statement assertions, and whether any misstatements identified are material.

Q: What happens if a misstatement is identified during substantive procedures?

A: If a misstatement is identified during substantive procedures, the auditor investigates it to understand the cause and extent, and to determine whether it is material. If it is material, it must be corrected before the auditor can issue their opinion.

Q: Can substantive procedures be performed by a junior member of the audit team?

A: Substantive procedures can be performed by a junior member of the audit team under supervision, but their work must be reviewed by a more experienced auditor.

Q: How do auditors use calculation in substantive procedures?

A: Calculation can be used in substantive procedures to check the accuracy of the client's calculations, such as depreciation or interest.

Q: How are substantive procedures used in the audit of revenue?

A: Substantive procedures for revenue might include cut-off tests, confirmation from customers, and analytical procedures comparing current revenue to prior periods or budgets.

Q: How are substantive procedures used in the audit of expenses?

A: Substantive procedures for expenses might include tests of details of expense transactions, analytical procedures comparing current expenses to prior periods or budgets, and tests of controls over expense approval and recording.

Q: How are substantive procedures used in the audit of liabilities?

A: Substantive procedures for liabilities might include confirmation from lenders or other creditors, reconciliation of loan statements to ledger balances, and analytical procedures comparing current liabilities to prior periods or budgets.

Q: How are substantive procedures used in the audit of equity?

A: Substantive procedures for equity might include confirmation from shareholders, inspection of share certificates or capital contracts, and analytical procedures comparing current equity to prior periods or budgets.

Q: Can substantive procedures be performed remotely?

A: Some substantive procedures can be performed remotely, such as analytical procedures or inspection of electronic documents.

However, some procedures may require the auditor to be physically present, such as observing the client's inventory count.

Q: How do auditors use reperformance in substantive procedures?

A: Reperformance involves the auditor independently carrying out the client's procedures to check their accuracy, such as recalculating depreciation or reperforming a bank reconciliation.

Q: What is the role of the audit manager or partner in substantive procedures?

A: The audit manager or partner is responsible for overseeing the performance of substantive procedures, reviewing the work of the audit team, and making key judgements and decisions based on the results of the procedures.

Q: How do auditors use computer-assisted audit techniques (CAATs) in substantive procedures?

A: CAATs can be used in substantive procedures to analyze large volumes of data, perform calculations, or test controls over computerized systems.

Q: How are substantive procedures used in the audit of cash?

A: Substantive procedures for cash might include confirmation from banks, reconciliation of bank statements to ledger balances, and tests of controls over cash handling and recording.

Q: Can substantive procedures identify all misstatements?

A: While substantive procedures are designed to identify material misstatements, they may not identify all misstatements, particularly if they are intentional or involve complex or unusual transactions.

Applications

Scenario 1: Inventory Misstatement

Suppose a company has reported an unusually high inventory level in its financial statements. As an auditor, you suspect that there might be an overstatement of inventory to inflate the company's assets. How would you use substantive procedures to resolve this issue?

Solution: To address this, we would conduct physical verification of the inventory. This involves counting the inventory items and comparing with the records. Additionally, we could review purchase and sales records to verify the existence and ownership of the inventory. We could also analyze the company's inventory turnover ratio to identify any discrepancies.

Scenario 2: Accounts Receivable Fraud

Imagine you are auditing a company that has shown a significant increase in its accounts receivable balances over the year. You suspect that there might be some fraudulent activity involved. What substantive procedures would you apply to investigate this?

Solution: To investigate this issue, we would first confirm the accounts receivable balances with the customers directly. Next, we would review the company's credit policy and check for any changes that might have led to the increase. We would also analyze the age of the receivables to check if there are any old accounts that might indicate fictitious sales.

Scenario 3: Revenue Recognition

Assume you are auditing a software company that recognizes revenue upon signing the contract rather than on delivery. You suspect that this might be in violation of the revenue recognition principle. What substantive procedures would you use to address this concern?

Solution: In this case, we would first review the contracts to understand the terms and conditions of revenue recognition. We would then verify if the revenue has been recognized in accordance with the terms of the contract and the accounting standards. Additionally, we would examine the timing of revenue recognition to ensure that it aligns with the delivery of the software.

Scenario 4: Understated Expenses

Suppose a company you are auditing has reported lower expenses compared to the previous years. You suspect that the company might be understating its expenses to inflate its profits. How would you use substantive procedures to investigate this?

Solution: To investigate this, we would first compare the current year's expenses with the previous years' to identify any significant variances. We would then review the expense accounts and check the supporting documents to verify the accuracy of the expenses recorded. Additionally, we would analyze the company's cost structure to identify any changes that might have led to the decrease in expenses.

Verification

Theoretical

Q: What is the purpose of verification in auditing?

A: The purpose of verification in auditing is to ensure that the assets and liabilities presented in the financial statements of a company are true and correct.

Q: How does verification in auditing differ from vouching?

A: Verification is a process of checking assets and liabilities, whereas vouching is the inspection of vouchers supporting the transactions.

Q: What are the key elements of verification in auditing?

A: The key elements include checking the existence, ownership, value, and disclosure of assets and liabilities.

Q: What is the role of an auditor in verification?

A: An auditor's role in verification is to confirm the authenticity of the information presented in the financial statements.

Q: Why is verification essential in auditing?

A: Verification is essential in auditing as it helps in detecting errors and frauds, ensuring accuracy and reliability of financial statements.

Q: What are the methods of verification in auditing?

A: The methods include physical verification, documentary evidence, third-party confirmation, and analytical procedures.

Q: How does physical verification work in auditing?

A: Physical verification involves the auditor physically checking the assets to confirm their existence.

Q: What is the significance of documentary evidence in verification?
A: Documentary evidence provides proof of the existence, ownership, and value of assets and liabilities.
Q: What is third-party confirmation in verification?
A: Third-party confirmation involves obtaining information from independent sources to confirm the accuracy of data.
Q: How do analytical procedures assist in verification?
A: Analytical procedures involve the analysis of financial information to identify inconsistencies, unusual transactions or trends.
Q: Why is disclosure verification important in auditing?
A: Disclosure verification ensures that all necessary information has been disclosed in the financial statements as per the accounting standards.
Q: What are the challenges in verification during auditing?
A: Challenges can include lack of proper documentation, inability to physically verify certain assets, and lack of cooperation from management.
Q: How can auditors overcome these challenges?
A: Auditors can overcome these challenges by using different methods of verification, seeking expert help, and enforcing audit rights.
Q: What is the impact of technology on verification in auditing?
A: Technology can automate verification processes, improve accuracy, and speed up the audit process.
Q: How does verification contribute to the integrity of financial reporting?
A: Verification ensures that the financial reports are accurate and reliable, thereby enhancing their integrity.
Q: How can verification help in risk management?

A: Verification identifies errors and frauds which can be potential risks, thereby aiding in risk management.

Q: How does verification ensure compliance with laws and regulations?

A: Verification ensures that the financial statements are prepared as per the applicable laws and regulations.

Q: What is the role of internal control in verification?

A: Internal control aids in verification by ensuring accuracy and reliability of financial information.

Q: How does verification enhance stakeholder confidence?

A: Verification assures stakeholders that the financial statements are reliable and free from material misstatements.

Q: What is the impact of verification on decision-making?

A: Verification provides reliable financial information which aids in informed decision-making.

Q: What are the consequences of inadequate verification in auditing?

A: Inadequate verification can lead to inaccurate financial statements, undetected frauds, and decreased stakeholder confidence.

Q: How does verification aid in fraud detection?

A: Verification involves checking the existence, ownership, and value of assets and liabilities, which can aid in detecting fraudulent activities.

Q: How does verification differ in different industries?

A: The verification process may vary based on the nature of assets and liabilities in different industries.

Q: How can auditors ensure objectivity in verification?

A: Auditors can ensure objectivity by maintaining professional skepticism and independence during the verification process.

Q: How does verification relate to audit opinion?

A: The results of verification form a basis for the auditor's opinion on the financial statements.

Q: What is the significance of materiality in verification?

A: Materiality concept helps the auditor to focus on significant items during the verification process.

Q: How does verification ensure completeness of financial statements?

A: Verification ensures that all assets and liabilities have been included in the financial statements.

Q: How does verification ensure valuation of assets and liabilities?

A: Verification involves checking the correctness of the value of assets and liabilities as per the applicable accounting standards.

Q: How does verification ensure ownership of assets and liabilities?

A: Verification involves checking the legal documents to confirm the ownership of assets and liabilities.

Q: How does verification ensure existence of assets and liabilities?

A: Verification involves physical checking or other methods to confirm the existence of assets and liabilities.

Q: How does verification in auditing ensure consistency?

A: Verification ensures that the accounting policies have been consistently applied in preparing the financial statements.

Q: How does verification ensure classification of assets and liabilities?

A: Verification ensures that the assets and liabilities have been classified correctly as per the applicable accounting standards.

Q: How does verification ensure accuracy of financial statements?

A: Verification involves checking the correctness of amounts and other details of assets and liabilities which ensures the accuracy of financial statements.

Q: How does verification ensure reliability of financial statements?

A: Verification ensures that the financial statements are free from material misstatements, thereby enhancing their reliability.

Q: How does verification ensure fairness of financial statements?

A: Verification ensures that the financial statements provide a true and fair view of the financial position and performance of the company.

Q: How does verification ensure transparency in financial reporting?

A: Verification ensures that all necessary disclosures have been made in the financial statements, thereby enhancing transparency.

Q: How does verification ensure accountability in financial reporting?

A: Verification ensures that the management is accountable for the accuracy and reliability of the financial statements.

Q: How does verification ensure comparability of financial statements?

A: Verification ensures that the financial statements are prepared as per the consistent accounting policies, thereby enhancing comparability.

Q: How does verification ensure relevance of financial information?

A: Verification ensures that the financial information is relevant to the needs of the users of financial statements.

Q: How does verification ensure understandability of financial statements?

A: Verification ensures that the financial statements are presented in a clear and understandable manner.

Q: How does verification ensure timeliness of financial reporting?

A: Verification ensures that the financial statements are prepared and presented in a timely manner.

Q: How does verification ensure conformity with Generally Accepted Accounting Principles (GAAP)?

A: Verification ensures that the financial statements are prepared as per the GAAP.

Q: How does verification ensure adherence to International Financial Reporting Standards (IFRS)?

A: Verification ensures that the financial statements are prepared as per the IFRS.

Q: How does verification ensure compliance with statutory requirements?

A: Verification ensures that the financial statements are prepared as per the statutory requirements.

Q: How does verification ensure compliance with tax laws?

A: Verification ensures that the tax liabilities have been correctly computed and disclosed in the financial statements.

Q: How does verification ensure compliance with Company Law?

A: Verification ensures that the provisions of Company Law have been complied with in preparing the financial statements.

Q: How does verification ensure compliance with Securities and Exchange Board of India (SEBI) regulations?

A: Verification ensures that the SEBI regulations have been complied with in preparing the financial statements.

Q: How does verification ensure compliance with banking regulations?

A: Verification ensures that the banking regulations have been complied with in preparing the financial statements.

Q: How does verification ensure compliance with insurance regulations?

A: Verification ensures that the insurance regulations have been complied with in preparing the financial statements.

Q: How does verification ensure compliance with environmental laws?

A: Verification ensures that the environmental laws have been complied with in preparing the financial statements.

Applications

Scenario 1: Inaccurate Physical Inventory

XYZ Corporation conducts an annual physical inventory check. As an auditor, you noticed a discrepancy between the physical count and the recorded inventory in the accounting system.

Resolution: The auditor should first verify the accuracy of the physical count, cross-checking it with the inventory report. If the physical count is accurate, the discrepancy might be due to theft, loss, or inaccurate recording. The auditor should recommend a thorough investigation to find the root cause of the discrepancy and suggest implementing stronger internal controls over inventory.

Scenario 2: Suspicious Write-offs

ABC Ltd. has recorded a significant amount of write-offs in the current year. As an auditor, you suspect that these write-offs might be used to hide fraudulent activity.

Resolution: The auditor should scrutinize the nature of the write-offs, checking the supporting documents and conducting interviews with the responsible personnel. If the write-offs are found to be legitimate, they should be accepted. If not, the auditor should report the fraudulent activity to senior management and suggest strengthening the internal controls over the write-off process.

Scenario 3: Unusual Revenue Recognition

During your audit of DEF Inc., you noticed that they recognize revenue as soon as an order is placed, instead of when the goods are delivered or the service is rendered.

Resolution: The auditor should verify that DEF Inc.'s revenue recognition policy complies with the applicable accounting standards. If it doesn't, the auditor should recommend that the company adjust its revenue recognition policy to match the standards. The auditor should also examine the impact of this policy on the financial statements and propose necessary adjustments.

Scenario 4: Inconsistent Fixed Assets Register

While auditing GHI Company, you found that the company's fixed assets register is not consistent with the general ledger and the financial statements.

Resolution: The auditor should verify the accuracy of the fixed assets register, cross-checking it with the general ledger and the financial statements. Any discrepancies found should be investigated, and the auditor should make sure that the company corrects these discrepancies. The auditor should also recommend implementing better controls over the recording and maintenance of the fixed assets register.

Scenario 5: Doubtful Trade Receivables

JKL Corp. has a significant amount of trade receivables that are overdue. As an auditor, you are doubtful whether these receivables are collectible.

Resolution: The auditor should review the aging report of the trade receivables and assess the collectability of the overdue amounts. If necessary, the auditor should recommend that the company provide for doubtful debts. The auditor should also advise the company to improve its credit control policies to reduce the risk of overdue receivables.

Vouching

Theoretical

Q: What is vouching in auditing?

A: Vouching is an audit process where an auditor examines the documentary evidence supporting a transaction to confirm its authenticity.

Q: Why is vouching considered important in auditing?

A: Vouching is important as it helps to verify the authenticity of transactions recorded in the books of accounts and detect any fraud or misrepresentation.

Q: What details does an auditor examine during vouching?

A: During vouching, an auditor examines details such as the date, amount, authorization, and evidence of the transaction.

Q: How does vouching help in preventing fraud?

A: Vouching helps in preventing fraud by ensuring that all transactions are backed by valid documents and have been correctly recorded.

Q: What documents can be used as vouching evidence?

A: Receipts, invoices, contracts, and bank statements are some of the documents that can be used as vouching evidence.

Q: How does vouching help in building a relationship of trust between the auditor and the client?

A: Vouching builds trust as it demonstrates the auditor's thoroughness and commitment to verifying the accuracy of the client's financial records.

Q: What is the main objective of vouching?
A: The main objective of vouching is to verify the authenticity of transactions and ensure they have been recorded accurately.
Q: What risks are associated with vouching?
A: Risks associated with vouching include overlooking fraudulent transactions, misinterpreting documents, or failing to detect errors.
Q: How does vouching add value to an audit?
A: Vouching adds value to an audit by enhancing its credibility and providing assurance about the accuracy of the financial statements.
Q: Can vouching be performed electronically?
A: Yes, vouching can be performed electronically by examining digital records and transaction evidence.
Q: Is vouching a mandatory step in auditing?
A: Yes, vouching is a critical step in auditing as it verifies the authenticity of transactions.
Q: What skills are needed for effective vouching?
A: To effectively vouch, one needs analytical abilities, meticulousness, and a comprehensive knowledge of accounting rules.
Q: How does vouching help in detecting errors in accounting?
A: Vouching helps in detecting errors by ensuring each transaction is supported by valid documents and has been recorded accurately.
Q: Can vouching guarantee the absence of fraud?
A: No, while vouching helps in detecting fraud, it does not guarantee its absence as fraudsters may use sophisticated methods to conceal fraudulent transactions.
Q: What is the role of internal control in vouching?
A: Internal control plays a crucial role in vouching as it ensures that transactions are properly authorized and recorded.
Q: How does vouching contribute to audit efficiency?

A: Vouching contributes to audit efficiency by helping auditors quickly identify errors or inconsistencies in the accounting records.

Q: What challenges can auditors face during vouching?

A: Auditors can face challenges such as incomplete documentation, lack of cooperation from the client, or complex transactions during vouching.

Q: How can auditors overcome the challenges of vouching?

A: Auditors can overcome the challenges of vouching by maintaining open communication with the client, using appropriate audit tools, and continuously updating their knowledge and skills.

Q: How is vouching different from verification in auditing?

A: While vouching involves examining documentary evidence to confirm the authenticity of transactions, verification involves checking the existence, ownership, and value of assets and liabilities.

Q: How does vouching help in complying with auditing standards?

A: Vouching helps in complying with auditing standards by ensuring that the audit is conducted with due diligence and the financial statements present a true and fair view.

Q: Does vouching involve a physical inspection of assets or inventory?

A: No, vouching mainly involves examining documents and records. Physical inspection of assets or inventory is part of the verification process.

Q: Can vouching be outsourced?

A: Yes, vouching can be outsourced to external auditors or audit firms who have the necessary expertise and experience.

Q: Can vouching detect all types of frauds?

A: No, vouching can't detect all types of frauds. Some sophisticated frauds may require specialized audit techniques or forensic auditing.

Q: How frequently should vouching be done?

A: The frequency of vouching depends on the auditor's judgment, the size and complexity of the business, and the effectiveness of the internal control system.

Q: Why is it important to vouch both income and expenditure?

A: Vouching both income and expenditure helps to ensure that all transactions are accounted for and there's no misappropriation of funds.

Q: Can an auditor rely solely on vouching to form their opinion?

A: No, while vouching is important, an auditor should also perform other audit procedures like inquiry, inspection, and analytical procedures to form their opinion.

Q: What is the impact of technology on vouching?

A: Technology has made vouching more efficient and accurate by enabling electronic validation of transactions and automated checking of large volumes of data.

Q: How does vouching help in audit planning?

A: Vouching helps in audit planning by identifying areas of risk or concern that may require further investigation or audit focus.

Q: Is vouching a time-consuming process?

A: Vouching can be time-consuming, particularly for large businesses with numerous transactions. However, the use of technology can make the process more efficient.

Q: What are the consequences of ineffective vouching?

A: Ineffective vouching can lead to undetected errors or fraud, inaccurate financial statements, and potential legal or regulatory consequences.

Q: Can vouching be skipped if a company has a strong internal control system?

A: No, even if a company has a strong internal control system, vouching should still be performed to confirm the authenticity of transactions.

Q: Can vouching be done by a non-auditor?

A: While non-auditors can assist in gathering documents for vouching, the actual vouching process should be performed by a qualified auditor to ensure accuracy and compliance.

Q: What is the relationship between vouching and materiality in auditing?

A: The concept of materiality in auditing helps determine the extent of vouching. If a transaction is considered material, it requires a higher level of vouching.

Q: What is the role of professional skepticism in vouching?

A: Professional skepticism in vouching involves questioning the authenticity of documents and not accepting them at face value. It's crucial for detecting fraud or misrepresentation.

Q: Can an auditor vouch for future transactions?

A: No, an auditor can only vouch for past transactions as they need documentary evidence which is not available for future transactions.

Q: What's the difference between positive and negative vouching?

A: Positive vouching involves checking all entries in the books of accounts, while negative vouching involves checking only those entries which are unusual or suspicious.

Q: What is the role of vouching in statutory audits?

A: In statutory audits, vouching helps ensure compliance with laws and regulations by verifying the authenticity of transactions.

Q: Can vouching detect errors of omission?

A: Vouching may not always detect errors of omission as it involves checking documentary evidence for recorded transactions. Errors of omission involve transactions that have not been recorded.

Q: Can an auditor be held liable for not vouching properly?
A: Yes, if an auditor fails to vouch properly and this leads to financial loss or legal issues, they could be held liable.
Q: How does vouching help in assessing audit risk?
A: Vouching helps in assessing audit risk by identifying errors or frauds that could impact the accuracy of the financial statements.
Q: How does vouching help in determining the audit scope?
A: Vouching helps in determining the audit scope by identifying high-risk areas that require more detailed examination.
Q: What's the role of vouching in cost audits?
A: In cost audits, vouching helps verify the accuracy of cost records and ensure that they comply with cost accounting standards.
Q: Can vouching be performed on a sample basis?
A: Yes, vouching can be performed on a sample basis, especially in large businesses with numerous transactions. However, the sample should be representative of the entire population.
Q: What's the role of vouching in tax audits?
A: In tax audits, vouching helps verify the accuracy of income and expense records and ensure compliance with tax laws.
Q: Can vouching be performed retrospectively?
A: Yes, vouching can be performed retrospectively to verify past transactions, especially if there's suspicion of fraud or error.
Q: How does vouching help in evaluating the effectiveness of internal control?
A: Vouching helps in evaluating the effectiveness of internal control by checking whether transactions have been properly authorized and recorded.
Q: What is the role of vouching in detecting related party transactions?

A: Vouching helps in detecting related party transactions by examining documentary evidence and looking for indicators such as common addresses, similar names, or unusual transaction terms.

Q: Can an auditor vouch for transactions that have occurred after the balance sheet date?

A: An auditor can vouch for transactions that have occurred after the balance sheet date to confirm their occurrence and ensure they are correctly classified as post-balance sheet events.

Q: How does vouching help in identifying contingent liabilities?

A: Vouching helps in identifying contingent liabilities by examining documents related to lawsuits, claims, or potential obligations that could become liabilities in the future.

Q: What's the role of vouching in confirming the going concern assumption?

A: Vouching helps in confirming the going concern assumption by verifying the accuracy of income and expense records and checking for any indicators of financial distress.

Applications

Scenario 1:

A new company has hired an auditor to assess the financial statements. The auditor came across a large purchase of office equipment, and while the invoice was provided, there was no supporting documents such as delivery notes or supplier's statement. How should the auditor vouch this transaction?

Solution: The auditor should ask for additional documentation to support the purchase such as delivery notes or vendor's statement. If these are not available, they should contact the supplier directly to confirm the transaction. If the transaction cannot be vouched, it should be considered a potential misstatement.

Scenario 2:

An auditor is reviewing a company's payroll expenses. They noticed that the payroll register does not match the general ledger and there are no supporting documents for many of the payroll transactions. How should the auditor vouch these transactions?
Solution: The auditor should ask the management for supporting documents such as time cards, pay rates approval, and payroll bank statement. If these are not available, they should perform analytical procedures or recompute the payroll to confirm the accuracy. If discrepancies still exist, it may indicate fraud or error.

Scenario 3:

A company has reported a significant increase in sales. However, upon reviewing the sales invoices, the auditor noticed that many of the sales were made to a new customer and there were no supporting shipping documents. How should the auditor vouch these sales?

Solution: The auditor should ask for shipping documents to support the sales. If these are not available, they should confirm the sales directly with the customer. If the sales cannot be vouched, it may indicate potential revenue recognition fraud.

Scenario 4:

A company has made a large donation to a charity. The auditor found the receipt for the donation, but there is no board of directors meeting minutes authorizing the donation. How should the auditor vouch this transaction?

Solution: The auditor should ask for the board of directors meeting minutes or other documentation showing the donation was authorized. If these are not available, it may indicate a potential misappropriation of assets.

Scenario 5:

A company has reported substantial repair and maintenance expenses. The auditor found the invoices for the repairs but there is no work orders or other supporting documents. How should the auditor vouch these expenses?

Solution: The auditor should ask for work orders or other supporting documents to confirm the repairs were actually made. If these are not available, they should inspect the assets to verify the repairs. If the expenses cannot be vouched, it may indicate potential overstatement of expenses.

Attestation

Theoretical

Question: What is attestation in auditing?

Answer: Attestation in auditing is the process where an auditor examines financial records to assess their accuracy and reliability. The auditor then provides a professional, independent opinion on the state of the organization's financial statements.

Question: What is the main purpose of attestation in auditing?

Answer: The main purpose of attestation in auditing is to provide assurance that the organization's financial statements are free from material misstatements, whether due to fraud or error.

Question: What is the difference between auditing and attestation?

Answer: While both auditing and attestation involve the examination of financial information, auditing typically involves a more comprehensive and detailed review. Attestation, on the other hand, is often focused on specific aspects of the financial statements.

Question: Who can perform attestation in auditing?

Answer: Attestation can only be performed by a certified public accountant (CPA) or an auditing firm that is independent of the organization being audited.

Question: What are the types of attestation engagements?

Answer: The types of attestation engagements include financial statement audits, reviews of financial statements, and examinations of internal control over financial reporting.
Question: What is the role of standards in attestation engagements?
Answer: Standards guide the planning, conduct, and reporting of attestation engagements, helping to ensure consistency, reliability, and accuracy.
Question: What is a negative assurance in attestation?
Answer: In a negative assurance, the auditor does not definitively state a conclusion, but instead mentions that they have not encountered any issues that would lead them to think the financial statements have been unfairly presented.
Question: What is the difference between a review and an audit in attestation?
Answer: A review doesn't provide as extensive an examination as an audit does. The aim of an audit is to provide a strong level of confidence that the financial statements contain no major mistakes, while a review only gives a certain level of confidence.
Question: What is the importance of independence in attestation?
Answer: Independence is crucial in attestation as it ensures the auditor's opinion is unbiased and free from any conflicts of interest.
Question: What is a management assertion?
Answer: A management assertion is a claim made by the management regarding certain aspects of the business, such as the accuracy and completeness of the financial statements.
Question: What are attestation standards?
Answer: Attestation standards are guidelines set by professional bodies that outline the responsibilities of the auditor in an attestation engagement.

Question: How does an auditor obtain evidence in an attestation engagement?

Answer: An auditor obtains evidence through a variety of procedures such as inspection, observation, confirmation, re-calculation, re-performance, and inquiry.

Question: What is a material misstatement in the context of attestation?

Answer: A material misstatement is an error or omission that could affect the decisions of users of the financial statements.

Question: What is the role of internal control in attestation?

Answer: Internal control plays a crucial role in attestation as it can affect the auditor's assessment of the risk of material misstatement and the nature, timing, and extent of audit procedures.

Question: What is an unqualified opinion in attestation?

Answer: A clean opinion, also referred to as an unqualified opinion, is given when the auditor determines that the financial statements are accurately represented in all significant aspects.

Question: What is a qualified opinion?

Answer: A qualified opinion is issued when the auditor believes that, except for certain issues, the financial statements are presented fairly.

Question: What is an adverse opinion?

Answer: An adverse opinion is issued when the auditor believes that the financial statements are not presented fairly or do not conform to the generally accepted accounting principles.

Question: What is a disclaimer of opinion?

Answer: A disclaimer of opinion is issued when the auditor is unable to form an opinion due to lack of sufficient appropriate audit evidence.

Question: What is the significance of professional skepticism in attestation?

Answer: Professional skepticism is important in attestation as it enables the auditor to critically assess audit evidence and make unbiased judgments.

Question: How do attestations enhance the credibility of financial statements?

Answer: Attestations enhance the credibility of financial statements by providing an independent and professional opinion on their fairness and accuracy.

Question: What is the relationship between risk assessment and attestation?

Answer: Risk assessment is a key part of attestation as it helps the auditor identify areas where there is a high risk of material misstatement.

Question: What is the role of audit evidence in attestation?

Answer: Audit evidence forms the basis of the auditor's opinion in attestation. The auditor gathers and evaluates audit evidence to determine whether the financial statements are free from material misstatement.

Question: What is the difference between reasonable assurance and absolute assurance in attestation?

Answer: Reasonable assurance provides a high degree of confidence, though not complete certainty, that the financial statements have no significant errors. Full assurance cannot be achieved because of the innate restrictions of an audit.

Question: What is an attestation report?

Answer: An attestation report is a document in which the auditor expresses their opinion on the subject matter of the attestation.

Question: What is the difference between attestation and assurance services?

Answer: While both attestation and assurance services involve assessing the reliability of information, attestation is more specific and focuses on the financial statements, whereas assurance services can cover a broader range of information and processes.

Question: How does an auditor determine materiality in attestation?

Answer: Materiality in attestation is determined based on professional judgment and considering the needs of the users of the financial statements.

Question: What is the purpose of an engagement letter in attestation?

Answer: An engagement letter outlines the scope of the attestation engagement, the responsibilities of the auditor and the client, and the terms of the engagement.

Question: What is the difference between financial statement attestation and compliance attestation?

Answer: Financial statement attestation focuses on the accuracy and fairness of the financial statements, while compliance attestation focuses on whether the organization is complying with specific laws or regulations.

Question: What is the role of management in attestation?

Answer: Management is responsible for the preparation and fair presentation of the financial statements, as well as the design, implementation, and maintenance of internal control.

Question: What is the difference between attestation and certification?

Answer: Attestation is the process of verifying the accuracy of financial statements, while certification is the process of confirming the qualifications or competence of an individual or organization.

Question: What is the role of an audit committee in attestation?

Answer: The audit committee oversees the attestation process, including the selection and supervision of the auditor, and the review and approval of the attestation report.

Question: What is the relationship between attestation and corporate governance?
Answer: Attestation supports corporate governance by providing an independent assessment of the accuracy and fairness of the financial statements, which can contribute to transparency and accountability.
Question: What is the difference between a positive and negative assurance in attestation?
Answer: Positive assurance is an explicit statement about the accuracy and fairness of the financial statements, while negative assurance is a statement that nothing has come to the auditor's attention that causes them to believe that the financial statements are not presented fairly.
Question: What is the difference between attestation and compilation services?
Answer: Attestation involves providing an opinion on the fairness and accuracy of the financial statements, while compilation involves merely presenting financial data in the form of financial statements without providing any assurance on them.
Question: What is the difference between a limited and reasonable assurance attestation engagement?
Answer: A limited assurance engagement involves less extensive procedures than a reasonable assurance engagement and results in a lower level of assurance.
Question: What is the difference between a single and multi-scope attestation engagement?
Answer: A single-scope attestation engagement focuses on one specific area, while a multi-scope engagement covers multiple areas or aspects of the financial statements.
Question: What is the difference between a first and third-party attestation?

Answer: A first-party attestation is provided by the organization itself, while a third-party attestation is provided by an independent auditor.

Question: What is the difference between attestation and inspection in auditing?

Answer: Attestation involves providing an opinion on the accuracy and fairness of the financial statements, while inspection involves the detailed examination of the financial records and transactions.

Question: What is the role of an auditor's judgment in attestation?

Answer: Auditor's judgment plays a crucial role in attestation, especially in determining materiality, assessing the risk of material misstatement, and interpreting audit evidence.

Question: What is the relationship between attestation and forensic accounting?

Answer: While attestation focuses on verifying the accuracy and fairness of the financial statements, forensic accounting involves investigating financial information to detect and prevent fraud.

Question: How does attestation contribute to financial transparency?

Answer: Attestation contributes to financial transparency by providing an independent and professional opinion on the accuracy and fairness of the financial statements, which can enhance the confidence of stakeholders.

Question: What is the importance of ethics in attestation?

Answer: Ethics is crucial in attestation as it guides the auditor's behavior and decisions, ensuring that they act with integrity, objectivity, and professional competence.

Question: What is a management representation letter in attestation?

Answer: A management representation letter is a document in which the management makes certain representations to the auditor, such as the completeness and accuracy of the financial information.

Question: What is the difference between a statutory and voluntary attestation?

Answer: A statutory attestation is required by law, while a voluntary attestation is not legally required but may be undertaken for various reasons, such as to enhance credibility.

Question: What is a scope limitation in attestation?

Answer: A scope limitation is a restriction that prevents the auditor from completing all aspects of the attestation engagement, which may affect the auditor's ability to provide an opinion.

Question: What is the relationship between attestation and financial reporting?

Answer: Attestation is an integral part of financial reporting as it provides an independent and professional opinion on the accuracy and fairness of the financial statements, which can enhance the reliability of financial reporting.

Question: What is the difference between a public and private attestation?

Answer: A public attestation is performed by an auditor who is independent of the organization, while a private attestation may be performed by an internal auditor or other employee of the organization.

Question: What is the role of technology in attestation?

Answer: Technology can assist in attestation by facilitating the collection, analysis, and interpretation of audit evidence, as well as enhancing the efficiency and effectiveness of the attestation process.

Question: What is the relationship between attestation and risk management?

Answer: Attestation contributes to risk management by identifying and assessing the risk of material misstatement in the financial statements, which can assist the organization in managing its financial risks.

Question: What is the relationship between attestation and stakeholder confidence?

Answer: Attestation enhances stakeholder confidence by providing an independent and professional opinion on the accuracy and fairness of the financial statements, which can enhance the trust of stakeholders in the organization's financial reporting.

Applications

Scenario 1:

ABC company has hired you to perform an audit on their financial statements. After a thorough examination, you discovered that there are significant discrepancies in their accounts receivables. How would you attest these findings in your audit report?

Solution:

In such a situation, an auditor should clearly state the discrepancies found in the accounts receivables section in their audit report. There should be a detailed explanation of the findings, including the nature of the discrepancies, the amount involved, and the possible implications on the financial statements. The auditor should also provide recommendations on how the company can rectify the issue.

Scenario 2:

You are auditing a tech startup that has just completed its first year of operations. The company has not maintained proper books of accounts and lacks internal control systems. How would you approach this attestation?

Solution:

In this case, the auditor should first advise the company on the importance of maintaining proper books of accounts and establishing internal control systems. In the audit report, the auditor should clearly state the absence of these critical accounting practices and the potential risks it presents to the company. The auditor should also recommend steps the company should take to address these issues.

Scenario 3:

You're auditing a company and found out that it's significantly overvaluing its inventory in the financial statements, which is inflating its profits. How would you attest this in your audit report?

Solution:

The auditor should clearly state in the audit report that the company is overvaluing its inventory, leading to an overstatement of its profits. The auditor should provide details of the overvaluation, including the extent of the overstatement and its impact on the company's financial status. The auditor should also recommend that the company revise its inventory valuation method to reflect a more accurate value.

Scenario 4:

You have been hired to audit a non-profit organization. During the audit, you discover that the organization has not complied with the specific grant requirements. How would you attest this non-compliance in your audit report?

Solution:

The auditor should state in the audit report that the organization has not complied with the grant requirements. The auditor should detail the nature of non-compliance, the specific requirements not met, and the possible repercussions, such as penalties or loss of the grant. The auditor should recommend that the organization take immediate action to comply with the grant requirements.

Scenario 5:

You're auditing a company and found out that it's not depreciating its assets correctly, resulting in an understatement of its expenses. How would you attest this in your audit report?

Solution:

The auditor should state in the audit report that the company is not correctly depreciating its assets, leading to an understatement of its expenses. The auditor should provide details of the incorrect depreciation method used and its impact on the company's financial status. The auditor should recommend that the company revise its depreciation method to properly reflect the wear and tear of its assets.

Substantive Testing

Theoretical

Q: What is substantive testing in auditing?

A: Substantive testing in auditing is a process used by auditors to assess the integrity of financial transactions and account balances in a company's financial statements.

Q: What is the purpose of substantive testing in auditing?

A: The purpose of substantive testing in auditing is to detect material misstatements in the financial statements and provide reasonable assurance that the statements are free from such errors.

Q: How does substantive testing differ from compliance testing?

A: While compliance testing checks whether a company follows internal controls, substantive testing aims to verify the accuracy of individual transactions and account balances.

Q: What are the two types of substantive tests?

A: The two types of substantive tests are tests of details and analytical procedures.

Q: What are tests of details in substantive testing?

A: Tests of details involve checking the accuracy of individual transactions and account balances.

Q: What are analytical procedures in substantive testing?

A: Analytical procedures involve comparing data and identifying inconsistencies or deviations from expected patterns.

Q: When is substantive testing performed in the audit process?

A: Substantive testing is performed in the middle stages of the audit process, after the internal controls have been assessed and before the audit opinion is formed.

Q: What factors influence the extent of substantive testing in an audit?

A: The extent of substantive testing in an audit is influenced by the auditor's perception of the risks of material misstatement, the effectiveness of internal controls, and the size and complexity of the organization.

Q: How does substantive testing contribute to the quality of an audit?

A: Substantive testing contributes to the quality of an audit by providing evidence to support the auditor's opinion on the fairness and accuracy of the financial statements.

Q: What is the role of substantive testing in detecting fraud?

A: Substantive testing can help detect fraud by identifying irregularities or discrepancies in the financial statements that may indicate fraudulent activities.

Q: What is materiality in the context of substantive testing?

A: Materiality refers to the significance of a misstatement or omission that could influence the decisions of a user of financial statements. Substantive testing aims to detect such material misstatements.

Q: How does an auditor decide which items to test substantively?

A: An auditor selects items for substantive testing based on their judgment of which items carry the highest risk of material misstatement.

Q: What is the relationship between substantive testing and audit risk?

A: Substantive testing is a key component of the audit risk model. By detecting material misstatements, substantive testing helps to reduce the risk of an incorrect audit opinion.

Q: What are some common methods used in substantive testing?
A: Common methods used in substantive testing include inspection of documents, observation, inquiry, confirmation, and recalculation.
Q: How does substantive testing differ from test of controls?
A: While test of controls assess the effectiveness of a company's internal controls, substantive testing examines the accuracy of the actual financial transactions and balances.
Q: What is the effect of strong internal controls on substantive testing?
A: When internal controls are strong, an auditor may reduce the extent of substantive testing as there is less risk of material misstatement.
Q: How does substantive testing relate to the concept of professional skepticism in auditing?
A: Substantive testing requires the application of professional skepticism, as auditors must critically examine and question the information provided in the financial statements.
Q: Why is substantive testing considered an essential part of the audit process?
A: Substantive testing is essential because it provides the evidence needed to support the auditor's opinion on the accuracy and fairness of the financial statements.
Q: Can an audit be completed without substantive testing?
A: No, an audit cannot be completed without substantive testing as it is a key source of audit evidence.
Q: What happens if substantive testing reveals a material misstatement?
A: If substantive testing reveals a material misstatement, the auditor must determine the cause and may need to revise their assessment of audit risk and their audit plan.

Q: How does an auditor document their substantive testing procedures?
A: Auditors document their substantive testing procedures in the audit working papers, which record the plan for the audit, the nature, timing, and extent of audit procedures performed, and the results of these procedures.
Q: What is cut-off testing in the context of substantive testing?
A: Cut-off testing is a kind of substantive testing that verifies if transactions are accurately recorded in the appropriate accounting period.
Q: Why are third-party confirmations used in substantive testing?
A: Third-party confirmations are used in substantive testing to independently verify the accuracy of information in the financial statements.
Q: What role does sampling play in substantive testing?
A: Sampling allows auditors to test a representative selection of transactions or balances, rather than every single one. This makes substantive testing more efficient and cost-effective.
Q: How does an auditor determine the sample size for substantive testing?
A: The sample size for substantive testing is determined based on the auditor's assessment of the risk of material misstatement, the desired level of assurance, and the tolerable misstatement.
Q: What is a substantive analytical procedure?
A: A substantive analytical procedure is a type of analytical procedure used as a substantive test to detect material misstatements in the financial statements.
Q: Can substantive testing be performed on interim financial statements?
A: Yes, substantive testing can be performed on interim financial statements to provide interim audit assurance.

Q: How does substantive testing contribute to the audit evidence gathered by an auditor?
A: Substantive testing contributes to audit evidence by providing independent verification of the accuracy and completeness of the transactions and balances reported in the financial statements.
Q: How does an auditor balance the cost and benefit of substantive testing?
A: Auditors balance the cost and benefit of substantive testing by focusing on areas with the highest risk of material misstatement and using efficient testing methods such as sampling and analytical procedures.
Q: What is the role of substantive testing in a limited review engagement?
A: In a limited review engagement, substantive testing is usually less extensive than in a full audit, but still important for providing a moderate level of assurance.
Q: Why is substantive testing important in a forensic audit?
A: In a forensic audit, substantive testing is crucial for detecting fraudulent transactions and providing evidence for potential legal proceedings.
Q: What is the difference between substantive testing and substantive procedures?
A: Substantive testing is the process of verifying the accuracy of transactions and balances, while substantive procedures are the specific methods or steps used in this process.
Q: How does an auditor use professional judgment in substantive testing?
A: An auditor uses professional judgment in substantive testing to determine which items to test, how extensively to test them, and how to interpret the results.
Q: What skills are required for effective substantive testing?

A: Effective substantive testing requires skills such as attention to detail, critical thinking, knowledge of accounting standards, and proficiency in audit techniques.

Q: How does an auditor report the results of substantive testing?

A: The results of substantive testing are reported in the auditor's working papers and may also be discussed in the audit report if they have a significant impact on the financial statements.

Q: What is the role of substantive testing in an integrated audit?

A: In an integrated audit, substantive testing is used to verify both the financial statements and the effectiveness of internal controls over financial reporting.

Q: What types of transactions or balances are typically targeted in substantive testing?

A: Substantive testing typically targets transactions and balances that are material, complex, volatile, or prone to error or fraud.

Q: How does substantive testing help in verifying the existence of assets?

A: Substantive testing helps in verifying the existence of assets by examining supporting documents, performing physical inspections, and confirming with third parties.

Q: How does substantive testing help in verifying the valuation of assets?

A: Substantive testing helps in verifying the valuation of assets by reviewing the methods and assumptions used in valuation, comparing with market values, and checking for impairment.

Q: How does substantive testing help in verifying the ownership of assets?

A: Substantive testing helps in verifying the ownership of assets by reviewing legal documents such as deeds or titles, and confirming with third parties.

Q: How does substantive testing help in verifying the completeness of liabilities?

A: Substantive testing helps in verifying the completeness of liabilities by reviewing agreements and contracts, performing analytical procedures, and confirming with creditors.

Q: How does substantive testing help in verifying the accuracy of income and expenses?

A: Substantive testing helps in verifying the accuracy of income and expenses by examining transaction documents, performing analytical procedures, and checking for correct classification and timing.

Q: How does substantive testing help in verifying the presentation and disclosure of financial information?

A: Substantive testing helps in verifying the presentation and disclosure of financial information by checking for compliance with accounting standards and reviewing the clarity, consistency, and comprehensiveness of disclosures.

Q: What is the relationship between substantive testing and materiality?

A: The relationship between substantive testing and materiality is that substantive testing aims to detect material misstatements that could influence the decisions of users of financial statements.

Q: Can substantive testing be automated?

A: Yes, some aspects of substantive testing can be automated using audit software, which can increase efficiency and accuracy.

Q: What is the relationship between substantive testing and audit assertions?

A: Substantive testing is designed to verify audit assertions such as existence, completeness, valuation, rights and obligations, and presentation and disclosure.

Q: What challenges can arise in substantive testing?

A: Challenges in substantive testing can arise from factors such as large volumes of transactions, complex calculations, lack of documentation, and resistance from the client.

Q: How can an auditor overcome challenges in substantive testing?

A: An auditor can overcome challenges in substantive testing by planning carefully, using efficient testing methods, applying professional skepticism, and communicating effectively with the client.

Q: How does substantive testing contribute to the auditor's understanding of the client's business?

A: Substantive testing contributes to the auditor's understanding of the client's business by revealing information about the client's transactions, balances, risks, and internal controls.

Applications

Scenario 1:

In a software development company, the auditor plans to perform substantive testing on the company's sales revenue. The auditor noticed that a significant revenue increase occurred in the last quarter of the financial year.

Solution:

The auditor should perform substantive testing on the sales transactions recorded in the last quarter. This would involve selecting a sample of sales transactions and verifying them against supporting documents such as sales invoices, delivery notes, and customer orders. The auditor should also perform analytical procedures, comparing the revenue trends with industry trends or the company's past performance. If the sales increase cannot be reasonably explained, it may indicate a risk of material misstatement in the sales revenue.

Scenario 2:

During an audit of a manufacturing company, the auditor identified that the company had significant inventory quantities.

The auditor is concerned about the potential risk of overstatement of inventory.

Solution:

The auditor should perform substantive testing on the inventory. This should involve physical verification of the inventory quantities at the company's warehouses. The auditor should also review the company's inventory counting procedures and perform test counts to verify their accuracy. They should also review the valuation of inventory, checking the cost calculations and ensuring that the inventory is valued at the lower of cost or net realizable value.

Scenario 3:

An auditor is auditing a financial institution and notices large loan amounts written off as bad debts in the financial statements.

Solution:

The auditor should perform substantive testing on the loan write-offs. This would involve reviewing the documentation for the write-off approvals and ensuring that they were in line with the company's policy. The auditor should also review the loan files for the written-off loans and ensure that all necessary steps to recover the loans were taken before they were written off. If the write-offs seem unjustified, it may indicate a risk of material misstatement in the loan write-offs.

Scenario 4:

During the audit of a retail company, the auditor identifies significant year-end sales returns that could impact the company's sales revenue.

Solution:

The auditor should perform substantive testing on sales returns. This should involve reviewing the sales return records and matching them with the credit notes issued. The auditor should also review the company's policy on sales returns and ensure that the returns were recorded in line with this policy.

If there are discrepancies, it may indicate a risk of sales revenue being overstated.

Audit Software

Theoretical

Q: What is audit software?

A: Audit software is a type of computer program that assists auditors in identifying and resolving compliance issues, inconsistencies, or deficiencies in the data they are examining.

Q: What is the primary purpose of audit software?

A: The primary purpose of audit software is to facilitate and automate the process of auditing, making it more efficient and less prone to human error.

Q: How does audit software help in the auditing process?

A: Audit software assists auditors by automating data analysis tasks, generating reports, and facilitating compliance with regulatory standards.

Q: What are some key features of audit software?

A: Key features of audit software include data import, data analysis, risk assessment, reporting tools, and compliance management.

Q: Why is data analysis important in audit software?

A: Data analysis is important in audit software because it allows auditors to identify patterns, trends, and anomalies in the data, which can indicate potential issues or areas of risk.

Q: How does audit software improve the efficiency of the auditing process?

A: Audit software improves the efficiency of the auditing process by automating routine tasks, reducing the chance of error, and allowing auditors to focus on higher-level analysis and decision-making.

Q: How does audit software support risk assessment?

A: Audit software supports risk assessment by providing tools for identifying and evaluating potential risks, as well as for planning and implementing appropriate risk management strategies.

Q: How does audit software help with reporting?

A: Audit software helps with reporting by generating detailed, customizable reports that provide a clear and concise summary of the audit findings.

Q: What is compliance management in audit software?

A: Compliance management in audit software refers to the software's ability to help organizations ensure they are meeting all relevant regulatory and industry standards.

Q: How does audit software facilitate compliance management?

A: Audit software facilitates compliance management by tracking compliance status, producing compliance reports, and providing alerts for potential non-compliance issues.

Q: How does audit software improve the accuracy of the auditing process?

A: Audit software improves the accuracy of the auditing process by reducing the chance of human error in data analysis and reporting.

Q: What is the role of audit software in internal auditing?

A: In internal auditing, audit software is used to review and assess the organization's internal controls, financial systems, and operational procedures.

Q: How does audit software support external auditing?

A: In external auditing, audit software is used to analyze an organization's financial statements and other documents to ensure they are accurate and comply with relevant regulations.
Q: Can audit software be customized to suit different types of audits?
A: Yes, most audit software can be customized to suit different types of audits, including financial audits, operational audits, and compliance audits.
Q: What types of organizations can benefit from using audit software?
A: Any organization that needs to perform audits, either internally or externally, can benefit from using audit software. This includes businesses of all sizes, non-profit organizations, and government agencies.
Q: How does audit software aid in fraud detection?
A: Audit software aids in fraud detection by identifying unusual patterns or discrepancies in the data that may indicate fraudulent activity.
Q: How does audit software support the audit planning process?
A: Audit software supports the audit planning process by helping auditors identify areas of risk, set audit objectives, and develop an audit plan.
Q: Can audit software be used for real-time auditing?
A: Yes, some audit software allows for real-time auditing, which means the software can continuously monitor and analyze data as it is being generated.
Q: What is the importance of data import in audit software?
A: Data import is important in audit software because it allows auditors to easily import data from various sources for analysis.
Q: How does audit software help in the documentation of audit processes?

A: Audit software helps in the documentation of audit processes by recording all audit activities, generating audit trails, and storing all relevant documents and evidence.

Q: Can audit software integrate with other business systems?

A: Yes, many audit software can integrate with other business systems, such as enterprise resource planning (ERP) systems, customer relationship management (CRM) systems, and accounting systems.

Q: How does audit software enhance data security during the auditing process?

A: Audit software enhances data security during the auditing process by ensuring that all data is securely stored and transmitted, and by providing access controls to prevent unauthorized access to sensitive data.

Q: What is the role of audit software in continuous auditing?

A: In continuous auditing, audit software is used to constantly monitor and analyze data, allowing for immediate detection and resolution of any issues or anomalies.

Q: How can audit software help in the detection of non-compliance issues?

A: Audit software can help in the detection of non-compliance issues by analyzing data against compliance rules and standards, and by providing alerts for potential non-compliance issues.

Q: How does audit software contribute to the transparency of the auditing process?

A: Audit software contributes to the transparency of the auditing process by providing a clear and detailed record of all audit activities, findings, and recommendations.

Q: How can audit software support decision-making in the auditing process?

A: Audit software can support decision-making in the auditing process by providing auditors with accurate, up-to-date information, and by helping them identify and evaluate potential risks and issues.

Q: What is the importance of user-friendly interface in audit software?

A: A user-friendly interface is important in audit software because it makes the software easier to use, reducing the learning curve for users and increasing their productivity.

Q: How does audit software support audit follow-up activities?

A: Audit software supports audit follow-up activities by tracking the implementation of audit recommendations and by providing tools for monitoring and evaluating their effectiveness.

Q: Can audit software be used for both internal and external audits?

A: Yes, audit software can be used for both internal and external audits. It provides tools and features that are useful for both types of audits.

Q: How does audit software assist in the evaluation of internal controls?

A: Audit software assists in the evaluation of internal controls by analyzing data related to the organization's control environment and by helping auditors identify potential control weaknesses.

Q: How does audit software facilitate the communication of audit findings?

A: Audit software facilitates the communication of audit findings by generating clear and concise reports, and by providing tools for sharing these reports with relevant stakeholders.

Q: How does audit software aid in the identification of operational inefficiencies?

A: Audit software aids in the identification of operational inefficiencies by analyzing operational data and identifying areas where resources may not be used effectively.

Q: What is the role of audit software in data reconciliation?

A: In data reconciliation, audit software is used to compare data from different sources and identify any discrepancies.

Q: How does audit software support the audit closure process?

A: Audit software supports the audit closure process by providing tools for finalizing the audit report, communicating the findings to relevant stakeholders, and documenting the audit process for future reference.

Q: Can audit software be used for auditing financial statements?

A: Yes, audit software can be used for auditing financial statements. It can analyze financial data, identify inconsistencies or anomalies, and generate financial reports.

Q: How does audit software assist in regulatory compliance audits?

A: Audit software assists in regulatory compliance audits by providing tools for assessing compliance with regulatory standards, identifying potential non-compliance issues, and documenting the audit process.

Q: How does audit software support the implementation of audit recommendations?

A: Audit software supports the implementation of audit recommendations by tracking the status of each recommendation, providing alerts for overdue actions, and evaluating the effectiveness of implemented actions.

Q: What is the role of audit software in quality audits?

A: In quality audits, audit software is used to assess the quality of the organization's products, services, or processes, and to identify areas for improvement.

Q: How does audit software facilitate the audit scheduling process?

A: Audit software facilitates the audit scheduling process by providing tools for planning and scheduling audits, and for managing audit resources.

Q: Can audit software be used for auditing information systems?
A: Yes, audit software can be used for auditing information systems. It can analyze data related to the organization's IT infrastructure, identify potential security risks, and assess compliance with IT standards and regulations.
Q: How does audit software enhance the reliability of audit findings?
A: Audit software enhances the reliability of audit findings by reducing the chance of human error in data analysis and by providing a clear and detailed record of the audit process.
Q: How does audit software support the audit review process?
A: Audit software supports the audit review process by providing tools for reviewing audit findings, evaluating the effectiveness of audit procedures, and making necessary adjustments to the audit plan.
Q: How does audit software assist in the audit preparation process?
A: Audit software assists in the audit preparation process by helping auditors gather necessary data, set audit objectives, and develop an audit plan.
Q: Can audit software handle large volumes of data?
A: Yes, most audit software can handle large volumes of data, making it suitable for auditing large organizations or complex systems.
Q: How does audit software support the documentation of audit evidence?
A: Audit software supports the documentation of audit evidence by providing tools for recording audit activities, storing audit documents, and generating audit trails.
Q: What is the role of audit software in performance audits?

A: In performance audits, audit software is used to assess the effectiveness and efficiency of the organization's operations, and to identify areas for improvement.

Q: How does audit software facilitate collaboration in the auditing process?

A: Audit software facilitates collaboration in the auditing process by providing tools for sharing data, communicating findings, and coordinating audit activities among team members.

Q: How does audit software assist in the evaluation of financial controls?

A: Audit software assists in the evaluation of financial controls by analyzing financial data and identifying potential control weaknesses or financial risks.

Q: How does audit software support the audit verification process?

A: Audit software supports the audit verification process by providing tools for verifying the accuracy and completeness of data, and for validating the findings of the audit.

Q: What is the importance of data visualization in audit software?

A: Data visualization is important in audit software because it allows auditors to easily understand and interpret complex data, identify patterns or trends, and communicate their findings effectively.

Applications

Scenario 1: Ensuring the accuracy of financial transactions

ABC Company is a mid-sized firm that has been using manual auditing methods. Recently, the finance department has noticed a few discrepancies in their financial records, which has led to some issues with their investors and stakeholders. ABC Company has decided to implement audit software to manage their financial records and transactions effectively.

Solution: The company can implement audit software such as ACL, IDEA, or Teammate. These software programs can help them to process large volumes of data, identify anomalies, and ensure accuracy in financial transactions. They can also assist in maintaining audit trails, reducing the chances of errors, and enhancing the overall efficiency of the auditing process.

Scenario 2: Time constraints

XYZ Company is a rapidly growing enterprise. With the increase in business operations, the auditing team is finding it challenging to complete the audit process within the stipulated time. The manual auditing method is too time-consuming and inefficient.

Solution: By implementing audit software, XYZ Company can automate repetitive tasks, reducing the time taken to complete the audit process. Software such as AuditFile and Onspring can provide real-time insights, enabling the auditing team to identify potential issues and address them promptly.

Scenario 3: Compliance with regulations

DEF Company operates in a highly regulated industry. They are required to comply with numerous regulatory standards and guidelines. The company is struggling to keep track of all these regulations and ensure compliance, leading to frequent fines and penalties.

Solution: Audit software can help DEF Company to monitor compliance with various regulations. Software like SAP Audit Management and MetricStream can provide customizable templates to keep track of different regulations, generate reports, and ensure compliance.

Scenario 4: Risk Management

GHI Company is facing several business risks, including financial, operational, and compliance risks. The company is finding it difficult to manage and mitigate these risks effectively.

Solution: By using audit software like LogicGate or AuditBoard, GHI Company can identify, assess, and manage risks. The software can prioritize risks based on their potential impact, allowing the company to focus their efforts on the most critical risks.

Scenario 5: Communication and collaboration issues

JKL Company has multiple departments spread across different locations. The auditing team is finding it challenging to collaborate with these various departments and share information efficiently.

Solution: Audit software can facilitate communication and collaboration among different departments. Software like HighBond or Arbutus Analyzer can centralize data, allowing the auditing team to access necessary information quickly and share it with relevant departments.

Assertions

Theoretical

Q: What is an assertion in auditing?

A: An assertion in auditing refers to the claims made by the management regarding the financial statements of an organization, which auditors then review for accuracy.

Q: How many types of assertions are there in auditing?

A: There are five types of assertions in auditing: existence, completeness, valuation, rights and obligations, and presentation and disclosure.

Q: What is the purpose of assertions in auditing?

A: Assertions help auditors to form a basis for their review of an organization's financial statements and to gather sufficient appropriate evidence about whether the assertions are free from material misstatement.

Q: What is the relevance of the 'existence' assertion in auditing?

A: The existence assertion confirms that assets and liabilities in the financial statements exist at the specific date of the balance sheet.

Q: What does the 'completeness' assertion imply in auditing?

A: The completeness assertion states that all transactions and accounts that should be presented in the financial statements are included.

Q: How does the 'valuation' assertion apply in auditing?

A: The valuation assertion implies that all assets, liabilities, and equity interests are included in the financial statements at appropriate amounts.

Q: What does 'rights and obligations' assertion mean in auditing?
A: The rights and obligations assertion implies that the entity holds or controls the rights to assets, and liabilities are the obligations of the entity at a given date.
Q: How does the 'presentation and disclosure' assertion impact auditing?
A: The assertion of presentation and disclosure claims that all elements of the financial statements are correctly categorized, detailed, and revealed in all significant aspects.
Q: How do auditors use assertions during their audit procedures?
A: Auditors use assertions to assess the risk of material misstatements and design audit procedures to address these risks.
Q: Who is responsible for the accuracy of assertions in auditing?
A: The entity's management is responsible for the accuracy of assertions in auditing.
Q: Why are assertions important in the auditing process?
A: Assertions are important in the auditing process as they guide the focus and direction of the audit, and help the auditor to gather sufficient evidence to form an opinion on the financial statements.
Q: How do auditors test the 'existence' assertion in auditing?
A: Auditors test the existence assertion by physically verifying the existence of assets or confirming balances with third parties.
Q: How do auditors test the 'completeness' assertion in auditing?
A: Auditors test the completeness assertion by reviewing reconciliations, tracing transactions to the general ledger, and reviewing cut-off procedures.
Q: How do auditors test the 'valuation' assertion in auditing?
A: Auditors test the valuation assertion by reviewing the basis for valuation, evaluating the method of valuation, and recalculating valuations.
Q: How do auditors test the 'rights and obligations' assertion in auditing?

A: The auditors test the rights and obligations assertion by reviewing contracts, agreements, and legal documents.

Q: How do auditors test the 'presentation and disclosure' assertion in auditing?

A: Auditors test the presentation and disclosure assertion by reviewing the financial statement disclosures for completeness and accuracy.

Q: What is the difference between a positive and negative assertion in auditing?

A: A positive assertion provides assurance that a statement is accurate, while a negative assertion provides assurance that a statement is not materially misstated.

Q: How can an auditor detect fraudulent assertions?

A: An auditor can detect fraudulent assertions through various auditing procedures such as analytical procedures, tests of controls, and substantive testing.

Q: Are assertions in auditing applicable to both financial and non-financial information?

A: Yes, assertions in auditing apply to both financial and non-financial information.

Q: Can an auditor rely solely on assertions made by an entity's management?

A: No, an auditor cannot rely solely on assertions made by an entity's management. The auditor must gather sufficient appropriate audit evidence to support these assertions.

Q: What happens if an auditor finds discrepancies in an entity's assertions?

A: If an auditor finds discrepancies in an entity's assertions, they must investigate further to ascertain the reasons for the discrepancies and potentially modify their audit opinion if necessary.

Q: What is the role of internal control in supporting assertions?

A: Internal control helps to ensure the accuracy and reliability of the assertions made by management by enforcing checks and balances in the entity's operations.

Q: Can an auditor make assertions?

A: No, an auditor cannot make assertions. Assertions are made by the entity's management.

Q: What is the relationship between assertions and audit risk?

A: Assertions and audit risk are inversely related. The more reliable the assertions, the lower the audit risk.

Q: Why is it important for an auditor to understand an entity's business environment?

A: Understanding the entity's business environment helps the auditor to assess the plausibility and consistency of the management's assertions.

Q: How does an auditor's professional skepticism relate to assertions?

A: An auditor's professional skepticism involves questioning the assertions made by management and not accepting them at face value without appropriate evidence.

Q: What is the effect of a material misstatement in an assertion?

A: A material misstatement in an assertion can lead to an incorrect interpretation of the financial statements, affecting decisions made by users of the statements.

Q: How does an auditor assess the reasonableness of an assertion?

A: An auditor assesses the reasonableness of an assertion by comparing it with other independent information, such as market data or previous year's data.

Q: What is the link between assertions and the audit opinion?

A: The audit opinion is based on whether the auditor believes the assertions in the financial statements are free from material misstatement.

Q: How does an auditor document assertions in the audit working papers?

A: An auditor documents assertions in the audit working papers by describing the procedures performed, the evidence obtained, and the conclusions reached.

Q: Can an assertion be both true and false at the same time?

A: No, an assertion cannot be both true and false at the same time. A claim is a declaration that can either be true or false.

Q: What should an auditor do if they are unable to obtain sufficient appropriate audit evidence about an assertion?

A: If an auditor is unable to obtain sufficient appropriate audit evidence about an assertion, they should consider the impact on their audit opinion and may need to issue a modified opinion.

Q: How does an auditor evaluate the appropriateness of an assertion?

A: An auditor evaluates the appropriateness of an assertion by considering its relevance and reliability, and by corroborating it with other evidence.

Q: What is the difference between assertions at the financial statement level and assertions at the class of transactions level?

A: Assertions at the financial statement level relate to the overall presentation of the financial statements, while assertions at the class of transactions level relate to individual transactions and balances.

Q: How does the auditor's understanding of the entity's industry affect the evaluation of assertions?

A: The auditor's understanding of the entity's industry helps them to assess the reasonableness of the assertions, as certain assertions may be more or less likely to be accurate depending on the industry.

Q: How does the auditor's knowledge of the entity's internal control system affect the evaluation of assertions?

A: The auditor's knowledge of the entity's internal control system helps them to assess the reliability of the assertions, as a strong internal control system increases the likelihood that the assertions are accurate.

Q: What is the role of analytical procedures in testing assertions?

A: Analytical procedures help the auditor to identify inconsistencies or unusual transactions that may indicate a misstatement in an assertion.

Q: Can an auditor accept an assertion without testing it?

A: No, an auditor should not accept an assertion without testing it. The auditor needs to gather sufficient appropriate audit evidence to support the assertion.

Q: What is the relationship between assertions and materiality in auditing?

A: The concept of materiality in auditing relates to the significance of a misstatement in an assertion. If a misstatement is considered material, it could affect the users' understanding of the financial statements.

Q: Can an auditor ignore an assertion if it is immaterial?

A: While an auditor may decide to perform less extensive testing on immaterial assertions, they should not ignore any assertion completely.

Q: How does the auditor's understanding of the entity's operations affect the evaluation of assertions?

A: The auditor's understanding of the entity's operations helps them to assess the plausibility of the assertions, as certain assertions may be more or less likely to be accurate depending on the nature of the entity's operations.

Q: How does an auditor determine which assertions to test?

A: An auditor determines which assertions to test based on their risk assessment. Assertions related to areas with a higher risk of material misstatement are likely to be tested more extensively.

Q: What happens if an auditor disagrees with an assertion made by management?

A: If an auditor disagrees with an assertion made by management, they should discuss the matter with management and may need to modify their audit opinion if the disagreement is not resolved.

Q: What is the role of professional judgment in evaluating assertions?

A: Professional judgment is important in evaluating assertions as it allows the auditor to assess the reasonableness and consistency of the assertions based on their knowledge and experience.

Q: What is the impact of a misstatement in an assertion on the audit report?

A: A misstatement in an assertion can lead to a modification in the audit report, depending on the materiality and pervasiveness of the misstatement.

Q: How does an auditor evaluate the consistency of an assertion with other information?

A: An auditor evaluates the consistency of an assertion with other information by comparing it with other evidence obtained during the audit, and with their understanding of the entity and its environment.

Q: Can an assertion be considered valid if it is not supported by sufficient appropriate audit evidence?

A: No, an assertion cannot be considered valid if it is not supported by sufficient appropriate audit evidence. The auditor needs to gather such evidence to support the assertion.

Q: How does the concept of audit evidence relate to assertions?

A: Audit evidence is the information that the auditor uses to evaluate the accuracy of the assertions made by management. The quality and quantity of audit evidence can affect the auditor's evaluation of the assertions.

Q: What is the difference between a direct and indirect assertion in auditing?

A: A direct assertion is a claim made by management about a certain fact, while an indirect assertion is a claim that can be inferred from other assertions or information.

Q: How do assertions in auditing affect the users of financial statements?

A: Assertions in auditing affect the users of financial statements as they rely on the accuracy of these assertions to make informed decisions. If the assertions are not accurate, the users may make incorrect decisions based on the misleading information.

Applications

Scenario 1:

The auditing firm ABC & Co. is conducting an audit for XYZ Ltd. The management of XYZ Ltd. asserts that all transactions related to their sales have been recorded in the books of accounts. As an auditor, how would you test this assertion?

Solution: ABC & Co. can sample a few transactions from the sales journal and trace them back to the source documents such as sales invoices and delivery notes. If the transactions are found in the source documents, it confirms the assertion of the management.

Scenario 2:

During the audit of LMN Inc., the management asserts that the company's inventory is in good condition and can be sold in the ordinary course of business. How would auditors validate this assertion?

Solution: The auditors of LMN Inc. can physically verify the inventory and assess its condition. They can also review the company's inventory turnover ratio and compare it with industry norms to check if the inventory is moving at a normal pace.

Scenario 3:

PQR Corp. asserts that the company has full ownership and rights over all the assets recorded in the balance sheet. How can an auditor review this assertion?

Solution: The auditor can review the legal documents related to the assets, such as title deeds for properties and car registration documents for vehicles. Additionally, they can check for any liens or encumbrances on the assets by examining the loan agreements and legal cases, if any.

Scenario 4:

During the audit of STU Ltd., the management asserts that all liabilities have been disclosed in the financial statements. How would auditors test this assertion?

Solution: The auditor can review the company's bank statements, loan agreements, and minutes of board meetings to identify any undisclosed liabilities. They can also perform a search for unrecorded liabilities by reviewing transactions near the end of the fiscal year.

Scenario 5:

The management of VWX Inc. asserts that the revenues recognized in the income statement have all been earned during the period. How would an auditor validate this assertion?

Solution: The auditor can review the company's sales contracts and invoices to determine if the revenue was indeed earned during the period. They can also check the timing of the delivery of goods or services to the customers to ensure it aligns with the revenue recognition.

Audit Engagement

Theoretical

Q: What is an audit engagement?

A: Audit engagement refers to the agreement between an auditor and a client to conduct an audit of financial statements.

Q: What is the primary purpose of an audit engagement?

A: The primary purpose of an audit engagement is to provide an independent opinion on the reliability and validity of a company's financial statements.

Q: What are some of the key components of an audit engagement?

A: Key components of an audit engagement include the audit plan, audit scope, audit procedures, and the audit report.

Q: Who initiates an audit engagement?

A: An audit engagement is usually initiated by the management of a company who hires an external auditor to conduct the audit.

Q: How is the scope of an audit engagement determined?

A: The scope of an audit engagement is typically determined by the auditor, based on their understanding of the company's operations, industry, and financial condition.

Q: What is the auditor's responsibility in an audit engagement?

A: The auditor's responsibility in an audit engagement is to conduct an independent and impartial review of the company's financial statements and to provide an opinion on their reliability and validity.

Q: What is the role of management in an audit engagement?
A: The role of management in an audit engagement is to provide the auditor with all necessary information and access to records, and to ensure that the financial statements are prepared in accordance with relevant accounting standards.
Q: What information is included in an audit engagement letter?
A: An audit engagement letter includes details about the scope of the audit, the auditor's responsibilities, the management's responsibilities, and the terms and conditions of the engagement.
Q: What are the potential outcomes of an audit engagement?
A: The potential outcomes of an audit engagement include an unqualified opinion (clean audit), a qualified opinion (some issues were found), an adverse opinion (serious issues were found), or a disclaimer of opinion (unable to provide an opinion).
Q: What factors can influence the outcome of an audit engagement?
A: Factors that can influence the outcome of an audit engagement include the quality and accuracy of the company's financial records, the effectiveness of its internal controls, and the level of cooperation from management.
Q: What types of risks are assessed during an audit engagement?
A: During an audit engagement, auditors assess various types of risks, including inherent risk, control risk, and detection risk.
Q: What is the importance of professional skepticism in an audit engagement?
A: Professional skepticism is important in an audit engagement as it enables the auditor to critically assess the information provided by the management and to identify potential issues or discrepancies.
Q: How does an auditor gather evidence during an audit engagement?

A: An auditor gathers evidence during an audit engagement through various means, including inspection of records, observation, inquiries, and confirmations.

Q: What is the role of internal controls in an audit engagement?

A: The role of internal controls in an audit engagement is to ensure the accuracy and reliability of financial reporting, which in turn aids the auditor in providing an accurate opinion on the financial statements.

Q: What is the impact of materiality on an audit engagement?

A: Materiality impacts an audit engagement by determining the level of errors or misstatements that could be considered significant enough to affect the users' understanding of the financial statements.

Q: What is a related party transaction and how does it affect an audit engagement?

A: A related party transaction is a business deal or arrangement between two parties who are related through ownership, control, or influence. It affects an audit engagement as it can lead to potential conflicts of interest and can affect the fairness and transparency of the financial statements.

Q: How is an audit engagement concluded?

A: An audit engagement is concluded with the issuance of an audit report, which provides the auditor's opinion on the financial statements.

Q: What is the importance of an exit meeting in an audit engagement?

A: An exit meeting in an audit engagement is important as it provides an opportunity for the auditor to discuss their findings and recommendations with management before finalizing the audit report.

Q: How does a change in accounting policies affect an audit engagement?

A: A change in accounting policies can affect an audit engagement by requiring the auditor to assess whether the new policies are in compliance with relevant accounting standards and if they have been properly applied and disclosed.

Q: What is the role of an audit committee in an audit engagement?

A: The role of an audit committee in an audit engagement is to oversee the audit process, liaise between the auditor and management, and review the audit findings and recommendations.

Q: How can fraud be detected during an audit engagement?

A: Fraud can be detected during an audit engagement through various means, including analytical procedures, testing of internal controls, and investigation of unusual transactions or discrepancies.

Q: What are some of the challenges in an audit engagement?

A: Some of the challenges in an audit engagement include lack of cooperation from management, inadequate records or documentation, complex accounting issues, and time constraints.

Q: How are audit findings communicated in an audit engagement?

A: Audit findings are typically communicated in an audit engagement through the auditor's report, as well as in meetings and discussions with management and the audit committee.

Q: What is the importance of independence in an audit engagement?

A: Independence is crucial in an audit engagement as it ensures that the auditor can provide an impartial and unbiased opinion on the financial statements.

Q: What is the difference between an audit engagement and a review engagement?

A: An audit engagement involves a comprehensive examination of the financial statements and provides a high level of assurance, while a review engagement involves a less detailed examination and provides a moderate level of assurance.

Q: What is the purpose of an engagement letter in an audit engagement?

A: The purpose of an engagement letter in an audit engagement is to formally establish the terms and conditions of the audit, including the scope, responsibilities, and expectations.

Q: How is audit quality ensured in an audit engagement?

A: Audit quality in an audit engagement is ensured through various means, including adherence to auditing standards, effective planning and supervision, thorough testing and evidence gathering, and a critical review of the audit findings.

Q: What is the role of ethics in an audit engagement?

A: Ethics plays a critical role in an audit engagement by guiding the auditor's conduct and decision-making, ensuring that they act with integrity, objectivity, confidentiality, and professionalism.

Q: How can conflicts of interest be managed in an audit engagement?

A: Conflicts of interest in an audit engagement can be managed through various means, including disclosure of the conflict, independence checks, and, if necessary, withdrawal from the audit engagement.

Q: What are some of the consequences of a poor-quality audit engagement?

A: Consequences of a poor-quality audit engagement can include financial loss, damage to the company's reputation, legal penalties, and loss of stakeholder confidence.

Q: What are the steps involved in planning an audit engagement?

A: The steps involved in planning an audit engagement typically include understanding the client and their business, assessing the risks, determining the audit scope, developing the audit plan, and communicating the plan to the client.

Q: What is the role of risk assessment in an audit engagement?

A: The role of risk assessment in an audit engagement is to identify, evaluate, and respond to the risks of material misstatement in the financial statements.

Q: What is a management representation letter in an audit engagement?

A: A management representation letter in an audit engagement is a letter from management confirming the accuracy of the information provided to the auditor and their responsibility for the financial statements.

Q: What is the difference between a statutory audit and a voluntary audit engagement?

A: A statutory audit is a legally required audit, while a voluntary audit engagement is one that is initiated by the company for its own purposes, such as to improve internal controls or to provide assurance to stakeholders.

Q: How is materiality determined in an audit engagement?

A: Materiality in an audit engagement is typically determined based on a percentage of a relevant financial statement item, such as revenue or total assets, or based on professional judgment.

Q: What is the importance of documentation in an audit engagement?

A: Documentation is important in an audit engagement as it provides evidence of the auditor's work, supports the audit findings, and enables the review and evaluation of the audit.

Q: How does an auditor use analytical procedures in an audit engagement?

A: An auditor uses analytical procedures in an audit engagement to identify trends, relationships, and anomalies in the financial data, which can help in identifying risks and testing the financial statements.

Q: What is the role of professional judgment in an audit engagement?

A: Professional judgment is crucial in an audit engagement as it guides the auditor's decision-making, particularly in areas that require interpretation or evaluation of complex information.

Q: How do changes in the business environment affect an audit engagement?

A: Changes in the business environment can affect an audit engagement by introducing new risks or uncertainties, requiring changes to the audit plan, or impacting the evaluation of the financial statements.

Q: What are the different types of audit opinions that can result from an audit engagement?

A: The different types of audit opinions that can result from an audit engagement include an unqualified opinion, a qualified opinion, an adverse opinion, and a disclaimer of opinion.

Q: What is the importance of communication in an audit engagement?

A: Communication is vital in an audit engagement as it ensures that all parties understand the audit process, the findings, and the implications, and it facilitates cooperation and resolution of issues.

Q: What is the role of an audit program in an audit engagement?

A: The role of an audit program in an audit engagement is to guide the audit process, outlining the steps to be taken, the procedures to be performed, and the areas to be tested.

Q: How is sampling used in an audit engagement?

A: Sampling is used in an audit engagement to select a representative subset of transactions or balances for testing, providing a basis for the auditor's opinion on the entire population.

Q: What is the role of technology in an audit engagement?
A: Technology plays a key role in an audit engagement by enabling efficient data analysis, documentation, communication, and reporting, as well as enhancing the detection of errors or fraud.
Q: How can disagreements between the auditor and management be resolved in an audit engagement?
A: Disagreements between the auditor and management in an audit engagement can be resolved through discussion, consultation with independent advisors, and, if necessary, escalation to the audit committee or board of directors.
Q: What is the importance of understanding the client's business in an audit engagement?
A: Understanding the client's business in an audit engagement is important as it provides context for the financial statements, aids in risk assessment, and guides the audit procedures and evaluation of the results.
Q: What is the role of a quality control review in an audit engagement?
A: The role of a quality control review in an audit engagement is to check the quality and completeness of the audit work, ensuring compliance with auditing standards and the accuracy of the audit report.
Q: What is the difference between a group audit engagement and a single entity audit engagement?
A: A group audit engagement involves the audit of a group of entities consolidated into one set of financial statements, while a single entity audit engagement involves the audit of an individual entity's financial statements.
Q: What is the role of an engagement partner in an audit engagement?

A: The role of an engagement partner in an audit engagement is to oversee the audit process, liaise with the client, make key decisions, and sign the audit report on behalf of the audit firm.

Q: How is the effectiveness of an audit engagement evaluated?

A: The effectiveness of an audit engagement is evaluated based on whether it achieved its objective of providing an independent and reliable opinion on the financial statements, and whether it complied with relevant auditing standards and regulations.

Applications

Scenario 1:

Company A has recently undergone an audit engagement. The auditors found several discrepancies in the financial statements. As the audit manager, how would you handle this situation?

Solution:

In this situation, the audit manager should first review the discrepancies identified by the auditors. If the discrepancies are real, the manager should discuss these issues with the auditors and the management team of Company A. The manager should then prepare an action plan to mitigate these issues and ensure that they do not reoccur in the future.

Scenario 2:

During an audit engagement, the auditors discovered that Company B has been underreporting its income to evade taxes. As an auditor, what steps would you take in this situation?

Solution:

As an auditor, it is my responsibility to ensure that the financial records of the company are accurate and compliant with the laws. In this case, I would first gather all the necessary evidence and then report my findings to both the management of Company B and the relevant tax authorities. I would also recommend that Company B hire a tax consultant to resolve this issue.

Scenario 3:

In an audit engagement, the auditors noticed that Company C has been overvaluing its assets to attract investors. How would you address this issue as an auditor?

Solution:

As an auditor, my primary responsibility is to ensure that the financial statements of the company are accurate and reliable. If I find that a company is overvaluing its assets, I would first discuss my findings with the management of Company C. I would then provide them with a detailed report outlining the discrepancies I found and the potential consequences of their actions. I would also recommend that they correct their financial statements and make them publicly available to maintain transparency with their investors.

Scenario 4:

During an audit engagement, the auditors were unable to access certain financial records of Company D. How should the auditors handle this situation?

Solution:

As an auditor, when faced with such a situation, I would communicate this issue to the management of Company D. The management should provide access to all necessary financial records for an accurate audit. If they continue to refuse, I would have to qualify my audit opinion, indicating that I was unable to obtain sufficient appropriate audit evidence.

Scenario 5:

In an audit engagement, the auditors found that Company E has been using outdated accounting methods which are leading to inaccuracies in their financial statements. As an auditor, what steps would you take?

Solution:

As an auditor, it is my responsibility to ensure that the company's financial statements are prepared using the correct accounting methods. I would discuss this issue with the management of Company E and recommend that they update their accounting methods. I would also offer training to their accounting staff to ensure that they are up-to-date with the latest accounting standards and practices.

Peer Review

Theoretical

Q: What is the purpose of a peer review in auditing?

A: The main purpose of peer review in auditing is to ensure the quality and integrity of the audit process. It is a process where the work of one auditor is reviewed by another to identify any errors or discrepancies.

Q: How does peer review enhance the audit process?

A: Peer review enhances the audit process by providing a second opinion on the work done, thus ensuring that the audit has been carried out thoroughly and accurately.

Q: Who conducts peer reviews in auditing?

A: Usually, peer reviews are conducted by another auditor or audit firm that is not involved in the initial audit process.

Q: What are the key elements of an effective peer review process in auditing?

A: The key elements of an effective peer review process in auditing are independence, objectivity, competence, and a systematic approach.

Q: What is the role of independence in a peer review process?

A: Independence is vital in a peer review process as it ensures that the review is unbiased and impartial.

Q: How does the peer review process relate to audit standards?

A: The peer review process ensures that the audit is conducted in compliance with the appropriate audit standards.

Q: What happens if errors or discrepancies are found during a peer review?
A: If errors or discrepancies are found during the peer review, they are reported to the original auditor for correction and re-evaluation.
Q: How often should peer reviews be conducted?
A: The frequency of peer reviews can vary, but it is usually suggested that they be conducted every three to five years.
Q: What is the impact of a peer review on the credibility of an audit?
A: A peer review can greatly enhance the credibility of an audit as it provides an additional level of scrutiny and verification.
Q: Can a peer review replace the need for an external audit?
A: No, a peer review cannot replace an external audit. It is meant to supplement the external audit process, not replace it.
Q: How does a peer review process ensure the reliability of financial statements?
A: A peer review process ensures the reliability of financial statements by providing a second layer of scrutiny and verification.
Q: What is the role of objectivity in a peer review process?
A: Objectivity in a peer review process ensures that the review is fair and impartial.
Q: What are the risks associated with a peer review process?
A: The risks associated with a peer review process include potential conflicts of interest and the possibility of overlooking errors or discrepancies.
Q: How can these risks be mitigated?
A: These risks can be mitigated through maintaining independence and objectivity, and by having a systematic approach to the review process.
Q: How does a peer review contribute to the professional development of auditors?

A: A peer review provides auditors with feedback on their work, which can be used for learning and professional development.

Q: How does a peer review process contribute to corporate governance?

A: A peer review process contributes to corporate governance by ensuring the accuracy and reliability of financial reporting.

Q: Can a peer review process be used in both internal and external audits?

A: Yes, a peer review process can be used in both internal and external audits to ensure quality and accuracy.

Q: What is the role of competence in a peer review process?

A: Competence ensures that the reviewer has the necessary knowledge and skills to effectively review the audit work.

Q: How does a systematic approach contribute to an effective peer review process?

A: A systematic approach ensures that the review process is thorough and consistent.

Q: What is the outcome of a successful peer review in auditing?

A: The outcome of a successful peer review in auditing is an audit report that is accurate, reliable, and in compliance with audit standards.

Q: How does a peer review process support transparency in auditing?

A: A peer review process supports transparency in auditing by providing an additional level of scrutiny and verification.

Q: What is the difference between a peer review and a quality control review in auditing?

A: While both are review processes, a quality control review focuses on the audit firm's systems and procedures, whereas a peer review focuses on the specific audit engagement.

Q: How does a peer review process uphold audit ethics?

A: A peer review process upholds audit ethics by ensuring that the audit is conducted in a fair, unbiased, and professional manner.
Q: What are the potential challenges in implementing a peer review process in auditing?
A: Potential challenges in implementing a peer review process in auditing include finding a competent and independent reviewer, managing conflicts of interest, and ensuring the thoroughness of the review.
Q: How can these challenges be overcome?
A: These challenges can be overcome through careful planning, clear communication, and adherence to audit standards and ethics.
Q: What is the role of communication in a peer review process?
A: Communication is key in a peer review process as it facilitates the exchange of ideas and feedback between the reviewer and the original auditor.
Q: How can a peer review process be improved?
A: A peer review process can be improved through ongoing training and development, regular feedback, and continuous refinement of the review procedures.
Q: What is the significance of a peer review report in auditing?
A: A peer review report is significant in auditing as it provides a formal record of the review process and its findings.
Q: How does a peer review process support the audit assurance process?
A: A peer review process supports the audit assurance process by providing an additional level of scrutiny and verification, thus enhancing the assurance provided by the audit.
Q: What is the relationship between a peer review process and audit risk?
A: A peer review process can help manage audit risk by identifying and addressing any errors or discrepancies in the audit work.

Q: Can a peer review process be used to review the work of an audit team?

A: Yes, a peer review process can be used to review the work of an audit team to ensure accuracy and compliance with audit standards.

Q: What is the relationship between a peer review process and audit evidence?

A: A peer review process verifies the audit evidence collected, ensuring its sufficiency and appropriateness.

Q: How can a peer review process contribute to the audit planning process?

A: A peer review process can contribute to the audit planning process by providing feedback and insights that can inform future audit plans.

Q: How does a peer review process support the decision-making process in auditing?

A: A peer review process supports the decision-making process in auditing by providing additional information and insights, thus enhancing the quality of audit decisions.

Q: Can a peer review process be automated?

A: While certain aspects of a peer review process can be automated, it still requires human judgment and expertise to ensure the quality of the audit work.

Q: How does a peer review process relate to the concept of professional skepticism in auditing?

A: A peer review process upholds the concept of professional skepticism in auditing by questioning and verifying the audit work.

Q: How does a peer review process support the audit documentation process?

A: A peer review process supports the audit documentation process by reviewing the audit documentation for completeness and accuracy.

Q: How does a peer review process contribute to the audit reporting process?

A: A peer review process contributes to the audit reporting process by ensuring the accuracy and completeness of the audit report.

Q: What is the role of a peer review process in the audit cycle?

A: A peer review process plays a key role in the audit cycle by providing a check and balance to ensure the quality and accuracy of the audit work.

Q: What is the relationship between a peer review process and audit scope?

A: A peer review process verifies that the audit scope has been appropriately determined and adhered to.

Q: How does a peer review process relate to the concept of materiality in auditing?

A: A peer review process verifies that materiality has been appropriately considered and applied in the audit.

Q: What is the role of a peer review process in audit engagements?

A: A peer review process plays a critical role in audit engagements by providing an additional level of scrutiny and verification to ensure the quality of the audit work.

Q: How does a peer review process support the principle of accountability in auditing?

A: A peer review process supports the principle of accountability in auditing by providing an additional check on the work of the auditor.

Q: Can a peer review process be used in the audit of financial statements?

A: Yes, a peer review process can be used in the audit of financial statements to ensure their accuracy and reliability.

Q: How does a peer review process relate to the concept of audit opinion?

A: A peer review process verifies the basis for the audit opinion, ensuring its accuracy and validity.

Q: How does a peer review process support the audit conclusion process?

A: A peer review process supports the audit conclusion process by providing additional verification of the audit findings and conclusions.

Q: What is the relationship between a peer review process and audit procedures?

A: A peer review process verifies that the audit procedures have been correctly applied and are appropriate for the audit.

Q: How does a peer review process contribute to the audit risk assessment process?

A: A peer review process contributes to the audit risk assessment process by providing an additional level of scrutiny that can identify and address audit risks.

Q: Can a peer review process be used in the audit of internal control systems?

A: Yes, a peer review process can be used in the audit of internal control systems to ensure their effectiveness and reliability.

Q: How does a peer review process relate to the concept of audit judgment?

A: A peer review process verifies the appropriateness of audit judgment, ensuring its validity and accuracy.

Applications

Scenario 1: A small-sized auditing firm, XYZ Auditors, has just completed the auditing process for one of their clients. The firm has a policy of conducting peer reviews to ensure the quality of their work. However, the peer review has identified several errors in the auditing process. The errors are minor but could have significant impacts on the client's financial statement.

Solution: To rectify the situation, XYZ Auditors should immediately inform the client about the errors and take corrective actions. The firm should also review their auditing procedures and provide additional training to their staff to prevent such errors in the future.

Scenario 2: ABC Auditors, a large auditing firm, has been conducting peer reviews for many years. Recently, they have noticed that the quality of their audits has been declining. The peer reviews are not identifying the issues that are resulting in the decline in quality.

Solution: ABC Auditors should reassess their peer review process. They may need to bring in an external peer reviewer to provide a fresh perspective. The firm may also need to update their peer review policies and procedures to ensure they are effective in identifying and addressing issues.

Scenario 3: A medium-sized auditing firm, DEF Auditors, has never conducted a peer review. They believe their audits are of high quality and see no need for peer reviews. However, one of their clients has requested a peer review as part of the auditing process.

Solution: DEF Auditors should respect the client's request and conduct a peer review. They may need to hire an external auditor to conduct the review. The firm should also consider implementing peer reviews as a standard part of their auditing process. It can help them ensure the quality of their audits and meet the expectations of their clients.

Scenario 4: GHI Auditors, a reputable auditing firm, has just conducted a peer review for one of their audits. The peer review has identified several major issues that could potentially lead to a lawsuit. The firm is unsure of how to handle the situation. Solution: GHI Auditors should immediately address the issues identified in the peer review. They may need to re-audit the client's financial statements to correct the errors. The firm should also consult with a legal expert to understand the potential legal implications. In addition, they should review their auditing procedures to prevent such issues in the future.

Audit Findings

Theoretical

Q: What is the purpose of audit findings in an auditing process?

A: The purpose of audit findings in the auditing process is to identify and document any discrepancies, non-compliance, or areas for improvement during the audit.

Q: What types of issues are typically identified in audit findings?

A: Typical issues identified in audit findings include non-compliance with regulations or policies, inefficient operations, financial discrepancies, and potential risks.

Q: How are audit findings typically classified?

A: Audit findings are typically classified into categories such as minor, moderate, and major, based on the severity and impact of the identified issue.

Q: What is the role of an auditor in the audit findings process?

A: The auditor's role in the audit findings process is to identify, analyze, and document the findings, and to provide recommendations for improvement.

Q: How can audit findings influence the decision-making process in an organization?

A: Audit findings provide valuable insights into the organization's systems and processes, helping the management to make informed decisions regarding process improvements, risk management, and compliance.

Q: What is the difference between an audit finding and an audit observation?
A: An audit finding is a discrepancy identified during the audit, while an audit observation is a minor issue that does not necessarily represent a breach of compliance or risk.
Q: How should audit findings be communicated to the auditee?
A: Audit findings should be communicated to the auditee in a clear, concise, and factual manner, usually through an audit report.
Q: What are the steps involved in the audit findings process?
A: The audit findings process typically involves identification of discrepancies, analysis of the issue, documentation of the findings, and providing recommendations for improvement.
Q: What is the significance of providing evidence to support audit findings?
A: Providing evidence to support audit findings ensures that the findings are based on factual data, enhancing the credibility and reliability of the audit.
Q: How can the audit findings process contribute to continuous improvement in an organization?
A: The audit findings process can contribute to continuous improvement by identifying areas for improvement and providing recommendations for enhancing efficiency, effectiveness, and compliance.
Q: What is the role of risk assessment in the audit findings process?
A: Risk assessment plays a crucial role in the audit findings process by helping to identify potential risks and areas of non-compliance that need to be addressed.
Q: Why is it important to follow up on audit findings?
A: Following up on audit findings is important to ensure that the recommended actions have been implemented and the identified issues have been resolved.

Q: What is the impact of audit findings on the overall audit opinion?
A: Audit findings can significantly impact the overall audit opinion, as they provide evidence of the organization's compliance with regulations and the effectiveness of its systems and processes.
Q: How should audit findings be documented in the audit report?
A: Audit findings should be documented in the audit report in a clear, concise, and factual manner, providing details of the identified issue, the evidence supporting the finding, and the recommended actions.
Q: What is the role of the audit committee in the audit findings process?
A: The audit committee plays a crucial role in the audit findings process by reviewing the findings, ensuring appropriate action is taken, and maintaining oversight of the organization's internal control systems.
Q: How can audit findings be used to enhance internal controls?
A: Audit findings can be used to enhance internal controls by identifying weaknesses and providing recommendations for strengthening the control environment.
Q: What is the relationship between audit findings and audit risk?
A: Audit findings can contribute to audit risk if they indicate significant non-compliance or weaknesses in the organization's systems and processes.
Q: How are audit findings used in the development of the audit plan?
A: Audit findings can be used in the development of the audit plan by identifying areas of risk and non-compliance that need to be addressed in the next audit.
Q: How can technology be used to enhance the audit findings process?

A: Technology can be used to enhance the audit findings process by facilitating data analysis, documentation of findings, and communication of the findings to the auditee.
Q: How can audit findings contribute to the achievement of the organization's objectives?
A: Audit findings can contribute to the achievement of the organization's objectives by identifying areas for improvement and providing recommendations for enhancing efficiency, effectiveness, and compliance.
Q: What factors should be considered when prioritizing audit findings?
A: Factors to consider when prioritizing audit findings include the severity and impact of the identified issue, the risk it poses to the organization, and the feasibility of implementing the recommended actions.
Q: What is the importance of maintaining objectivity in the audit findings process?
A: Maintaining objectivity in the audit findings process is important to ensure that the findings are based on factual data and are not influenced by personal bias or prejudice.
Q: How can audit findings contribute to the development of the organization's risk management strategy?
A: Audit findings can contribute to the development of the organization's risk management strategy by identifying potential risks and areas of non-compliance that need to be addressed.
Q: What is the role of management in the audit findings process?
A: The role of management in the audit findings process is to review the findings, implement the recommended actions, and ensure continuous improvement in the organization's systems and processes.
Q: How can audit findings be used to evaluate the performance of the internal audit function?

A: Audit findings can be used to evaluate the performance of the internal audit function by assessing the effectiveness of the audit in identifying and addressing issues and risks.

Q: What is the importance of confidentiality in the audit findings process?

A: Confidentiality is important in the audit findings process to protect sensitive information and uphold the integrity of the audit.

Q: How is the materiality concept applied in the audit findings process?

A: The materiality concept is applied in the audit findings process by focusing on issues that are significant or material to the organization's financial statements or operations.

Q: What is the role of the audit scope in the audit findings process?

A: The audit scope plays a crucial role in the audit findings process by defining the areas to be audited and the depth of the audit.

Q: How can audit findings be used to enhance the organization's compliance with regulations?

A: Audit findings can be used to enhance the organization's compliance with regulations by identifying areas of non-compliance and providing recommendations for corrective action.

Q: What are the potential consequences of ignoring audit findings?

A: Ignoring audit findings can lead to potential risks, non-compliance with regulations, financial losses, and damage to the organization's reputation.

Q: What is the role of the internal control system in the audit findings process?

A: The internal control system plays a crucial role in the audit findings process by providing a framework for the identification, analysis, and resolution of audit findings.

Q: How can audit findings contribute to the organization's strategic planning process?

A: Audit findings can contribute to the organization's strategic planning process by providing insights into the organization's strengths, weaknesses, opportunities, and threats.

Q: What is the importance of communicating audit findings in a timely manner?

A: Communicating audit findings in a timely manner is important to ensure that the identified issues are addressed promptly and effectively.

Q: How can the audit findings process contribute to the organization's corporate governance?

A: The audit findings process can contribute to the organization's corporate governance by enhancing transparency, accountability, and compliance.

Q: How should audit findings be presented to the board of directors?

A: Audit findings should be presented to the board of directors in a clear, concise, and factual manner, highlighting the key issues and recommendations.

Q: What is the importance of considering the organization's business environment in the audit findings process?

A: Considering the organization's business environment in the audit findings process is important to ensure that the findings and recommendations are relevant and applicable.

Q: How can audit findings contribute to the organization's financial management?

A: Audit findings can contribute to the organization's financial management by identifying financial discrepancies and providing recommendations for financial control and efficiency.

Q: What are the potential challenges in the audit findings process?

A: Potential challenges in the audit findings process include lack of cooperation from the auditee, inadequate documentation, and complex or ambiguous regulations.

Q: How can audit findings contribute to the organization's operational efficiency?

A: Audit findings can contribute to the organization's operational efficiency by identifying inefficient operations and providing recommendations for process improvements.

Q: What is the role of the external auditor in the audit findings process?

A: The role of the external auditor in the audit findings process is to provide an independent and objective assessment of the organization's systems and processes, and to identify and document audit findings.

Q: What is the difference between audit findings and audit recommendations?

A: Audit findings are the discrepancies identified during the audit, while audit recommendations are the actions suggested to address these discrepancies.

Q: What is the importance of maintaining professionalism in the audit findings process?

A: Maintaining professionalism in the audit findings process is important to uphold the integrity of the audit and to ensure that the findings are based on factual data and unbiased analysis.

Q: How can audit findings contribute to the organization's quality management?

A: Audit findings can contribute to the organization's quality management by identifying quality issues and providing recommendations for quality improvement.

Q: What is the role of the audit methodology in the audit findings process?

A: The audit methodology plays a crucial role in the audit findings process by providing a systematic approach to the identification, analysis, and resolution of audit findings.

Q: What is the importance of documenting audit findings?

A: Documenting audit findings is important to provide a record of the identified issues and the actions taken to address them, and to facilitate communication and follow-up.

Q: How can audit findings be used to enhance the organization's risk awareness?

A: Audit findings can be used to enhance the organization's risk awareness by identifying potential risks and providing recommendations for risk management.

Q: What is the impact of audit findings on the organization's reputation?

A: Audit findings can impact the organization's reputation, as they provide evidence of the organization's compliance with regulations and the effectiveness of its systems and processes.

Q: How can audit findings contribute to the organization's sustainability?

A: Audit findings can contribute to the organization's sustainability by identifying areas for improvement and providing recommendations for enhancing efficiency, effectiveness, and compliance.

Q: What is the role of the audit program in the audit findings process?

A: The audit program plays a crucial role in the audit findings process by defining the audit objectives, scope, methodology, and procedures.

Q: What is the importance of considering the organization's culture in the audit findings process?

A: Considering the organization's culture in the audit findings process is important to ensure that the findings and recommendations are culturally sensitive and applicable.

Applications

Scenario 1: In the case of XYZ Corp, the auditors discovered discrepancies in the financial statements where the accounts receivable were overestimated by 20%. It was found that the company was inflating its sales numbers to appear more profitable.

Solution: To rectify this issue, the auditors must adjust the financial statement to reflect the correct numbers. Also, they should recommend the implementation of controls to ensure accurate recording of sales. The management of XYZ Corp should be held accountable for the misrepresentation of financial data.

Scenario 2: In an audit of ABC Ltd., the auditors found that the company had not recorded a significant liability, causing an understatement of liabilities and overstatement of net income.

Solution: The auditors should adjust the financial statements to reflect the omitted liability. They should suggest that the company improve its process for identifying and recording all liabilities. ABC Ltd. should also review its internal control system to prevent such errors in the future.

Scenario 3: During the audit of PQR Inc., the auditors found that the company had been using an incorrect method for depreciating its assets. This resulted in the understatement of the depreciation expense and overstatement of the asset's book value.

Solution: The auditors must correct the depreciation method and adjust the financial statements accordingly. They should recommend that PQR Inc. uses the correct depreciation method as per the applicable accounting standards. The company should also provide training to its accounting staff to avoid such errors in the future.

Scenario 4: In the case of LMN Enterprises, the auditors found that the company had been recognizing revenue before the delivery of the goods, which is against the revenue recognition principle.

Solution: The auditors should require the company to adjust its revenue to reflect only the revenue earned from delivered goods. They should also recommend that the company follow the revenue recognition principle strictly. LMN Enterprises should implement controls to ensure that revenue is recognized only when earned.

Scenario 5: During the audit of RST Inc., the auditors found that the inventory was overstated due to the inclusion of obsolete items.

Solution: The auditors must adjust the financial statements to exclude the value of obsolete inventory. They should recommend that RST Inc. implements a system for regular review and write-off of obsolete inventory. The company should also improve its inventory management system to avoid similar problems in the future.

Management Letter

Theoretical

Question: What is a management letter in auditing?

Answer: A management letter in auditing is a formal document prepared by an auditor at the end of an audit process. It contains the auditor's observations, recommendations, and potential improvements for the management's consideration.

Question: What is the purpose of a management letter in auditing?

Answer: The purpose of a management letter is to communicate the auditor's findings and recommendations to the management. It aids in improving the organization's operational efficiency and control environment.

Question: Who usually prepares the management letter?

Answer: The management letter is usually prepared by the auditor who conducted the audit.

Question: To whom is the management letter addressed?

Answer: The management letter is usually addressed to the senior management or the board of directors of the company being audited.

Question: What should a management letter contain?

Answer: A management letter should contain the identified control weaknesses, risk areas, non-compliance issues, and suggestions for improvement.

Question: Does a management letter include financial reporting?

Answer: No, a management letter primarily focuses on operational and administrative issues and not on financial reporting.

Question: When is a management letter issued?

Answer: A management letter is typically issued after the completion of the audit process.

Question: Is the issuance of a management letter mandatory in an audit?

Answer: The issuance of a management letter is not mandatory. However, it is considered good practice as it communicates the auditor's observations and recommendations for improvement.

Question: How does a management letter aid in risk management?

Answer: By identifying key risk areas and providing recommendations for improvement, a management letter aids in mitigating potential risks.

Question: How is a management letter different from an audit report?

Answer: An audit report is a formal opinion on the company's financial statements, while a management letter focuses on the operational and administrative observations and suggestions for improvement.

Question: Can a management letter identify fraud?

Answer: Not directly, but a management letter can identify control weaknesses and risk areas that may lead to fraud if not addressed.

Question: How does a management letter promote operational efficiency?

Answer: A management letter can promote operational efficiency by identifying operational inefficiencies and recommending corrective actions.

Question: Is a management letter a confidential document?

Answer: Yes, a management letter is generally considered confidential and is not typically disclosed to the public.
Question: What is the relationship between a management letter and internal control?
Answer: A management letter can identify weaknesses in internal control and suggest ways to strengthen it.
Question: How should management respond to a management letter?
Answer: Management should review the recommendations, take necessary corrective actions, and communicate their plans to the auditor.
Question: How does a management letter contribute to corporate governance?
Answer: By identifying control weaknesses and suggesting improvements, a management letter can contribute to better corporate governance.
Question: How can a management letter influence decision-making?
Answer: The observations and recommendations in a management letter can provide valuable insights for management's decision-making process.
Question: What is considered a serious issue in a management letter?
Answer: A serious issue in a management letter is one that poses significant risk to the organization if not addressed promptly.
Question: Do all audit engagements result in a management letter?
Answer: Not necessarily, the issuance of a management letter depends on the auditor's judgement.
Question: How long should a management letter be retained?
Answer: The retention period for a management letter can vary depending on the company's policy and regulatory requirements.

Question: How often is a management letter issued?
Answer: A management letter is generally issued after each audit engagement.
Question: How should the management implement the recommendations in a management letter?
Answer: The management should develop an action plan to address the recommendations and monitor their implementation.
Question: Are management letters only for internal use?
Answer: Generally yes, management letters are typically for internal use and not disclosed to the public.
Question: Can a management letter reveal a company's strategic direction?
Answer: Not directly, but a management letter can provide insights into operational and administrative issues that may impact the company's strategic direction.
Question: How can a management letter contribute to business growth?
Answer: By identifying areas for operational improvement and risk mitigation, a management letter can contribute to business growth.
Question: What role does a management letter play in stakeholder communication?
Answer: A management letter can help communicate the auditor's findings and recommendations to key stakeholders, such as the board of directors.
Question: Does a management letter have legal implications?
Answer: A management letter itself does not have legal implications, but it can highlight legal or regulatory compliance issues that need to be addressed.
Question: How does a management letter reflect the auditor's independence?

Answer: By providing objective observations and recommendations, a management letter reflects the auditor's independence and impartiality.

Question: What is the role of a management letter in audit planning?

Answer: A management letter doesn't directly contribute to audit planning, but the issues highlighted in it could inform the planning of future audits.

Question: Can a management letter be used as evidence in legal proceedings?

Answer: While it is not typically used as evidence, a management letter could be requested in legal proceedings if it is relevant to the case.

Question: Is a management letter a public document?

Answer: No, a management letter is usually confidential and not disclosed to the public.

Question: What happens if the management ignores the recommendations in a management letter?

Answer: Ignoring the recommendations could lead to operational inefficiencies, increased risks, and potential non-compliance issues.

Question: Can a management letter predict a company's future performance?

Answer: Not directly, but it can highlight operational and risk issues that could impact future performance.

Question: Is a management letter a regulatory requirement?

Answer: The issuance of a management letter is not a regulatory requirement, but it is considered good auditing practice.

Question: Does a management letter need to be audited?

Answer: No, a management letter does not need to be audited. It is itself a product of the audit process.

Question: Can a management letter be revised?

Answer: Generally, a management letter is not revised. However, the auditor may issue a supplementary letter if necessary.
Question: Can a management letter be disputed?
Answer: Yes, the management can discuss and dispute the findings with the auditor before the final letter is issued.
Question: How does a management letter contribute to transparency?
Answer: A management letter promotes transparency by communicating the auditor's findings and recommendations to the management.
Question: Can a management letter be used for benchmarking?
Answer: While not typically used for benchmarking, a management letter can provide insights into operational and risk issues for comparison with industry standards.
Question: Does a management letter guarantee the accuracy of financial statements?
Answer: No, a management letter focuses on operational and administrative issues, not the accuracy of financial statements.
Question: Can a management letter be issued without an audit?
Answer: No, a management letter is a product of the audit process and is not issued without an audit.
Question: Can a management letter include personal observations?
Answer: Yes, a management letter can include the auditor's personal observations, as long as they are relevant and professional.
Question: Who signs the management letter?
Answer: The management letter is usually signed by the lead auditor or the audit engagement partner.
Question: Can a management letter result in disciplinary action?

Answer: While a management letter itself does not result in disciplinary action, the issues highlighted in it could lead to disciplinary action if not addressed.
Question: How does a management letter contribute to accountability?
Answer: A management letter contributes to accountability by communicating the auditor's findings and recommendations to the management.
Question: Can a management letter be issued electronically?
Answer: Yes, a management letter can be issued electronically, provided it meets all the necessary requirements.
Question: Does a management letter need to be presented at an annual general meeting (AGM)?
Answer: While not a requirement, the content of a management letter may be discussed at an AGM if it is deemed relevant.
Question: Can a management letter be ignored?
Answer: Though a management letter can technically be ignored, it is highly discouraged as it contains valuable insights for improving the organization's operations.
Question: How does a management letter aid in the improvement of business processes?
Answer: A management letter aids in the improvement of business processes by identifying weaknesses and recommending solutions for improvement.
Question: Is a management letter a tool for change management?
Answer: Yes, a management letter can be a catalyst for change management by identifying areas of improvement and recommending changes.

Applications

Scenario 1: Misclassification of Expenses

John is an auditor of WYZ Ltd, which is a manufacturing company. During the audit, he noticed that the company has classified some of their capital expenditure as revenue expenditure in the financial statements. This misclassification can lead to an overstatement of profits.

Solution: John should mention this issue in his audit management letter. He should suggest the company to review the classification of their expenditure and adjust the financial statements accordingly. Proper training should be provided to the accounting personnel to avoid such errors in the future.

Scenario 2: Inadequate Internal Control over Cash

Sarah, an auditor of ABC Ltd, observes that the company lacks proper control over cash handling. There have been instances of cash shortages and no one seems to be held accountable.

Solution: Sarah should highlight this issue in her management letter. She should recommend that the company implements stringent internal control measures over cash handling, such as segregation of duties, regular cash counts, and reconciliation of physical cash with book records.

Scenario 3: Inaccurate Inventory Valuation

Peter, an auditor of PQR Ltd, discovers that the company is not following the correct method for inventory valuation. This can lead to incorrect valuation of inventory in the balance sheet.

Solution: Peter should bring this to the attention of the management in his audit letter. He should recommend them to follow an appropriate method for inventory valuation as per the accounting standards. This would ensure that the value of inventory is stated accurately in the balance sheet.

Scenario 4: Non-compliance with Tax Laws

During the audit of XYZ Ltd, Lisa, the auditor, finds that the company has not complied with certain tax laws, resulting in potential penalties and interest.

Solution: Lisa should mention this in her management letter. She should advise the management to review their tax compliance process and ensure adherence to all applicable tax laws. The company should also consider seeking advice from tax experts to avoid similar non-compliance issues in the future.

Scenario 5: Incorrect Depreciation Calculation

While auditing DEF Ltd, Robert discovered that the company is not calculating depreciation correctly on its assets, leading to an overstatement of assets and understatement of expenses.

Solution: Robert should include this issue in his audit management letter. He should recommend the company to review its depreciation calculation method and correct the inaccuracies. The company should also consider providing training to its staff on accurate computation of depreciation.

Audit Opinion

Theoretical

Q: What is an audit opinion?

A: An audit opinion is the conclusion made by an auditor at the end of an audit process. It gives a clear picture of a company's financial position and confirms whether the financial statements are accurate and comply with generally accepted accounting principles (GAAP).

Q: How many types of audit opinions are there?

A: The four types of audit opinions are: Unqualified opinion, Qualified opinion, Adverse opinion, and Disclaimer of opinion.

Q: What does an unqualified opinion represent?

A: An unqualified opinion represents that the financial statements are presented fairly and in accordance with the GAAP.

Q: What does a qualified opinion imply?

A: A qualified opinion implies that the financial records have been maintained in general, in accordance with GAAP but there are some exceptions that need to be addressed.

Q: When is an adverse opinion given?

A: An adverse opinion is given when the auditor believes that the financial statements seriously deviate from the GAAP.

Q: What is a disclaimer of opinion?

A: A disclaimer of opinion is issued when the auditor is unable to form an opinion on the financial statements due to insufficient information or inability to perform an effective audit.

Q: How does the audit opinion affect stakeholders?

A: The audit opinion affects stakeholders as it helps them make informed decisions. A negative audit opinion can result in a decrease in stock prices, while a positive one can increase investor confidence.

Q: Why is an audit opinion important?

A: An audit opinion is important because it provides an impartial view of a company's financial health, ensuring transparency and building trust with stakeholders.

Q: Can an audit opinion be changed?

A: Yes, an audit opinion can be revised if the auditor discovers new information that significantly impacts the financial statements.

Q: How is an audit opinion formed?

A: An audit opinion is formed after a thorough examination of a company's financial records, internal controls, and consistency with the GAAP.

Q: What factors can influence an audit opinion?

A: Factors like errors in financial records, fraudulent activities, inconsistencies in accounts, or non-compliance with GAAP can influence an audit opinion.

Q: What happens if a company receives an adverse opinion?

A: If a company receives an adverse opinion, it might face difficulties in securing investments or loans and may be required to redo its financial statements.

Q: What role does an audit opinion play in corporate governance?

A: An audit opinion plays a crucial role in corporate governance by ensuring transparency, accuracy, and adherence to financial regulations, thus fostering trust among stakeholders.

Q: How does an audit opinion impact the credibility of financial statements?

A: An audit opinion impacts the credibility of financial statements by validating their accuracy, completeness, and compliance with GAAP, thereby enhancing their reliability.
Q: What steps does an auditor take to form an audit opinion?
A: An auditor examines the company's financial records, checks for compliance with GAAP, evaluates internal controls, and verifies the consistency and accuracy of financial data to form an audit opinion.
Q: How does an unqualified opinion impact a company's reputation?
A: An unqualified opinion enhances a company's reputation as it signifies that the company's financial statements are accurate and comply with GAAP.
Q: What is the difference between a qualified and unqualified opinion?
A: A qualified opinion implies some exceptions to GAAP, while an unqualified opinion denotes full compliance with GAAP.
Q: What is the implication of a disclaimer of opinion for investors?
A: A disclaimer of opinion can create uncertainty for investors as it indicates that the auditor couldn't form an opinion on the company's financial health.
Q: Can a company still operate with an adverse audit opinion?
A: Yes, a company can still operate with an adverse audit opinion, but it might face challenges in securing financing, and its reputation may be damaged.
Q: How often is an audit opinion given?
A: An audit opinion is typically given annually, at the end of a company's fiscal year, after the auditor completes the audit process.
Q: What is the role of an auditor in giving an audit opinion?
A: The auditor's role in giving an audit opinion is to examine the company's financial records, assess internal controls, ensure GAAP

compliance, and provide an impartial evaluation of the company's financial position.

Q: How does a positive audit opinion impact a company's stock prices?

A: A positive audit opinion can boost a company's stock prices as it increases investor confidence in the company's financial health.

Q: What information does an audit opinion provide to shareholders?

A: An audit opinion provides shareholders with an impartial evaluation of the company's financial position, accuracy of its financial statements, and compliance with GAAP, helping them make informed decisions.

Q: Why are there different types of audit opinions?

A: There are different types of audit opinions to accurately represent the varying levels of accuracy, compliance, and transparency in a company's financial statements.

Q: How does an audit opinion reflect on a company's financial transparency?

A: An audit opinion reflects on a company's financial transparency by confirming the accuracy of its financial statements and compliance with GAAP, promoting trust among stakeholders.

Q: How does an audit opinion contribute to business growth?

A: A positive audit opinion can stimulate business growth by enhancing investor confidence, improving credibility, and enabling access to better financing opportunities.

Q: Can the audit opinion influence a company's credit rating?

A: Yes, an adverse audit opinion can negatively impact a company's credit rating as it indicates financial inconsistencies or non-compliance with GAAP.

Q: What actions can a company take after receiving a qualified opinion?

A: After receiving a qualified opinion, a company can review and correct the exceptions identified, improve its internal controls, and ensure better compliance with GAAP.

Q: How does an audit opinion affect the company's relationship with its bank?

A: An audit opinion can affect the company's relationship with its bank. A positive opinion can enhance the trust, while a negative opinion can create doubts about the company's financial health, possibly impacting the terms of loans or credit facilities.

Q: Can an audit opinion be disputed by a company?

A: While companies may disagree with an audit opinion, they cannot dispute it as it is formed by an independent external auditor based on a thorough evaluation of the company's financial records.

Q: What is the significance of an audit opinion in mergers and acquisitions?

A: In mergers and acquisitions, an audit opinion provides valuable insights into the target company's financial health, aiding in informed decision-making.

Q: What is the impact of a disclaimer of opinion on a company's market position?

A: A disclaimer of opinion can create uncertainty in the market and potentially weaken the company's market position due to perceived financial instability.

Q: What role does the audit opinion play in risk management?

A: An audit opinion plays a crucial role in risk management by identifying financial discrepancies, non-compliance with GAAP, and weaknesses in internal controls, thus helping in mitigating financial risks.

Q: How does an audit opinion impact a company's financial planning?

A: An audit opinion can significantly impact a company's financial planning as it reveals the accuracy of financial statements and compliance with GAAP, helping in strategic decision-making and future planning.

Q: Can an audit opinion indicate potential bankruptcy?

A: Yes, an adverse audit opinion can indicate potential bankruptcy if it reveals severe financial discrepancies and non-compliance with GAAP.

Q: How does an audit opinion affect a company's credibility in the market?

A: An audit opinion significantly affects a company's credibility in the market. A positive opinion enhances credibility, while a negative opinion can damage it.

Q: What impact does an audit opinion have on a company's financial stability?

A: An audit opinion provides an assessment of a company's financial stability. A positive opinion indicates good financial health, while a negative opinion may suggest financial instability.

Q: How does an audit opinion influence a company's decision-making process?

A: An audit opinion can influence a company's decision-making process by providing insights into the accuracy of financial statements, internal control effectiveness, and compliance with GAAP.

Q: How does an audit opinion affect a company's public image?

A: An audit opinion can significantly affect a company's public image. A positive audit opinion enhances the company's image, whereas a negative opinion can tarnish it.

Q: How does an audit opinion impact investor's confidence in a company?

A: An audit opinion significantly impacts investor's confidence in a company. A positive opinion can boost confidence, while a negative opinion can lead to loss of trust.

Q: What is the role of an audit opinion in financial reporting?

A: An audit opinion plays a critical role in financial reporting by validating the accuracy, completeness, and compliance of financial statements with GAAP.

Q: How does an audit opinion contribute to the financial health of a company?

A: An audit opinion contributes to the financial health of a company by ensuring transparency, accuracy, and adherence to financial regulations, thus fostering trust amongst stakeholders and promoting financial stability.

Q: How does an audit opinion reflect on the management's performance?

A: An audit opinion can be a reflection of the management's performance in maintaining accurate financial records, ensuring compliance with GAAP, and implementing effective internal controls.

Q: What is the impact of an audit opinion on the company's operational efficiency?

A: While an audit opinion primarily focuses on financial records, it can indirectly reflect on the company's operational efficiency by highlighting issues in internal controls or financial discrepancies that may stem from operational inefficiencies.

Q: Can an audit opinion reveal fraudulent activities?

A: Yes, an audit opinion can reveal fraudulent activities if the auditor identifies significant inconsistencies or discrepancies in the financial statements.

Q: How does an audit opinion contribute to the corporate culture?

A: An audit opinion contributes to the corporate culture by promoting financial transparency, accountability, and integrity.

Q: How does an audit opinion affect the company's competitive advantage?

A: A positive audit opinion can provide a competitive advantage by enhancing investor confidence, credibility in the market, and access to better financing opportunities.

Q: How does an audit opinion impact a company's strategic planning?

A: An audit opinion impacts a company's strategic planning by providing insights into its financial health, which is crucial for making strategic decisions and future planning.

Q: How does an audit opinion affect a company's tax obligations?

A: An audit opinion doesn't directly affect a company's tax obligations, but it can highlight discrepancies or errors in the financial statements that could lead to miscalculations in tax liabilities.

Q: Can an audit opinion influence a company's growth prospects?

A: Yes, an audit opinion can significantly influence a company's growth prospects. A positive opinion can attract more investments, while a negative opinion can deter investors, affecting the company's growth potential.

Applications

Scenario 1:

ABC Company is a manufacturing firm that recently finished its financial year. The company's external auditor, XYZ & Co., is tasked with giving an audit opinion on the company's financial statements. The auditor discovered that the company has been using an incorrect method to account for its inventory, which significantly affects the reported profit.

Solution: In this scenario, the auditor should issue a qualified opinion. A qualified opinion indicates that, except for the effects of the matter to which the qualification relates, the financial statements present fairly, in all material respects, the financial position of the company. The auditor should clearly explain the reasons for the qualification in the audit report.

Scenario 2:

DEF Company, a public corporation, has just completed a major acquisition. The company's auditor, PQR & Co., found discrepancies in the valuation of the acquired company's assets. The auditor also noticed that DEF Company has not disclosed this acquisition in its financial statements.

Solution: This scenario calls for an adverse opinion by the auditor. An adverse opinion is given when the financial statements are not presented fairly or are materially misstated. The auditor should explicitly state that the financial statements are not fairly presented and explain the reasons why in the audit report.

Scenario 3:

GHI Company is a small business that has been operating for one year. The company's auditor, UVW & Co., was unable to obtain sufficient appropriate audit evidence about the company's inventory. The inventory represents a significant portion of the company's assets.

Solution: In this case, the auditor should issue a disclaimer of opinion. A disclaimer of opinion is issued when the auditor is unable to obtain sufficient appropriate audit evidence on which to base an opinion, and the possible effects on the financial statements could be both material and pervasive. The auditor should indicate the reason for the disclaimer in the audit report and state that they were unable to form an opinion.

Scenario 4:

JKL Company, a retail company, has provided all necessary documentation and access to its financial records for the annual audit. The auditor, ZYX & Co., has found no material misstatements or discrepancies.

Solution: In this situation, the auditor should issue an unqualified or clean opinion. This is the most excellent kind of report a business can get.

The auditor's report would state that the financial statements give a true and fair view in accordance with the relevant financial reporting framework.

Auditor's Report

Theoretical

Q: What is an auditor's report?

A: An auditor's report is a document prepared by an auditor that provides an opinion on the validity and reliability of a company's financial statements.

Q: What purpose does an auditor's report serve?

A: The auditor's report serves to give stakeholders, such as investors and creditors, assurance that the company's financial statements are accurate and comply with accounting standards.

Q: Who is responsible for preparing the auditor's report?

A: The external auditor, who is independent of the company, is responsible for preparing the auditor's report.

Q: What are the main components of an auditor's report?

A: An auditor's report typically consists of the title, addressee, introductory paragraph, scope paragraph, opinion paragraph, and auditor's signature.

Q: What does the introductory paragraph of an auditor's report contain?

A: The introductory paragraph identifies the entity whose financial statements have been audited and describes the financial statements.

Q: What is the role of the scope paragraph in an auditor's report?

A: The scope paragraph describes the nature of the audit, including the standards used, and provides a description of the work the auditor did.

Q: What is the opinion paragraph in an auditor's report?

A: The opinion paragraph contains the auditor's opinion on whether the financial statements present a true and fair view of the company's financial position and comply with accounting standards.

Q: What does a clean or unqualified opinion in an auditor's report mean?

A: A clean or unqualified opinion means the auditor believes the financial statements are free from material errors and misstatements and are in accordance with accounting standards.

Q: What does a qualified opinion in an auditor's report mean?

A: A qualified opinion means the auditor has found issues with the financial statements but believes they are fairly presented except for the effects of these issues.

Q: What is an adverse opinion in an auditor's report?

A: An adverse opinion is a declaration that the financial statements are not a fair representation of the company's financial position and do not comply with accounting standards.

Q: What is a disclaimer of opinion in an auditor's report?

A: A disclaimer of opinion is a statement by the auditor that they are unable to form an opinion on the financial statements due to limitations in the scope of their audit.

Q: What factors could lead an auditor to issue a qualified opinion?

A: Factors such as inconsistencies in the application of accounting standards, misstatements, or insufficient evidence could lead an auditor to issue a qualified opinion.

Q: What is the significance of the auditor's signature on the auditor's report?

A: The auditor's signature signifies the report is the product of an independent and objective audit process carried out in accordance with professional standards.
Q: How does an auditor's report impact investor decisions?
A: An auditor's report can significantly impact investor decisions as it provides an independent assessment of the company's financial health.
Q: What is the difference between an auditor's report and an audit report?
A: An auditor's report refers to the opinion issued by the auditor on the financial statements, while an audit report is a broader document detailing the audit's findings and conclusions.
Q: When is an auditor's report typically issued?
A: An auditor's report is typically issued at the conclusion of the audit process, which is usually annually for most companies.
Q: What is the responsibility of a company's management in relation to the auditor's report?
A: The company's management is responsible for the preparation and fair presentation of the financial statements, which are then audited to form the basis of the auditor's report.
Q: What happens if there are significant changes in a company's financial condition between the date of the auditor's report and the issuance of the financial statements?
A: If significant changes occur, the auditor may need to revise their report or perform additional audit procedures.
Q: What is the relationship between an auditor's report and the concept of audit risk?
A: The auditor's report is directly influenced by the idea of audit risk. This risk involves the possibility that the auditor might inadvertently fail to adjust their viewpoint on financial statements that are significantly misrepresented.
Q: Can an auditor's report be used as a tool for fraud detection?

A: While an auditor's report can highlight discrepancies and inconsistencies that may indicate fraud, it is not specifically designed as a tool for fraud detection.

Q: What is the role of an auditor's report in corporate governance?

A: An auditor's report plays a vital role in corporate governance by providing an independent assessment of the accuracy and fairness of the company's financial reporting.

Q: In what ways does an auditor's report promote transparency in financial reporting?

A: An auditor's report promotes transparency by providing an unbiased examination of a company's financial statements, potentially identifying any inaccuracies or misrepresentations.

Q: How can the credibility of an auditor's report be assessed?

A: The credibility of an auditor's report can be assessed by considering the reputation and independence of the auditor, the thoroughness of the audit process and the standard of the audit.

Q: What is the impact of an adverse auditor's report on a company's reputation?

A: An adverse auditor's report can significantly harm a company's reputation, leading to a loss of investor confidence and potential regulatory scrutiny.

Q: Can an auditor's report help in identifying the company's areas of improvement?

A: Yes, an auditor's report can help identify areas where the company's financial controls or reporting procedures may need improvement.

Q: How does an auditor's report contribute to the decision-making process of the company's stakeholders?

A: The auditor's report provides independent, reliable information on the company's financial performance, which stakeholders can use to make informed decisions.

Q: Can a company dispute the findings in an auditor's report?
A: While a company can discuss the findings with the auditor, the final report represents the auditor's independent and professional opinion.
Q: What is the role of auditing standards in an auditor's report?
A: Auditing standards guide the audit process, ensuring the report is based on an in-depth, consistent and unbiased review of the financial statements.
Q: In what circumstances can an auditor withdraw their report?
A: An auditor can withdraw their report if they find that the financial statements contain material misstatements that were not identified during the audit.
Q: Why is the independence of the auditor crucial to the credibility of the auditor's report?
A: The independence of the auditor is crucial as it ensures the report is free from bias and reflects a true and fair view of the company's financial position.
Q: How does an auditor's report affect the company's access to credit?
A: A positive auditor's report can enhance a company's creditworthiness, while a negative report can make it difficult for the company to obtain credit.
Q: Does the auditor's report address all financial aspects of the company?
A: While the auditor's report provides an opinion on the overall financial statements, it does not address every specific financial transaction or aspect of the company.
Q: Can the auditor's report be relied upon for investment decisions?
A: While the auditor's report provides valuable information, it should not be the sole basis for investment decisions. Investors should also consider other factors and seek professional advice.

Q: Does an unqualified auditor's report guarantee the company's future financial performance?

A: No, an unqualified auditor's report only attests to the fairness and accuracy of the financial statements at a specific point in time. It does not guarantee future performance.

Q: What is the implication of a disclaimer of opinion in an auditor's report?

A: A disclaimer of opinion usually indicates that the auditor was unable to obtain sufficient audit evidence to form an opinion, which may raise concerns about the company's financial reporting.

Q: How does the auditor's report reflect the concept of materiality in auditing?

A: The auditor's report reflects the concept of materiality as it provides an opinion on whether the financial statements are free from material misstatement.

Q: What does an emphasis of matter paragraph in an auditor's report signify?

A: An emphasis of matter paragraph draws attention to a matter that is appropriately presented or disclosed in the financial statements but is of such importance that it is fundamental to users' understanding of the financial statements.

Q: How does an auditor determine the type of opinion to issue in the auditor's report?

A: The type of opinion is determined based on the auditor's assessment of the financial statements, considering factors such as materiality of errors, compliance with accounting standards, and adequacy of disclosures.

Q: What is the role of professional skepticism in the preparation of an auditor's report?

A: Professional skepticism involves the auditor having a questioning mind and a critical assessment of audit evidence, which is essential in forming a fair and unbiased opinion for the auditor's report.

Q: How does an auditor's report impact public confidence in the company?

A: An auditor's report can significantly impact public confidence in the company. A positive report can enhance confidence, while a negative report can cause concern and decrease confidence.

Q: What is the role of the auditor's report in regulatory compliance?

A: The auditor's report helps ensure regulatory compliance by verifying that the company's financial statements are prepared in accordance with applicable accounting standards and regulations.

Q: Can an auditor's report be revised?

A: Yes, an auditor's report can be revised if the auditor becomes aware of facts that existed at the report date that might have affected the report.

Q: What is the impact of an auditor's report on the company's stock price?

A: The auditor's report can influence the company's stock price as investors use it to assess the company's financial health.

Q: Can an auditor issue more than one type of opinion in an auditor's report?

A: No, the auditor issues one overall opinion on the financial statements as a whole in the auditor's report.

Q: What is the importance of the date of the auditor's report?

A: The date of the auditor's report indicates the end of the auditor's responsibility for the audit of the financial statements and is typically the date when the auditor has obtained sufficient appropriate audit evidence.

Q: What is the implication of a going concern emphasis of matter in an auditor's report?

A: A going concern emphasis of matter indicates that there may be significant doubt about the company's ability to continue as a going concern.

Q: How does the auditor's report assist in financial analysis?

A: The auditor's report provides a basis for financial analysis by providing assurance that the financial statements present a true and fair view of the company's financial position.

Q: What is the role of internal control in the preparation of an auditor's report?

A: The auditor's assessment of the company's internal control over financial reporting can impact the audit procedures performed and the findings reported in the auditor's report.

Q: How does the auditor's report support accountability within the company?

A: The auditor's report supports accountability by providing an independent check on the company's financial reporting, which can help identify any inaccuracies or misrepresentations.

Q: How does the auditor's report contribute to the integrity of financial markets?

A: The auditor's report contributes to the integrity of financial markets by enhancing the reliability and credibility of financial information, which is crucial for the functioning of the markets.

Applications

Scenario 1: Lack of Independence

Suppose you are an external auditor for a major corporation, XYZ Ltd. You realize that your sister recently got a job in the finance department of the same company. How do you maintain your independence?

Solution: Since independence, both in fact and appearance, is critical in auditing, the first step to take would be to disclose this relationship to your audit team and the management of XYZ Ltd. If your sister's role doesn't directly impact the financial statements, you may be able to continue with the audit. However, if there is a potential conflict of interest, it would be best to recuse yourself from the audit of this company.

Scenario 2: Material Misstatement

You are auditing a company ABC Ltd. You notice that there is a material misstatement in the financial statements relating to the valuation of inventory. The management insists that the figures are correct. What do you do?

Solution: In this scenario, you should gather sufficient appropriate audit evidence to confirm if the misstatement is indeed material. If the misstatement is material and pervasive such that it distorts the view given by the financial statements, you should issue a qualified or adverse opinion, depending on the circumstances. You should also communicate with those charged with governance about the misstatement.

Scenario 3: Inadequate Documentation

While auditing a startup company, you find that the company has poor documentation of its transactions. The management explains that they have been too busy growing the business to maintain proper records. What action do you take?

Solution: It is an auditor's responsibility to obtain sufficient and appropriate audit evidence to form an opinion on the financial statements. In this case, the lack of documentation is a limitation in the scope of your audit. You should communicate this issue to the management and those charged with governance of the company. If the issue is not resolved, it may lead to a qualified opinion or disclaimer of opinion in your auditor's report.

Scenario 4: Fraud Detection

You are auditing a large retailer and find evidence of fraud. The management is not aware of the fraud and there is pressure on you to ignore it. What do you do?

Solution: As an auditor, your responsibility is to act in the best interests of the shareholders. You should gather enough evidence to support your findings and report the evidence of fraud to the senior management and the audit committee. If appropriate action is not taken, you may need to report the fraud to the appropriate legal or regulatory body.

Scenario 5: Going Concern Issues

You are auditing a company that has been making losses for the past few years. There is substantial doubt about the company's ability to continue as a going concern. How do you address this in your audit report?

Solution: If there are material uncertainties related to events or conditions that may cast significant doubt on the entity's ability to continue as a going concern, the auditor should express a qualified or adverse opinion. The auditor's report should clearly state the reasons for the concern and the basis for the opinion.

About the Author

The author is an accomplished professional with an MBA in Finance, ACCA (Knowledge Level), BBA (Finance), and a major in Finance for their O and A levels. With over ten years of practical investment experience

Milton Keynes UK
Ingram Content Group UK Ltd.
UKHW010712140823
426838UK00001B/104